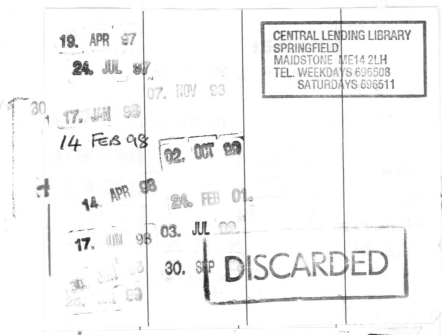

GERMAN
MOTORCYCLES
ROAD & RACING BIKES

MICK WALKER

GERMAN
MOTORCYCLES

ROAD & RACING BIKES

OSPREY

Published in 1989 by Osprey Publishing Limited
59 Grosvenor Street, London W1X 9DA

© Mick Walker 1989

British Library Cataloguing-in-Publication Data

Walker, Mick
German Motorcycles
1. German motorcycles, history
I. Title
629.2'275'0943

ISBN 0-850-45759-9

Contents

Introduction

Today, West Germany is known around the world for its quality engineering, especially its cars and cameras. It's also held in high regard for its expertise in trade and industry which have worked over recent times to ensure the strength of the *Deutschmark*. In addition, the West German trade fairs are outstanding amongst those of other countries. All this has given the population one of the highest standards of living anywhere in the world – all a far cry from what was a shattered country at the end of the Second World War.

Germany's political (and with it economic) structure was thrown on its head after the conflict when four zones of occupation – American, British, French and Russian were established, and the pre-war capital Berlin was divided into four sectors. At the Potsdam Conference in 1945, the Allied Control Council laid down rules for the eventual reconstruction of Germany's political life on a democratic basis, with the country treated as a single political and economic unit. But as Winston Churchill, accurately predicted, this high ideal failed because of conflict between the capitalist partners in the West and Communist Russia in the East.

The Western powers then proposed to the political parties in their zones of occupation, the creation of a separate West German state.

Following free elections in the West German *Länder* (regions or provinces), the first constitutional bodies of the Federal Republic, were formed in September 1949, with its capital at Bonn. The next month, the Russians proclaimed their occupied zone a state, calling it the German Democratic Republic, with its seat of power in the eastern sector of Berlin.

The Federal Republic (West Germany) gained full sovereignty in 1955 with the lifting of the Occupation Statute, and within a few short years West Germany had become a founder member of the EEC (European Economic Community).

The partitioning of the communist run GDR (German Democratic Republic) was reinforced by the building of the Berlin Wall in August 1961. This was an attempt to stem the tide of people attempting to shift from east to west. One has to remember that prior to the 'wall' being completed some *14 million* refugees and expellees had fled westwards!

Today, West Germany has 61.5 million inhabitants and is the world's fourth largest industrial power.

Why then did the West German motorcycle industry rise like a phoenix from the ashes of the Second World War to a position, which by the mid 1950's was the envy of the two wheel world, but was to almost disappear by the end of the decade? This book will answer those questions and reveal why the 1960's was to witness a miniature rebirth. It lasted almost intact to the early 1980's when, once again the German motorcycle almost became extinct.

The answer to these questions really lies in the success of the German people themselves.

German post war motorcycle production had got underway seriously in 1947. At that time the standard of living was for the majority only just above the very bare existence level. These circumstances conditioned the type of machines produced, hence they were, in the main, simple utility models. In the early 1950's the accent switched to technical innovation, performance and luxury, and clearly showed the vast improvement in living standards. By the mid-1950's the economic 'miracle' was in full swing. Only Belgium, Switzerland and Sweden outstripped the Federal Republic in the European prosperity league.

As a result, the requirements of the German road user switched from two to four wheels, even though for a short period this was partially masked by large sales of scooters and micro cars (with either three or four wheels). Many of the latter were produced by the traditional motorcycle manufacturers.

Initially a high level of road taxation and insurance rates for cars plus the high price of petrol in Germany, increased the ranks of the motorcyclists. Many people including doctors and businessmen, who in Britain and America would have normally used a car, in Germany rode a motorcycle or scooter.

By the end of 1953, for example, there were more than 2,10,000 motorcycles, mopeds and scooters registered in West Germany. Total output for the industry in 1953 was 437,500 machines. Not only was this a record for Germany but it was higher than in any other country's output of two-wheelers. All this created in reality was a false sense of security within the industry. Many companies over-extended themselves in the headlong rush for new, more complex (and expensive) models. By the time they appeared in 1955/56 these were largely unwanted. Potential buyers melted away to purchase their first cars.

The author with his BMW K75S, October 1987.

Those few manufacturers who survived into the 1960's were then able to enjoy a second boom, albeit a much more modest one, of sales of ultra-lightweight motorcycles and mopeds to a teenage population hungry for their own independent transport.

Then, as the 1980's dawned, the depression which hit the industrial world finally sealed the remaining manufacturers' fate, as these young customers were the ones who bore the brunt of an upsurge in unemployment.

Today, only BMW survives in anything which could be labelled a major operation and the majority of its sales go to the affluent business executive who has his or her machine very much as a leisure vehicle – certainly not as an every day form of transport.

Despite the reverses of manufacturing, German motorcycles have excelled in sport. Not only road racing, but motocross and enduro – the last 40 years has seen some of the very best machinery and designs seen in many respective classes made in the Federal Republic.

This title was originally intended as a companion volume to my earlier work; *Spanish Post War Road Racing Motorcycles* (Osprey Publishing). However, I soon found that the sheer number of manufacturers compared to the Spanish industry posed a major problem – space. And consequently more time and effort to compile. The result is, I hope, the definitive history of the post-war German motorcycle, at least on tarmac, in the English language.

Once again I am indebted to a large number of friends both new and old, without whose help this book would have been much more difficult, if not impossible to compile.

My close associate Doug Jackson as usual opened his extensive archives to me which not only include information, but many rare photographs and brochures. Don Mitchell supplied me with several items of literature from his comprehensive stock of second hand motorcycle handbooks, parts catalogues and leaflets. And thanks to John Fernley for assistance with the Hercules/DKW Rotary engined machines.

Then came the marque specialists; Fred Secker (BMW), David Cameron (Hercules), Phil Higston (Maico),

Vast crowds packed each hall at the 1950 Frankfurt Show. The motorcycle was a NSU 100 Fox. The figure on top was constructed from some cycle parts and had fully articulating limbs. It was considered novel at the time.

Emlyn Evans (NSU), Peter Robinson (Scooters), and Frenchman Dominique Tellier (Horex). Graham Sanderson, now with the British Honda arm, provided useful information on Friedel Münch, the man behind the Münch Mammoth.

Of the manufacturers, BMW proved just why it has survived longer than most. It provided more assistance than I have ever received from any other company while writing any of my previous titles. Their publicity machine, like their motorcycles, can only be described as superb.

Other photographs came from a wide range of sources, including my own collection and some from the famous EMAP archives, run by that arch enthusiast Brian Wooley. Some photographs used carried the imprint of professionals.

If I have overlooked anyone, I can but apologise, it was not my intention.

Finally, as always, my thanks to the Osprey team of Catherine, Caroline, Helen, Tony Thacker and editor Nicholas Collins, with a *very* special thanks to Andrew Kemp, for their usual first-class assistance, in this my largest effort in the series – and the one which caused most blood, sweat and tears to produce.

MICK WALKER
Wisbech, Cambridgeshire
September 1988.

Adler

Originally established by Heinrich Kleyer as Adler Fahradwerke AG in 1886 to manufacture bicycles, the company began to supplement this business with typewriter production in 1895 and the name was changed simply to Adler Werke. This was not to say that it had been unsuccessful in the original venture, for by 1898 it had built its 100,000th bicycle.

A year later, Adler (Eagle) joined the ranks of the automobile pioneers when its first car was produced, and then in 1902 it tried its hand at motorcycles. This venture cannot have been as profitable as their other parts of the business for it lasted only until 1907. Adler then concentrated on bicycles, cars and typewriters for over four decades and it was not until 1949 that the decision was taken to re-enter the motorcycle market.

The first positive results of this appeared the following year in the shape of the M100 designed by Hermann Friedrich, Adler's managing director and chief engineer. It was a simple single cylinder 98 cc (50 × 50 mm) commuter machine primarily designed to help fill the void which existed for anyone needing basic personal transport in the post-war era.

The power output from its 5.7:1 compression ratio was just 3.75 bhp at 4,800 rpm and with a foot-operated three-speed gearbox provided a maximum speed of 43.75 mph. But the ride was well up to the standards of any of its rivals with a good level of comfort thanks to a sturdy twin-tube frame plus both front and rear suspension. The front was sprung by a peculiar combination of a leading link and blade design using an internal coil spring, while plungers took care of the rear. Other details included a 7-litre tank and 2.50 × 19 inch tyres.

Adler introduced the M200 in 1951. The engine produced 11.4 bhp and was mounted in a duplex frame. This was the first of the company's post-war twin cylinder models and had plunger rear suspension, which was appreciated by the German public.

In 1951 three larger brothers joined the M100 – the M125/150 singles and the M200 twin, although the latter only appeared late in the year. The M125's 123.5 cc (54 × 54 mm) engine gave 6.8 bhp at 5,750 rpm on a compression ratio of 5.4:1 and had the same 6 volt 25/30 watt flywheel magneto and 6 amp/hour battery electrical system as the M100. The frame was of similar design to the M100 but with a larger 12-litre fuel tank and 150 mm full-width brake hubs. Top speed was 55 mph.

The M150 was a substantially larger bike even though its capacity of 147 cc (59 × 54 mm) on paper appeared as only a modest advance in displacement. It shared most of its cycle parts with the M200 twin. The latter had a 195 cc (48 × 54 mm) power unit which was to lead directly to Adler's most popular model, the 250 twin.

On both models the suspension system was similar to the smaller bikes but was more substantial, and used bottom links with a clock-type coil spring. Not only did the two share the same basic frame, forks, suspension system, 3.25 inch tyres and 16 inch wheels with 150 mm full-width hubs, but the modular design also went much further with the same 170 mm headlight, 12-litre fuel tank, deeply valanced mudguards, seat and parcel carrier. Both were available in either black or metallic grey and from the side even the engines appeared the same, with identical stroke and four-speed gear cluster. Performances were not vastly different either at 59 mph and 63 mph – although the larger bike was faster on acceleration despite being some 10 kg heavier at 130 kg. This was almost entirely due to an extra cylinder and a larger flywheel alternator.

A new M250 model, which was to prove (in various forms) far and away Adler's most popular and best-selling model was launched in 1952. At its heart was a 247 cc (54 × 54 mm) piston port two-stroke twin owing much to the M200. In its original form it produced 16 bhp at 5,590 rpm with 5.75:1 compression ratio from flat top three-ring pistons.

Externally, the motorcycle appeared similar to the smaller twin except for its larger 180 mm brakes, a different paint finish on the tank and a pair of silencers with fishtail ends.

All Adler engines shared an unusual transmission arrangement. The 200 and 250 used an engine-speed clutch mounted on the crankshaft, *outside* the primary drive which was by helical gears. But the 98 and 123 cc models used an even more unusual configuration with the engine mounted off to the right of the machine with the clutch and then the gearbox in line with it to the left. Drive to the rear wheel was taken from a sprocket adjacent to the clutch between the engine and gearbox and concentric with the crankshaft – an arrangement unique to Adler.

At the 1952 Warsage 24-hour race for production machines the winner in the up-to-250 cc class had

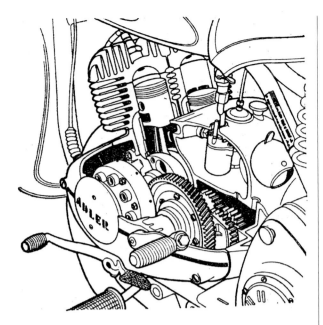

In this cutaway drawing of the Adler M250 power unit the engine speed clutch is particularly interesting

been an Adler, which also beat all the machines in the 350 cc class and was to come second overall! And in the 27th International Six Day Trial (ISDT) in Austria, four Adler twins had started – and four had finished, three with golds and one with a bronze medal.

For the Amsterdam Show in March 1953 a production ISDT version of the new Adler 250 made an appearance for the first time. External changes were limited to a high-level exhaust, wider handlebars and a chrome headlight grille. There were also miniature shock absorbers in the bottom of each fork link, and the engine had been tuned to produce an additional 2 bhp.

When five Adler twins started in the 1953 ISDT in Czechoslovakia, all finished – but this time all five gained gold medals. All were members of the German Vase teams. In the Warsage 24-hours, Adler again shone, with the first four places in the 250 class and second, fourth, fifth and sixth overall.

There were more competition triumphs, including golds throughout Germany in endurance-type trials. In the Luttich-Monaco-Luttich Rally Adler gained a 100 per cent record with all four twins that started gaining gold medals and taking the team prize. A carefully-prepared standard production Adler M250 achieved the remarkable speed of 74 mph for the flying kilometre under strict test conditions. And in the Monaco Rally Adler took two golds and the Ladies Cup as well as the 250 cc class.

The year also witnessed Adler's entry into road racing events. One machine, modified and ridden by Hallmeier of Nurnberg was used at the 20th Eilenriede Rennen held at Hanover on 27 September. Although the race was won by NSU works rider Werner Haas, the Adler twin commanded considerable attention for its speed of almost 100 mph and vivid acceleration – not least from the factory who then decided to build a prototype production racing version of the M250 roadster. This was entered in German National events by Walter Vogel.

Much of the success generated in competition was due to a separate race shop within the factory staffed by men such as Kurt Grasmann and Jan Friedrich Drkosch.

October's Frankfurt Show saw the debut of the MB250S – a sports version of the standard model which was on sale for the 1954 season with 18 bhp on tap and several changes including high-level exhausts.

Another major innovation was new front forks on all 1954 models except the 98 and 123 cc motorcycles. The new fork was a leading link type providing 4 inches of vertical movement for the front wheel and designed to keep weight to a minimum forward of the steering axis. The fork tubes were thus in a continuous line with the 63° steering head and light alloy castings clamped to their base carried 20 mm diameter bushes in which the chromed steel fork links pivoted. At the top an alloy casting carried the handlebars as well as a steering

Adler's MB250S was first produced in 1953. It shared many common parts with single cylinder bikes in range.

damper and a lock. The steering head had been raised to allow a deeper, larger capacity tank to be fitted, which dramatically improved the riding position.

The Frankfurt Show also introduced a novel exhibit – a special customised M250 with fully-enclosed bodywork by Freiss. This hid from view everything but the lower half of the front wheel, the bottom of the rear wheel and the tail of the silencers. Despite gaining considerable comment from onlookers at the show, the Freiss-inspired futuristic idea never went any further.

At the end of 1953 the M150, M200 and M250 were replaced by the MB150, M2011, MB201, MB200 and MB250 – plus the sports MB250S. All these were Frankfurt debutantes and had four-speed gearboxes.

The 150 had the same engine as before with flywheel magneto, rectifier and 6 amp/hour battery. The frame was revised and there was a 15-litre tank. The 2011 was a 199 cc (65 × 60 mm) single with 10.5 bhp, battery and coil ignition and chain primary drive – an economy version of the MB201 using the 150 mm front brake and 15-litre tank. The MB201 was a heavier machine but its version of the engine gave 11.4 bhp at 5450 rpm. The MB200 was an update of the discontinued M200 twin. Again, the power output was 11.4 bhp at 5450 rpm, while the 250 was an improved version of the earlier M250 with 16 bhp at 5600 rpm giving it a 74 mph maximum speed. Top of the range, the MB250S sports version delivered 18 bhp and was good for 77 mph.

ADLER MB 250 S

Grabbing attention at the 1953 Frankfurt Show, Adler's MB250 is shown in de luxe form with Denfold dual seat. Most examples of this model were produced with a simple, sprung single saddle. Germany at this time was building towards a consumer boom.

The first MB250 to reach Britain came in early 1954 when Fred Ager of Ealing, London had one specially imported after seeing the description of an M250 in *Motor Cycling*. He had written to the Frankfurt factory to enquire if one could be bought, and while the factory was not at that time interested in exporting to Britain because a 30 per cent import levy against European machinery denied Adler a chance to sell at a competitive price, it nonetheless offered to sell Ager one privately. A suitable deal was struck.

Even though Ager had already paid for a 1953 M250 model, following the Frankfurt show and the intro-duction of the improved MB250, Adler, unasked substituted one of the latest machines in its place. A gesture which was deeply appreciated by the recipient. On its arrival in Britain, the MB250 so fulfilled its owner's expectations (he had previously run a BMW) that he wrote to John Thorpe of *Motor Cycling*. Ager offered the journalist the loan of the machine for a few days as soon as the machine was run in.

Thorpe was impressed from the start, finding the design first class and, as he put it, 'neat, clean and eminently practical'. He reported 'Workmanship and finish are of the highest order', and indeed they were.

Many details gave evidence of a machine planned down to the last nut and bolt. Knurled top rings adjusted the hydraulically damped plunger rear suspension for load, the Yale-type lock in the steering damper, the same security on the toolbox lid which would lay flat when released to form a work tray, the rubber buffers for the centre stand, and the quick-

release wingnuts on the hinged rear mudguard were all evidence of coherent engineering practice.

Thorpe found that a mere dab on the inward folding kickstart was enough to bring the machine into subdued life. There was an uncanny lack of mechanical noise except from a distinctly audible primary transmission. The high silencers coped admirably with the exhaust note by reducing it to little more than a drone except when the machine was accelerating hard.

Clutch take-up was adjudged to be somewhat fierce and it was found best to use just the front portion of the rocking, heel-and-toe gear lever on the left of the engine. Adler had solved the problem of an evasive neutral by positioning it at the bottom of the gear selection, thus all gears were 'up' – a system which was found very efficient once a rider had become used to it. In addition, there was even an easily visible neutral warning light in the headlamp-mounted speedometer.

The change from first to second needed some care to avoid a 'crunch' but thereafter changes in either direction were found to be effortless, *provided* that a pause was made.

Whether accelerating or cruising, the engine was both smooth and vibration-free, except for a slight roughness at around 30 mph in top and some high-frequency vibration at over 55 mph. For the rest, the twin produced its power in so fussless a manner that as John Thorpe put it, 'one would have hardly realised that there was an engine at work at all had it not been for the road racing past'.

Although the maker's claim of 72 mph was adjudged pretty accurate, acceleration in the intermediate gears once 30 mph was reached was more pronounced than this would suggest. It was also stated that as much of the performance was located at the upper end of the rev range, intelligent use of the gearbox was essential if the best was to be obtained in this respect.

The brakes were more than adequate for the performance. Thorpe considered them 'the sort of which one dreams – powerful, smooth, fadeless'. Either was powerful enough to lock its wheel, yet pull up was always dead straight unless the machine was leaned to the right when the front anchor was applied, in which case a slight deviation was noticeable.

Despite link-type front forks, there was no tendency for the machine either to lift under acceleration or to dip under braking as was normal with this type of suspension assembly. Thorpe found the front and rear suspension was 'truly-excellent', especially in combination with the soft springing of the saddle. A rock-steady stability added to the characteristics of the engine and transmission, and the steering did not disgrace the rest of the machine. The MB250 could be heeled over well on any surface and the only fault found was that on bumpy left-handers when the stand fouled the ground. It is interesting, however, to note Thorpe's comment that 'naturally, the small wheels (tyres are 3.25 × 16 front and rear) did not permit that ultimate refinement which gives hair-line navigation'.

Surprisingly for a high performance two-stroke twin, fuel consumption averaged out at 70 mpg when the top end performance was used and at lower speeds well over 100 mpg could be reasonably expected. These were amazing figures, especially when one considers the poor fuel consumption of the same engine configuration thirty years later.

Equally remarkable, in view of later development was that, like several lightweight machines of the day, Adlers were often hitched to a sidecar – in fact the factory brochure showed the MB200 and a single seat sports chair stating: 'Even when the MB200 is fitted with a sidecar, average speeds can be attained which used to be possible only with a far heavier machine'.

Development of the production racing Adler continued apace. At the important International

Hockenheim meeting on 10 May 1954 the Adler ridden by Vogel came home seventh, a most creditable result bearing in mind that there were only the works NSUs and Guzzis in front. This followed its first victory when another Adler ridden by Hallmeier won the 250 class of the 'Three Corner' Dieburger meeting held on 11 April. The winning Adler finished one minute ahead of the DKW ridden by Lottes and the Guzzi of Thorn-Prikker. Hubert Luttenburger was another rider to figure well on Adler machinery at this time.

The power output of the Adlers was now up to 26 bhp at 7500 rpm, which corresponded to a maximum road speed reputed to have been around 105 mph. Weight was 98 kg dry (220 lb) and while the front suspension was based on the latest production roadster 250's, full swinging arm suspension was used at the rear.

At the French GP staged at Rheims on the 31 May, Adler came home ninth and tenth – the first machines behind the pack of factory NSU and Guzzi entries. Without a doubt, the outstanding performances were those of Hallmeier and Vogel. The former finished third behind the works NSU Rennmax twins of Haas and Hollaus at the German GP at Solitude, while Vogel came in sixth. Vogel also managed the same position in the Swiss GP at Berne, and later took a gold medal on a 250 twin in the 1954 ISDT in Wales. Two other Adler riders, Kramer and Steindl, also managed golds while Bilger took a bronze.

Late in 1954 came the news that Adlers were to be imported officially into Britain by Avon Autos of London W7. To begin with, the only model imported was the MB250 twin in either black or green colour schemes at a price of £220. Soon afterwards, *Motor Cycling* for the 17 February 1955 issue published a full road test under the headline 'An Up-to-the-minute German Luxury Machine with an Impressive Performance'. This was witnessed by the following extract: 'Acceleration from a standing start was, to put it mildly, little short of fantastic . . . an adjective applied by several incredulous owners of 500 cc twins who found themselves hard put to stay with the smart green Adler as it got away from the traffic lights with the steady, heady surge of power'. In fact, the whole test was full of praise except for one item, the mudguarding, which drew the criticism that it was 'not as efficient as it is extensive'.

Throughout 1955 Adlers continued to shine within the German national racing scene but rarely ventured abroad. One of the most successful riders that year was Siegfried Lohmann, who finished 9th in the Belgian GP and 16th in the German GP at the Nurburgring. Adlers

Adler water-cooled, streamlined 250 at 1955 Dutch TT.

Air-cooled racer developed from plunger framed M250.

came home second, fifth and seventh in the 1,500 mile Liege-Milan-Liege Sporting Rally organised over the weekend of 24/25 July by the Belgian Royal Motor Club. And in the Dutch TT that year, the first water-cooled Adler twin appeared complete with a full dustbin fairing constructed in hand-beaten aluminium.

Sales however, were declining throughout the industry and in an attempt to stem the tide, 1955 saw the introduction of Adler's entry into the scooter market. Unfortunately for the company, the Junior, as it was called, found the opposition extremely tough both at home and in their export markets.

Powered by a fan-cooled 98 cc two-stroke single (50 × 50 mm) rated at 3.75 bhp on a 5.5:1 compression ratio, it had a three-speed foot-operated gearbox. At 40 mph the top speed was very similar to the technically

comparable DKW Hobby, and like the Ingoldstadt design, the Junior was a large machine. If nothing else, its 14 inch wheels proved that its designer was more used to motorcycles than scooters, even if Adler claimed instead that the 'long stretched double swinging arm gear and large 14 inch wheels ensured truly ideal roadholding'. As if that was not sufficiently enticing, the brochure also went on to say that 'The power and economy of the proven Adler engine, its quick starting, easy hill climbing and steady perseverance on the motor highway can be taken for granted and need hardly be mentioned at all.'

In reality, despite advertising claims that it was fully suitable for transporting two in comfort, the Junior

The race winning ability of privately produced water-cooled machines attracted riders of the quality of Falk, Beer, Lohmann and many others who remained loyal. It was the vivid acceleration of the motorcycles which gave the marque an edge.

hardly had power to transport its rider. Perhaps its only selling point, which was hardly mentioned in the sales brochure was the luxury of an electric starter. Although a larger-engined 125 cc version was built, this was only ever a prototype and never entered production.

The time spent (wasted?) on trying to develop and market the Junior scooter showed on the rest of the production front. The 1956 range announced in October 1955 showed nothing new. It consisted of the Junior, plus six motorcycles (M100, M2011, MB201, MB200, MB250 and 250S). Despite Adler's attempts to get in on the small capacity mass commuter market, it was still the quarter-litre twins which sold in the greatest numbers and gained most respect for the marque, for both provided a blend of smooth, silent power with exceptional power delivery for the time.

In addition, 1955 was hardly a successful year for Adler in the ISDT. Only one machine was entered and this retired early in the event. The 1956 event was the 31st in the series, and was held on Adler's home soil at Garmisch-Partenkirchen. This time, the factory entered a proper manufacturer's team and were rewarded by seeing all the riders, Steindl, Bilger and Vogel, gain golds on their 247 cc twins. However, this was to be their last official fling at the ISDT.

There were signs of a resurgence at the Frankfurt Show in October 1956 when one of the highlights was the appearance of a new Adler sports twin, the 250 Sprinter, among a range of other new 250 twins. The newcomer featured a swinging arm frame developed by factory riders in the rigours of the ISDT and racing events. It was also adopted for the Favorit roadster, Six Days enduro and Motocross dirt racer, all of which made their appearance at the same time in a determined move by the Frankfurt company.

The Sprinter boasted a tuned MB250S engine,

chrome tank panels, two-tone dualseat, narrow sports handlebars and greatly improved styling. The top speed of almost 80 mph was some going for a fully-equipped roadster at the time. The Favorit replaced the MB250 and had identical performance, but was fitted with only a single foam-padded seat.

Most exciting of all were the two off-road competition bikes. The Six Day 250 was an exact replica of the factory's successful ISDT machines and it was displayed flanked by the three gold medal winning bikes. With 18 bhp at 5300 rpm, the factory claimed a maximum road speed of 75 mph. It came fully equipped for battle with high level exhaust, tanktop map case/tool bag, braced bars, headlamp and sump guards, additional front suspension dampers, uprated rear dampers for the swinging arm suspension, single seat, competition number plates, knobbly tyres (3.00 × 19 front and 3.50 × 18 rear), and a host of additional items including modified gearing both in the gearbox and final drive ratios.

The Motocross sported a bright red finish and was more of a one-off special and less closely related to the roadsters. It had an even higher state of tune with 20 bhp at 6300 rpm, and used a totally different frame with Earles-type front forks and angled (as opposed to vertical) twin rear dampers. The tank held a mere 7 litres, mudguards were abbreviated, there was a slim racing style seat and twin chromed racing expansion pipes. Virtually the only parts it shared with the standard models were the brakes, and weight was down to 130 kg against 172 kg for the Six Days.

Surprisingly, in view of the specialist nature of these machines, Adler had taken the decision to axe all the older models for the 1957 season, except the Junior Scooter. This was now offered in two guises: standard and Luxus, which had a slight increase in power to 4 bhp and boasted several refinements. There was also a moped on their stand at Frankfurt, thanks to a tie-up with Triumph (TWN) and Hercules – a badge-engineered Triumph Fips model. They had also appointed a new importer for Britain, R&C Autocars of London W1. This company was to concentrate their efforts on the Junior Scooter which sold for £163 1s 3d and the 250 Favorit which went for £262 17s 8d. From mid-season the 250 Motocross was also available to special order.

Both the Six Day enduro and Motocross dirt racer were reliable and fast in their chosen fields, although the latter went better in a straight line than over the more demanding sections of the motocross circuits. Observers commented that it went 'like a jack rabbit across the field'. But both were only ever produced in small numbers and the new swinging arm 250 roadsters came at a time when motorcycle sales in Germany were on the floor.

By 1958 Adler was finding motorcycle sales an ever-more difficult task. For Britain the range was increased and the price structure updated. The Junior sold at £162 16s 0d; the Favorit £255 14s 9d; Sprinter £294 8s 8d and Motocross £283 3s 8d.

Despite commercial difficulties, Adler had continued to do well on the race track even at international level. Typical of this was the Rhein-Pokal-Rennen meeting staged over the 4.8 mile Hockenheim circuit on 12 May 1958, where many of the world's top riders gathered. These Included Geoff Duke, Keith Campbell and the East German MZ star Ernst Degner.

In the 250 race, a number of converted Adler roadsters were entered, and drama ensued. From the start, German champion Horst Kassner took the lead on an NSU Sportmax ahead of Australian Eric Hinton on another NSU. For 16 laps Hinton lay a safe second only to have his gearbox seize on the East Curve. His machine shot between the trees and into the crowd and injured several spectators. Hinton was examined in hospital but had suffered only a fractured bone in one ankle and another break in his other foot.

From then on the race was anything but a procession, as Heiss on a NSU who had worked his way up the field after a bad start became involved in a superb dice for third and then second with the leading Adler twin of Dieter Falk. Meanwhile, another pair of NSUs fought tooth and nail with Adler riders Gunter Beer and Siegfried Lohmann.

Even though Kassner led all the way to win at the end, Falk was second and Lohmann came out top in the other scrap to take a brilliant fourth place. The speed of the event can be witnessed by Kassner's fastest lap of 102.22 mph – some motoring. For a roadster-based twin cylinder two-stroke Adler to put up such a competitive performance was a great achievement, for it should be remembered that at the time the NSU Sportmax was a world-class machine that had taken the 1955 championship.

But shortly after this in July, there came news that the giant Grundig Corporation had acquired a controlling interest in Adler Werke. This act was to seal the fate of Adler motorcycles, because shortly afterwards senior management was instructed to concentrate their efforts solely upon typewriter production – a business which survives to this day.

Strangely, it was not until this final year that Adler really began to shine in the World Championships, finishing fifth in the series after the marque had already passed into history! Falk and Beer put up some brave performances in that year's title race, with Falk finishing fifth in the Isle of Man, third at the Dutch TT and the Nurburgring, and sixth at Monza in Italy, while Beer finished fourth in Sweden and at Monza.

Even though this was the peak of Adler's achievements, the Frankfurt 'strokers' continued to give a good account of themselves until well into the 1960s, particularly where the circuit demanded optimum acceleration rather than top speed.

Many interesting specials were produced using the Adler 250 twin engine as a base. Usually they were water-cooled. One was built by Fritz Klager featuring a homebuilt crankshaft, water-cooled cylinders and five-speed 'box. It breathed through two 30 mm Bing carbs, and was reputed to turn out 38 bhp at 11,000 rpm and to be good for 130 mph on full chat. All this was mounted in a special one-off frame built by Dieter Busch of Frankfurt (later a driving force and tuner behind several world sidecar champions of the 1970s). The front forks were from an Aermacchi Ala d'Ora racer with a brake from an NSU Sportmax, while the rear was an Italian Oldani.

But perhaps the most amazing Adler-based racing special was the Kestermann water-cooled *four* cylinder. This started life as early as 1962 when it was built for German solo rider Karl Hoppe using a pair of Adler 250 racing units carried across the frame on a common crankcase to make an extremely neat and purposeful unit. Initially, it sported four British Amal GP carbs, later changed to Amal Monoblocs. Its first competitive outing was in the 1962 Freiburg Hill Climb, an internationally famous event in the Black Forest. Here Hoppe rode it to a record fifth fastest time – only five seconds slower than Canadian Mike Duff who took his very quick Matchless G50 into fourth spot.

It was then sold to Swiss sidecar ace Fritz Scheidegger as an alternative power unit to his flat-twin BMW Rennsport four-stroke. Although the Adler four never totally supplanted the BMW twin, he did nevertheless devote a considerable amount of time to its development until the summer of 1964 when the project was finally abandoned.

Apart from racing, the twin cylinder Adler engine was a popular choice with specials builders wanting a roadster with a difference. The most unusual of these was spotted at the Elephant Rally in January 1965. An Adler twin had been very neatly grafted into a 200

Kestermann developed 500 four used Adler components and was raced by sidecar ace Fritz Scheidegger in 1963.

Above **Richard Williats is pictured taking second place in the final of the national races held at Castle Combe 20 April 1963. The motorcycle is his Adler 250 twin.**

Ducati Elite frame and the machine had a single seat sports sidecar attached. Amazingly, this unusual combination looked so good it could have been a factory job.

Even today, Adler is recalled with strong affection by many enthusiasts – and not all of them two-stroke buffs. The abiding memory is of what was in its day a trend-setting engine – the 247 cc, 54 mm 'square' two-stroke parallel twin which found its forte as the provider of smooth, economical power for street use, gold medal-winning reliability in endurance trials, rip-snorting dirt bike racing and even Grands Prix. How many other power units can claim such a wide range of truly *successful* roles?

Below **The Elephant Rally attracts some fantastic machinery. This Ducati Elite powered Adler MB250 is believed to be unique. It was seen, along with its sports chair, at the 1965 event. Notice that the motorcycle has only a single seat.**

BMW

production models

The story of BMW, Germany's last remaining large-scale motorcycle manufacturer, has not always been one of the commercial buoyancy it enjoys today. During its long history, the firm has often had to take second place to other makers and at one time even stared total ruin and bankruptcy in the face.

BMW's origins are found in the 19th century when in 1896 a well-known industrialist of the time, Heinrich Ehrhart, opened a factory at Eisenach with a view to making military equipment. This was not to be, and soon production concentrated on bicycles and electric vehicles, the first of which appeared in 1898 and were chiefly notable for their transmission. Not the common chain or belt, because Ehrhart used toothed gear wheels and shafts with universal joints.

These early vehicles were hand built by a group of enthusiastic engineers, with the result that Ehrhart's business sense forced him to drop this line of development in favour of producing Decauville cars under licence from France. Production of these began in 1900 and the car was called Wartburg after the local castle in Eisenach. In totally different hands after World War II, the name was used for a series of East German three-cylinder two-stroke cars owing much to DKW influence – but that is another story.

Both Eisenach and Wartburg names were used for the licence-built Decauville models. Two were entered for the 1902 Paris-Vienna race – one with a five-speed gearbox! Both finished, but this promising beginning in the field of motor sport was not followed up.

Ehrhart soon tired of this particular business enterprise and left the company the following year. The original factory was taken over by a new organisation founded by some of Heinrich Ehrhart's former associates, although his son continued car manufacture at one of the firm's other plants. Ehrhart still used the Decauville designs and called them Ehrhart-Decauvilles.

The new management decided that a totally fresh range of cars was what was needed, and chose the name Dixi. The products marketed under this new brand name were most definitely designed for what we would today refer to as an upmarket clientele.

By 1911 the next piece slotted into the BMW jigsaw, and it was aviation, rather than motoring, which provided the key. In that year, Gustav Otto (son of Nikolaus Otto, creator of the four-stroke Otto cycle),

opened an aircraft factory on Lerchenauerstrasse at the eastern end of Munich's Oberwiesenfeld Airport. Two years later, Karl Rapp started the aero engine factory Repp Motorenwerke GmbH.

At the outset of World War I in 1914, the Eisenach, Otto and Rapp companies were all completely separate and unconnected in any way – but each was to play a vital role in the emergence of BMW over the following years.

The first step was on 7 March 1916 when Otto and Rapp as two of Munich's smaller aircraft factories amalgamated to form Bayerische Flugzeugwerke AG (BFW), with the intention of concentrating their energies and resources into the design and production

Having returned to motorcycle production BMW was able to roll the 1000th R24 off the end of the line as early as 1949. Publicity for the event was modest because public relations resources were still scarce for the war-scarred manufacturer.

of aero engines. Its two directors were Karl Rapp and Dr Ing E. Max Friz. The foundation of their company coincided with a rapid expansion of the fledgling German Air Force. Soon, many of Germany's front line fighter squadrons, including the legendary Richthofen unit commanded by the highest-scoring air ace of the war, Baron Manfried von Richthofen (the Red Baron) used aircraft powered by BFW's products.

BFW's fame soon spread outside Germany's borders to the Austro-Hungarian empire, where a naval engineer on detachment with the Austro-Daimler aircraft engine company, Franz Josef Popp, came to hear of their excellence. Popp decided to take his special skills to BFW AG in Munich. They were gratefully accepted. On 29 July 1917, Bayerische Motoren Werke GmbH (BMW) came into existence with Popp as its managing director – a post he was to hold until 1942.

A year later, in the summer of 1918 the company went public, and became BMW AG.

The company was then at the peak of its war production. It employed over 3500 people. Among these was one particular director, Fritz Neumeyer, who was later to become a deadly rival for over two decades as boss of Zündapp.

Aero engine production was at its height. Fokker's new D VII was then arguably the world's finest fighter aircraft – and though not especially fast, its strong point was its great manoeuvrability at high altitudes. The power unit was either a 160/180 hp Mercedes, or the 185 hp BMW. The latter, neatly cowled and fitted with a frontal radiator, had superior performance and was much sought after by Germany's air aces.

But the war was nearly over, and just as BMW's rise had been meteoric, so its fall after Germany's defeat was equally spectacular.

Even as the victors and vanquished were assembling for the signing of the Armistice at Compiège, chief designer Max Friz was completing the final preparations of a brand-new six cylinder in-line watercooled BMW engine. Rated at an amazing 300 hp, the engine was installed into a BFW biplane at the Munich production complex and underwent a series of secret tests. It achieved the then world record height of 9,760 metres (32,022 feet) on 17 June 1919. Following the record-breaking flight virtually all BMW's aviation interests – including the new engine and all the technical data – were confiscated by the Allied Control Commission.

BMW was forced to turn its hand literally to anything in order to remain in existence. Materials which had been intended for aero engine production were diverted into a vast number of new uses including agricultural equipment, tool boxes and even office equipment. Slowly, BMW hauled itself back from the abyss of commercial and financial disaster. Supplying metal castings to other enterprises led to a vital contract to manufacture components for railway braking systems. Then followed engine manufacture

First of the post-war BMW flat twins the 494 cc R51/2 was introduced to an eager market in 1950.

again with a new Friz design for an 8-litre power unit for use in heavy trucks, buses and boats.

Eventually this opened up a completely new avenue – motorcycles. In 1920 development work began using a proprietary Kurier 148 cc two-stroke single designed by Curt Hanfland, as the basis of a lightweight machine with direct belt drive. Perhaps fortunately, this sold not as a BMW, but under the name Flink. The Flink was not a commercial success for BMW.

Shortly afterwards in 1921, the old Gustav Otto works were sold. It was used until 1937 manufacturing Flottweg motorcycles and clip-on engines, after which BMW was to buy it back as its own production expanded.

Meanwhile, 1921 also saw the introduction of an engine which was to be the true beginning of the *real* range of BMW motorcycles. Designed by Martin Stolle and designated the M2B15, it was a 493 cc flat-twin side valve with square bore and stroke measurements of 68 × 68 mm.

The M2B15 was supplied to Victoria, SMW, Bison, SBD and other smaller companies.

It was also used by BMW in 1922 to power the Helios motorcycle in which the M2B15 was mounted fore-and-aft like a contemporary Douglas, driving the rear wheel by chain. The Helios was not a BMW design, although the complete machine was built at the Munich plant. And nor was it a very good motorcycle – partly, perhaps, because the men at BMW were more interested in aviation and in fact *hated* motorcycles. But as a gifted engineer, Friz could see the machine's shortcomings, and as a realist he knew that for the present at least there was no possibility of returning to aircraft manufacture. So he set to work to create a new machine and ensure that it would be good enough to carry the blue and white BMW emblem. The quartering was supposed to portray a whirling aircraft propeller blade and have resemblance to Bavaria's chequered flag.

When results of his efforts were unveiled at the Paris Show in 1923, they created a sensation. The R32, as the new machine was called, used what was virtually a direct descendant of the 493 cc engine. But it was now mounted transversely in unit with a three-speed gearbox with shaft drive to the rear wheel. The frame was a full twin triangle design and the front fork was sprung by a quarter-elliptic leaf spring. It was the beginning of a design format which was modern enough to last until today.

Although the R32 was not as powerful as some of its contemporaries, the BMW design was superior in several important areas and offered a truly modern concept in a world still dominated by unreliable engines, flimsy frames and temperamental trans-

missions. Over the next three years 3,100 were produced.

Max Friz returned to aircraft design in 1924 when formal restrictions which had been in force since the end of hostilities were lifted. That year Rudolf Schleicher developed the R37 with an ohv engine which offered nearly double the 8.5 bhp power output of the R32, with 16 bhp at 4000 rpm.

By 1927, BMW had manufactured its 25,000th motorcycle, and shortly after this, launched its first 750 class machine, the side valve R62. This appeared in 1928, the same year that BMW took over the Dixi plant in Eisenach.

During the First World War, the Eisenach works built military trucks but, like BMW, the Armistice had left Dixi in dire trouble. They were taken over by the railway manufacturers Gothaer Wagenfabrik, whose new subsidiary was dubbed Dixi Werke, Einsenach AG. With an injection of cash it had been able to return to car production again in 1920. For much of the 1920s, its business was concentrated upon one model, the 1596 cc 6/24 model.

In 1927, after several years steady growth, Dixi found it had new owners again because Gothaer Wagenfabrik was itself taken over by Shapiro. The following year came a licence to build the British Austin Seven, but before production had properly got under way, Shapiro decided to sell off both plant and product range.

It was at this point that BMW stepped in, as it considered that the time was right to make an entry into the car market. BMW acquired the Eisenach factory for 2.2 million Reichsmarks (RM). And so the three roots of the BMW family tree finally merged to present a common corporate front to the world.

The first BMW car was therefore born out of the Austin. It was sold first as a Dixi, but by 1929 as a BMW. It was not until 1933 that the first all-BMW car design, the 303 appeared. About 2300 examples had been built when the model was dropped in 1934 in favour of the new 303. From this point onwards the history of the company started to see-saw between cars and bikes as to whether four wheels or two would call the tune (except for a short period when three wheels dominated proceedings).

In 1928 an ohv version of the 750 flat-twin motorcycle, called the R63 was also introduced. On the aviation side business was growing rapidly, especially since the acquisition of a licence to build American Pratt & Whitney radial engines.

Some 2630 people were now employed and in the following year this number increased to 3860 as a result of greatly increased car production. Like other firms which had grown at this time (see also NSU) this left BMW very vulnerable to the storm which was about to hit Germany. The Great Depression began to bite at the end of the 1920s. BMW, like NSU, had just completed a major investment programme, and the economic collapse which bankrupted 17,000 German companies in just 1931 alone, hit the firm terribly hard. Even so, a policy of diversification and skilled financial management managed to keep BMW from the ultimate catastrophe of ceasing to trade.

In the early 1930s BMW introduced pressed steel frames for the first time anywhere in the world. These were used on the 740 cc R11. And although 1930 was a black year for most German companies, BMW aero engines sold well in Russia and Japan and so provided a lifeline to the struggling business. Yet more help was provided by the R2, a 198 cc ohv single commuter lightweight. Its potential owners not only had the advantage that it was cheap but they could also avoid having to take the stiff German driving test.

With 15,300 sales between the end of 1930 and the beginning of 1936, the little R2 sold in greater numbers than any previous BMW motorcycle.

However, it was the 398 cc R4 which really helped BMW's motorcycle recovery in the first half of the '30s. From 1932 onwards, the R4 was delivered to the German Army in sizeable numbers, and the abolition of

First manufactured in 1952 the R68 was the sports model in BMW's range at the beginning of the decade. Most had low-level exhausts but some, as seen on this machine, had siamesed high-level systems. Inspiration for the exhaust design came from the ISDT and other off-road competitions.

vehicle licence tax the same year helped its chances with the civilian population. By 1933, the year when Adolf Hitler came to political power, BMW had almost fully recovered from the crisis. The company boasted record production and a total workforce of 4720.

Its turnover in 1934 of 82 million RM compared with 19 million in 1932 was remarkable. But even more startling figures were to emerge in 1935 with a staggering total of 128 million RM and 11,113 employees. This was the year of the introduction of the 745 cc R12 flat twin, which became the company's most successful model of the inter-war years. It had one outstanding feature above all else – not the first-ever telescopic forks, but the first ever to incorporate hydraulic damping on a production machine. The R12 also had a four-speed gearbox whereas earlier BMWs had three speeds.

Between 1935 and 1938 36,000 R12s were sold. But 1935 also saw the introduction of a machine whose total production would be no more than 450 in the next two years. This was the prestigious R17, a super-sporting mount with a twin-carb 730 cc flat-twin engine giving 33 bhp at 4300 rpm. It was the most powerful production roadster built by BMW until the introduction of the much later post-war R68 model in 1952.

In the same year AFN Ltd of Falcon Works, London Road, Isleworth, Middlesex (now a Porsche dealership) became the first British importers of BMW. It was an inauspicious time, for in 1936 the first signs of another world conflict began to emerge. As if to meet this possibility, BMW set up a military equipment division at its Eisenach works to manufacture lightweight field

BMW's stand at the 1953 Frankfurt Show revealed the company's confidence in its future.

guns. Motorcycle developments continued apace, however, with a couple of new production models, the R3, a 305 cc single and the R5 with a much-improved version of the venerable 494 cc engine first used on the original R32.

BMW 'retook' the Flottweg factory in 1937. This was the same establishment it had sold back in 1921. It was a period of intense activity on record-breaking and competition fronts (see Chapter 3) and it was only a short time afterwards that the racing technology was carried through into the BMW roadster line. In 1938 (the year that the 100,000th BMW motorcycle rolled off the production line) both the R51 and R61 models appeared, equipped with spring frames and telescopic forks.

By 1939 and the eve of war, the BMW empire was still putting on weight with a workforce now standing at 26,919. And in Britain, AFN was offering a full range of BMW production models for the 1939 season: the 250 ohv R23 at £59, the 350 ohv R35 for £85, the 500 ohv R51 at £123, 600 ohv R66 for £135 or 600 sv R61 for £118, and the 750 sv R71 for £123. Soon, however, the storm clouds of war were to blot out the scene and by September, Europe was once again torn apart by conflict.

BMW was obviously preoccupied with production of aero engines. However, the efforts of the motorcycle division were also in demand because the *Wehrmacht* (German Army) required large numbers of machines as troop transport and fighting vehicles. These were provided by three main companies, Zündapp, NSU – and of course BMW. There were single cylinder BMW military bikes, but without doubt, the definitive German motorcycle of the war was the BMW R75 (or essentially similar Zündapp) flat-twin. Many of these R75s were used for sidecar duties, although they also found favour in solo form.

The war brought management changes. Karl Popp, the first managing director, retired and his place was taken by Kurt Donarth. Just before the end of the conflict, on 11 April 1945, Hitler ordered Donarth to destroy all production facilities immediately.

Heavy bombing had already taken its toll of the BMW facilities and by 1945 about a third of the Munich plants had been destroyed. But Donarth wisely chose to ignore the order. He did so again when it was later repeated. But this time it was the American garrison in Munich who decreed in October that the plant should be dismantled and destroyed. Anything of value should have been shipped back to the States. When the American forces had taken over Munich they removed many of the remaining machine tools. While in the East, Eisenach was occupied by Soviet forces and found itself in the Russian sector of post-war Germany.

Because Munich had been the centre of BMW's wartime aero engine production, Eisenach had been used as the car and motorcycle plant. It was all commandeered by the Red Army. Later, in the hands of the civilian Communist government, it was used to construct the Russians' own BMW motorcycles and cars. First from spare parts and later from parts manufactured by the new owners. Motorcycle production was then transferred to the Soviet Union. While the cars, originally BMWs, then EMWs (Eisenach Motoren Werke) were built from pre-war BMW designs, continued at Eisenach. From 1956, the East German plant produced three-cylinder two-stroke cars under the Wartburg name.

In its stripped, shattered Munich factory meanwhile, BMW was fighting for its existence again. Under the Allied Control Commission, immediately following the war, German companies were prohibited from making motorcycles. So by September 1945 BMW were undertaking limited peacetime production of anything which would sell – cooking utensils, wood planing equipment and even bicycle parts. Later, in early 1946, the plant (like NSU's) was used to service American military vehicles. Later still, production began of baking machines and household equipment.

As Germany's need to become mobile again became more and more pressing, the Allied Control Commission began to relax its regulation of transport. Permission was granted to allow BMW to assemble 100 R23 247 cc ohv singles from spare parts, and to build 21,000 bicycles. The workforce had reached a total of 1800 men and women.

Launch of the first *real* post-war BMW came in 1948, with the appearance of the R24. The 247 cc (68 × 68 mm) single was a development of the immediately pre-war R23, but produced an additional 2 bhp for a total of 12 bhp at 5600 rpm. It employed a rigid frame, spindly undamped telescopic forks, 3.00 inch tyres on black painted rims, small fuel tank made smaller still by having the toolbox built into its top, and single sided brakes. Altogether, comfort was not one of the machine's strong points, but it proved popular in a country short on even the most basic necessities.

In 1949, the 1,000th R24 rolled off the production line (and it should be remembered that quotas had been imposed by the Allies). After 12,010 had been manufactured by May 1950, the R24 was replaced by the more comfortable R25 which had a similar specification to the earlier machine with the addition of plunger rear suspension.

The other model introduced in 1950 was the R51/2, an updated version of the popular pre-war R51. This 494 cc (68 × 68 mm) ohv flat twin gained the following comment in the *Motor Cycle* dated 23 March 1950, in that magazine's report of the Geneva Show, 'The reintroduced 500 cc BMW transverse twin is a very trim, workmanlike looking mount'. Workmanlike indeed, with substantial mudguards – including the renowned 'elephant's ear' voluminously flared front guard – and well shrouded suspension.

The next week, the show bandwagon rolled into Frankfurt, to stage Germany's first really important motorcycling event since the end of the war. As revealed in the Introduction, by the spring of 1950 the domestic industry had already begun its rapid expansion programme. Like many of its rivals, BMW was out in strength at the event, which was organised by the German Association of Cycle and Motorcycle Manufacturers.

At around the same time, Arthur Bourne, then editor of the well-known British magazine *Motor Cycle*, undertook a 2600 mile journey around Europe on an Ariel Square Four. It consisted of a run across France, an amble through Switzerland and into Italy (where he visited several Italian factories including Moto Guzzi and Lambretta), followed by a hasty passage through the Dolomites and the Austrian Tyrol before entering Germany. In all, a total of fourteen companies were visited – six in Italy and eight in Germany – and 15 different machines ridden, amongst them the new 500 class BMW R51/2.

Bourne was no stranger to the marque having first sampled one as far back as the 1927 ISDT. He found riding the new R51/2 was very much 'like returning to an old friend'. He described the changes that had taken place since pre-war days, listing 'new cylinder heads, the incorporation of a cam-type transmission shock absorber in the gearbox, and the employment of a new and much improved four-speed gearbox'.

Each of these features had been first adopted on the 250 single. Earlier, during the previous year, Bourne had tested a sample of the single, an experience which added to his past knowledge of the twins to give him a good idea of what to expect with the new R51/2 – summing it up in the following manner. 'It is one's old friend plus further endearing characteristics. There is greater power at medium revs (which BMW's have sought, rightly maintaining that this gives higher average speeds), improved – much improved – flexibility and a better gearchange. The flexibility impressed me. I found it possible to go down to about 16 mph in top gear with the ignition fully advanced and then to accelerate smoothly..... A very short vibration period occurred at roughly 43 mph (69 kph). At higher speeds, the engine was delightfully smooth'.

There was some criticism of the transmission – a gearchange which despite improvement was 'still not 100 per cent' and a tendency for the clutch to grab – while the rear suspension was rated as too hard. However, Bourne considered the BMW's outstanding production, and wrote 'this latest machine, with its greater flexibility and added power is, I consider, easily the best BMW yet – lively, lusty, beautifully made'.

Even so, BMW saw fit to replace the R51/2 the following year with the R51/3 – essentially a modernised and improved version. Although the power output of 24 bhp was identical, the engine was considerably

With a 590 cc engine the 1954 BMW R67/2 was equally acceptable in either solo or sidecar roles.

different and set a style which in general appearance was still to be visible as late as 1969 on the R69S.

The crankcase – a 'tunnel' casting had an outstandingly clean appearance. Behind a rounded timing cover at the front was the gear drive to the camshaft and magneto ignition. The rocker boxes atop the cylinders on each side were of a new shape and carried cooling fins, while the Bing carburettors were fully waterproofed and ducted into the top of the gearbox, above which was bolted a housing for the external air filter. The gearbox bolted to the back of the crankcase, carrying on its smooth lines, and for the first time it contained a switch which activated a light in the headlamp shell when neutral was selected.

Running gear also saw changes, with the first use of full width brake hubs on a production BMW, front fork gaiters and alloy wheel rims, a larger capacity fuel tank and new exhaust pipes and silencers (now without tail fins).

News of the R51/3 was released at the Brussels Salon in January 1951, where rumours were rife that they were also about to reintroduce a 600 cc ohv twin. This was confirmed the following month when at the Amsterdam Show the R67 made its debut. Powered by a 590 cc

(72 × 73 mm) ohv engine unit which followed the general design of the R51/3 and produced 26 bhp at 5500 rpm. Oddly, it used the cycle parts of the earlier R51/2 – including the fishtail silencers, black painted steel wheel rims and less powerful single-sided brakes.

In fact, the main reason for its appearance was market demand from sidecar users who were looking for a suitable power unit with which to haul a third wheel. However, it was the first appearance of a BMW of over 500 cc in the post-war period, and for that reason alone is noteworthy, despite only 1470 examples ever being produced.

Not only was the R67 replaced by the improved R67/2 at the end of 1951, but the R25 also gained a '2' suffix at the same time. The third bike in the range, the R51/3, remained unchanged for the season, and it was in this form that it was shown at the Swiss Motorcycle Exhibition in Geneva during March 1952. German products dominated this show, and without doubt the sensation was a new BMW, the R68, for which the factory claimed a genuine 105 mph. Although the power was up to 35 bhp at 7000 rpm, largely as a result of engine tuning (including a higher compression ratio), the appearance and general specification followed the rather dated R67/2. Notable additions were a pillion seat as standard equipment, lighter mudguards and a twin leading-shoe front brake operated (like those of

BMWs for the next two decades) by the cable inner pulling one shoe on while the cable outer pushed the other.

The R68 did not replace the R67/2, so BMW's 1952 line contained two 600s, as well as the R51/3 and R25/2. Another notable display at Geneva was one of the 250s hitched to a single seat sports sidecar. All four models were listed the following spring by the British importers AFN Ltd at exotic prices – £215 18s 11d for the R25/2, £339 17s 9d for the R51/3, £343 14s 5d for the R67/2. No price was given for the top of the range R68.

At the important Frankfurt International Motorcycle Show which took place in October, BMW's star exhibit was a *real* show surprise – no less than a 498 cc Rennsport production racer of which the company stated that between 30–50 would be manufactured early in 1954. In fact the bike was *almost* a replica of the bikes campaigned by the factory works riders in '53, but carried telescopic forks instead of the leading link Earles forks on the works bikes and carburettors in place of their fuel injectors. The bike's dry weight was quoted at 297 lb and a maximum speed of 124 mph was claimed – but no price was given!

The only 'new' roadster was the R25/3, which now offered 13 bhp (at the same 5800 rpm), hydraulically damped front forks, an air filter housed within the fuel tank (with a long induction pipe to the carburettor), and the toolbox moved to the side of the tank rather than the top. But perhaps the most obvious change was the introduction of full-width alloy brake drums of a similar design to those first used on the R68 model. When the new 250 went into production, the R25/2 was

BMW motorcycles have seen police service around the world. This photograph was taken when Queen Elizabeth II visited Melbourne, Australia at the end of the 1950's. The motorcycles are R60s, which were launched by BMW in 1955.

discontinued after 38,651 had been made from 1951–3, making it the most popular model BMW had produced up to that time.

For 1954 all three flat twins – the R51/3, R67/2 and R68 – were equipped with the new type of air filter system introduced on the R25/3, and a modified exhaust system whereby both the intake and exhaust silencing were improved. The telescopic front forks on all three models featured improved hydraulic dampers offering not only a softer ride but also improved roadholding. The R68, which in solo form was capable of over 100 mph remained Germany's fastest standard production machine, and for 1954 was available with sidecar attachment lugs.

And so things appeared set into a steady pattern. While other German manufacturers – rather like the Japanese today – were unveiling new designs at a seemingly frenetic pace in a bid to stay competitive, BMW relied on steady improvements and refinements to their basic 250 single, 500 and 600 twins, and remained true to shaft drive and traditional all-black finish with white pinstriping.

At least that was the face they presented to the world. But within the company things were slightly different, for BMW's management was concerned about an uncertain future. Although BMW's 100,000th post-war motorcycle had been built towards the end of 1953 and sales were at record levels, management felt that the company was too exposed to the whims of the enthusiast market when other manufacturers were getting involved with scooters and mini cars. Even on the car front, BMW was then concentrated on the luxury end of the market (actually a similar position to the one which they hold today, but in a vastly different economic climate).

So to broaden BMW's appeal, first came a scooter built in 1954, using a four-stroke ohv engine – but this

never left the prototype stage. But far more important was the Isetta 'bubble car', which did reach production at an early stage in its development.

This was not a BMW original, but a tried and tested design from the Italian Iso concern from which BMW had obtained a licence during 1954. When it first entered production in 1955, it was a four-wheeler – although the twin rear wheels were so close as to make it technically a three-wheeler in some countries. However, it was soon produced as a true three-wheeler to take advantage of tax and insurance concessions available in several other markets, including Britain.

Power was by a fan-cooled version of the R25 engine (later R26 and 27 units) in both the original 245 and later 295 (72 × 73 mm) form from December 1955 onwards. From 1955 to 1962, when production finally came to a halt, 74,312 of the 250 Isettas and 87,416 of the 300 cc models were built. Add to this 34,813 of the stretched 600 version powered by the 594 cc flat twin and it is evident what an important part the Isetta played in BMW history during the late '50s. Later, more use was made of motorcycle power by boring out the 600 flat twin to 698 cc (78 × 73 mm) and fitting it to the excellent 700 light car which was offered in both standard and coupe versions from 1959 to 1964.

While the full story of these vehicles (like the history of BMW's conventional cars) is outside the scope of this book, it is very clear how the use of motorcycle engines gave the company an added bonus of making the most of its design work.

Meanwhile, it had also been exploiting its motorcycle development to the full. The 38th Brussels *Salon* which opened on 15 January 1955 saw a sensation on the BMW stand – two sensations, actually – in the form of a pair of brand new models. The newcomers were the five hundred R50 and the six hundred R69. Both had Earles-type front forks and full swinging arm rear suspension bearing a close resemblance to the factory racers.

However, the treatment of the rear frame was virtually unique in that it also bore a marked resemblance to the old plunger design, with main loops which extended down and back almost as far as the wheel spindle. But instead of the rear frame carrying top and bottom mounts for the old-style plunger boxes, the rear shock absorbers were supported from the middle by the upper portions of the loops. A welded bracket extended rearwards to form the base of a top shroud for the spring/damper unit, which was held in from the top by a threaded alloy boss. The upper portion of the shrouds also formed rear mudguard mountings. This arrangement made for a very rigid frame and was built in this form for the benefit of BMW's many sidecar users. For the same reason, the front forks had dual mountings for the swinging bottom link and suspension units, allowing trail to be adjusted with relative ease. The rear suspension pre-load could be varied simply by turning a handle built into the base of the unit.

A journalist from *Motor Cycling* **road testing a BMW R69. Rural England in the summer of 1960 was more open than today for putting a machine through its paces.**

The rear swinging arm pivoted on taper roller bearings from two adjustable stub spindles screwed into the frame just behind the gearbox. And where previous BMWs had always had an exposed shaft drive, the driveshaft was now enclosed within the right leg of the swinging arm, which bolted to the rear bevel drive casing.

Other differences from earlier models included a deeper fuel tank (still with 17-litre capacity) which featured a large lockable toolbox whose lid formed the left knee grip. There were smaller 18 inch alloy wheel rims, new silencers, new mudguards (although the rear still had a much-appreciated hinged rear section for wheel removal).

Engines were largely unchanged, but power was now up to 26 bhp at 5800 rpm on the R50 and 35 bhp at 6800 rpm on the R69 – both a considerable improvement on the earlier models. The R50's 494 cc (68 – 68 mm) unit had a compression ratio of 6.8:1 (6.3:1 on the R51/3) 24 mm (22 mm) Bing carbs and slightly higher-lift cams. On the larger 594 cc (72 × 73 cc) R69 engine, only the compression ratio was changed to 8:1 instead of 7.5 or 7.7:1 – the cams and 26 mm carbs remained the same.

However, both engines gained a new diaphragm clutch and a new three-shaft gearbox in a redesigned housing, the rear of which carried the output flange to which bolted the universal joint for the drive shaft, and also mounted the rubber gaiter which covered the joint. Although the gearbox was basically a similar four-speed design with a cam lobe shock absorber on the input shaft, it was successful in speeding up what had previously been rather a super-slow gearchange. Ratios were 1st, 5.33:1, 2nd 3.02:1, 3rd 2.04:1, and top 1.54:1.

These two new flat-twins replaced the three previous models, which were all taken out of production at the very end of 1954. Of the trio, the R51/3 had been by far the most successful, with a total of 18,425 produced from 1951–54. Next came the 594 cc R67/2 with 4,260 from 1952–54, and finally the sporting R68, with only 1453 examples during its 1952–54 lifespan.

A R69 was tested by *Motor Cycling* in the 19 April 1956 issue. Top speed was found to be 102 mph with 61 mph being achieved for the standing quarter mile. But the tester made the underlying point that even though the R69 was the 'sports' model in the BMW range, it was still a tourer at heart – albeit a fast, luxury one. As the tester put it, the model represented 'a vast improvement over its predecessors, which themselves held an enviable reputation'.

Despite having two significantly improved flat twins, and an updated 250 in the pipeline (it was soon to emerge as the R26), BMW was beginning to be affected by the upsurge in the popularity of scooters and small cars. Even with the Isetta, things were tough and getting tougher.

High prices did not help. In October 1955, AFN Ltd announced the line-up for Britain in 1956, where the R25/3 would be £220 16s 0d, the R50 and R67/3 £366, and the R69 £476 8s 0d.

Though BMW were to do well in sports (see next chapter) 1956 was not a success commercially. In September, hard on the heels of other factories (including NSU) laying off workers, came the first serious problems for the Munich factory when it was reported that BMW had dismissed 600 workers owing to falling sales. The year's end revealed the full extent of the problems, when it became clear that compared with 1955, production figures had slumped to 15,500 – scarcely half of the previous year's total.

This was despite the fact that all the machines had only recently been updated. Among them, at the end of 1955, the updated 250, the R26 had appeared, superseding the R25/3 of which 47,700 had been built during a three year life.

Very much echoing the R50/69, the R26 gave the visual impression of being much larger than its true capacity of 247 cc (68 × 68 mm). The engine was virtually identical to the R25/3, but had a higher 7.5:1 compression ratio, larger 26 mm Bing carb and other more minor changes giving it a healthy increase in power to 15 bhp at 6400 rpm. The gear ratios were identical to the R50 and R69.

To the eye, the most obvious difference to the power unit was the use of larger finning on the cylinder head to give improved cooling. This also made it look more at home in the cycle parts which were virtually identical to the larger flat twins, other than the front brake (single leading shoe) and the tank which had a 15-litre capacity (2 litres more than the R25/3) with the toolbox in its top. The air filter housing became a massive affair under the seat, which also housed the battery.

Electrics were 6 volt, with a 60 watt Noris generator mounted on the crankshaft, 6.5 inch Bosch headlamp with a 35/35 watt bulb, a substantial stop/tail light, warning lights and electric horn.

This model was well received by the press. *Motor Cycling* tested one in its 27 September 1956 issue. A sub-heading read: 'A Lightweight to a Luxurious Specification'. Costing £256 13s 7d, the R26 was the most expensive 250 on the British market. For that substantial outlay, the purchaser got a machine which was capable of 73 mph, but more importantly, one of high quality which was both mechanically quiet and civilised with its shaft drive, powerful lights, high standard of roadholding and superb comfort.

Other advantages brought out in the test included the ultra-clean engine/gearbox/shaft drive combination, and routine maintenance which was cut to the bare minimum and kept simple. For example, without a secondary chain to adjust, back end fettling consisted solely of occasional oil changes, and moving – by hand – the levers that altered the rear springing from soft to hard as required for the task ahead. The spark plug was 'eminently' accessible, and the valve clearance could be adjusted without having to remove the tank.

The only real criticisms centred around the twistgrip mechanism, which in the tester's opinion 'called for as many as three bites at the cherry to achieve full throttle from the tick-over position' and that bottom gear 'was too low to be other than a hindrance unless take-off was on an adverse gradient of some magnitude'. And like the flat twins, the kick-starter which swung out to the left was best dealt with when the machine was on its stand. No choke was fitted.

Again like the twins, upward gearchanges could only be made progressively and quietly if due allowance was made for the engine clutch by pausing before actual re-engagement of the dogs after declutching. A speedier change, although entirely possible, produced an audible 'clunk' as the cogs went home, and a forward surge as the clutch's excess kinetic energy was absorbed at the rear wheel. However, *Motor Cycling*'s tester was entirely satisfied with the downward gearshift.

The other new model for 1956 was the R60 – basically a replacement for the R67 and aimed at the same sidecar enthusiast market. It therefore had a low compression, 28 bhp engine in the cycle parts of the R50, together with the option of various sidecar ratios in the rear bevel gear. In fact, BMW offered a wide range of special fittings for sidecarrists, including their own 'Spezial' complete sidecar – basically a badged Steib TR500 with flat sides (and not the 'Zeppelin' style Steib almost universally associated with BMWs). Other options were wide handlebars, heavy duty suspension springs, strengthened wheels, sidecar ratios in the gearbox/rear bevel box (and speedometer geared to suit), sidecar wheel brakes using a hydraulic linkage in the motorcycle rear brake rod, and interchangeable wheels all round with a spare on the sidecar rack. That little lot complete would have cost about as much as *three* British 500 cc bikes!

Despite the depressed market, the same spirit which kept up BMW's commitment to the sport ensured their presence at the various international exhibitions which were staged in all the major capitals of Europe. Even though the vitally important domestic show at Frankfurt was a mere two weeks distant, 5 October 1956 saw BMW put on an impressive stand at the 43rd French Motorcycle Show in Paris. At the time, France retained a vibrant two-wheel industry itself with almost five million machines on the roads. And during 1955 a total of 1,145,750 machines (830,575 mopeds, 125,657 scooters and 179,518 motorcycles over 50 cc) were built in the Republic.

Then came the Frankfurt colossus – 'Germany's Third Monster Motorcycle Exhibition' as *Motor Cycling* called it on the 25 October. Superficially, the '56 Frankfurt Show put on a buoyant display as ever, but behind the veneer, things were very, very different for the German motorcycle industry in general, and BMW in particular. In reality, as the event was taking place, no BMW motorcycles were being produced at all and even the previously successful Isetta three-wheeler introduced some two years earlier was proving an embarrassment to the company's management. Production was down almost half to 120 a day and stocks were rising rapidly in

BMW R50/60-series engine.

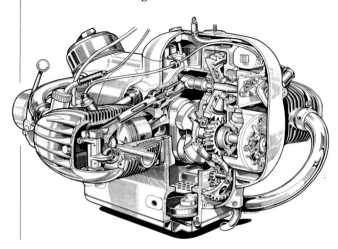

the firm's warehouse. In fact, had it not been for BMW's local Munich bank providing additional working capital, the famous company could well have folded there and then.

That all was not well had been evident to the outside world despite the Frankfurt pazzazz. *Motor Cycling's* Show report had mentioned that 'BMW had nothing new to report', while rivals *Motor Cycle* chose a particularly apt headline above their offering: 'Re-trenchment in Germany'.

As if things were not already bad enough, in 1957 events were to prove even worse, when a total of only 5,400 bikes left the production lines, although Isetta sales did show a slight improvement. This allowed BMW to reduce the level of its overstocks. But at least the situation was not entirely apparent to the outside world, with BMW outwardly at least retaining an air of confidence, assisted in no small part by the company's continued participation in sporting events.

In Britain, BMW continued to attract an enthusiastic following. In October AFN listed four models for 1958. All were on view a month later on Stand number 80 at the Earls Court Show in London. *Motor Cycle's* special Show edition said that 'quietness, smoothness and excellence of design are the outstanding features of the BMW range'. Prices were: R26 £258 4s 8d, R50 £380 9s 9d, R60 £392 19s 3d, and R69 £495 5s 2d. Both three and four-wheel versions of the Isetta were now available in Britain, although the bubble car sales were not handled by AFN, but by Isetta of Great Britain Ltd, based at Brighton, Sussex. Prices ranged from £270 7s 2d for the standard three-wheeler to £365 19s 6d for the Plus (de luxe) four-wheeler.

Financial problems meant no new models for 1958 or 1959, and as expected the Annual Financial Report presented in December 1959 showed BMW heavily in the red. Prior to the meeting, it was widely expected that BMW would accept a take-over bid from Daimler-Benz, but under the leadership of Dr Herbert Quandt, the shareholders came to the rescue with a new business plan. This was accepted by the creditor banks, but it was very much a touch and go operation. The success of the new corporate plan would rest on a series of moves to raise capital not only from the banks but also from the realisation of assets. Hence one of the first moves was to dispose of the aero engine business to MAN Turbo GmbH.

New products called for by the plan, included the development of the 700 saloon car mentioned earlier, and as a side benefit, improvements to the motorcycle line. Ultimately this meant that a whole series of new models appeared in September 1960 at the Frankfurt Show, in time for the 1961 model year. Most notably altered of these was a new 250, the R27. There was also more power for the flat twins, with sports versions of the R50 and R69 – the R50S and R69S – while the R60/2 superseded the earlier R60.

The last of the BMW singles, the R27, was available both in Germany and in other markets 1960–67.

When the R26 was phased out, a total of 30,328 had been built, but the new model seemed well able to shoulder the mantle. Power was increased to 18 bhp at 7400 rpm (formerly 15 bhp at 6400) mainly due to increasing the compression to 8.2:1. To cure vibration, the complete engine assembly, plus the exhaust system, was rubber mounted at front and rear of the crankcase as well as on rubber buffers above and behind the cylinder head. Another improvement was the introduction of an automatic timing chain tensioner using a spring and blade to damp out the chain vibration sometimes noted before. The frame was identical to the R26 except for the modified engine mounts and as before either a single or dual seat could be specified.

Except for minor changes to improve reliability, and an increase in compression ratio from 6.5:1 to 7.5:1 which upped power to 30 bhp at slightly higher revs, the R60/2 was identical to the R60.

Most interesting were the R50S and R69S sportsters – which in traditional BMW fashion really meant sports tourers, although BMW were truthfully able to claim the R69S was 'The fastest German machine – of royal standard indeed – [and] represents the top line of BMW motorcycle production: 42 bhp – 110 mph'.

Motor Cycle went even better on the superlatives when they tested the new top-of-the-line model in 1961 and writing 'Luxury roadster with superb high-speed performance yet docile traffic manners; magnificent steering, roadholding and brakes'. The magazine's fastest one way speed of 108 mph in a very strong side wind proved BMW's 110 mph claim accurate. Perhaps the only real drawback for potential purchasers in Britain at least was the staggering £530 15s purchase

price – almost double that of a home-built vertical twin!

While the extra power of the R69S endowed it with a top speed of 110 mph, the smaller twin was capable of a genuine 100 mph – and all without sacrificing in any way the high degree of comfort and silence of their touring brothers. Both sportsters used the same cycle parts as the earlier R50/60/69 models, with only the addition of a hydraulic steering damper and handlebar end direction indicators as obvious external differences. Engines could be told apart externally by their rocker covers – the sportster engines had two horizontal ribs while the touring models had six (although the high attrition rate of these items in even a minor accident means that they are a less than reliable guide to the provenance of the engine of a second-hand machine). The extra performance was due to modified engines with a compression ratio of 9.2:1 on the 500 giving a resultant power increase to 35 bhp at 7650 rpm, while the figures for the 600 were 9.5:1 and 42 bhp at 7000 rpm. The engines also had a timed rotary breather disc mounted at the front end of the camshaft and connecting it with passages into the crankcase. The only other major difference was to the gear ratios, which were now closer so as to enable the rider to pilot his machine in a more sporting fashion if he wished.

The R69S was to prove much more popular than the R50S, which was discontinued in 1963 after only 1636 had been sold. Interestingly enough, in the earlier range only 2819 R69s had been sold compared to the production of 32,532 R50s.

However, what really ensured BMW's long-term survival was the new 1500 medium car which was launched at Frankfurt in September 1961. Not only did the success of this model transform the company fortunes, but it also pointed the way for the future – which has meant that the ratio of car/motorcycle production has been at around 10 to 1 for the last two decades. One is bound to ask, why did BMW bother to carry on with motorcycles at all? A difficult question with no clear answer, but it could be tradition, prestige, or any manner of other reasons. What is certain is that it wasn't profit.

In fact, the 1960s was largely a period of advance for BMW on four wheels and stagnation for two. Even so, the company never lost its name for quality during this period. Two examples of the attention lavished even on small details: the tank badges on an early 1960s BMW were still made of genuine glass enamel, while the rear brake rod linkage comprised six major parts (plus 18 fasteners, etc), designed to ensure that the pedal was unaffected by suspension movements. From March 1965, British imports were handled by BMW Concessionaires of Victoria Road, Portslade, Brighton, Sussex. Four models were now available – the R27 at £384 14s 10d, R50 at £449 16s 5d, R60 at £451 13s 10d, and the top of the range R69S at £524 9s 10d.

The following month *Motor Cycle* for 22 April carried first details of a new range of flat twins, then in the early prototype stage, and editor Harry Louis was treated to a test ride on one. The essence of the new-look boxer was lighter weight. Over the preceding years, BMWs had put on weight rather than taking it off, as their specification had become more lavish. At 445 lbs, the R69S was in danger of becoming ponderous – even if it could not be accused of lacking performance.

So BMW engineers decided that the next generation of the venerable twins had to be leaner and fitter – but at the same time retaining the company's traditional quality. The first inkling of what was on the way had come when the machines prepared for the 1964 ISDT had appeared with telescopic front forks, a light duplex frame and a souped-up engine reputed to develop 54 bhp.

The machine Louis rode weighed 380 lb, some 50 to 60 lb lighter than the current models. He immediately noticed the weight difference, even when easing it off the stand. And galloping it around Bavaria, it became in Louis' words; 'sheer joy to heel through fast corners, to switch from one angle of lean to the other in an 'S' bend, to take it round tight hairpins, to wiggle slowly along slippery farm tracks'. He summed up the appeal of the concept like this; 'Like middle age spread, the weight climb of luxury bikes is usually in small stages with the cost in convenience and handling going almost unnoticed. Only when the weight is cut back is the deceit really exposed. That's how it is with the Bee-Em'.

Lower weight was not the whole story. There had also been a complete face-lift which had given the bike a much tidier front end, neater, narrower handlebar, blade mudguards, shallower seat, deep tank tailored to fit the frame, and a redesigned exhaust system.

Louis commented 'Yes, my guess is that when the lean look roadster *does* appear it will be very much a plus on the BMW escutcheon. Trouble is, a long, long wait is certain. Like Rolls-Royces, the Munich men set their sights high and won't be hurried'.

It was to be a prophetic statement. The existing range soldiered on for nearly five years, unchanged except for the dropping of the R27 in 1967 and the launch of the 'American only' R50 US, R60 US and R69 US which were sold in North America from early 1968 on. The only difference between these and the standard European machines was that the Earles forks were replaced with telescopics and the handlebars were higher and wider. This was a reflection of the growing interest for Stateside riders in taking their machines off the freeways and interstates on to the dirt roads and rough byways. The teles coped better with this sort of going and BMW responded to the needs of the giant US market accordingly. In July 1968 the price for the R60 US was $1376.

BMW's long-awaited 'new breed' did not appear until 1969, but the machines launched at the Cologne Show that September were indeed very close to the prototype tested by Louis nearly half a decade earlier.

View of 245 cc R27 engine showing operation of the overhead valve system.

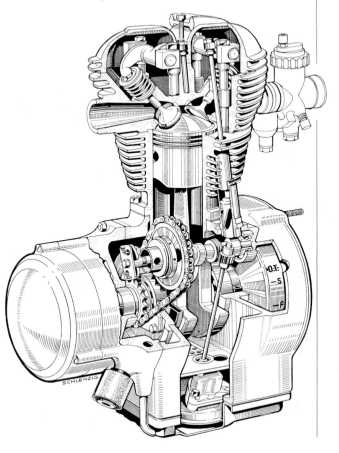

There were three new bikes, the R50/5, R60/5 and R75/5. The 'Stroke 5s', as they became known, appeared just at the right time. Spearheaded by the Japanese new wave, motorcycling was heading out of recession. The first of the superbikes had appeared and the market was ready and waiting for the new bikes from BMW.

The newcomers totally replaced the old models. While the engines were still the traditional flat twins continuing the layout pioneered by Max Friz back in 1923, there were some important changes. The most important of these were to the crankshaft and the position of the camshaft.

The earlier crank had been a pressed-up assembly, which was replaced by a simple but strong two-throw forging. To improve the balance of the flat twin layout, BMW engineers devised small counterweights which were bolted onto the crankshaft web and chosen to suit the weight of the respective pistons. These changes enabled the engines to have a larger capacity than would otherwise have been possible.

The crank was mounted in plain bearings at each end. The rear bearing was housed directly in the large light-alloy crankcase casting, while the forward bearing was held in a detachable support plate. The one-piece assembly meant that split shell big-end bearings were needed, which in turn required a new higher pressure lubrication system. An Eaton-type oil pump (a new departure for BMW) was driven from the end of the camshaft and supplied the lubricant via a proper car-type filter. And where on the earlier models the camshaft had been gear-driven and mounted above the crankshaft, it was now carried below the crank and driven by chain.

A distinctive feature of the old cylinder barrels had been the pair of pushrod tubes on the top, but these had now disappeared underneath. And the barrels themselves were now cast in light alloy instead of iron, with pressed-in cast-iron liners. The cylinder heads were light alloy as before, but of improved design and with the traditional detachable one-piece rocker covers.

Each of the three engines used a stroke of 70.6 mm, with cylinder bore sizes of 67, 73.5 and 82 mm giving 498, 599 and 746 cc (the otherwise near-identical specification gave rise to a quip that only BMW could charge more money for a bigger hole!).

Carburettors on the smaller models were conventional Bing instruments but on the 750 were of the CV (constant vacuum) type. The power outputs were 32 bhp for the R50/5, 40 bhp for the R60/5 (both at 6400 rpm), and 50 bhp at 6200 rpm for the R75/5. All three shared a common three-shaft gearbox with the same internal ratios.

Another change was the replacement of the former 90 watt dynamo/magneto electrics with an 180 watt alternator with coil ignition – and for the first time, 12 volt electrics. Electric starting was standard on the two larger models, and although the headlight was similar to the old type built-in speedo and ignition switch on top, another innovation was the full set of four direction indicators with rectangular lenses.

The most obvious change to the whole bike was that the redesigned engine assembly was mounted into a frame which was not only considerably lighter than the old one, but used a completely different layout. It was built up using oval section tubing joined by an inert gas welding process which produced not only very strong, but well-finished joints.

The frame was in two sections – there was a separate main duplex cradle around the engine, and a rear sub-frame carrying the seat and the top mountings for the rear suspension, which bolted to the main frame loops at four points. The main section was based around a single, substantial top backbone welded to the base of the headstock. A pair of tubes ran down diagonally and splayed out from the top of the headstock, curved round and back to form a double cradle under the engine, then up and round to meet the main backbone under the nose of the seat. There was a cross brace just below the steering head and a further tube ran back from this to the underside of the backbone.

The rear suspension pivot points and swinging arm arrangement were similar to the earlier models, and the rear suspension units retained the old load adjuster handles. As on the '65 prototype, a telescopic front fork was used, developed from the ISDT mounts – because on the long distance trials models rubber fork gaiters were fitted. The front wheel spindle was carried ahead on lugs cast into the front of the forks, rather than at the end as on most machines, and so a greater spring/damper length was possible. One loss regretted by some owners was that the interchangeable wheels had gone, for where these had both previously been of 18 inch diameter and had identical (very expensive) hubs with splines for the rear drive, the front tyre was now 3.25 × 19 inch and the rear was 4.00 × 18.

To many died-in-the-wool BMW enthusiasts and not a few others, the new/5 machines did not have the air of quality or the charisma of their forerunners – even though they might be more efficient motorcycles. There was more use of plastic, for example, and simplification in production engineering. Some people were suspicious of the soundness of the bolted-up rear subframe, and it was noted that for the first time BMW did not recommend the /5 machines for sidecar use. And almost sacrilegiously, the new owner was even offered a choice of a wide range of colours! Previously, the only alternative to black with white coachlines had been a 'negative image' white with black lines.

There was another break with tradition, too. For where the company had always been linked with the Bavarian capital, Munich, it came as a shock to many enthusiasts to realise that the new twins were actually

being made at a new factory in Spandau, West Berlin. This had become almost inevitable with the car side booming and needing all the space available at Munich. A start had been made on the Spandau site at the end of 1966, and it was partly the need to get this ready that had accounted for the long delay between the prototype and the first appearance of the new range of bikes in 1969.

In fact, the 'new' site had been used for aero engine manufacture until the end of the Second World War. It initially employed 850 workers. The chief executive there was Horst Spintler (40 years old at the time) whose official title was managing director of the motorcycle sales division. Spintler had joined BMW early in 1964 after four years with the German branch of Agip, the Italian oil giant, and five years with the German industrial conglomerate, Krupp.

Initially, the Spandau complex was essentially an assembly, rather than manufacturing plant. However, after five years and several millions spent on tooling, the only part of the motorcycles still manufactured at BMW's Munich headquarters were crankshafts and gearboxes – components which were soon to be made at Spandau.

By then the workforce had risen to 1500, with over half of these non-German, with a high percentage being Turkish *gästarbeiter*. There was even one Irishman on the line who had ridden all the way to Germany in search of work – on his own BMW! Today, with high

BMW replaced the Earles-forked R50/60 series in 1969 with the /5-series. The new models not only were significantly lighter but had telescopic forks. R60/5 is shown.

unemployment throughout Europe it may seem strange, but being in Berlin in the early 1970s, BMW had great difficulty finding labour. Management was openly making serious attempts at recruiting workers throughout Europe, including some of those formerly employed within the once great British motorcycle industry.

Throughout 1970 and 1971, the new range remained unchanged. In August 1970, British prices were R50/5 £762 8s 10d, R60/5 £826 8s 5d, and the R75/5 £998 14s 10d . . . the day of the £1,000 BMW had almost arrived.

A little known fact of the early 1970s was that BMW and the Austrian Puch discussed a plan to join forces to produce a completely new range of 250 and 350 overhead cam parallel twins – the idea being that Puch would build these in its Graz factory and that they would be marketed as BMW-Puchs. Unlike BMW, Puch had spare factory capacity, while BMW could easily accommodate the new models within its substantial export and marketing divisions. It was also hinted that Puch might be able to help solve the labour shortage at Spandau by producing components for the flat twins. But although several prototypes appeared, the BMW-Puch parallel twins never entered production – even though it was stated in 1971 that production would commence early the following year with a planned output of 25,000 machines per annum.

For 1972, several alterations were introduced to the /5 range. Mechanically, these were mostly small modifications, although within the engine, the flywheel weight was reduced. This made a slightly more revvy power delivery – particularly on the smaller unit. The size of the rear wheel rim was increased from WM2 to WM3, although the tyre size remained the same at 4.00 × 18 (there was in any case little clearance alongside the shaft to fit a larger one) and on the 750, the rear bevel box ratio was lowered. In an effort to improve the bend swinging capability, the rear suspension units were modified, and as a safety measure the propstand was changed for one which automatically sprang up as soon as the dead weight of the motorcycle was removed. However, this 'mousetrap' device was not popular with many riders.

There were also more cosmetic changes, and it was undoubtedly these that drew the most adverse comment. The capacity of the fuel tank was reduced to 17.5-litres, giving it a flatter appearance, and chromium plated panels were added to its sides. The gap between the main and subframe tubes on each side was filled by chromed metal panels, and the twin grab-handles on the pillion seat were merged to loop round the rear. But the smaller tank (and to a lesser extent the garish side panels) were never popular, and in fact for 1973 BMW were forced back to the original 21-litre tank (without the chrome panels) for most models sold in Britain.

The only other change for that year was a significant one, for the swinging arm was stiffened and lengthened by 50 mm to produce the so-called 'long wheelbase' frame. This was intended to cure a previous tendency for a see-sawing effect to become apparent when opening or closing the throttle.

In May of 1973, two standard production R75/5s were entered in a successful attempt to win the coveted Maudes Trophy. The Trophy was originally the gift of Mr. Pettyt from Maudes of Exeter and was first known as the Pettyt Trophy. Only awarded to motorcycle manufacturers for *really* meritorious performance, it had been won pre-war nine times. In the post-war period prior to BMW's attempt, the judges had rewarded BSA in 1952 and Honda in 1963. Since 1973 it has only been awarded twice more.

BMW's submission indeed deserved to join this select band. A team of 14 riders made up mainly from the British press but including racer Tony Jefferies and TT Chief Travelling Marshal Alan Killip were to ride the two R75/5s for seven continuous days and nights over the Isle of Man TT course. For seven days and seven nights it rained almost incessantly. One machine crashed, and one suffered clutch problems, but despite the conditions, at the end of the week the machines had covered 16,658 miles. Even so, BMW and their team of riders and back-up crew were kept waiting for many

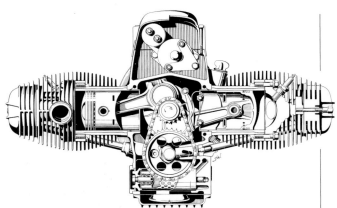

A major engine change between BMW /5-series and what went before was the replacement of the helical gears at the front of the crankcase with cheaper chain and sprocket.

months until October, when the ACU finally announced that their performance had been successful and that the Maudes was theirs.

In fact, the machines were already about to be supplanted. On 2 October, at the Paris Show, the company made its next move in the evolution of its classic flat twin design. The choice of Paris was no doubt deliberate, for it was there 50 years before that BMW had presented its very first motorcycle, the R32, to the public.

Now, not only had the company made significant changes to its existing models, so that the /5 range was now totally replaced by the /6 series, but it had also hurled itself headlong to the top of the Superbike League with a pair of brand-new 900 cc models. The first was a superb sports model, the R90S, which *Motor Cycle News* called the 'BMWunderbike!' In its styling it represented a milestone in BMW history featuring a dual 'racing-style' seat, fairing cowl, twin hydraulic front disc brakes and an exquisite airbrush custom paint job in smoked silver-grey for the tank, seat and fairing which not only took time but meant that no two R90Ss were ever absolutely identical. The fairing not only provided a surprising degree of protection for the rider, but also housed a more powerful 180 mm halogen headlamp, a voltmeter and electric clock. For the first time BMW had employed a stylist on their motorcycles – Hans Muth.

The second 900, the R90/6, was the touring model and shared much the same specification as the other two new models, the R75/6 and R60/6. The styling was more sporting than the /5 machines, with new plastic side panels and silencers, together with a much more modern treatment of the headlamp, instruments and handlebar controls.

The increase in engine size for the largest BMW had come about as the factory had watched the buying public becoming more and more capacity conscious,

To mark 50 years of motorcycle production BMW launched sporting R90S in 1973. Highly regarded by riders the engine delivered 67 bhp and top speed of around 125 mph.

sounding the death knell of the 500 unit, an engine size which they had employed for half a century.

In reality, the 900 cc BMW was not really 'new' at all. As far back as July 1971, *Motor Cycle* had carried a story by Ernst Leverkus – a leading journalist and father of Germany's famous Elephant Rally – in which he related that despite non-committal comments by the factory, he had proof that some 900 engines (rumoured for years) had been provided for top trials riders Sebastian Nachtmann and Karl Ibschar. Unbeknown to BMW, Leverkus had actually tried a stock R75/5 fitted with just such an engine.

The R90/5 as he called it showed a significant increase in both power and torque. From a standstill, 62.5 mph was reached in a mere 4.6 seconds, and 87 mph came up in 10 seconds, 100 mph in less than 15 seconds and 112 in 25 seconds. This was on standard R75/5 gearing, which undergeared the 900 to the extent that it revved 750 rpm beyond the power peak of 6000 rpm, which gave a top speed of 120 mph prone and 106 mph sitting bolt upright.

Finally, Leverkus posed several significant technical questions – with all that power and torque, he would prefer a longer wheelbase. And how would the

crankcase, transmission and even wheel spokes stand up? Interestingly, the factory showed it had done its own testing, as by the time the 900 finally appeared in production these criticisms had largely been answered.

All the new models had crankcases with stronger internal webs to cope with the extra power and (as with the /5s) used the same 70.6 mm stroke, with different bore sizes – which made the 898 cc engine (identical in dimensions to the prototype) very much a short-stroke with its 90 mm bore. At the time development engineer Hans von der Marwitz said that had they gone any bigger the cylinder liner would have been too thin. The crankshafts again were the same but the 900 had heavier tungsten inserts in its counterweights. All the new models featured five-speed gearboxes – another first on production BMWs.

The R90S also used two huge 38 mm Dell'Orto PHF carbs, featuring accelerator pumps to ensure instant punch without flat spots. The sportster also had larger exhaust valves, a hotter cam profile and a series of holes at the rear of the crankcase for better air supply. All this boosted the power up to 67 bhp.

Vents in the front of the engine casings on all the new models allowed more cooling air to the larger 280 watt alternator. They were also given larger batteries – up from 15 to 25 amp/hour.

Frames remained virtually the same, with a bolt-up rear section and just the addition of extra gussets at the steering head. Rear suspension was three-way adjustable – still with a hand lever, while the front forks on the R90/S had an additional 30 mm movement compared to the other models. BMW's reason for doing this was stated simply by development boss von der Marwitz, 'We did this because the twin discs at the front are so fantastic. And we also want big comfort. With tougher forks you lose comfort'.

The twin discs of the R90S were indeed a revelation in braking power although hydraulic disc brakes had been available as an aftermarket accessory for the /5s. These were marketed by BMW sidecar star Heinz Luttringhauser. British Lockheed calipers were used on these conversions, with a double disc unit mounted on a conventional drum-type hub. Now there were single disc front brakes on the R90/6 and R75/6, too – the R60/6 was the only model to retain drums front and rear, but without the chrome trims which had graced the /5 models. Unusually, BMW's hydraulic brakes featured remote master cylinders hidden under the tank and operated by a short cable from the handlebar lever. And the calipers, mounted behind the fork leg, were also unusual in that they 'floated' on an adjustable pivot, rather than being rigidly mounted.

The 1975 range, announced towards the end of 1974 saw several modifications, including perforated discs on the R90S. BMW claimed at the time that these gave better braking in the wet, removing the previous heart-stopping lag as the water was evaporated off the discs. But their most notable achievement from the rider's point of view was to create a new sound dimension to motorcycling – siren brakes! And nothing had been done to lessen the braking effort required with the single brakes on the R75/6 and R90/6. The forks and fork spindles were stiffened on all models.

The kickstart was finally dropped as a standard option (but was available to special order). The starter motor was uprated to lessen the possibility of failure in sub-zero conditions, and the battery was increased in size.

All models now had Hella switchgear and cranked Magura control levers that required shorter hand reach. The switches had tell-tale messages as required by American law, but ergonomically they appeared to be no better than the old units.

There was also a new range of colour options, with the R90S now also available in Daytona orange, a smoked finish similar to the previous (and continuing) grey. In Britain the new models were launched at Donington Park, just opened as a new museum and race circuit, at prices of £1244.47 for the R60/6, £1464.79 for the R75/6, £1598.40 for the R90/6, and £1874.88 for the R90S.

The biennial Cologne Show in September 1976 heralded the announcement of the /7 series in 600, 750 and new 1000 cc capacities. It also saw, more significantly, the introduction of a completely new concept for BMW – the fully-faired R100RS. Its fairing had absorbed the lion's share of the development budget, and represented a new era not only for BMW,

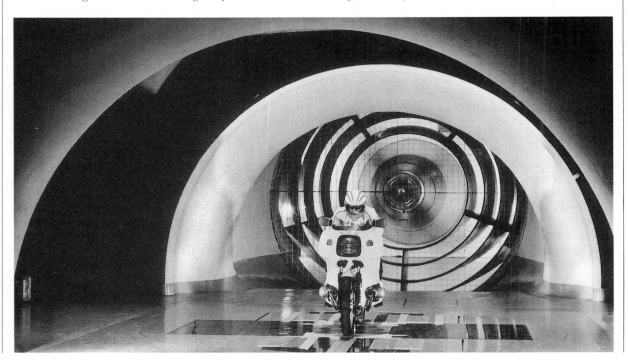

but also for motorcycling in general. Certainly, comprehensive fairings had been offered by manufacturers before, but the R100RS was to be the world's first truly successful series production motorcycle with full protection.

To achieve an optimum shape, BMW hired the famous Pininfarina wind tunnel in Italy – at a cost of £2,500 per day. Tufts of wool and strategically placed electrodes allowed scientists to measure the airflow in the tunnel at speeds in excess of 100 mph. As a result of these experiments, the fairing gained small spoilers level with the front mudguard to enhance the downthrust on the front wheel, and a lip on the screen which left the rider cocooned in a pocket of still air.

The 600 and 750 retained most of their internals, and the only outward difference was new-style finning on the barrel, squared-off rocker covers and new crankcase badges. Internally, the valve gear had small changes, including the use of alloy tappets. The 600 now had a disc brake in place of the old front drum.

A larger engine capacity for the top models had been achieved by boring out the cylinders even more than on the discontinued 900, to 94 mm, giving 980 cc. The touring R100/7 had a 9:1 compression ratio, upped to 9.5 on the R100RS sports engine – which also had 40 mm Bing carbs in place of 32 mm instruments. Larger bore exhaust pipes were also used.

Without doubt, the R100RS set new standards for the ultimate riding machine – Futureshock! as one magazine called it. And superlatives were common amongst the ranks of the road testers.

Above all, there was the price to be justified. At that time, none of its main rivals cost more than £2,000 – the Honda Gold Wing GL1000 was £1,600, Moto Guzzi's 850 Le Mans was £1,999, Benelli's 750 Sei was £1,798, a Kawasaki Z900 cost £1,369, a Dunstall Honda 900 £1,750, and a Ducati 860GTS £1,499. BMW's had always been costly compared to the rest, but the R100RS was staggeringly expensive at £2,899.

Even so, that did not stop the plaudits. *Motor Cycle Mechanics* said in January 1977 'Quite Simply, An Outstanding Bike' and tester Bob Goddard found that although 'the BMW is not perfect – in fact there are quite a few things wrong with it . . . in all the major requirements of a very serious motorcycle for a very serious (and wealthy) motorcyclist the R100RS is outstanding'. He achieved a maximum speed of 116 mph and an average fuel consumption of 47 mpg over track testing and relatively sedate touring. With the large tank, this gave a range of well over 200 miles.

Star features included the riding position and superb level of protection offered by the injection moulded fairing. 'You can cruise the R100RS at 100 mph plus all

Optimising the fairing shape of BMW's R100RS demanded the sophisticated facilities of the famous Pininfarina wind tunnel in Italy. A bargain at £2,500 a day to hire.

Neale Shilton rode the 2000th British police service BMW from Munich to Earls Court. He arrived to display the machine at the 1980 Motorcycle Show.

day without the strain of being buffeted by a hurricane'. The engine torque (greatly improved over the R90S) gave it a 'long-legged gait' while there was praise for the 'superlative suspension and handling, instrumentation and windtone horns which let out enough noise 'to wake a sleeping policeman'.

But as Goddard also revealed, there were for such an expensive machine quite a few detail disappointments. Things like 'the screen edge trim which peeled off during the test' and 'the headlamp window in the fairing which leaked allowing dirt-contaminated water to dirty the inside of the glass where it reduced headlamp power and was impossible to clean'. A lasting problem for many owners was also that as if to prove that not even top-of-the-tree motorcycles are perfect, on early machines the bellows which sealed each fork leg to the fairing persisted in defying attempts to fix them in place and responding to gravity by drooping down the fork leg to the embarrassment of the rider.

But if these things were relatively minor annoyances, another area of disappointment was the braking from the twin drilled discs at the front. These 'lacked bite and needed quite a lot of pressure to haul the bike down from high speeds in a hurry'. And the seat came in for harsh criticism. On the early models there was a massive hump at the rear giving it very odd dimensions. 'It is big enough for one-and-a-half people, making it almost as unsuitable for solo use as with a pillion passenger cramped in behind'. It was also poorly padded – 'the edges of the seat pan were so thinly covered with sponge that they dug into the thighs when stopped at traffic lights, etc' – and although the

British R100RS seen at a BMW rally in 1980. Banner in background celebrates joy of riding motorcylces.

hump lifted to reveal a handy compartment and lift-out tray, this unfortunately again 'let the water in'.

When the new model range was introduced towards the end of 1977, there were 19 improvements to the old models. These included a hydraulic single disc at the rear on the R100RS and twin discs on the front for the R100/7. There were improved gearchange linkages, redesigned instruments, a first aid kit, single key locking, a foam cover over the handlebars to reduce injuries in head-on shunts, and an audible warning for the direction indicators. There were many who would not consider the irritating squawk of the latter to be an 'improvement'.

The R75/7 was to be dropped and replaced by the new 797 cc (84.8 × 70.6 mm) R80/7 costing £1899. *Motor Cycle News* considered it 'Probably the best compromise of all the flat twins: smooth power delivery, but with plenty of low down torque', while *Motorcycling Monthly* asked whether the new 800 was 'an improvement or just a replacement for the 750?'

In the autumn of 1978 BMW made its biggest ever drive into the medium weight market with the introduction of the 473.4 cc R45, its smallest-ever flat twin, and the 649.6 cc R65 which replaced the long-running R60/5/6/7.

There was also a third model for the German domestic market only. This was the R45N, with its engine down-graded to 27 bhp to take advantage of the large insurance saving offered to German riders of bikes with power outputs below that figure.

For the last decade BMW had reorganised their marketing and retreated more and more into the sale of high-priced machines for well-heeled enthusiasts. With the introduction of these middleweights, all that changed overnight as if the company now considered it was time to go onto the attack and challenge the mass market.

Apart from the obvious difference in capacity, the newcomers were almost identical, with a common stroke of 61.5 mm, the same 9.2:1 compression ratio, and identical 32 mm exhaust valves. The smaller engine had a 70 mm bore and 34 mm inlet valve, while the R65 had an 82 mm bore and 38 mm inlet. The carbs were 28 and 32 mm CV Bings, respectively. Of the two sizes, the R45 was smoother, but the R65 was much the nicer and more relaxing to ride because of the larger capacity and increased torque. A new ignition system offered dynamic ignition advance and helped to even out the already smooth power delivery, although there were those who found a vibration period on the R65 sufficiently bad to discourage cruising exactly on Britain's 70 mph limit. However, an important change was the addition of a torsion damper to the driveshaft to smooth the ride during acceleration and braking. It almost totally eliminated the previous torque reaction from the flat-twin layout.

The frame was argon-arc welded in the same gauge tubing as the /7's and to similar dimensions, although the main backbone was a single tube rather than double as on the larger models. The wheelbase was shorter by 50 mm thanks to a shorter swinging arm, and there were new front forks with the calipers mounted higher on the sliders and the spindle carried at the end rather than in front. These forks had different damping rates compared to the larger twins, but still gave 175 mm travel.

Wheels were a spider's web of pressure cast alloy. Available as options on the /7 models, on which they proved prone to failure, they were standard on the smaller machines, although both were 18 inch diameter with 3.25 front and 4.00 rear tyres.

Both models' petrol tanks now had a sharper styling but a typically-BMW generous capacity of 22-litres. There was neater switchgear and a comprehensive unit enclosing the instruments and offering space for additional switches, plus a clock. The Bosch headlamp was smaller at 160 mm compared with the earlier 180 mm unit but was still powerful as it was provided with the same H4 quartz halogen 60/55 watt bulb.

The two machines weighed exactly the same – 452 lb dry. Even in its export form the R45 only produced 35 bhp (below many Japanese *250s* of the period) and was to prove generally unpopular because of its poor acceleration, even though BMW claimed a top speed of 99 mph against 108 mph for the R65. The 27 bhp home-market R45 was quite frankly one of the most lifeless motorcycles that BMW ever produced.

In retrospect, the R45/R65 middleweights were very much a stop-gap solution to BMW's by now ageing larger flat twins. Though in late 1978 yet another 'new' large twin – the R100RT with voluminous touring fairing – was introduced alongside an improved R100RS with 70 bhp on tap, cast alloy wheels and a choice of either the original 1½ seat or a more practical conventional dualseat.

By winter 1978 it became known that BMW was planning for a major programme of change to enable the motorcycle division to survive into the 1980s – and beyond. As part of this process, a major reconstruction of plant and machinery at Spandau had been under way for some time and was completed during 1979.

The essence of the strategy was that both new three and four cylinder water-cooled engines were already under development. For many years rumours – often pure fantasy – had surfaced concerning various new designs, including four cylinder models. But the 1978 story was based on fact, as later events were to prove.

One of the main reasons for at long last looking away from the flat-twin concept were the problems besetting

Laverda was a partner in the development of BMW R80 G/S. It was an excellent roadster. Still available in the late 1980's the model pioneered Monolever rear suspension.

sales in the lucrative North American market. A slump had left some 7,000 units of the BMW range unsold out of a budgeted 30,000. Where they had been the leading European make in 1977, they had slipped from sixth overall to eleventh behind the Swedish low-volume off-road bike builders Husqvarna.

Not only this, but at home BMW had slumped to a lowly seventh place in the market share table, largely due to keen price competition (dumping, in other words) from Japanese imports. In October 1978 the chief manager Count Rudolph von der Schulenberg resigned, and the new man at the helm was now Dr Eberhardt Sarfert. Schulenberg's departure was soon followed by a drastic bid to get the balance of the motorcycle division right, when all three of the chief engineer, sales and financial directors were 'relieved' from their jobs and transferred within the company.

At the time, BMW's press relations manager Michael Schimpke denied that the company was in dire straits, but did admit that the problem was critical, even going as far as to comment, 'It doesn't take a lot to see that it could have become very serious indeed if we had not been quick to make management changes'. He was also confident that BMW could 'redistribute' the 7,000 unsold machines in the USA.

Chief reason for the predicament was the falling

price of the dollar against the strong Deutschmark which had prompted two price rises during 1978. However, another reason was the friction between BMW and their long-term concessionaires, Bulter and Smith of New York City.

The American company had known for some time that BMW would try to dispense with its services sooner or later, and set up its own subsidiary. And when the contract term expired at the end of 1979, relations between the two companies rapidly soured, accounting for a very large part of the poor US sales record of BMW in the late 70s.

BMW's export fortunes, despite the USA, were not uniformly bad. British sales of the flat twins had never been better. In the year ending December 1979, BMW Concessionaires GB Ltd increased their market share from 0.88 to 1.45 per cent – a rise of 61 per cent – accounting for total sales of 2,518 machines. A major cause of this had been the massive increase in the use of BMWs as police machines. Dominance was so great that 44 of the 50 British constabularies which used motorcycles had BMWs in service. By then the police and various British government departments had 1,262 BMWs on the road and orders placed for another 322 machines.

Parts and accessories sales amounted to almost £1 million, and the motorcycle side of BMW Concessionaires was looking increasingly profitable. The network had 86 dealers around the country. General manager Ian Watson commented, 'We've had a superb year, latterly taking 27 per cent of the over 750 cc market and plan on capitalising and building on that success in 1979'. What form that would take was not said, but at the same time an official denial was given

regarding the machines which would ultimately replace the boxers at the top of the market. Anton Hille, managing director of BMW Concessionaires stated, 'BMW are not planning to introduce a new, shaft-driven water-cooled four-stroke triple or any other superbike in the foreseeable future'.

But all was not to remain sweetness and light between the British importers (in reality a private company, TKM) and BMW. Although TKM had held the concession for over 10 years, from 1 January 1980 a factory-controlled and financed operation took over. As Pat Myers, general manager of the new BMW (GB) Ltd explained, 'It's the policy of BMW in Germany to have its own subsidiaries to import their cars and motorcycles. As a sister company we have a long-term commitment to BMW. Of course, we have to make a profit, but it's the future we're interested in and that's why we plan to spend more on marketing. As far as the factory is concerned, they can take the overall view of all their markets and that helps them to control their production'.

BMW's new wholly owned, multi-million pound headquarters in Bracknell, Berkshire was a reflection of the German company's world-wide approach to marketing for the new decade. Although it must be stressed that this was in the main due to the success of BMW cars around the globe, and the profits they generated, rather than anything achieved by the motorcycle division.

But as an indication of just what could be achieved with the flat twin layout, the Cologne show in September saw a BMW exhibit called the Futuro, with turbocharged 800 cc engine capable of over 125 mph from 75 bhp output. That speed mainly came from the

Below **All BMW road-going twins, triples and fours now feature Monoshock suspension. The R80 ST was given this form of suspension for its debut in 1982.**

Opposite above **At the 1980 Cologne Show the wraps were taken off the Futuro flat twin design project.**

Opposite below **Futuro with streamlined cladding removed.**

Below **Computers drove Futuro instrument cluster.**

aerodynamics of the carbon-fibre reinforced plastic fairing. The designers had also gone to considerable lengths to pare weight from the running gear, including spun aluminium solid disc wheels, alloy disc brakes and frame in a mixture of tube and alloy sheet.

Although more of a design exercise than a serious production possibility, the Futuro nevertheless gave an interesting insight into the wide range of technical features then under consideration within the BMW research department.

The turbo system closely followed similar work being carried out by the Japanese. Perhaps BMW was fortunate from a financial point of view that the Futuro project never entered production – as no doubt corporate chiefs of the Big Four Japanese makers would concur, with the benefit of hindsight, regarding their respective embarrassing production turbo sales failures.

The Futuro's boost pressure was controlled by a microprocessor which took full account of the revs and running temperature of the engine. The fuel injection by Bosch LH Jetronic system had hot wire air metering to register the airflow into the engine. This gave what BMW claimed was the smoothest possible torque curve with lowest fuel consumption.

BMW's future looked, if not brilliant, at least healthy. And as *Motor Cycle Weekly* was able to report on 15 November 1980, the drastic fall in sales that had by then started to take its toll on the motorcycle industry around the world did not seem to have affected BMW, certainly not in Britain. By then, falling profits and redundancies were starting to become common in an industry which was to be affected more than most by the recession which hit the industrialised world in the early 80s. But as *Motor Cycle Weekly* stated 'BMW GB is above its target for sales and registrations . . . A lantern in the gloom'.

The same issue carried an exclusive 'first time' test of the new R80G/S trail bike. Tester Graham Sanderson began his test report with 'How's this for a sweeping statement: BMW's new 800 cc R80 G/S trail bike is their best roadster and certainly the most memorable machine of the year'.

There had been off-road BMWs for many, many years, but the new model was able to cash in on BMW's successful return to long distance trials in 1978 and comprehensive triumphs in the ISDT the following year. Further success in the gruelling Paris-Dakar rally of 1980 had also helped with the launch of the R80 G/S – the G stood for *Gelände* – off-road.

But BMW made it plain that the G/S was not intended as a serious off-road challenger, rather to provide a special dirt bike style on road, where the 797 cc (84.8 × 70.6 mm) engine produced 49 bhp and catapulted the lightweight G/S to a 107 mph maximum. The true competition bikes were a mere 304 lb, while the production model was some 96 lb heavier.

Additionally, their engines were both more powerful and peakier, making them the preserve of truly expert riders only.

This said, the production G/S was not only radically styled (the project had been conceived with the close collaboration of the Italian bike builders Laverda) but also saw a number of innovative departures from BMW's conventional roadster practice.

Engine weight was reduced by 15 lb, for example, by using aluminium cylinders with a Galnikal bore coating and by paring dead weight from the single plate diphragm clutch assembly. The latter was reduced in diameter without reducing friction area, while the housing was trimmed and slotted for better cooling. This not only lessened the effort of clutch operation, but also virtually eliminated noise when changing gear.

But it was the rear drive and suspension layout which made the G/S so distinctive amongst other production BMWs, for there was simply a swinging arm containing the drive shaft on the right, the wheel was completely unsupported on the left, effecting a considerable weight saving. There was no loss of structural rigidity, claimed BMW. In practice, this 'monolever strut' was a boon – not only did it facilitate quick and easy removal of the rear wheel, but it was also largely responsible for the newcomer's excellent handling. The point was not lost by BMW and by 1985 was to be used on the whole model range.

Other weight saving features compared to the normal roadsters were a high-level two-into-one exhaust, plastic mudguards, a simpler control console without a rev counter, fibreglass seat pan, and a single perforated brake disc now operated by a Brembo caliper and pads with a high metal content.

At a British price of £2,449 in November 1980, the R80G/S slotted squarely into the middle of the BMW price range. The remainder of this consisted of the R45 at £1,950, R65 at £2,194, R100 at £2,594, R100CS (with R90S style cockpit fairing) at £2,975, and R100RS and R100RT at £3,497. For the 1981 model year, all these machines adopted the new coated alloy bores in place of the older cast liners. This allowed substantial reductions in piston/bore clearance and new piston rings were fitted. The whole range also benefited from modifications to the clutch, bringing improvements in gear changes.

To improve lubrication, the oil passages were redesigned, and a deeper sump ensured that sloshing during braking or acceleration would not starve the oil pick-up point. A Bosch transistorised ignition system finally replaced the twin points on the end of the crankshaft and a new type of electronic voltage regulator was used. A new air filter and box reduced intake noise, while throttle control was simplified so that a single cable operated a junction box to feed both carbs. The choke moved from under the petrol tank to the handlebar, and the optional kickstarter was

Touring scene typical of the country in Southern Germany close to where this R80 RT was built in the early 1980's.

redesigned so that its gearing turned the engine over quicker.

There was little modification to the frame apart from an alteration which allowed easier removal of the battery, although some models had their swinging arms lengthened while others received stronger driveshaft tubes to improve swinging arm strength. A new rear drive shell improved both cooling and torsional rigidity; as well as holding more oil.

The braking systems, however, were changed much more extensively. The floating calipers were replaced by fixed units which needed no adjustment for pad wear. And a new pad material was used which contained no asbestos (now recognised as a potential health hazard) but which was claimed to give as much as a 40 per cent improvement in wet weather braking.

And so the twins remained until late 1981, when BMW announced that it had started to tool up for production of a new 1000 cc water-cooled four. It was reported that the company had set aside £35.5 million in a dramatic bid to double its motorcycle production by the mid-1980s, meaning in effect a sales target of 60,000 machines a year by 1985. This was the year when the new model was first expected to hit the streets. In reality, this starting date was to prove over-pessimistic.

BMW also announced a new 650 twin, the R65LS. It was basically a restyled sports R65. It had a 'flow line' treatment of the seat and tank, together with a small nose fairing, plus a new front mudguard and new cast alloy wheels. Colours were more flamboyant, red with white wheels or all silver, with matt black silencers and other parts. The handlebars were dropped, weight was down, and the engine was more powerful, but otherwise it was still very much an R65 in prettier clothing.

The next development of the twins appeared in the autumn of 1982 at Cologne. The R80ST was a successful roadster conversion of the G/S trail bike, and although it was only available for a relatively short period, it was nevertheless a popular rider's mount. It retained the same single shock, monolever rear suspension, tall chassis and high level siamesed exhaust system. But in place of G/S's 21 inch front wheel was a 19 inch rim carried on R100 stanchions with a R45/65 slider so that the spindle was central rather than on the front of the forks. Wheel travel was also reduced, but the total effect combined to keep the trail and castor angle much the same as the G/S, so retaining light but positive steering. At the rear, the shock absorber was shortened to give slightly less travel, but overall seat height remained a problem.

Most of the other changes from the G/S involved taking parts from the R45/65 range to convert the bike into a true roadster. These included a close-fitting front mudguard, larger halogen headlamp and the double instrument console with a tacho, plus high bars courtesy of the American spec. R65.

BMW published this poster to mark sixty years of manufacturing flat twin motorcycles with shaft drive on the eve of revealing its new generation of K-series multis.

Power output and gearing remained the same as the G/S, although the ST was some 36 lb heavier at 404 lb. Even so, it was actually a very light machine for its class. On performance, *Motorcycling* got a timed best speed with rider prone of 103.65 mph, which was useful rather than earth shattering. But perhaps the true spirit of the machine was better captured by a piece in *Motor Cycle Sport* for October 1983 which said that 'the rationale behind the R80ST has been to capture the handling qualities of the big trail bike in a roadster of almost equally light weight . . . on the eve of the launch of the K series, BMW's first venture beyond two pots, pushrods and some other elementals in motorcycle circles, we publish an appraisal of the company's most up-to-date twin. Ironically, the 80ST – light, a fine handler, relatively simple, powerful enough for most out of reach of the home country's autobahnen – impresses as the most persuasive argument yet advanced by BMW in support of its policy of keeping the dizzier heights of Jap style hi-tech out of motorcycle design'.

As was said, it was in some ways ironic that at long last, in October 1983, came the machine BMW enthusiasts and many others had awaited for years – a four-cylinder 'new era' superbike. Just three months before a special rally was organised to celebrate 60 years of BMW, *60 Jahre BMW Motorrad*. It was flat-twin motorcycles, all the way.

The first superbike model to appear was the basic K100, launched in Britain at the bargain basement price (at least as far as BMWs go) of £3,290.

There had been considerable speculation about the possible layout of a new BMW four, not least because the conventional Japanese across-the-frame layout was considered impossible since it would place BMW as just another competitor to the Big Four Japanese giants. Such a configuration was also unthinkable, because more critically, it would have done away with the low centre of gravity that had for so long been a big selling point for the twins. Shaft-drive would also have been awkward to arrange, although the Japanese had been doing it for years. BMW's solution to the problem was radical in terms of what the conservative buying public had come to expect, but like all the best solutions very simple.

The result was the model's most interesting technical feature. It was the Compact Drive System (CDS) which was to form the key ingredient of all K series machines. This used the engine and transmission very much as an integral part of the chassis design, by taking a four cylinder power unit and turning it through 90 degrees so that the crankshaft lay along the longitudinal axis of the motorcycle, then laying it on its side. This kept the crankshaft, gearbox and driveshaft in one more-or-less straight, compact line – and solved all BMW's headaches without creating any further problems. The rear wheel was automatically accommodated, while a minimal framework above the engine could support the seat, tank and steering head. It was functional, it had a low centre of gravity, and above all, it was different. Different enough to justify granting of various patents on the design, although there were those who pointed at some undeniable similarities between it and a prototype produced by the great British designer Val Page for Ariel, decades before BMW.

First of the new BMW multis, the K100 appeared in 1983. Its Compact Drive System formed a fundamental part of overall design. Later three-cylinder K75 used many common components.

The 1986 K-series in parade order.

Nevertheless, the execution was wholly original. Apparently, once the concept had been accepted, the BMW R&D team went out and obtained a Peugeot car engine and set about matching it to an existing BMW transmission, then strapping the whole lot into a motorcycle frame. This was as long ago as 1976, and once the experiment had proved that the idea was workable, they beavered away to build their own engines. At first they tried both three and four cylinder variants in sizes ranging from 800 to 1300 cc, and with plenty of car experience to draw upon, it will come as no surprise that the fruits of these early labours produced power units with strong four-wheel connections.

Finally, after much prototype work, it was decided to adopt in modular fashion a three-cylinder 750 and a four-cylinder 1000, with the 1-litre unit appearing first. Both were double-overhead cam designs, using chain drive at the front of the engines, and a feature of these engines was their lightness, aided by measures such as

The author testing one of the latest R80's with Monolever suspension in June 1987.

West Germany's *Motorrad* **magazine voted the BMW K100 RS 'Motorcycle of the Year' for three consecutive years. BMW celebrated this notable event by building the all-black limited edition K100 RS Motorsport in 1987.**

an all alloy cylinder block with a bore coating of a combination of nickel and silicon – this having just recently been adopted on the twins. The capacity was 987 cc from 67 × 70 mm bores, and for the first time on a production BMW, the engine was water-cooled and fuel injected. Both measures aimed at improving reliability, as well as emissions and noise levels. This activity happened against a background of increased environmental legislation. The exhaust was well silenced by a huge single silencer fed by four small-diameter pipes, all in stainless steel. For the clutch, a dry single plate design was used and there was a five-speed gearbox, bolting straight onto the back of the engine.

The model received an almost unparalleled amount of publicity. After all the ballyhoo surrounding the K100's launch had subsided, the general view was that BMW had almost got it right, but not quite. In truth, perhaps the original K series machine was not quite as good as everyone had expected. Although at 473 lb it was claimed to be the lightest machine in its class, as one tester put it, 'the bike falls between two stools, being a good tourer and an exciting scratcher, but not excelling in either mode'. Handling was in fact very reasonable, with a monolever rear suspension like that

first seen on the 1980 R80 G/S, and massive 41.5 mm front fork stanchions. An equally massive front wheel spindle was employed to brace the legs firmly from the base. The front wheel was cast alloy with twin discs, and of 18 inch diameter (at a time when fashion trends were to smaller 16 inch wheels for lighter handling). The rear rim was 17 inches with a single disc.

But it was still no out-and-out sports machine, and by now, perhaps a higher standard of equipment was expected of a touring motorcycle – thanks as much to any manufacturer as BMW.

Some pundits found the slab of sump on one side, rocker cover on the other, ugly – dubbing the K the 'Flying Brick'. And there were those who had cause to bemoan a K100 habit of smoking profusely after a night left on its side stand – even if this stopped after a few minutes and the bike never seemed to use any oil.

But a few months later, the press were able to report, as *Motor Cycle News* so aptly put it; 'Finished product'. They were referring to the appearance of the K100RS in January 1984. Surprisingly enough, this essentially had only a purpose-built sports fairing and no engine tuning to distinguish it from the K100 – and cost exactly a thumping £1,000 more! But still it seemed to come up to everyone's expectations and left the standard naked first-born very much a poor second.

Far from being a poseur's accessory, the admittedly expensive new plastic (and certain other smaller changes) managed to transform the package into something worthy of all the expense lavished on the new generation of multis. Although at 132 mph the top speed had gained some 6 mph over the standard K100, the big improvement was its willingness to cruise happily at high speed without causing rider fatigue and to impart a feeling of security which the unfaired bike just could not match.

Then in early summer there appeared the fully-faired K100RT with the same frame and engine but even more protection, plus touring panniers. But having justified the RS almost solely in terms of its fairing, I found that the RT's weather protection was possibly going too far, as I wrote in a road test I carried out for the December 1984 issue of *Motorcycle Enthusiast*, 'It completely divorced the rider from the road, and was more akin to driving a two-wheel car'. Okay perhaps for touring or for high-mileage all-weather riders, but certainly not for actually enjoying oneself on two wheels. It could also prove uncomfortably warm on a hot day, although this was more than made up for by its performance in winter – especially if the rider opted for the optional and excellent heated handlebar grips.

At the Cologne show later that year, BMW Chairman Dr Eberhardt Sarfert openly slammed the Japanese for causing a disastrous slump in new motorcycle sales, even though this trend had missed BMW. Sales for his company's products were increasing in virtually every market. In Britain they were up by nearly 20 per cent, but in the Netherlands where BMW then led the over 750 cc market, the gain was an astonishing 138 per cent.

Before the end of 1984 came the first 'public' press picture of the three-cylinder 750 version of the K series engine, which was expected to be launched on the home market the following May. The cylinder dimensions were the same 67 × 70 mm giving 740 cc. The engine was effectively just a pot shorter, meaning that the frame 'pulled back' more from the steering head to suit a revised front engine mounting point. One of the immediate giveaways for the new model was its three-sided silencer, which was much more attractive than the rather ugly slab-sided creation which had drawn so much bad press on the fours.

October 1984 also saw the introduction of new R80 and R80ST flat twins with 'monolever' rear suspension. These effectively replaced not only the older R80ST, but also the only two other existing twins except for the G/S trail bike. These were the R65 and R65LS. The poor-selling R45 was phased out over a year before.

By the time another twelve months had passed, the K100 series was already firmly established and although the K75C had been launched in the export markets only a month before, it had become a runaway success. At home in Germany, however, its sales were disappointing. For example, it immediately took a seven per cent share of the hotly contested British 750 cc market, and as it was only a little more than £100 cheaper than the standard K100. Many, including myself, asked the question – why?

The answer was quite simple. It combined a

smoother engine with sportier and easier handling than its bigger brother. *Motorcycling Weekly* got a 124 mph maximum from their test K75C, and Chris Myers summed up the feeling of many who had previously ridden the various K100s by writing, 'The engine, for example, is so smooth, responsive and refined it's in danger of becoming a modern classic. And it even *looks* better than the K100 lump with much better proportions'. British journalists Terry Snelling and Bruce Preston undertook a real marathon ride on a pair of K75Cs from the northernmost point of Norway to the south of France. Both agreed afterwards that it was the 'journey of a lifetime'. Preston reported using 64 gallons of petrol and just a half pint of oil during the trip at an average of 58.25 mph.

In June 1986 I attended the British press launch of the

The world's largest production enduro, BMW's 1988 R100 ES proved that the flat twin had a future.

more sporting, faired K75S in Scotland – little realising that exactly a year later I would be taking delivery of my very own K-series triple, paid for with my own hard-earned money. I offer this as proof that out of the many, many machines which I have tested in my capacity as a journalist, the BMW three comes out top as the best *overall* motorcycle.

With a record number of 14 models also including the K100, K100RS, K100RT, K100LT (a deluxe RT), K75S, K75C, R65, R80, R80LT, R80G/S and R80 G/S Paris Dakar, BMW can currently offer a motorcycle for just about every serious enthusiast's needs. And with the car division doing ever better from the 3-Series (beloved of young executives with generous company leasing arrangements) right up to the luxurious, quick and to some, expensive 750iL costing well over £53,000 in Britain, BMW would seem in an enviable position.

But as if to show that one never can tell in the dog-eat-dog commercial world, Graf Goltz, Chairman of the supervisory board of BMW AG felt it necessary to issue a press statement after BMW's Annual General Meeting at Munich on 2 July 1987. For some time, Stock Exchange information sources and the press had been claiming that BMW was up for take-over. This followed

Three cylinders and a sporting character gives the 1989 K75S a special place in the K-series.

the death of Dr Herbert Quandt – who had been instrumental in saving the company back in the dark days of 1959. And now there was talk that the Quandt family intended to sell its majority shareholding.

Speaking with the express authorisation of the Quandt family executors Graf Goltz plainly affirmed their continuing commitment to BMW's future and said 'We shall continue with great confidence to make our contribution towards ensuring that BMW's success will be maintained in the future'.

What all this goes to prove is that even during arguably its most successful-ever period in the company's history – even for such a large and seemingly powerful organisation as BMW had become by the late 1980s, with thousands of employees around the world – world stock-market speculators and the press could still cause more than a few corporate hearts to flutter with anxiety. Which begs the question, just what future does the BMW motorcycle have as we approach the end of the twentieth century?

Odds are that after all the decades of trauma, somehow it must surely survive into the next millenium by a combination of what has carried it through to date – sound engineering and detail improvement together with that all-important reputation for quality which makes owning a BMW the two-wheeled equivalent of driving, if not a Rolls-Royce, perhaps even more aptly . . . a BMW!

BMW

the racing machines

It was the R37 which first put BMW's sporting efforts on the map in 1924, when Fritz Bieber aboard a tuned version of the company's new sports roadster won the German national road racing championship. From then on until comparatively recently, race breeding played a vital part in the future of the BMW motorcycle, and added greatly to the company prestige within the motorcycle world.

The R37's designer Rudolf Schleicher was not only responsible for the preparation of Bieber's championship winning racer, but rode a BMW successfully in the 1926 ISDT held in Britain. His gold medal-winning performance gave the company additional publicity in one of the export markets in which BMW were just starting to take an increasing interest.

In all, BMW built some ten special racing versions of the R37, using them to experiment not only with tuned engines, but also an improved frame and for the time, novel alloy cylinder heads. Its last major success was a victory in the 1926 German Grand Prix by Paul Koppen.

In the late 1920s, prior to the onset of financial austerities brought on by the Great Depression, Ernst Henne showed the BMW flag by breaking a number of world speed records on his 735 cc speedster. Henne raced against the stopwatch at the heavily banked Avus circuit in Berlin and on Germany's first autobahn at Ingoldstadt near Munich. Among these records, he achieved the world's fastest for a motorcycle, at 137.58 mph. This set a pattern for another run of outstanding performances by BMW, next demonstrated by Henne again in 1932 when he retook the record which had been lost to Joe Wright's Zenith-JAP, with a speed of 151.77 mph at Tat, Hungary in the summer of 1932.

The next year was the year Adolf Hitler came to power, and for BMW a year of competition success at the ISDT in Wales. The works trials team, mounted on R4 machines, took ISDT golds at Garmisch Partenkirchen in its native Bavaria in 1934.

There were more speed records, too, when Ernst Henne hoisted his own record to 152.81 mph at Gyon – again in Hungary. On a different front, a 12-cylinder BMW aero engine was used to power an experimental propellor driven train to a world train record speed of 143 mph.

Already a sporting hero before the Second World War, Schorsch Meier is seen at one of his 1948 victories.

Meier leads team mate Walter Zeller at the German Motorcycle Championships, 31 May 1951.

Henne broke his own new record again in 1935, this time on a new section of autobahn just outside Frankfurt, with an average speed of 159.01 mph. The following year he was back again at the same venue, but this time with a new, supercharged 495 cc engine, as competitions manager Schleicher acknowledged that the 750 had finally been superseeded. Also new was an all-enclosing body shell for machine and rider, which featured a prominent tail fin. This took the speed up to 168.92 mph.

Some six months later, lone Englishman Eric Fernihough shattered BMW's record on his home-built and tuned 996 cc supercharged JAP. But it was only his for a short time before it fell again to Piero Taruffi's supercharged, water-cooled Gilera four. Within some five weeks of the Italian teams triumph, on 28 November 1937, Henne had his BMW back in the record books again – hoisting the world record to 173.57 mph where it was destined to stay for fourteen long years until 1951.

The supercharging technology that helped to make this possible for Henne and BMW had been under development since 1929 when a production R63 had a positive displacement blower mounted on the top of the gearbox and driven by the magneto shaft.

Lessons learnt from this were applied not only to record breaking, but also to the BMW Kompressor 500 works road racers which bore a close resemblance to Henne's machine under the skin. Both were fitted with a Zoller blower built onto the front of the crankcase assembly and coupled to the rearward facing inlets by long pipes passing over the cylinders. The capacity was 492.6 cc (66 × 72 mm) and the dohc twin generated in excess of 80 bhp at 8000 rpm, offering a maximum speed of around 140 mph – subject to circuit conditions.

The first of these 500 racers appeared in 1935 and used telescopic front forks at a time when none of the other racing teams used them. But it was not until the end of 1936 that BMW began using plunger rear suspension as well – and when it came, the plunger type

Zeller leading Norton rider Ken Kavanagh during 1953 500 cc Swiss Grand Prix at Berne.

A highly versatile rider, Zeller was selected for Germany's Trophy team in the 1953 ISDT. His machine's universal coupling, however, failed on the third day of the event hosted by Czechoslovakia.

still did not automatically give the Munich factory a competitive edge or even equal other machines, notably the British Norton singles.

By 1937, the 500s were in contention throughout Europe. And that included Germany, where BMW veteran Karl Gall became the national champion. On the Isle of Man, after finishing sixth in the Senior TT, Jock West went on to win the Ulster Grand Prix in Northern Ireland aboard one of the rapid BMW supercharged twins. There were high hopes for the following year, 1938, but Karl Gall was injured during practice for the Isle of Man, while Georg Meier (destined to become European champion that year) was forced to retire on the starting line. This left West. He rode his BMW on the limit and succeeded in taking the flat twin into fifth spot.

Georg Meier was also involved in long distance trials, gaining several medals on BMW machines. And in 1939 Meier became the first foreign rider to take the Isle of Man Senior TT, then the most important motorcycle race in the world.

Meier's team-mate Jock West came home second, but this resounding 1-2 was tinged with sadness owing to the death in practice of the third member of the team, Karl Gall, a great BMW rider throughout his long career. Following the TT, Kraus joined the works team in his place, with additional riders usually being recruited from the host country as the Grand Prix circus moved around. For a short time, the four-cylinder Gilera offered BMW a real challenge, but all too soon such contests would be shelved by the Second World War.

One of the first bright spots for BMW in the immediate post-war period was when racing restarted albeit in a very limited way. BMW was forced to use pre-war machines including the BMW Kompressor 500 twin, on which Georg Meier, now 36, was once again in winning form. Several of the work's machines had survived the war either to race on German soil again, or to end their days as war booty. Today, both John Surtees in Britain and Walter Zeller in Germany claim to own Meier's actual TT winning machine – a controversy which will probably never finally be resolved.

In 1946, Meier formed the Veritas team and chose a BMW for his campaign to win the German road racing championship. And in 1949, Georg Meier was voted Sportsman of the Year in Germany – the first time a motorcyclist had received the honour.

The factory selected its own fuel injection system for the works 1953 Rennsport engine.

Conventional carburettors on a 1954 production machine were less advanced but could be set-up at home.

All this was in local competitions only, for German factories and German riders were still banned from FIM-organised international events. But competition still began as eagerly as ever for the 1950 season, and there were some notable battles between supercharged BMW and NSU twins ridden by such luminaries as Meier for BMW and Fleischmann for NSU. All this was due to come to end as Germany was re-admitted to the FIM, but which had banned the use of supercharging.

Even so, BMW was ready for the world stage again as it demonstrated by the debut of a new flat twin on 29 April 1951 at the Eilenreide Rennen meeting near Hanover. Unlike the also-new NSU four (described in Chapter 13), the BMW not only lasted the distance, but took the victor's spoils. There was a new rider, too, and new star for the company, 23 year old Walter Zeller who took the flag from veteran Meier, also BMW mounted.

But in the wider field of international competition, there was still some way to go. After eight rounds of the Grand Prix circuit, there were still no placings in the top six. Although, in the future, BMW was to make greater impact in the sidecar class, the best it could manage was a fifth in the season's opener at Barcelona. The Austrian pair of Vogel and Vinatzer were BMW's only scorers for 1951.

Oddly, BMW had actually begun to make its mark in the sidecar field by gaining several World Championship points as early as 1949, the year when an official FIM World Championship was instigated. Despite BMW and German riders being banned, points were won by foreigners Benz and Hirel (Switzerland) who were sixth in the Swiss GP. They also came fourth in the Belgian, while the Belgians Rorsvort and Lemput were sixth. In

1950, BMW's only classic success was Masuy (Belgium) and Denis Jenkinson (Britain) who took a sixth in Switzerland.

In 1951, even though Germany was now officially admitted to international competition, the Grand Prix results did not alter significantly from the performances previously turned in by the privateers. Top six placings still eluded BMW in any of the enlarged, eight-round 500 cc solo series. And in the chairs, the Austrians Vogel and Vinatzer were the only points scorers with a BMW, scoring a fifth in the season's first race at Barcelona, Spain.

As the '52 season opened, BMW received a considerable amount of publicity regarding their projected racing plans – solo and sidecar – and much was expected. The official team announced early in April comprised Georg Meier and Walter Zeller on solos, and Kraus/Hauser as sidecar teams – plus two reserve riders. One of these was Hans Baltisberger (formerly rider of a 1950 dohc Norton single) and the other was Ernst Riedlbauch, who already had a number of wins as a privateer aboard BMWs.

However, when the first classic opened at Berne in Switzerland, no BMWs had entered for the Swiss GP, and it was only later in June that an official reason was given. This was the factory's preoccupation with the ISDT. It was widely rumoured that the German Trophy team were to use 500 and 600 BMWs and that the race team was being entered in all possible long distance trials since the final team selection was to be based on those results. The team was said to include Hans Meier, Georg's 20 year old brother.

By mid-July, almost on the eve of the German GP at Solitude which was to be held on 20 July, the new BMW

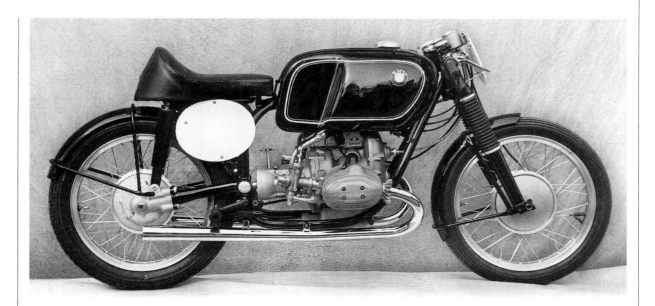

Above **Production version of Rennsport with telescopic forks was first seen at 1953 Frankfurt Show.**

racing bikes were still very much in the development stage. Four different types of 500 were in evidence. All four had short-stroke engines with dohc valve operation – a design which was eventually to emerge as the Rennsport model. They also sported a new, more shapely tank and a pair of long, narrow-tapering megaphone exhausts. But otherwise, there were notable variations from machine to machine.

Two of them had new frames with widely-splayed front downtubes, additional bracing in the region of the rear bevel drive, and horizontal tubes below the fuel tank acting as additional engine supports. Georg Meier's mount had the cardan shaft housed inside the right-hand leg of the rear swinging arm – the first time this drive/suspension layout had been used. However, Meier was none too happy about the steering of his machine in the early testing sessions, but after attention to the suspension system improvement was noticable. It had much the same telescopic fork as before, but now a pair of bridge pieces were used. Meanwhile, Hans Baltisberger's bike was fitted with newly modified brakes.

Early in September, the final selection of the German teams for the ISDT was announced. It transpired that in the Trophy, Maicos machines and NSUs had been preferred to the larger BMW flat twins, although three R68 models were to be used by members of the Vase team – Georg Meier, Walter Zeller and Hans Roth. The factory also entered a manufacturer's team consisting

A pensive Walter Zeller waits for the start of a race at the beginning of the 1954 season.

of Wiggerl Kraus and Max Klankermeier on R66/2 sidecar outfits, and Hans Meier riding one of these machines in solo trim.

The 27th ISDT was held in Austria between the 18–23 September, where 260 riders battled over a strenuous 1,250 mile course. And at its end, had it not been for an amazing piece of misfortune when a valve parted on the left cylinder of Roth's machine, the Vase would have been won not by the victorious Czech team, but by Germany's BMW-mounted trio. In the closing stages of the trial, they were the only team unpenalized, but when it came to the speed test Hans Roth was unable to persuade his machine to fire. Losing a mark for every minute absent from the one-hour test this cost his team 60 precious marks. Nevertheless, the BMW performance was superb – reflected in gold medals for Hans and Georg Meier, Zeller and the sidecars of Klankermeier, Kraus, Thornblom and Vandernoll.

Rumours were rife in Germany and abroad at the end of 1952 that Georg Meier would be retiring from racing. However, the pundits were proved wrong when early in January 1953 an official statement from BMW listed the team men for the new season. There were the names of both Meiers, Baltisberger, Zeller – plus Kraus with a sidecar outfit.

On a cold, windy day on which the snow-capped tops of the nearby Black Forest emphasised that winter had only just past, 120,000 enthusiasts gathered at the 4.75 mile Hockenheim Ring near Heidelberg. DMV's annual international Rhein Pokal Rennen held on Sunday 10 May. Four works BMWs were entered, sporting Earles forks for the first time and using auxiliary dampers to give increased control.

The race was a *tour de force* for the brand-new four cylinder in-line Moto Guzzis. Fergus Anderson recorded the fastest lap before retiring, and Enrico Lorenzetti raced to victory. But it was to be the new model's only major win, and following another retirement by Les Graham's MV Agusta, the second and third places went to Meier and privateer Mette's BMWs.

The sidecar event provided a photo-finish between Kraus and the World Champion Eric Oliver. Victory went to the Englishman only by the narrowest of margins. Kraus' machine had no carburettors, and instead fuel was injected directly into the inlet ports by a pump driven from the front of the timing cover. There

Fritz Hillebrand at the 1954 Belgian Grand Prix was already showing the form which was to make him World Champion.

The R68 which was victorious at Australia's first 24-hour race for production motorcycles. Staged 3/4 October 1954 it was won by the team of Jack Forrest, Don Flynn and Les Roberts. Roberts is shown riding with considerable panache in the 23rd hour.

was a pair of inward-angled air control slides mounted between the injectors and the cylinder heads, which were operated by conventional throttle cables.

BMW's lone entry for the solo class in the Isle of Man (IoM) TT was Walter Zeller, who *Motor Cycling* described as 'Very good indeed' during the practice session. It was his first visit to Mona's isle. After trying both conventional carburettors and fuel injection, he opted to use the latter system. However, no opportunity was available to study performance in the race owing to Zeller's early retirement following a spill at Signpost Corner on lap two after lying ninth at the end of lap one.

After the TT, Zeller with the rest of the solo riders concentrated his efforts within the German borders. Typical of the results gained was Zeller's victory at the Avus circuit in East Germany, near Berlin on 16 August. Despite tropical heat, Zeller established a new class record by averaging 112.1 mph for the entire race. To make it a BMW double, Kraus took the sidecar race from another BMW rider Noll.

In the world championships, Kraus and Noll shared the best result, with third places in Belgium and Switzerland respectively. The only other points scorer that year on one of the flat twin outfits was Fritz

Hillebrand. He gained a sixth in the final round in Italy.

Following the poor showing of the NSU entries in the 1952 ISDT and the good record achieved by BMW, Germany's team selectors opted for a mix of BMW and Maico machines for the 1953 Trophy event staged in Czechoslovakia.

Under a clear, blue sky, with the rising sun rapidly dispelling the vapours of a very cold night, the 28th ISDT got under way at 7.00 am on Tuesday 15 September. The German Trophy team consisted of a pair of 175 cc Maicos, together with three 590 cc BMWs ridden by Roth, Georg Meier and Zeller, while BMW had also entered their own manufacturer's team as in the previous event.

Disaster awaited the Trophy team, for on the third day the universal joint of Zeller's mount began to break up. After falling badly behind time, he was forced to retire at Frenstat. This set-back was to drop the German team to fourth, with 460 marks lost. The only other

John Surtees had his only ride on a works BMW at the 1955 German Grand Prix. Mid-way through the race he was forced to retire with mechanical trouble.

BMW retirement, however, was a private entry on an R68 solo. It was Florian Camathias who was later to become a world famous name for his sidecar racing exploits. BMW gained a total of seven gold medals – five solo, two sidecar.

The 1954 season started for the BMW team with an entry in the international Rhein Pokal road races at Hockenheim in South West Germany on Sunday 9 May. This was an important meeting, with not only members of BMW's team in attendance, but also representatives of Guzzi, NSU and MV Agusta, plus world sidecar champion Eric Oliver's Norton outfit in contention.

In the 500 race, after retirement by Fergus Anderson on the in-line four Guzzi, victory finally went to Ken Kavanagh on the new Guzzi single. Walter Zeller made it a well-deserved second ahead of Nello Pagani's MV four, followed by BMW new boy Hans Bartl.

The sidecar race saw Eric Oliver take victory a split second ahead of Willie Noll's BMW, after a wheel-to-wheel battle throughout the entire event. Fritz Hillebrand on another of the flat twins came in third and had the satisfaction of setting the fastest lap at 100.73 mph.

Following quickly after the Hockenheim success came an even bigger one for BMW, when four short days later on 12 May the factory gained their first post-war international speed records. Using a streamlined version of the 494 cc Rennsport racing model, this put them on top of the world in the 8 and 9 hour bracket for the 500, 750 and 1000 cc solo classes. The venue was Montlhery, outside Paris where riders Georg and Hans Meier and Walter Zeller set up speeds of 103.55 mph (166.64 kph) and 102.70 mph (165.28 kph) for the 8 and 9 hour respectively.

Next came the 17th international Eifelrennen over the famous 14.16 mile Nurburgring. The event took place under dull, clouded skies on a bitterly cold day – but still attended by large crowds. A notable experiment was carried out at the meeting by BMW, with a hydraulically-operated front brake system on one of their solos.

A non-starter in the 500 race was Walter Zeller, who had come off in practice. Up to the time of his accident, he had been the fastest rider in his class, but his injury, a broken ankle, was unfortunately serious enough to make him a non-runner not only in this race, but also for the Isle of Man TT. Without Zeller, the race was won by Norton works rider Ray Amm. But the real surprise was the second place taken by Georg Braun on a single cylinder Horex. He proved faster than all the remaining BMWs, including Hans Meier, who came third.

In the sidecar race, Noll appeared to have more speed than Oliver on his Norton, but the English rider still had the upper hand on the corners, which were a feature of the long Nurburgring circuit. At the finish Oliver took victory by performing one of his famous manoeuvres of slip-streaming and swinging out to overtake as he approached the line – even though Noll set the fastest lap.

Then came the TT. Without Zeller, BMW's only solo entry was Bartl, riding a production Rennsport, rather than an official works bike. And as things turned out, he too was a non-starter.

The sidecar event was being run over the shorter Clypse circuit, on which Hillebrand earned the following comment from *Motor Cycling* after his practice performance; 'For sheer neatness, Hillebrand (BMW) was outstanding, particularly on the uphill section through the Nursery Bends after the "Manx Arms" at Onchan'. Hydraulic brakes were used on all the BMW sidecar entries, and proved to be entirely satisfactory, with a minimal amount of wear. In the race itself, Oliver won, but Hillebrand, Noll and Schneider took all the next three places for BMW. Schneider was in the points despite a practice crash which badly damaged his outfit.

Although Eric Oliver then went on to take victory in the next two classic rounds in Ulster and Belgium, Noll came back to win the remaining three races in Germany, Switzerland and Italy and to take the title – BMW's first.

This was to prove a turning point in the world of sidecar racing, with BMW taking a record nineteen world championships between 1954 and 1974. An achievement which has only been surpassed by Helmut Fath in 1968 on his home-built four and Horst Owesle in 1971 on the Munch four developed from the Fath design.

The record of the BMW sidecar champions is as follows: Wilhelm Noll/Fritz Cron 1954 and 1956; Willy Fraust/Karl Remmert 1955; Fritz Hillebrand/Manfred

Grunwald 1957; Walter Schneider/Hans Strauss 1958 and 1959; Helmut Fath/Alfred Wohlgemut 1960; Max Deubel/Emil Horner 1961–64; Fritz Scheidegger/John Robinson 1965 and 1966; Klaus Enders/Rolf Engelhardt 1967, 1969, 1970, 1972, 1973 and 1974. As well as these champions, several other notable sidecar exponents were to emerge over the next two decades of BMW dominance of the three-wheel class.

Although the company found success on the three-wheel racing front, achieving the same fortunes in the solo classes was something altogether more difficult. While Noll and BMW were taking their first classic victory in the sidecar race at the German Grand Prix held at the Solitude circuit on Sunday 25 July before record crowds, things were going decidedly differently for Zeller and Co in the 500 race. Zeller, now recovered from his accident at the Nurburgring in May, retired with little more than a lap completed when his engine suddenly ceased firing. The first BMW home was privateer Knijnenburg in eleventh spot.

At Solitude, modified fuel injection systems were

On the Munich–Ingoldstadt autobahn 4 October 1955 Wilhelm Noll, sidecar ace, had several highly successful record-breaking runs with an unsupercharged 500 Rennsport equipped with a strutted wheel.

seen on Zeller's solo and the sidecars used by Noll and Hillebrand, with Bosch injector pumps replacing the BMW units previously fitted. Mounted on the front of the timing covers and driven from the timing gear, the new pumps each contained two plungers operated by a swash plate on the pump spindle. Fuel was injected directly into the combustion chambers on the side remote from the spark plug. Injection was regulated by induction pressure – the control pipe being taken from a point between the guillotine throttle slide and the inlet valve.

Zeller's machine also featured duplex single-leading shoe front brakes in place of the former single, twin-leading shoe design. And for the first time on a solo BMW racer streamlining was used. However, unlike the fully-enclosed shells of contemporaries like NSU and Guzzi, this was a modest affair in hand-beaten alloy, around the steering head and handlebar. Of the sidecar crews, only Noll's outfit used streamlining – first seen at the Belgian GP.

Despite difficulties during the season, on 8 August Zeller became the new German 500 champion because of his win in the last but one of the German Championship series. It was staged over the 10 mile Schotten circuit, the scene a year earlier of the sensational riders' strike at the 1953 German GP.

In front of around 170,000 spectators, Zeller got away to a good start. But with the roads still very wet after a heavy shower, Ray Amm (Norton) collided with Carlo Bandirola (MV). The Norton star was delayed until the rest of the field had departed, but nonetheless fought back to second place, although he was unable to catch the flying Zeller. In the sidecar race, BMWs dominated, with Fraust taking victory from Schneider and Noll.

On the same day at Tubbergen in Holland, Knijnenburg took his production Rennsport to victory in the 500 race ahead of Norton-mounted Frank Perris (later to become a Suzuki star in the 1960s).

With NSU back in favour, the German selectors did not use a single BMW for any of their three teams in the 1954 ISDT. Surprisingly, there were no BMW entries at all that year.

In Australia, 3–4 October 1954 saw the inauguration of a 24-hour race for production motorcycles. It was to be the first of its kind. Staged at the Mount Druitt circuit near Sydney, the rules specified teams of three riders for each machine. From the start Jack Forrest took the lead on a 600 cc R68. A lead which he and team mates Don Flynn and Les Roberts succeeded in maintaining throughout. They put in 648 laps of the 2.25 mile circuit at an average speed of nearly 60 mph and covered 1,433 miles in the allotted time. In the combined 250 solo and sidecar class, an R25 came home first.

The Paris Show opened on 7 October with BMW making full use of Noll's world sidecar championship performance. His outfit acted as a centrepiece of the company's stand – and the man himself was back in action by the end of the month. But this time, he was piloting a fully-streamlined BMW sidecar record breaker at Montlhery. On Friday 29 October, he gained the 10 mile world record at an average speed of 114.43 mph and the 50 kilometre at 114.92 mph. On Sunday 31 October, Noll captured more records – the 50 mile at 112.63 mph, the 100 kilometres at 113.06 mph and the 100 miles at 105.95 mph. Finally, he gained the one hour record with a speed of 106.39 mph. All these records were in Category B, and held not just for the capacity of his engine (500 cc), but also for the 750 and 1200 classes as well.

The 1955 road racing season saw Willy Fraust and Karl Remmart take the world sidecar title with a tuned production Rennsport engine and conventional carburettors. This followed wins at Barcelona, Nurburgring and Assen. But just prior to the final GP at Monza, they were the victims of a horrific crash during testing at Hockenheim. It resulted in the death of Remmart and a long period in hospital for Fraust, who never raced again.

Noll and Cron finished second in the table with wins in Belgium and Italy. In fact, the title could well have gone to Noll after he had set the fastest lap in the Isle of Man TT, but then he crashed near the end of the race while in the lead. The race was then won by Schneider on another BMW.

BMW's only solo rider in the TT that year was the Australian Jack Forrest, but he was a non-starter. However, at the German GP, Walter Zeller was to give a hint of what might have been had he been allowed to compete. Both he and John Surtees – on his one and only BMW ride – were entered on BMWs with an interesting modification in the form of a hydraulic steering damper between a bracket on the frame and the top of the left fork stanchion.

The event was held at the legendary and demanding Nurburgring circuit for the first time since 1931. However, this appeared to pose no problem for the BMW team leader. He proceeded to emerge as the chief threat to the World Champion Geoff Duke on his mighty-four cylinder Gilera 'fire engine'. For Zeller was a very experienced rider on the twists and turns of the tortuous 14.16 mile circuit, having lapped only 2.6 seconds slower than the champion. Duke had not previously raced on the circuit, and in his determination to off-set the handicap, had covered 55 laps by car before practice commenced. On his second practice lap on the Gilera, he broke the lap record.

In the race itself, Duke made a super-slick start, and powered into the lead as the flag dropped. Building up a 15 second lead over Zeller in the early laps, he maintained this position virtually constantly for the next five laps. Then, piling on the coals, he swept his Gilera on to gain another three seconds from Zeller. For the first two and a half laps, Bandirola on an MV four held third spot, but was then passed by Armstrong on another Gilera four, although the Irishman was soon doomed to retire.

While Armstrong had been displacing Bandirola from third place, the number three Gilera rider Colnago had ousted Masetti on another MV from fifth place. Surtees on the second BMW had also passed Masetti, but was then slowed by a serious misfire. After a call at his pit, he dropped to 14th position and then retired.

Meanwhile, Duke and Zeller were circulating so fast that the German in second place was 90 seconds in front of third man Bandirola by half distance. So it remained until the end, with the two leaders pulling even further ahead of the field. For Zeller to have so displaced all but one of the Italian multis must rate as one of the best, if not the best, of the performances by a post-war BMW rider.

A month later at the end of July, almost a quarter of a million spectators invaded Solitude to witness Walter Zeller and Willy Fraust give BMW a popular double victory in the 500 and sidecar races. Zeller's race winning time was an improvement on Geoff Duke's record, but his best lap of 4 minutes, 42 seconds (a speed of 91.04 mph) still left Duke in possession of the lap record for the circuit at 91.35 mph.

Though BMW was not having a full attempt at the

world title, they certainly made up for it on the record breaking scene. Another 24 world records fell to BMW in the autumn of 1955. After unsuitable weather had foiled record attempts by the company during the last week of September, a return was made to the Munich-Ingoldstadt autobahn on Tuesday 4 October, where two dozen records were set. These included 18 in the sidecar classes, for capacities of 500, 750 and 1200 cc, and six in the solo classes for 500, 750 and 1000 cc.

Weather conditions were absolutely ideal, with a gentle breeze over the autobahn and just sufficient moisture in the atmosphere to let the engines develop maximum power.

The sidecar record breaker was ridden by Wilhelm Noll, and was a fully-enclosed unsupercharged 500 BMW, fitted with fuel injection and reputed to rev to 10,000 rpm. Noll's machine carried a 'strutted wheel' type sidecar. An outstanding feature of the outfit was an unusually-high stabilising fin at the rear. It had a Plexiglas canopy over the rider's compartment and in an emergency this could be jettisoned using a quick-release device.

Noll returned a speed of 174 mph for both the flying start kilometre and flying start mile. Over 5 kilometres he notched 168.5 mph and over 5 miles 165.5 mph. The

Fergus Anderson campaigned a factory sponsored Rennsport in the spring of 1956. The former World Champion who had taken laurels on Moto Guzzi machines was killed at Floreffe, Belgium, 6 May. The Scot was widely missed.

standing start figures were 86.5 mph and 103 mph at the kilometre and the mile marks. Although everything went to plan, he reported that petrol fumes inside the shell had given him some anxious moments during a couple of the runs.

Walter Zeller rode the solo machine, a conventional works road racing Rennsport carrying frontal streamlining only. Over 10 kilometres he returned a speed of 145 mph, and over 10 miles he managed to increase this to 150 mph.

For 1956, BMW made two major changes on the road racing front. First, to fit full streamlining to their solos, and secondly, to sponsor ex-world champion and former Moto Guzzi team manager Fergus Anderson on works machinery.

Then aged 47, Anderson had begun motorcycling on a Douglas back in 1923, making his competition debut four years later in a grass track event on a Levis borrowed from his sister. His first road race was in 1932 at the Spanish Grand Prix, and in 1938 he had ridden for NSU, switching to DKW in 1939.

After the war he rode a Velocette, and then the start of his long association with Moto Guzzi. As related in my book *Moto Guzzi Singles* (Osprey Publishing), Anderson then chalked up a vast array of successes on Mandello machinery. But a dispute with the Italian factory late in 1955 led to his alliance with BMW after testing the three cylinder DKW two-strokes.

His first appearance on one of the Munich twins came at Imola, Italy on Easter Monday 1956. Then came the Circuit de Mettet international in Belgium on 29 April, where Anderson came home third behind winner Surtees and Lomas in second place. There had been some teething problems, but with the machine sorted out, he took the BMW to Floreffe in Belgium on the 6 May. Opposition included John Surtees on an MV four plus Bill Lomas and Dickie Dale on works Guzzi singles. Anderson put up a fine performance with a meteoric ride on the straight where his machine was visibly faster than Surtees' MV four. But tragedy struck a few miles from the start line. There on an S-bend, Fergus Anderson, one of the great riders of his generation, crashed and was killed instantly.

Following this tragedy, BMW's solo effort was understandably overshadowed. But it had at last succeeded in producing really competitive solos. The latest flat twins were faster than they had ever been, and with it came improved handling and reliability. The speed that had been visible at Floreffe was demonstrated again by an impressive performance the same month by Zeller at Hockenheim, where he built up a 25 second lead over the Gilera four of Reg Armstrong.

The resurgence had come about thanks partly to new engine tuning, but mainly to streamlining, which now completely enveloped the frontal area of the machine. The speed was claimed as over 150 mph.

Walter Zeller caught by the camera as he pilots his fully streamlined flat twin to third place in the 1957 German Grand Prix at the Hockenheim circuit.

Following the untimely death of Fergus Anderson, BMW fielded two solo riders, Walter Zeller and new boy Ernst Riedelbauch, but only Zeller was entered for the IoM TT. During practice, he used full streamlining, but chose a naked bike in the race – this may have been a wise decision. On race day gusty conditions prevailed. At the end of the first lap Zeller lay sixth, but by the end of six laps he had moved up to fifth. Then with Guzzi rider Lomas in trouble to open up another place, the seventh and final lap saw Zeller move up to finish a creditable fourth behind race winner Surtees' MV four and the Norton singles of Hartle and Brett.

In the sidecar race BMW paid the price for not having a system of team orders for its three outfits. Instead of a 1-2-3 victory in the sidecar TT, mechanical trouble eliminated first Schneider and then Noll, but the remaining team man Hillebrand went on to win at record speed from a pack of Norton singles headed by Pip Harris. Before his retirement, Noll put in the fastest lap, but failed to beat his own record established the previous year.

Noll was the only one of the trio not to use a fuel-injected engine. However, in 1956 each sidecar outfit was equipped with full streamlining, unlike the previous year when one team member employed full streamlining, another partial enclosure, while the third rode a 'naked' machine. This standardisation was due to a long period of experiments by the factory on Noll's machine.

Following the Isle of Man, the Dutch TT at Assen a couple of weeks later saw Hillebrand again the winner, but this time Noll finished second. Other notable BMW finishers were Camathias in fifth and Fath seventh – both riders whose names would feature prominently later.

In the last race of the day, the 500, Kavanagh came to the line on a Guzzi V8, while Lomas rode one of the same marque's fleet singles. Surtees on the MV four made a quick start, followed by Zeller on the sole factory BMW in second place. With several retirements including both Guzzi riders and Masetti on another MV four, Zeller maintained his second place to the end. Another BMW (a production Rennsport) piloted by Ernst Hiller came home sixth.

The following week, Zeller made it a carbon copy result with another second behind Surtees in the ultra-fast Belgian GP at Spa Francorchamps. With a host of four cylinder models in attendance, ridden by the world's finest riders, this result was superb. Referring to his move up to second when Duke's Gilera retired, *Motor Cycle* said of Zeller's performance; 'riding brilliantly, he was never passed'. His average speed for the 15 lap, 131.6 mile race was 113.34 mph. At the same venue, Noll won the sidecar race, with the next BMW, Hillebrand's, in fourth place.

Then came the important German round held at Solitude. BMW's star Walter Zeller was on the front row of the grid together with Duke on a Gilera four, Lomas on a Guzzi V8, Armstrong and Monneret on Gileras, and finally Masetti, who formed the MV challenge in the absence of John Surtees, who was hurt in the previous day's 350 race.

At the end of the first lap, Zeller was sixth, and gradually pulled up to fourth by dint of some superb riding, thus splitting the Italian exotica. This effort, however, proved to be just too much for the BMW's engine, which clanked miserably as the bike pulled into the pits, its race run. With it went Zeller's chances of heading the world.

But if the 500 was a disappointment, not so the sidecar event, with a BMW 1-2-3-4 from Noll, Hillebrand, Fath and Schneider. In the process, Noll succeeded in breaking both the lap and race records.

August brought the Ulster GP, where Zeller made the journey with vital points at stake, but retired with clutch trouble. Noll once again won the battle of the chairs, while Hillebrand retired. And so the circus came to the final round at Monza in Italy on 9 September. But this was not a good day for the German team. A Gilera won the sidecar race and Zeller finishing down in sixth place following a hurried pit stop. Three other BMWs finished, with Klinger ninth, Hiller tenth, and Riedelbauch eleventh.

The final positions in the 1956 World Championship, with Zeller's 16 points against Surtees' 24, gave BMW's star second place – and no doubt he thought that except for machine problems he could have been world champion. It was the nearest a BMW solo rider was ever to get in the title hunt. Noll meanwhile became sidecar champion for the second time and then promptly announced his retirement from the sport. In 1957 he tried car racing, but without success.

As early as June, BMW had announced that they would be preparing three special machines for the ISDT that year, the 31st event in the series, to be held on home ground at Garmisch-Partenkirchen. At the time, they stated that a 500, a 250 and a sidecar outfit would be entered as an official manufacturer's team. Then, at the beginning of September it was announced that the Munich factory were fielding machines with all three engine capacities (250, 500 and 600) using both fuel injection and conventional carburation.

Skills learned as a Luftwaffe pilot aided Hillebrand. His partner is Manfred Grunwald at the Isle of Man TT, June 1957. They won this race and went on to win the World Sidecar Championship during the same year.

The competition, organised by the German ADAC and DMV, under the auspices of the FIM, began on 17 September. Although there was once again no BMW selected for either the German Trophy or Vase team, the four factory entries nevertheless put up a truly excellent performance with gaining a gold medal.

Sebastian Nachtmann (later to emerge as the factory's leading rider in long-distance events) and Hartner were riding 250 singles, while Hans Meier had a 500. The quartet was completed by a 600 sidecar outfit piloted by Kraus with Prutting as crew. This machine used conventional carbs and featured high-level exhaust pipes and crashbars.

There was one other BMW in the 1956 ISDT. It was a private entry by the Swiss rider Bracher, who gained a bronze medal on his 500 after losing 34 points.

As far as BMW's road racing team was concerned, the 1957 season opener was the Circuit de Mettet in Belgium on 5 May. Where, despite atrocious weather conditions, Hillebrand won the sidecar race and Hiller came home second in the 500 race behind Dickie Dale's Guzzi single. There were several retirements in this event, notably John Surtees' MV four and Keith Campbell's V8 Guzzi.

The following week, Hillebrand won again at the non-championship Austrian GP held at the 3.25 mile Salzburg circuit on 11 May, but it was the 500 solo event which caused the most surprise. Riding a production Rennsport, Austrian champion Gerold Klinger came out top after a close tussle with BMW team leader Walter Zeller, who led after the Austrian crashed on lap 7 of the 15 lap 47.71 mile race. Remounting, Klinger

Jack Forrest riding hard and setting a new Australian speed record of 149.06 mph at Coonabarabran, New South Wales, in early October 1957.

caught Zeller on the last lap and won by a few lengths to the great excitement of the home crowd.

The official World Championship commenced at Hockenheim on Sunday 19 May. Zeller rode superbly to finish a gallant third behind Liberati and McIntyre on Gilera fours, but he was in front of Dale on a Guzzi, Shepherd on an MV and Hiller in sixth place on another BMW. Hillebrand won the sidecar race, in which BMW took the first five places.

Saturday 25 May was the start of official practice for the 1957 Isle of Man Man TT – the Golden Jubilee of the event. BMW had only entered one man – Zeller – but as *Motor Cycling* reported; 'The large crowd of watchers at Quarter Bridge seemed to agree that Walter Zeller took a lot of beating for speed combined with ease'. His fastest time for this first session was 25 min 14.8 sec at a speed of 89.67 mph.

However, following this excellent start, things did not go quite according to plan. On Monday 27, the BMW rider struck mechanical trouble at Glen Helen, followed the same evening by a crash at Laurel Bank on wet tar. But in typical see-saw pattern Zeller topped the morning practice session again two days later on the 29 May with a lap at 96.91 mph – impressive stuff!

In the race itself, Zeller and the BMW seemed set for glory as at the end of lap one they came through holding third place behind Bob McIntyre's Gilera and John Surtees' MV. These positions remained unchanged as the leaders completed the third lap. But then came disappointing news when the loudspeakers announced 'Zeller retired at Ramsey'. The cause was dead ignition, and Zeller's racing was over for the day.

Despite Zeller's misfortune on the solo, BMW's other star maintained the factory's ascendancy in the Sidecar TT. *Motor Cycle* reported that 'The favourite, Fritz Hillebrand (BMW), wins Sidecar TT at record speeds for the second year in succession: half of starters retire'. In fact, it was a BMW 1-2-3, as in the previous year, with Schneider second and Camathias third. Hillebrand's fastest lap (of the 10.79 mile Clypse circuit) was at 72.55 mph, and his race average was 71.89 mph.

There were some surprising mechanical details associated with all the 1957 TT machines. The successful sidecar crews, and Zeller on his solo all used Dell'Orto carburettors. In two cases, these used 'home made' float chambers and dash pots, whereas Hillebrand opted for two float chambers. BMW stated that the 1957 flat twins were capable of 9500 rpm and had excellent torque at low speeds – hence their particular suitability for sidecar duty.

Perhaps the strangest aspect of BMW's 1957 TT machines was the use of streamlining on Zeller's solo mount. Fearing a wet and windy Senior race, Zeller had handed his machine over to the scrutineers prior to the race in naked form (after using a streamlined dustbin fairing in practice). But when race day proved fine, he somehow managed to fit the dustbin back on again

Zeller sits with obvious pleasure astride the specially constructed supercharged 590 cc roadster presented to him by a grateful BMW board in 1958.

within the allotted half hour. Even more surprising was the statement he made at the time that his streamlining made a difference of 35 mph to his maximum speed. When questioned about this statement prior to the race and asked whether he surely did not mean 35 kilometres per hour, he shook his head and affirmed that he meant 35 miles per hour. Many observers could not really believe this was possible, but Zeller was adamant, and he should have known.

Next race in the classic calendar was the Dutch TT at Assen on Saturday 29 June. Here Hillebrand won again, but the real news was Zeller, with another third, this time behind Surtees on a MV and Liberati on a Gilera. Hiller did well again coming in fifth, a position which Klinger had held on another flat twin until forced to retire.

At the Belgian GP a week later Schneider won the sidecar event from Camathias and Hillebrand, with the fastest lap set at 99.88 mph by Camathias – a new record. To show how close things were, Schneider's race winning average was 99.02 mph for the eight lap, 70.08 mile race.

The 500 solo race witnessed only seven of the 23 starters reaching the finish. One of the earliest in trouble was Zeller, who tumbled at Stavelot on the first lap. Klinger was holding fifth spot by mid-distance – but then missed a gear, with resultant damage which forced him to retire two laps later. No BMW finished. It was a muddled race where even the winner Liberati was denied victory when he was excluded from the result for taking over Geoff Duke's entry and not informing the organisers.

Zeller was not to score any more world championship points that season, even though he retained his national title. Hiller and Klinger proved successful in international non-world title races, for example taking several victories in Czechoslovakia, Holland and France as well as in Germany.

Meanwhile, Hillebrand and his passenger Grunwald had secured their world title after four of the five rounds that year, and took in a series of races in Spain during August. They had won a number of these when on 24 August, Hillebrand lost control during practice for a race at Bilbao. The outfit crashed heavily, and the 39-year old Hillebrand died instantly. Although Grunwald eventually recovered, he decided to retire.

Without its champion, the best that BMW could do in the final round at Monza was a third place. However, this win for a Gilera was to be the last for anything but a BMW in a world title race until Chris Vincent's historic

Six times World Champion Geoff Duke rode for BMW in 1958. Here he is snapped as he competes in that year's Senior TT on the Isle of Man.

BSA victory in the 1962 Isle of Man TT some five years later. And thanks to Hillebrand's unbeatable points score, BMW still retained the world title.

Meanwhile, on the commercial front, BMW was in deep financial trouble. It was maintaining a strong sidecar presence, plus being well represented in the solos and was prominent at all the various international shows. All this cost money, and something had to be cut from the budget. And so in 1957 the factory took no part in long distance trials, including the ISDT.

It was a difficult period for BMW's competition department but there were still plenty of privateers to fly the BMW flag. One was Jack Forrest, who had stamped his authority on Australian road racing that year. After winning several small events, he took part in the important Queensland TT races at the 2.7 mile Lowood airstrip-cum-road circuit near Brisbane on 16 June. Riding a fully-streamlined-BMW 500, he set the fastest lap of the day in the Senior race, but then crashed while well in the lead. At the time he was reported to have suffered severe abrasions and fractured a leg, but he was back in action in October on the rebuilt BMW – and in sensational style. Forrest raised the Australian speed records for 500, 750 and 1000 cc to 149.06 mph at Coonabarabran, New South Wales.

In 1958, Schneider and Strauss succeeded in taking up where Hillebrand left off, gaining the sidecar crown for BMW yet again, but only after a fiercely-contested four round series against the privateers Camathias and Cecco. Three rounds, including the Isle of Man went to Schneider, with Camathias second each time, while the

positions were reversed in the remaining event at the Dutch TT. Third place in the series went to future champion Helmut Fath passengered by Rudolf. Camathias employed swill pots on the Dell'Orto carburettors fitted to his machine, which eliminated fuel starvation caused by centrifugal force when cornering. The Swiss star also used a dustbin fairing from a works Mondial. He claimed it was good for an extra 5 mph compared to his previous fairing.

In the solo classes, the surprise news was that the ex-Norton and Gilera star, multi-world champion Geoff Duke would race a factory-backed Rennsport of the type used so successfully by Walter Zeller over the last few seasons. Zeller had decided to retire from competitive motorcycle sport. Later in the year as a token of its appreciation of his efforts, the company presented Zeller with a specially-built 589.5 cc (72.2 × 72 mm) supercharged racer in road trim to mark his retirement. This machine's engine came from the sidecar outfit which Max Klankermeier had campaigned in the 1949 600 cc German sidecar championship.

Backing up Duke in international events were ex-Guzzi star Dickie Dale, Australian Jack Forrest, Gerold Klinger and Ernst Hiller. Despite Zeller's retirement, on paper at least, this was BMW's strongest-ever team. This might have seemed odd at a time when BMW was in the depths of its worst financial crisis. But there was an important external factor. Just a few months before, in October 1957, both Gilera and Moto Guzzi had announced that they would not be entering works machines during 1958. Apart from the ageing British singles, this left MV Agusta and BMW as effectively the only contenders for the world crown. No doubt it was this alone that brought BMW and Geoff Duke together.

The first benefits of the partnership was seen on 17 April at the BMCRC (British Motor Cycle Racing Club) 7th International Silverstone Saturday. As *Motor Cycling* put it 'What a day to remember!'. Held in fine conditions it brought an immense crowd to see Duke making a bid to prove that he was still 'the Master' after almost two years away from week-in, week-out competitive racing.

Riding a Manx Norton in the 350 race, Duke did not disappoint, winning in fine style. But the keenest race of the day was the 500, for which Duke brought his dolphin-faired works BMW on to the front row of the grid. This was the flat twin's first outing since it had been collected in Munich a couple of days before. Reputed to be an ex-Zeller machine, the BMW had not been handling too well in practice and now sported a pair of completely untried Girling rear shock absorber units. . . . It was wait and see, and the crowd held its breath as the flag dropped and the riders pushed their machines into motion.

Florian Camathias in 1959 enabled BMW to claim 24 of the 27 world records open to motorcycle combinations.

Forty-three starters snarled and weaved away in a close-knit bunch, with Duke among the initial leaders. But this early promise was soon to be dashed when at the end of the first lap Duke and the BMW came past the packed grandstands opposite the start and finish line in eighth position, with, as *Motor Cycling* commented, 'the BM's acceleration making no visible impression on the majority of the singles'. Next lap and Duke was down to eleventh place. And three laps later he halted a silent BMW just past the start line, with what were reported later as 'unspecified gremlins in the transmission'. It was not a promising start.

Meanwhile, things were going a little better for Hiller. He started his season at the non-championship Spanish GP. It was raced around the twisty Montjuich circuit near Barcelona where he finished fifth in a race won by Surtees on a MV four.

In the Austrian GP, again non-championship, BMWs showed up well again. Klinger led from the start but had to retire early with gearbox trouble. The race was won by Hiller with Forrest third, Dale fifth, Huber sixth, Jaeger seventh and Duke eighth. To complete a highly successful day, BMW also took the first six places in the sidecar event which was won by Schneider from Camathias, Strub, Neussner, Fath and Scheidegger.

A week later, with less than a month to go to the Isle of Man Senior TT, Geoff Duke at long last got to grips with his mount. In one of the closest and most hotly-contested races of his career, he scored a superb win on the fast 4.8 mile Hockenheim circuit at the annual international Rhein Pokal Rennen. Duke headed Ernst Hiller over the line by little more than four lengths.

At the start, the only non-BMW on the front row was a Norton ridden by Australian Harry Hinton Jnr, who took off at a savage pace with Duke, Hiller, Dale and Forrest in hot pursuit. At the end, Hinton made third, ahead of Huber and Klinger on BMWs, and another Norton ridden by 1957 350 cc world champion Keith Campbell in sixth place.

The first classic of the season was the Isle of Man TT. Commenting on his choice of a BMW for this event, Geoff Duke offered some personal views in an article in *Motor Cycling* for the 22 May 1958:

'When I was a child my family frequently took me to the Isle of Man, but I was 16 before I saw my first TT race there. This was in 1939, when Georg Meier, on a German BMW, won the Senior at 89.38 mph and achieved the fastest lap of 90.75 mph. I am accepting this fact as a happy omen – because, unfortunately missing the TT for two seasons, I am, in June this year, returning to what I regard as the world's greatest event on a BMW. If 19 years ago, as I stood amazed and thrilled by Meier's performance, someone had suggested that one day I also would be riding a works

entered BMW and in the fabulous TT too. . . . well, I would have just told them that they were quite mad!'

Both Duke and Dale were entered for the Senior TT. Although both showed up well in practice, the race was another matter. First Dale was reported as motoring slowly at the end of lap one. This was followed soon afterwards by Duke pulling into his pit shaking his head ruefully as he talked to his mechanic and after a careful examination decided to retire. The cause was front brake trouble. Dale, however, at least kept going, finally finishing in tenth place at an averge speed of 92.46 mph, in a race won by John Surtees' MV.

Hiller during this time had chalked up important wins in Helsinki, Finland and Chimay, Belgium. And it was Hiller who performed best for BMW in the next classic, the Dutch TT, where he scored fourth and Dale sixth. Duke once again suffered problems with his front brake, even though it had been relined since his IoM retirement.

Seven days later at the Belgian GP, however, Duke at last seemed to have beaten the problem, when he finished fourth, one place ahead of Dale. Duke's average speed for the 15 lap, 131.42 mile ace was 113.59 mph – compared to winner Surtees' 115.32 mph.

Next came the German GP at the Nurburgring, where despite another victory for Surtees, the home

World Champions in 1959, Walter Schneider and Hans Strauss are seen winning the Belgian Grand Prix in that season.

crowd had at least something to shout about as the new national hero Ernst Hiller led for the first few miles – finally finishing fourth ahead of Dale.

At an international meeting at Thruxton early in August, Hiller came very near to taking the victory from British champion Derek Minter, but had to settle for the runner-up spot. At the Ulster GP, Dale was sixth, then at the final round in Italy rode superbly to clinch fourth, splitting a quartet of MV Agusta fours. Even Duke on his Norton could not match Dale at Monza in seventh spot. Two laps adrift, Klinger and Hiller filled ninth and tenth places respectively. It was enough to give Dale third place in the 1958 championships, followed by Duke in fourth who had ridden both BMW and Norton.

Away from the Grand Prix scene, John Lewis and Peter James brought an R69 into fourth place overall in the Thruxton 500 Mile production machine race. The men behind the venture were partners in MLG Motorcycles of Shepherds Bush, London – Vin Motler and Charlie Lock. Both were very much long-term BMW enthusiasts. It was a more impressive result than the mere statistic might suggest, as borne out by *Motor Cycle's* report of 26 June which said 'So unobtrusive that its high placing surprised many onlookers, a 595 cc BMW R69 was ridden into fourth place. Quietly, smoothly and cleanly the German flat twin, one of the most ordinary looking (*read standard*) models on the course, circled with admirable regularity, calling at the pits only for fuel and change of riders, never for oil or repairs'.

Out of the ISDT for the previous year, BMW machines were back in contention for the 1958 event staged on home ground amongst the mountains of Bavaria in late September. Gold medals were gained by a trio of converted R50s ridden by Hartner, Hans Meier and Roth – an impressive performance, even though none were members of an official team.

There was record-breaking galore at the end of the year at Monza on 16 December, where Florian Camathias broke the 100 kilometre world speed record in the 500, 750 and 1200 cc sidecar categories on a specially-prepared Rennsport outfit. His time was 120.73 mph, 3.312 mph better than Albino Milano's Gilera four record. Continuing his ride in an effort to break the one hour record, Camathias had to abandon the attempt a few minutes after completing the 100 km, when large sections of tread stripped from his front tyre.

Later, at the end of March 1959 on the Martigny-Charat road in the Simplon area, Camathias gained more records to add to his earlier success. On the same machine, he broke 500, 750 and 1000 cc sidecar records for the kilometre in 23.40 seconds, averaging 95.60 mph – beating the previous record (again held by Milani) by 0.37 mph. As a result of this, BMW were able to claim to hold 24 of the possible 27 world sidecar records.

Sebastian Nachtmann at 1960 ISDT on his BMW 600.

In many ways, this helped to hide the deepening crisis at the factory. These difficulties resulted in 1959 being something of a 'dead' year for BMW motorcycles on both the production and the sporting fronts. This was not assisted by the fact that although they won the sidecar championship, the 1958/59 winning team of Schneider and Strauss announced their retirement at the end of the year. Dale was unable to maintain his 1958 form in the solo world championship series with only two fourth places in France and Holland to show for his efforts. Huber was the only other BMW solo rider to score points, with a sixth at Hockenheim.

One bright spot in an otherwise moribund 1959 season was when the American rider John Penton checked in on his R60 at the Western Union office in Los Angeles on 10 June. Penton had covered the 2833 mile transcontinental journey from New York in a motorcycle record time of 52 hours, 11 minutes and one second – an average of over 50 mph.

Another high point was when John Lewis partnered by Bruce Daniels rode to an impressive victory in the 1959 Thruxton 500 Mile event. Lewis then left for Spain where he teamed up with Peter Darvill to win the Barcelona 24-hour race.

The Sixties saw mixed fortunes for BMW's sporting achievements. The new decade started with the amazing prospect of a Japanese rider, Fumio Ito, campaigning a Rennsport in the 500 Grand Prix series, but after a superb sixth in the French GP during April 1960, he could not sustain his form. Later, in 1963, he finished third in the 250 world championship on a Yamaha. He even won in Belgium, before returning to Japan.

The factory's last solo world championship points came in the 1961 German GP at Hockenheim, where Jaeger was third, Hiller fifth and Lothar sixth.

In sidecar competition, the story was different. There was a succession of BMW champions which began with Helmut Fath in 1960 and ending with Klaus Enders as champion yet again in 1969 following Fath's success on his home-built four in 1968.

Early in 1961, a specially-prepared R69S established the first of a series of successes for the model in record breaking and production racing. The 12 and 24-hour records fell to an Anglo-German effort with a BMW entered by MLG Motorcycles. Although pipped to the post by Velocette for the honour of being the first to complete 24 hours at over 100 mph, the BMW shattered the week-old record by almost 10 mph. Over the bumpy French speed bowl at Montlhery, Ellis Boyce,

George Catlin, John Holder and Sid Mizen completed the first 12 hours at an average speed of 109.39 mph and went on at a barely reduced speed to turn in 109.24 mph for the complete 24-hours. The total distance covered was 2621.77 miles and fuel consumption worked out at 34 mpg.

Fitted with a specially-made Peel dolphin fairing, the R69S carried a Marchal headlamp to supplement the track lighting during the hours of darkness. Other preparation consisted of stripping off any unnecessary equipment and fitting special high-compression Mahle pistons, long, shallow-taper megaphones (fitted with silencers), a Smiths 8000 rpm magnetic rev counter, a racing seat, reversed foot controls and a pad over the

rear of the tank enabling the rider literally to 'lay' on the machine for considerable periods.

At the end of the marathon, the engine was stripped and found to be in perfect condition – the only problem having been a slight misfire at high revs around a quarter distance, which vanished as mysteriously as it had come. When tested later by *Motor Cycling*, the

MLG R69S was certified at the MIRA test track as having a top speed of 118.3 mph with the rider crouching behind the screen.

At the time, it was little known that MLG had made an earlier attempt on the 24-hour record at Montlhery using another R69S. But this attempt in October 1960 had ended in tragedy when 25 year old Bill Sawford piloting the machine went over the banking and sustained a broken arm, broken leg, and broken pelvis, as a result of which he died. The accident happened on the first lap of his opening stint. Before it, Bruce Daniels, Sid Mizen and Phil Read had done an hour apiece, each averaging between 106 and 108 mph in darkness.

Following the successful record bid came more successes in 1961 at Thruxton, Barcelona and Silverstone – where a BMW won the 1000 Kilometre race. After this, MLG cut down its racing activities at the end of 1962, but BMW management took up the challenge, entering Helmut Hutten and Karl Hoppe in the 1963 Coupe de Europa endurance series. I can well remember seeing this pair perform at Thruxton, where they maintained steady, trouble-free progress to finish seventh in their class and 10th overall. Completing 216 laps (against the winner's 288) Hutten and Hoppe had an average speed of 65.1 mph.

There was also success in a completely different branch of the sport. One of the unforgettable sights of the 1960s was a result of BMW's continuing participation in the ISDT. The 'gentle giant' Sebastian Nachtmann controlled his massive flat twin with complete authority while mere mortals on much smaller, handier machinery could only look on in amazement. His performances were rewarded with a string of gold medals spanning the decade.

An interesting development off the main stream in the late 1960s was the work of Dutch BMW dealer and enthusiast Henny Van Donkelaar, who had grown tired of waiting for Munich to produce a 750 cc twin. So using 80 mm bore (as opposed to the standard 72 mm of the 594 cc engine) light alloy cylinders with cast-iron liners from West German specialist Wolfgang Kayser, he began converting customers' R60 and R69S models to 730 cc. The machines were offered with various forged Mahle pistons. These yielded a range of compression ratios from 7.5–9.5:1. These engines were used not only on the road, but some were raced with considerable success in long distance trials and even sidecar motocross in the late 1960s. Meanwhile, in Germany, several R50 type engines were converted to 700 cc.

Not since the 1950s and the days of Walter Zeller had BMW enthusiasts been able to claim their very own solo racing hero, but in 1967 a man who was to emerge as

Fritz Scheidegger and passenger John Robinson in action during 1964 Dutch TT at Assen. Next year they became the World Sidecar Champions.

the BMW solo rider *par excellence* of the next decade took part in his first road race. He was Helmut Dahne, and he had served his apprenticeship with BMW as a mechanic.

But Dahne was also an enthusiastic private rider – a real privateer, who prepared his own bike in his own time. Almost the only occasion on which he had official works help was after winning the Sudelfeld Bergrennen classic in 1968 in the face of strong opposition. His mount for the occasion was a home-built R69S special, but after the race, his boss Alex von Falkenhausen lent him a works engine. Almost overnight the young mechanic converted it to a 500. Dahne won first time out with the new power unit, with the result that von Falkenhausen gave him the works engine!

Later, after progressing to chief tester, Dahne quit BMW to work for the tyre giants Metzeler. But the parting was on good terms, and Dahne continued to campaign BMW flat twins. Still very much a privateer, his mentor was Helmut Bucher, who looked after the engine while Dahne concentrated on the chassis. He received a little support from the factories to whose fame he contributed, since Metzeler allowed him time off to race and paid all travelling expenses, BMW assisted by supplying limited quantities of spare parts.

To some extent it could be said that Dahne limited his career because of his loyalty to 'his' factory – BMW. For this reason Dahne never really got involved with the Grand Prix circus, as quite simply BMW had no suitable bike. Because of this, he concentrated his efforts on the

Below **BMW mechanics work on a Rennsport engine 'out in the field' during 1968 Sidecar TT, Isle of Man.**

Right **Pip Harris leading Florian Camathias a lap before Camathias' fatal crash, Brands Hatch, 11 October 1965.**

long-distance production machine races and real road circuits. The Isle of Man mountain circuit was his first choice, with the Nurburgring ran a close second. He believed that both of these were 'natural' courses and difficult to learn.

Why class Dahne with such luminaries as Zeller or Meier? Just his Isle of Man exploits crowned by victory in the 1976 1000 cc Production TT is enough to guarantee his claim to stardom.

BMW would not have been able to chalk up this famous victory without Dahne's tenacity as demonstrated at the end of practice for the 1976 TT, when a loose valve seat caused an exhaust valve to break. The result was a badly damaged cylinder head, but Dahne had no spare bike or engine. So, he had to cannibalise another person's machine to repair his own engine.

'Sheer power was not the most important factor', he once said about his racing success. Dahne was a man of few words, but was firmly of the opinion that modern GP two-strokes should have been banned, because as he put it, 'they represent a waste of energy and create pollution'. As the 1970s came to a close, even Dahne was forced to accept that no four-stroke was competitive any longer – certainly not one with only two cylinders. But for a period in the late 1960s and early 1970s Dahne managed to defy the trend. Truly a great rider, it was a pity that he had not lived in an earlier age.

Another notable BMW protagonist and special builder was the German Mike Krauser. Krauser had ridden BMW machinery in competition during the 1950s, and then run a team of Rennsport sidecars in the 1960s. This finally led to his takeover of the works' sidecar racing effort in the mid-1970s when the belt-driven dohc, four valve Rennsport engines were achieving 74 bhp. At this point a combination of competition from the Konig and Yamaha 'strokers', together with the stringent FIM noise regulations, finally killed them off.

Krauser went on to make a name for himself as a producer of fine luggage and other aftermarket accessories from a factory based in Mering. During 1975 and 1976, he worked for BMW and was responsible for its endurance racing effort. By then the venerable boxer engine was beginning to feel its age as big bore Japanese multis gradually began to take over from Ducati, Moto Guzzi, BMW, and other European marques.

In compensation for the Japanese lead in engines, chassis technology came to the fore for the Europeans.

Right **Klaus Enders and Ralf Englehardt winning the 1973 Czech GP at Brno. The partnership became World Champions on BMW's six time between 1967 and 1974.**

British BMW specialist Gus Kuhn entered several BMW's in both production and open class racing in the early 1970's. Pictured here is one of the uncompromising racers that sported leading link forks.

Frame rigidity and sure-footed handling were seen as the only way to make the most out of what was the basically outdated power unit which the Germans were committed to.

Riders for Krauser's BMW team at this period were Freddie Habfeld and Peter Zettelmeyer. Zettelmeyer was involved in engineering research at the University of Munich. He designed the fully-triangulated, light-weight chassis which formed the basis for the endurance racer and would also later spawn Krauser's own 'production special'. However, while the new frame certainly proved a notable improvement over the standard production version, it was not enough to stem the tide of Japanese power. BMW's official racing effort was shelved after Habfeld was injured at Barcelona in 1976.

Even so, March 1976 saw BMW triumphant on the race-track again at Daytona, USA. A headline of the time could not have hit it harder, 'Production One-two for undisputed BMWs'. Californian Steve McLaughlin riding a Bulter and Smith prepared R90S snatched victory from under the nose of team-mate Reg Pridmore in the 50 mile Superbike road race for production roadsters.

In fact, the specially-prepared flat twins had looked set to take the first three places until favourite Gary Fisher, who had set fastest qualifying time the previous day, struck engine trouble with only three of the 13 laps to go.

Only one other man could keep up with the flying BMWs – Cook Nielson, editor of *Cycle* magazine. Riding his own Ducati 900SS, time and again, Nielson split the battling BMW riders as the lead changed half a dozen times per lap. In the elbow to elbow contest, continuing right round the 150 mph banking, the crowd in the massive Daytona grandstand were on their toes with excitement.

Fisher, Nielson, McLaughlin and Pridmore all held the lead at some stage in the race and despite Fisher's retirement, the battle continued all the way to the finish line. British-born Pridmore looked to have a slight edge over team-mate McLaughlin as the pair hurtled around the steep banking at over 140 mph towards the chequered flag – but McLaughlin found the last ounce of power and took victory with inches in it. Both BMWs had the same winning average of 99.714 mph, which would easily have qualified them for the full Daytona 200 event that year. Nielson finished third a long way behind, followed by Californian Wes Cooley, who

Left **John Cowie rode this Gus Kuhn entered BMW in the Barcelona 24-hour endurance race.**

sweated it out all the way with a bucking, headstrong Kawasaki Z1 900.

In the same period, there were other production machine successes for British riders, both at home and in the Barcelona 24 hours and Bol d'Or marathon. Among the riders were Dave Potter, Gary Green, Graham Sharp, Ray Knight, John Cowie and Bernie Toleman.

During 1978, BMW dealer Werner Fallert created what may rank as the most technically interesting 'private' BMW ever, provided the factory racing effort is ignored. His dream was that the ultimate flat twin BMW would be like the works Rennsport racing engines of the 1950s boosted to 1000 cc. The result, based on the pushrod R100 production engine, was the FM1000. It was the most powerful BMW flat twin of all, with a top speed of nearly 160 mph.

Very little of the original engine was left after Fallert had dispensed with the cylinder heads, camshaft and valve gear, and replaced them with new ohc four-valve heads with bevel gear drives on the top of the crankcase. The factory-fitted oil pump was retained, but the oil filter was now a replaceable paper element type. Capacity was enlarged to 999.8 cc by using oversize 94.95 mm pistons, and with special 45 choke Dell'Orto carburettors, the engine developed an incredible 110 bhp at 8500 rpm.

Drive was through a special six-speed gearbox manufactured by Wolfgang Kayser. The complete engine unit was mounted into a purpose-built tubular frame which was the work of Werner Dieringer, chief designer at the Kreidler factory.

Perhaps the most amazing aspect of the whole machine was that it was not in reality a flat twin at all. In an attempt to provide better ground clearance, each cylinder had been angled by five degrees from the

Helmut Dahne won the 1000 cc Production TT on the Isle of Man in June 1977.

BMW returned as an official team to off-road sport in 1979. The specially prepared 750 cc flat twins produced 55 bhp. The investment was not cheap, but it paid.

horizontal – making it actually a 170 degree V-twin.

In 1979, ex-BMW endurance racer Habfeld, recovered from his 1976 Barcelona injury, joined forces with Michael Neher and Franz Wiedemann. Wiedemann was a noted designer. Together, they developed a prototype road-going machine based on the layout of the ill-fated endurance racer. Mike Krauser was then asked if his company would sponsor the new spaceframe BMW,

Although Krauser agreed, the task was to prove anything but quick or simple. One major hurdle was that Federal TUV standards approval had to be

BMW earned considerable prestige from its victories in the Paris–Dakar rallies of the early 1980's. Works team rider Eddy Hau is pictured in the 1986 event. It was the last year that BMW entered as a manufacturer.

obtained. Development costs ran far in advance of the original budget, but Krauser was not a man to admit defeat easily, and he maintained his backing.

Finally, in 1980 the machine was unveiled and went into production as a prestigious sports tourer, the MKM1000. As the supreme accolade, the model was even offered with a full BMW factory warranty. While it used many standard parts, including the R100RS engine, plus wheels and forks, it was truly a hand-built special constructed around Zettelmeyer's latticework frame. It also sported striking bodywork by Zettelmeyer finished in brilliant white, with orange, pink and blue stripes. This paint scheme included fairing, seat and tank cover. Fuel was actually held in an alloy tank concealed underneath.

Production was strictly limited. The initial batch was 200, but even at their high price (£6,500 in Britain) there was no shortage of customers. Perhaps the biggest disappointment was that the machines lacked one of Krauser's own accessories as a standard option. This was his four-valve head kit which he marketed as an aftermarket fitting for standard BMWs. Not only did it offer a substantial power increase but it was actually narrower than the original BMW two valve units. However, thanks to BMW's warranty, it could only be offered as an accessory kit for the MKM1000 from 1982 onwards.

At least one MKM1000 was constructed purely as a racing machine. This was campaigned by Englishman Paul Iddon in the 1984 Battle of the Twins series, sponsored by LAC of Royal Tunbridge Wells, Kent. Besides usual race tuning, the LAC machine featured the four valve heads, an oil cooler, larger discs and three-spoke wheels. In pure speed, it proved a match for anything on the track, but its handling was not up to

that of the Ducati V-twin. It finished the year in second spot in the series.

A different kind of BMW special continued to break records into the 1980s. This was a 94 bhp streamlined 1000 cc flat twin constructed by the Italian rider Elio Zanini with help from BMW. Sadly, Zanini was killed in 1981 while setting three new speed records at the Nardo circuit in southern Italy. He had already established new records for the hour at 140.3 mph, six hours at 133.27 mph, and 1000 kilometres (625 miles) at 138.05 mph average, when a gust of wind caught him out.

Another Italian was involved with a noteworthy BMW flat-twin special of the early 1980s. The work of former MV Agusta race chief Arturo Magni, the MB2 used an R100 power unit and made its debut at the Cologne Show in September 1982. Described in detail in my book *MV Agusta* (Osprey Publishing), it was marketed, unlike the Krauser machine, as a complete rolling chassis into which the customer could slot his own engine. Frame, forks, wheels, brakes, tank, fairing,

Fritz Witzel on a BMW won the over-750 cc category in the 1979 International Six Day Trial.

seat and other cosmetics were all Italian.

Although BMWs were hardly ever seen on the race circuits during the early 1980s, they made their authority felt in a new, challenging form of motorcycle sport – the ultra-demanding Paris-Dakar marathon. The organisers billed it as 'The World's Toughest Race'. BMW took victory in 1981, '83, '84 and '85. But after this record of four wins, and a poor result in the 1986 event, the factory announced its retirement from the rally towards the end of the year.

The Paris-Dakar machines were developed from the BMW enduro machines used so successfully in the 1979 ISDT which were ridden by a team of six works-supported riders. A special 1040 cc 70 bhp version of the flat twin provided a maximum speed of 115 mph and offered torque figures of 87 Nm (64 ft/lb). With a full 60-litre (13.2 gal) tank of fuel, spares, tools and water bottles, the famed 'King of the Desert' weighed 230 kg (507 lb). Riders included Gaston Rahier, Hubert Auriol, Raymond Loizeaux and Eddy Hau. BMW's days of offering a real challenge on the road racing circuits might well have been over – but it was a timely reminder that the old boxer was not out of the ring yet. . . .

DKW

In several important aspects DKW ranks equally with BMW and NSU in the history of the German motorcycle. For many years the company was the world leader in two-stroke design – using a successful formula which it adhered to consistently but by no means slavishly.

The story of this great marque really began with the birth on 30 July 1898 of Jorgen Skafte Rasmussen in Nakskow, Denmark. The young Rasmussen moved to Düsseldorf, Germany in 1904 and then in 1907 to Zschopau, 20 kilometres south of Chemnitz in Saxony. After the Second World War it was renamed Karl Marx Stadt, and is now in East Germany. Here, Rasmussen held a number of engineering posts, and after the first world war, formed his own company in 1919 – JS Rasmussen.

The saga of how the company came to adopt the famous initials DKW is in itself quite a tale, and one with more than one ending. In 1963, at the celebration of his 85th birthday, Rassmussen put forward three reasons for the name. The first, *Dampf Kraft Wagen* came from his first engine – a steam powered unit for cars. The initials stuck, and when, between the wars, the company's racing machines were cleaning up at Berlin's Avus circuit the second slogan was invented: *Der Knabische Wunsche* – the schoolboy's dream. If that was not enough the introduction of a small car in 1928 brought the third twist: *Das Kleine Wunder*, meaning 'the little miracle', and it is this last version which has been the most accepted one over the years.

The fledgling company's first full year of trading was 1920 and it was very much one of development and research. A major milestone was passed in 1921, with the introduction of the Hugo Ruppe-designed 122 cc auxiliary engine. This could be 'clipped' to a conventional pedal cycle, driving the rear wheel by means of a leather belt. By mid-1922 some 25,000 of these miniature engines had been sold, with the two-stroke motor gaining an excellent reputation for reliability.

This sources was quickly followed by the scooter-like 122 cc Golem (1921) and 142 cc Lamos (1922) models. Although both of these offered 'armchair' comfort, they were unsuccessful sellers. But not ready to give up at these setbacks, the combination of Rasmussen's business acumen and the engineering skill of Ruppe saw development of other more successful ideas.

One of these appeared in 1924, with the advanced SM (steel model) which highlighted the pioneering type of design work coming from the team. The SM was a 173 cc single cylinder powered motorcycle, but its main claim to fame was its trendsetting pressed steel frame. It was soon copied by several other motorcycle manufacturers. Even so, DKW was able to stay ahead of the pack of copyists, and by 1927 it had absorbed 16 other companies and had a workforce of over 15,000.

Three years later, with even more rapid growth it could claim to be the world's largest motorcycle manufacturer. However, this level of growth had created side effects, and the main one was high losses and massive bank debts. However, Rasmussen was able to solve this problem with a business method which would characterize the motor industry in the 1960s and 1970s. This was the grouping of companies through mergers and takeovers.

In DKW's case it happened in 1932 when they merged with Horch, Audi and Wanderer to became Auto Union AG, headed by Dr Ing Carl Hahn. The new combine took as its trademark the four silver interlinked circles which over sixty years later are still to be found on Audi cars. But unlike today, this amalgamation of four companies was not purely a badge-engineering exercise. The other three concentrated upon four wheel manufacturing and DKW continued to be a motorcycle producer, and a good one at that.

The cloud of the Great Depression showed signs in 1932 of finally starting to lift and with its new alliance, DKW were ideally organised to take full advantage of an upturn in both domestic and export markets.

Production of DKW engines had been greatly assisted by the company's introduction in 1929 of the loop scavenge system designed by Ing Schnuerle. This was a major step in the evolution of the two-stroke engine. Hitherto, 'strokers had been hampered by breathing problems and it was for this reason that DKW had earlier revived the ancient Bichrome layout, using a separate cylinder acting as a charging pump. This could deliver the mixture with a degree of supercharging at normal atmospheric pressure. However, the Schnuerle system with its flat top pistons soon proved far more effective than either this system or the earlier designs incorporating a piston with a crown in the centre that formed an asymmetric deflector.

Schnuerle's principle offered superior power, improved flexibility and more even firing. It achieved this with angled inlet ports. These allowed the mixture taken in during the induction stroke to proceed up the cylinder, across the combustion chamber and down the other side of the cylinder, taking the course of escaping exhaust gas through its conventional control port. Considerable experimentation ensued before the optimum shape and positioning of the ports was finalised.

In the late 1920s DKW switched some of its attention to cars. They were progressive for the time with transverse-mounted engines (two-stroke, of course!) and front wheel drive. They were introduced at the 1931 Berlin Motor Show. But far more significantly for the present story, 1925 had seen DKW enter the motorcycle racing world with 175 and 250 cc machines using intercooling and the Bichrome system of supercharging. By 1929 the factory was building 175, 250 and 500 cc machines, but it was not until 1931 when the adoption of the Hermann Weber-designed split single layout appeared that the marque began achieving any outstanding competitive success.

August Prussing, who worked in the racing department alongside Weber, was also involved with their successful development. During the next few years just about every one of Germany's top riders

At the Milan Show, December 1950, DKW exhibited three versions of the 125 cc two-stroke single. It was a machine developed from the company's pre-war trendsetting design. All versions had swinging rear suspension with coil springs housed within fork arms and blade front forks.

raced DKW machines at one time or another. They included men of the calibre of Fleischmann, Herz, Steinbach, Klein, Müller, Ley, Rosemeyer, Wünsche, Kluge and Winkler.

The first of the new generation of split singles was a 0.25-litre machine with its supercharging piston working in front of the crankcase. And it was models based on this machine which went on to achieve an amazing array of wins and lap records throughout what were for DKW, the golden 30s. Soon the racing 'Deeks' became known outside the German frontiers, and in their day those 0.25-litre machines were often winning in faster time than the 350 cc bikes. One disappointment, however, came in 1935 when DKW entered the Isle of Man TT for the first time, with three 250s. Only one finished, gaining seventh spot and ridden by Arthur Geiss.

The Berlin show that year saw the debut of a production racer, the SS250, based on the successful factory bike and using the same basic split single watercooled engine. The show also revealed a full range of DKW roadsters up to 350, which were generally well accepted. In an era when four strokes tended to dominate proceedings this was quite something.

Geiss improved his Isle of Man showing in 1936 with an excellent third place that averaged 72.49 mph, behind race winner Foster's New Imperial and Tyrell-Smith's Excelsior. This was after the legendary Stanley Woods on another DKW had led the race only to be forced to retire on the last circuit after setting the fastest lap at 76.20 mph.

The following year an English rider, Ernie Thomas, brought a DKW home third again in the Lightweight TT,

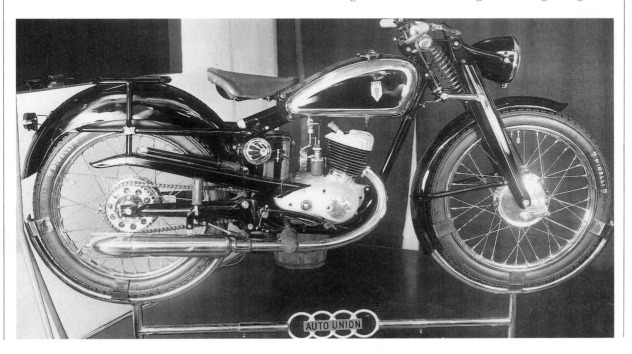

Based on the successful 125, the 1951 RT200 not only offered more power but also telescopic forks.

averaging 73.17 mph for the 264.25 mile race. But without doubt the greatest performance came in the 1938 event, when Ewald Kluge (who had led in the early stages of the 1937 TT) became the first German to win an Isle of Man race. Kluge led from the start to win comfortably and in the process established a new class lap record at 80.35 mph, as well as a race average of 78.48 mph. This was even though he had to make at least one more pit stop than the others due to the poor fuel consumption of his two-stroke engine – at that time it was around 15 mpg.

Besides road racing, DKW did well in ISDT-type events during the late 30s, winning a number of gold medals with a riders line-up that included Hermann, Schertzer, Demelbauer, Fahler, Leppin and Beckhusen. Machines used in these events ranged from 100 to 500 cc.

DKW's all-round success was reflected at the 1938 Berlin Show. This was the biggest yet, with sales reaching record levels and DKW playing a major part in Germany's overall prosperity. The future looked bright, even if the same could not be said of the political situation.

In 1939 DKW not only had the largest racing department in the world, with around 150 men working in it, but also some potent machinery, including the 250 US, a supercharged double piston twin, which gave 40 bhp at 7000 rpm and a similar 350 producing 48 bhp. One engine of each capacity was prepared for speed records, and running on alcohol fuel they pumped out 49 and 60 bhp respectively. These machines were the last designs of the brilliant Hermann Weber, who died after the war in the Soviet Union.

For the IoM TT in 1939 DKW fielded the strong team of Fleischmann, Wünsche, and the 1938 Lightweight class victor Kluge – with entries in both the 250, and 350 classes. The Lightweight TT saw not only a strong

challenge from Britain, but from Italy too, with blown Guzzis piloted by Tenni and Woods, and it was these two riders who led the field at the end of the first lap.

However, Mellors on the lone Benelli single then took over after Woods dropped out on the next lap. Soon the remaining Guzzi expired, leaving Mellors leading from Kluge in second. The other DKWs ridden by Wünsche (7th) and Thomas (8th) were still going. At the end Kluge retained his place behind Mellors, averaging 72.97 mph, whilst Wünsche came home 5th and Thomas 8th.

In the Junior TT, Kluge was a non-starter, but Fleischmann was third behind winner Stanley Woods (Velocette) and Harold Daniell (Norton) at an average speed of 82.51 mph. Wünsche was sixth. Privateer Fergus Anderson on another 'Deek' retired on the fifth lap, but the wily Scot used the same machine to finish 28th in the Senior TT.

After the Isle of Man came the Dutch TT, when *Motor Cycling* headlined, 'Germany Sweeps the Board'. This was rather an overstatement, although it was true that German machines and riders had won all three classes. In both the 250 and 500 categories they had been very seriously challenged by Moto Guzzi and Gilera machinery before retirements gave DKW and BMW their victories. Kluge won the 250 while Wünsche took the 350 class.

A month later in the Grand Prix of Sweden, DKW again took honours in the 250 and 350 classes, with Fleischman winning the 350, while in the smaller capacity event the first four riders home were all DKW-mounted.

The 250 winner Kluge then proved that he could do other things besides race motorcycles. He had taken an Auto Union 6-litre racing car which should have been driven by Meier, and together with Rudolf Caracciola in a Mercedes, drove a couple of high speed laps. But in spite of the enormous speed potential of the cars – attaining almost 200 mph on the straights – they did not manage to lap any faster than Serafini had done on his four cylinder Gilera when winning the 500 cc race earlier.

Before long came the ISDT and high drama. Germany had won in 1933–35. Britain had then taken the honours for the next three years – so the stage was set for a clash of the giants. The scene was played out on the Austro-German border, where the greatest ISDT up to that time attracted more entries than ever and was a model of superb organisation. Even this could not blot out the realities of the greater international situation. And sadly, the 1939 ISDT was memorable not for the quality of its motorcycling, but because the event was deserted during the week by most of the foreign competitors (including Britain) owing to the threat of conflict. Instead of sport, Europe was about to become locked in another struggle – the Second World War.

With the declaration of war the DKW factory, like the majority of other motorcycle plants, was forced to turn over motorcycle production to the war effort. Between 1939 and 1945, it built a number of middleweight military machines, including the NZ 250 and 350, and also a smaller number of the twin cylinder NZ 500. But of all the motorcycles which the war brought into being, DKW's smallest model would have the most enormous significance for post-war developments. This was the RT125 – a lightweight which not only provided the Wehrmacht with a perfect form of transport for one soldier, but was also ideal for a vast number of other tasks.

It was powered by a unit construction 122.2 cc (52 $\times$ 58 mm) engine with three speed gearbox. The RT125 was produced in large numbers during the war years, but the model's main claim to fame was that it was destined to become the most copied motorcycle of all time. The BSA Bantam, Harley Davidson Hummer, Moska 125 and even the original Yamaha YA1 (Red Dragon) all reveal DKW inspiration.

If wartime had brought its problems then peace, when it came in May 1945, was equally traumatic for the DKW marque. Not only had all four of Auto Union's main factories been severely damaged by Allied bombing but DKW was placed in the Russian sector when Germany was partitioned. The former DKW plant went on to make motorcycles for the Warsaw Pact countries, first under the name Ifa and then MZ – Motorrad Zschopau.

Auto Union elected to move West. For its rebirth in the newly emerged West Germany, DKW selected Ingolstadt on the river Danube, in Upper Bavaria, for its first post-war factory. It was here that DKW started with servicing of ex-military vehicles, rather than manufacture of any new machinery. But 1947 saw the formation of Auto Union GmbH while currency reforms in the summer of the following year allowed some of the pre-war Auto Union chiefs to raise enough capital to restart manufacturing vehicles. This decision, in effect, refinanced the Auto Union as a company.

The first project within the new Auto Union group was the re-introduction of the RT125 motorcycle. It entered production in 1949. That year some 500 examples of the 'born again' single cylinder piston-ported lightweight were built. With a power output of 4.75 bhp at 5000 rpm, a three speed gearbox, chain primary drive, 19 inch tyres and 9.5-litre tank, the 68 kg bike could reach 46.75 mph. This was hardly anything to get excited about, but in a country hungry for any cheap personal transport every RT125 made in 1949 was snatched up eagerly.

Re-introduction of the RT125 roadster had been preceded by DKW machines appearing on the race circuit again. As early as 1947, some of the pre-war 250s had been given an airing. Then on 8/9 May 1948 at Hockenheim, a racing version of the reborn RT125 appeared, which showed up well against mainly NSU opposition. Later ridden by Kluge, Wünsche and Müller it appeared in modified form with rear-facing twin exhaust, high level megaphone silencers, magneto ignition (in place of the former battery/coil), left side mounted carb, rev counter (originally none was fitted), plunger rear suspension, oil damped telescopic front forks and a larger full width front brake hub.

By 1949 both the racing 125 and 250 DKWs were

Works rider Siegfried Wünsche astride the then new 250 twin racer in June 1951.

becoming feared for their speed. Just how fast they were, particularly the larger model, is made plain by leading racer Fergus Anderson in a 'Racing News Letter' in his Continental Chatter column in the 17 November 1949 issue of *Motor Cycling*. Anderson said; 'Most memorable incident at Cologne: I was doing a little training on my 500 cc Gambalunga (Moto Guzzi) just in case the powers-that-be said "yes", and had it wound up to maximum revolutions in the biggest gear – when a machine came creeping inexorably past me in the middle of a long straight. It was Walfried Winkler on the four-piston 250 cc DKW!'

However, not only were DKW (like other German marques at the time) banned from international competition, hence Anderson's reference to 'the powers that be', but would have had difficulty competing anyway as the 250 was still supercharged. Forced induction was banned by the FIM from 1946 onwards. Meanwhile the newly 'racerised' RT125 would have been no match for machines such as the FB Mondial and Morini dohc four strokes. This is best illustrated by the lack of success demonstrated by the leading 125 cc 'strokers in the late 1940s Grand Prix events. It was a pack headed by Italy's MV Agusta and Spain's Montesa.

By 1950, DKW's recovery was in full swing, producing over 24,000 motorcycles (all RT125s) and some 6,800 *Schnell-laster* (high speed-trucks). The latter was a sleek delivery van powered by a 700 cc twin cylinder engine (two-stroke of course).

In March 1950 two important motorcycle exhibitions took place within a week of each other at the end of the month. The first was in Geneva where the latest blade-forked RT125 featured rubber as the suspension medium and described as having 'workmanlike appearance' by the *Motor Cycling* reporter.

At the Frankfurt Show a week later, the first of its kind in Germany since the war, DKW could have been expected to use the event to launch something new – but nothing of the sort happened. Only the RT125 was on display. This was in contrast to the many new exhibits from such rivals as NSU, Hercules and Tornax – and it underlines how the effect of having to uproot the factory hindered DKW's post-war development and regeneration, compared to say, NSU.

There was something new at the 23rd Milan Show which opened on 2 December. It ushered in an improved version of the RT125. The RT125 was now supplied with a swinging arm rear suspension that housed the coil springs inside the fork blade. The front forks remained unchanged. December also brought news that DKW would be racing in the 125 class of the World Championships. This followed an announcement in the spring of 1950 that Germany was to be readmitted to the FIM for the 1951 season. Riders were named as Kluge, Müller and Wünsche. There also appeared to be every likelihood that the team would

At the Swiss GP, 22 May 1952, the 250 had a massive hand beaten alloy tank and improved duplex frame.

compete in the Isle of Man TT, which was scheduled to stage a 125 race for the first time.

January 1951 a tele-forked RT 125 was unveiled at the Brussels show. And it was at this time that the factory also first mentioned plans for the introduction of 200 and 250 cc roadsters. The first of these, the RT200, arrived mid-year. Like the RT125 it was aimed very much at the person who needed reliable everyday transport, without many frills – or thrills. In appearance it followed the RT125 closely, but the machine was not simply a machined out smaller model, as both the bore and stroke at 62 × 64 mm were different. This added up to a capacity of 191 cc and unlike the 125, a four speed gearbox was fitted. The power output of 8.5 bhp (later increased to 9.2 bhp) at 4500 rpm, provided a 56.25 mph top speed. Wheels were both 19 inch, and as with the latest RT125, the RT200 sported telescopic front forks, but strangely, the frame was totally unsprung, a seemingly backward step compared to the smaller mount. The fuel tank held 12 litres, and the dry weight was 255 lb (compared to only 150 lb for the smaller bike).

At the first meeting of the new road racing season at the Eilenriede-Rennen, Hanover on 29 April, the Ingolstadt marque paraded its very latest hardware – as did NSU and BMW. DKW's offerings were 250 cc parallel twins, which had their cylinders inclined slightly forwards from the vertical. Each pot had its own Dell'Orto carburettor and the sparking plugs were placed in the middle of the heads – ignition was by flywheel magneto. The clutch was mounted on the nearside, with exposed chain primary drive. Suspension was by telescopic front fork and pivoted rear fork with twin fully-enclosed oil damped shocks. The frame was a welded tube, full duplex cradle type. All this was capped by a massive hand-beaten fuel tank in unpainted alloy. The combined rear mudguard/number plate and front mudguard were also in the same material, and on some machines a small alloy fairing was fitted.

Power output was around 20 bhp at first, rising to 23 bhp after some development work during the season. Both the new 250 twin and the improved 125 were the work of the young Erich Wolf, who had previously tuned Puch and earlier DKW engines before joining the famous two-stroke specialists. But try as he might Wolf just could not make the 250 twin competitive against the top four-strokes of the day in international events. For this was the realm ruled by Benelli, Moto Guzzi and Parilla.

In his attempt to improve performance, Wolf not only tried numerous induction systems with different discs, pistons, cylinder heads, barrels etc, but additionally carried out a weight paring exercise until the 250 DKW was the lightest machine in its class. This

resulted in better acceleration times, shorter braking distances and improved handling, but it also led to an increased level of unreliability, which in itself was self-defeating.

It was really not until 1952 that the first results of Wolf's and DKW's efforts were seen. First the 250 parallel twin was significantly improved by fitting a Bosch magneto in place of the previous flywheel magneto, a single Dell'Orto carburettor, and most importantly by replacing the megaphone using a pair of expansion chambers. This was one of the first – if not the first – machines to be so equipped anywhere in the world. And with this simple modification to the exhaust system, Ing Wolf was able to gain the significant improvement in performance which he needed.

First appearance of the latest twin was at Hockenheim on 11 April 1952. The DKW race team for the season was announced at the end of March.

The line-up was: veterans Ewald Kluge and Siegfried Wünsche – plus two new boys – 25 year old Karl Hoffman from Frankfurt and Rudi Felgenheier, a 21 year old from the Rhineland. No mention was made of Müller, who had been associated with the marque for

several years. It was rumoured that he would be mounted on Italian Mondial machinery, but eventually he appeared in the NSU team.

The really sensational news at Hockenheim was of a brand new 350 DKW. In reality, it was not a 'new' design at all. Plagued by difficulties with ignition systems, Wolf had earlier modified the 250 twin by fitting the magneto (and also the inlet disc) in front of the crankcase. It was this arrangement which had provided inspiration to fit another cylinder in place of the magneto at the front of the crankcase. This is how the new 350 DKW three cylinder was born, with two near vertical cylinders and a horizontal one. The angle between the two banks of cylinders was actually 75 degrees.

Both the 125 single and 250 twin 'Deek's had the square bore and stroke dimensions of 54 × 54 mm. But for the new three, in order to restrict the swept volume to 350 cc the bore of each cylinder was reduced to 53 mm and the stroke was fixed at 52.8 mm, giving each cylinder a capacity a shade over 116 cc and totalling 348.48 cc. A six cylinder car type magneto, bevel driven at half engine speed was employed – and the engine was fitted with three 28 mm Dell'Orto SS1 carbs and a

Prototype 350 triple made its first appearance at Hockenheim in May 1952. Its running gear made free use of that fitted to current 250 twin.

four-speed close ratio gearbox. And as the larger engine was fitted into the rolling chassis of the 250 twin, it had every chance of excelling due to its outstanding power-to-weight ratio. Sadly, the initial results were disappointing.

Both the latest 250 and new 350 made their debut in Grand Prix racing over the 4.5 mile Bremgarten circuit, Berne, Switzerland on Saturday 17 March. In contrast to the Swiss GP of a year earlier, which had been dismally wet, the weather was magnificent. Bright, uninterrupted sunshine bathed the scene as competitors came to the line for the 250 cc race. With three factory Moto Guzzis among the 13 starters, there seemed little doubt of its outcome. Also in the entry was a works Benelli single ridden by Les Graham – formidable competition for the two DKW twins.

At the end of the first lap Fergus Anderson led on a Guzzi, then Graham, followed by Siegfried Wünsche on the first of the DKWs. Soon the other DKW runner, Kluge, was out of the race on the third lap, paddling his silent 'Deek' into the pits to retire where he was followed on the tenth lap by Wünsche, who had held fourth place all the way.

As the 28 starters in the 350 race, which was the next event, wheeled their machines from the pits to the

starting grid, there was no doubt as to who was favourite to win. Norton team leader Geoff Duke had achieved record breaking times in practice, but it was the unknown quantity of the three cylinder DKW to be ridden by Wünsche which created the most comment.

After a sluggish start to the race, Wünsche got his DKW through the field to move ahead of Lawton, Amm and Kavanagh into fifth spot. The DKW demonstrated a promising turn of speed until lap 12, when engine trouble forced its retirement.

Although it was rumoured earlier that DKW would appear at the IoM TT, in reality no entry was made. It is sensible to assume that at the time their record of reliability was so suspect that in such a long and arduous race the team stood little chance of even finishing. Nor did they compete in the next two rounds, the Dutch TT and Belgium GP, but at the German GP staged at Solitude near Stuttgart on Sunday 20 July, DKW were out in force. With 400,000 spectators packing every square inch of the 7 mile circuit, the stage was set for some fast and exciting racing between works teams from Britain, Italy, Spain and Germany.

In the 125 event none of the DKWs finished in the top ten places. The 350 race saw two DKW threes entered – Kluge and Wünsche. Both provided high drama. On lap 12 Kluge caught up the leading factory Nortons at the front of the field, only to fall. With his shoulder blade broken he retrieved the machine, remounted and came in sixth, but was rushed straight to hospital after

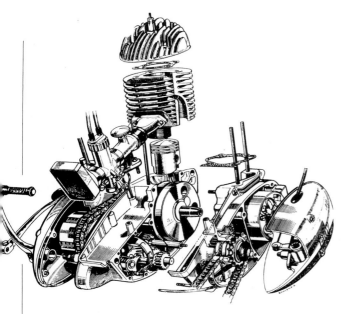

finishing the race. Meanwhile Wünsche battled on for most of the race after losing his nearside footrest, to finish 11th and gaining a great hand from the partisan crowd in the process.

But it was the 250 race which created the biggest sensation of the day. The mixed field comprised mostly Moto Guzzis, with a sprinkling of NSU twins, Parillas, Velocettes and a few DKWs. On one of these was Rudi Felgenheier. A last minute entry for DKW following the Kluge accident, and it was this newcomer who took victory when on the penultimate lap the two leading Guzzi riders Lorenzetti and Ruffo crashed. This left Bill Lomas on a NSU twin with victory in sight, only to be robbed almost at full distance by a broken conrod, letting Felgenheier into the lead which he held till the end. This gave DKW its first post-war Grand Prix victory.

Felgenheier, on a 250 parallel twin, was also the most

Above **Engine details of the RT250 single which came onto the market in 1952. Essentially it was an enlarged RT200 with a capacity of 244 cc (70 × 64 mm).**

Below **Siegfried Wünsche was an undieing competitor. At the Solitude circuit during the 350 race of the 1952 German Grand Prix he rode his three-cylinder 'Deek' without a nearside footrest. He finished 11th.**

successful of the DKW riders in home events that year. But this machine was no match for the new NSU Rennmax four-stroke twin.

On the international front, next came the Ulster and Italian GPs. DKW missed both of these, but at the Spanish GP – the final round in the 1952 Championships – held at Montjuich Park Barcelona on Sunday 5 October, Ewald Kluge made his comeback partnered by team mate Siegfried Wünsche.

In the 125 event only Kluge entered. Although he finished ninth he was three laps adrift of the winner Mendogni on a Morini. Both riders took part in the 500, where Kluge entered a 350 three as there was no separate 350 cc class. He came in 11th, while team mate Wünsche finished a creditable seventh behind MV, Gilera and Norton works bikes – and in front of local veteran Aranda on a Gilera four and Ray Amm on a Norton single.

One of the main reasons for the improved reliability of the 350 triple was without doubt the introduction of a new lubrication system in August. Earlier seizure problems had caused several retirements at a time when straight petroil lubrication was used. This was at first supplemented, and then replaced completely by direct lubrication to cylinder walls and main bearings. The oil was carried in the top frame tube and fed by gravity through a multiplicity of small pipes and needle valves.

DKW riders also appeared in another form of motorcycle sport for the first time since before the war – the ISDT. This was at the 27th event, held around the town of Bad Aussee, Austria. It started on Wednesday 17 September. Several DKW riders gained medals, with golds for Hasselrot, Landstrom, Eriksson, Finkenzeller, Sensburg (250 solos), Ischinger and Kirchberg (250 sidecar). Bronze medals went to Hobl (125) and Tamplin (250). With only one retirement, this was a most pleasing result for DKW.

Two points of special interest were that Hobl was later to race the works triples, and also that the 250s used were based on a new roadster introduced that year. This was the RT250, a machine which used essentially the same three-speed engine unit as the RT200 introduced the previous year, but with a capacity of 244 cc (70 × 64 mm) and a compression ratio of 6.3:1, giving 11 bhp at 4000 rpm. The carb was a Bing AJ 2/26/15 and the fuel capacity was 13 litres. Both wheels were 19 inch with a 3.25 × 19 front tyre and 3.50 × 19 rear. Rear suspension was controlled by plunger, while up front were telescopic forks and a full width 160 mm hub like those fitted to the RT125/200. Unlike the earlier models the rear drive chain was fully enclosed. Dry weight was 134 kg and maximum speed was 62.5 mph.

With the three roadster singles DKW was in a much stronger position to meet the influx of orders which had been thrust upon the company over the previous

couple of years. Even though the RT125 remained the best seller, the RT200/250 both not only sold well, but proved reliable and long-lasting in service.

At the end of the racing season in October 1952, the news in Germany was rife about a 500 DKW. This was rumoured first to be a twin, then a larger version of the three cylinder model and later even a four. In fact, none of these reports were accurate, as later events were to prove.

The DKW racing team was announced in early January 1953 for the new season. This was unchanged. Veterans Ewald Kluge and Siefried Wünsche, were backed up by Rudi Felgenheier and Karl Hofmann. Tantalisingly, there were no hints about a new machine, and while the 250 and 350 had been further developed the 125 had been dropped.

As had been a tradition with DKW, the basis of both the 1953 250 and 350 was a small frame with brakes which were just able to provide adequate stopping power. This was all part of an attempt to maintain the correct power-weight ratio. So seriously was the weight-saving issue taken, that four sizes of aluminium alloy fuel tank (interchangeable between the two models) were employed for different length races. These held 12, 22, 28 and 32 litres.

The IoM TT was the first of the 1953 classics. Prior to this in May, team leader Kluge had broken a leg at the Nurburgring in a German national championship meeting, and although their entry was not withdrawn, most observers believed the factory would give the TT a

Later swinging arm version of DKW RT350 at the 1953 Frankfurt Show. It was the factory's first post-war twin-cylinder roadster.

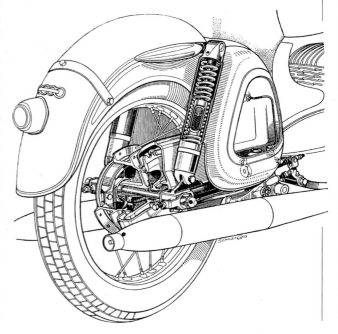

miss. On the contrary, Wednesday 3 June saw the DKW *equipe* arrive in the island with Siegfried Wünsche and the substitute for Kluge, Rudi Felgenheier, accompanied by race chief Wolf and mechanics.

They had a major task in front of them if they were to qualify on their 250s and 350s, for there were only two practice periods left for each class. Designer Wolf conducted much of the testing himself, and could claim to be the only man in his position who actually rode at full bore the machinery he designed. He was actually seen out on the Mountain section of the course early one morning before breakfast, in shirt sleeve order and with trousers rolled up to just below his knees while testing the 350 triple at well over 100 mph – and no crash helmet!

On the Thursday evening (their first practice session) quite a cheer went up when the two DKW riders made their appearance. They were such a long time arriving that it was feared that they would not be able to get in the necessary qualifying laps. Later it transpired that on showing up at the starting line, their helmets had been condemned. Finally, they borrowed the helmets of two travelling marshals, Bob Foster and George Mills.

Any doubts as to the ability of the pair in finding their way round were quickly dispelled. Rudi Felgenheier did his first lap at 70.32 mph and a second in 74.6 mph. Wünsche's standing start lap was done in 81.01 mph and his flyer at 84.65 mph. But after this successful start, disaster was literally just around the corner.

At 8pm on the evening of Saturday 6 June, DKW's last minute entry, Felgenheier, was returning from an unofficial exploratory trip around the course on a roadster when he rounded a curve between the Mountain Box and the Black Hut. He collided with a van which was being used by some highway personnel to repair a break in the wire fence. He suffered quite severe injuries, including a broken leg which it was feared at one time would have to be amputated. A sequel to this was that he was subsequently charged with dangerous driving and fined £7 in a local court.

Back on the race circuit his team mate Wünsche was ready to ride in the Junior TT on Monday 8 June with his three-cylinder model. *Motor Cycling* had this to say about its start; 'Ouch! What an attack on the eardrums as No 90 Siegfried Wünsche's DKW screams up to its high pitched war song!' However, the DKW did not stay on song – at Ramsey on lap 2, when around 15th in the running, Wünsche was forced to retire with engine trouble.

Wednesday 10 June saw him lined up against three works Guzzis and a lone NSU Rennmax twin ridden by Werner Haas – plus a large private entry of Guzzis and various British machines (mainly Excelsior and Velocette). Conditions were extremely wet, and the start was postponed for an hour. At the end of the first lap Fergus Anderson led on a Guzzi, Haas was second, followed by Enrico Lorenzetti on another Guzzi, with

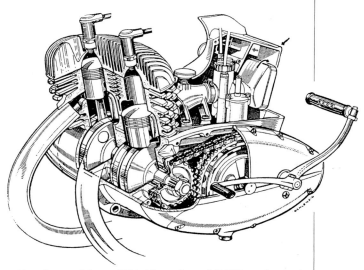

Manufactured from 1955, this variant of RT350 engine had Teves interrupted cylinder finning. Other features included duplex chain primary drive.

Wünsche in fourth. Towards the end of the third lap Lorenzetti dropped his machine and retired, leaving Wünsche in third place. And there he remained until the end, averaging 81.34 mph for the four laps.

After the race Wünsche, who had ridden for DKW in the 1937–39 Lightweight TTs, said that although very pleased with his third place he could have made a faster time except for acute 'pins and needles' caused by vibration transmitted through the footrests. On some occasions he had even been forced to change gear by hand!

Next in the classic calendar came the Dutch TT at Assen on Saturday 27th June. Here the, 250 race, which came first, saw three of the Ingolstadt strokers entered, with Wünsche joined by August Hobl and Dutchman Piet Knijenburg. At the start Wünsche made a flashing getaway and led the field down towards Juliana's Bend by nearly 100 yards. However, this lead was short lived and soon he had been overtaken by both Haas (NSU) and Anderson (Guzzi). Wünsche went on to finish fifth, with Hobl close behind in sixth, although Knijenburg retired.

Next came the 350 race with three DKW triples entered. These were expected to provide opposition to four works Nortons and three three-valve AJS 7R3s plus two 345 Moto Guzzi singles.

Then drama! The field was reduced by three. With warming up completed no DKWs had appeared – quite simply they had been withdrawn as it was considered that their speed was too low for the Dutch circuit.

In practice the threes had appeared in modified form. Cylinder finning was now square on the two upright cylinders, and much deeper on all three cylinders than before. The outer head fins on the upright 'pots' were cast at an angle to assist the passage of air.

A week after the Dutch GP, on Sunday 5 July, the team had obviously found a new head of pressure because they had decided to contest the 350 class at the ultra-high speed Spa Francorchamps circuit during the Belgian Grand Prix. This meeting was run in blazing sunshine, but DKW had only one opportunity for victory as there was no 250 class event for the day.

The 350 race was the first on the programme and was due to cover 11 laps of the 8.81 mile circuit. Only one DKW – Hobl's – appeared on the line as Wünsche had bent his machine, and himself, by falling off on the fast Blanchimont curve first time out in practice. The remaining DKW never showed in the top 10, and Hobl retired early in the race. Obviously there was a lot more development work needed.

Two weeks later and it was the home classic – or so it should have been. For never in the history of motorcycle racing had a situation arisen like the one which occurred at Schotten in central Germany, where the German Grand Prix was due to be held on Sunday 19 July. After inspecting the circuit before practice began, the AJS, Norton, Gilera and Moto Guzzi teams decided unanimously, that they would not compete.

This was not only because they thought that the circuit was too narrow for the larger, faster machines, but because in their opinion the surface was so slippery that it would have been guaranteeing disaster to run a championship meeting in the conditions.

However, the meeting went ahead with practice ending for the remaining teams on Saturday 18 July in dismally wet weather. Both NSU and DKW factory entries remained in the programmes. So did the Englishman, Len Parry, who had put in the fastest practice lap in the 350 class as a member of the Ingolstadt team aboard one of the three-cylinder 'strokers'.

The following day, the sun came out to dry the circuit for the 125 race which was the first event of the day. This had no DKW entries. Next came the 350s. On the line for 10 laps of the 10.5 mile course was the Italian Bandirola, with an MV four, and a DKW trio consisting of Hobl, Hofmann and Parry. The rest of the field was made up of private owners, mainly on British machines.

Parry set the pace all the way from the start to the top of the long climb to Poppestruth, but then retired. And at the end of the lap Hobl led by a small amount from a New Zealander Leo Simpson on an AJS 7R and the MV-mounted Bandirola. Then on the next lap Hobl set the fastest lap of the race at 77.25 mph, coming very close to Geoff Duke's 1952 lap record. But just when it looked as if the DKW rider had the race in the bag (he was gaining 15 seconds over second place man Bandirola on each lap), he coasted in on the long run down to the start/finish area at the end of the fourth circuit with all three plugs oiled up. Although he eventually rejoined the race, he was doomed to retire with the same problem later.

Meanwhile Hofmann, who had fallen on the opening lap, had moved up to third place – and to the great excitement of the crowd, overhauled AJS rider Ken Mudford to take second. There was no change amongst the leaders after that so the screaming three-cylinder 'Deek' had finally achieved something – albeit without any real opposition.

The 250 race came next, where amongst the twenty competitors were five factory NSU Rennmax twins and the same DKW trio who had just competed in the 350 race, plus Alano Montanari on a works Guzzi. Parry had a serious problem getting his DKW to start and eventually got under way some two minutes after the rest of the field had gone. Only Hobl was able to provide a challenge to the NSUs during the early stages of the race. It was led throughout by Werner Haas, lapping at a higher speed than Bandirola had ever achieved in the 350 race. Towards the end, Montanari forced his Guzzi past Hobl to claim second spot, a position he retained until the end. Only the one DKW finished.

The French GP, which came next, was by-passed as it only had a 350 class. The next DKW outing was in Germany again, where amidst the magnificent Schwarzwald scenery and in wonderful weather a crowd of over 150,000 assembled on Sunday 9 August to watch the 1953 Freiburg hillclimb. In many respects it was a veterans' day, for the best performances came from the ranks of pre-war stars. For example Siegfried Wünsche on his three cylinder 350 DKW not only won the 350 class, but set up a new record for the 8 mile series of climbs through the tortuous Schavinsland Pass road which reach a height of 3500 ft at the summit. Each competitor had two runs and the average time was the final result.

A new record set up by the DKW rider was a time of 7 min 59.16 seconds, bettering the figures established in 1936 by NSU star Heiner Fleischmann by 22.54 seconds. Wünsche's speed of 55.95 mph proved the fastest of the day – and superior to anything that the four wheel brigade could manage.

In the 125 class, Petruschke won on an Eastern zone Ifa (MZ), breaking the record set up in 1951 by Muller's DKW, by 1.40 second. Then in the 250 category Wünsche clocked 8 min 9.59 seconds (54.77 mph) on his first run, but retired on the second with ignition trouble, leaving Karl Hofmann on another DKW twin victor.

No DKWs were at the Ulster GP the following week, but a fortnight later on Sunday 23 August the Swiss GP saw the DKW team back in action, contesting both the 250 and 350 classes. There was a total of only three motorcycle events, (the other being the sidecar) as a prelude to the afternoon's car Grand Prix.

Covering 18 laps of the circuit, a distance of 81.5 miles, the 250s got under way in bright sunny weather, although the road remained damp in patches beneath the trees. Four DKWs came to the line mounted by

Wünsche, Hobl, Hofmann and Parry. Wünsche took the lead from the start, but superior speed soon put NSUs and Guzzis at the front. After Wünsche retired, the first DKW machine home was Parry's in eleventh followed by Hobl in twelfth.

From the fall of the flag, the 350 race was a similar story with Wünsche streaking into an early, short-lived lead, until Anderson soon had his Guzzi at the front of the pack. Even though the DKWs might not have been quick enough, they certainly made their presence felt as the following extract from *Motor Cycle* so aptly put it; 'Then come Farrant and Brett – for all the world like men who have disturbed a beehive – with all four DKWs angrily buzzing in pursuit!'

Soon there were two, for another lap saw Hobl and Parry disappear. The order at half distance saw the remaining pair of DKW riders seventh and eighth, and only one DKW survived to the three quarter stage, because Wünsche retired at the pits. At the end of the 21 lap, 94.9 mile race Anderson took the flag, with Hofmann down in sixth, the last of the riders not to be lapped by the winner.

In the Italian GP at Monza on Sunday 6 September DKW made a massive effort. Although the Swiss GP quartet had been joined by Englishman Tommy Wood, only one bike finished in the 350, which was Hobl in fourth spot, and none in the 250! Finally in October at the final round in Spain, Hobl finished sixth on the 250 parallel twin, there was no 350 class.

All-in-all it was very much a season dominated by retirements. Hobl emerged as the most consistent performer – and finisher. And the 250 twin, rather than the more glamorous 350 triple, had proved itself more reliable and competitive.

Strangely, after their excellent debut the previous year, only two DKW machines appeared in the 1953 ISDT. Neither was part of the official German Trophy or Vase teams. Both were specially prepared RT250s and the two riders, Pellikaan and Sensburg, both gained gold medals.

On the production front the RT125, 200 and 250 continued, the RT200 now sporting the plunger rear suspension of the larger single.

However, with increased profits and production figures being exceeded every week it was only a matter of time before DKW introduced more up-to-date designs to meet the challenge coming from a host of other manufacturers.

The second of Germany's post war International Motorcycle Exhibitions at Frankfurt was chosen as the launch pad. This opened to the public on Sunday 18 October and was held in what was virtually a small town of large buildings, open spaces and private roads. The whole mammoth area was devoted entirely to one week's exhibition of motorcycles and bicycles, together with all their side attractions.

Practically taking up Hall 8 by itself was the 1954 DKW model line. It featured two brand new models, and one updated one. The latter was a four-speed version of the RT250 – the RT250/1 – which not only had the addition of another gear but more power, up to 12 bhp at 4650 rpm, offering 65.75 mph. It also had a larger 13-litre tank, more chrome and wider 3.50 × 19 tyres.

The RT175 was new, but in reality owed much to existing models – an RT200 engine and RT250/1 chassis. To achieve the smaller capacity the 174 cc engine shared the same 62 mm bore as its 200 brother, but had the stroke reduced from 64 to 58 mm – whereas the 250 had used the 200's stroke and increased its bore to achieve the desired result.

But the only really new machine was the factory's first post-war roadster twin, the RT350. This was a handsome and well-equipped machine, with an air of quality, clean styling and the expectation of a good performance. *Motor Cycle* commented; 'If a prize were to be offered for sleekness of design, a serious contender would undoubtedly be the 350 cc DKW RT350. From stem to stern, this machine has considerable eye approval to enthusiast and layman alike and the finish of the parts, whether cast, plated, polished or enamelled cannot be faulted at any point.'

The piston-ported parallel twin had a capacity of 348

DKW team member Wünsche with one of the RT175 machines entered for the 1953 ISDT.

cc producing 18 bhp at 4800 rpm. It had cast iron cylinders and alloy heads, with a compression ratio of 6.3:1 and a Bing 2/24 carb. The silencers on the RT350 were best described as immense and simply by removing the baffles the machines top speed of 74 mph was *reduced* by around 10 mph.

Primary drive was by duplex chain, while the rear drive chain was fully enclosed and a large moulded rubber section sealed the joint between the moving rear chaincase and the engine unit. Other features included a 16-litre fuel tank, 180 mm front and 160 mm rear full width alloy brake hubs built onto 19 inch chromed steel rims with 3.25 front and 3.50 rear tyres. An interesting detail of the machine was its hydraulically operated rear brake, the master cylinder of which was housed in the right hand tool box. Suspension was luxurious with soft damping for the heavy-duty forks, and plunger rear suspension. The bike's other memorable feature was its exhilarating acceleration, which compensated for its relatively low maximum speed.

Also in 1953 the Ingolstadt factory launched the first of its many cars powered by a 900 cc two-stroke triple engine. And by the beginning of 1954 the workforce had more than doubled compared with 1950. Around 10,000 workers were employed on all aspects of DKW two and four wheeled production. DKW was now in a much stronger position financially and was, therefore, able to devote more development funds to both the standard production line and its competitions department.

It was in early 1954 that another figure came onto the scene who was to have a great influence on the racing side of the company. Robert Eberan von Eberhorst was originally a student of the Vienna Technical College and a genuine motorcycling enthusiast in the late 1920s. He later joined Auto Union at Chemnitz in the 1930s where he became an assistant in the development team of the great Professor Ferdinand Porsche. After the war, von Eberhorst went to work in England, where his appointments included periods at the Aston Martin and BRM, but in early 1954 he returned to Germany and became a technical director of DKW.

He was given the responsibility for the racing department. Having such a senior voice as von Eberhorst on the management team pumped new life into the competition effort. A less forceful and able character might well have scrapped the racing programme following the poor results of the past few seasons.

In an ensuing reorganisation, Ing Hellmut Georg was put in charge of the day-to-day running of the competition shop, and instructed by von Eberhorst to give top priority to sorting the 350 triple out once and for all. His task was to make it competitive both in terms of speed and reliability.

One of Georg's earliest decisions concerning GP racing was to concentrate efforts exclusively on the three cylinder design and shelve the 250 parallel twin.

Georg's immediate task was to dismantle a complete three and then redraw in full the original blueprints. The redesign which followed this curious exercise showed a

By 1955 DKW's 350 triple had been completely redesigned by Helmut Georg. Styling was now aggressive.

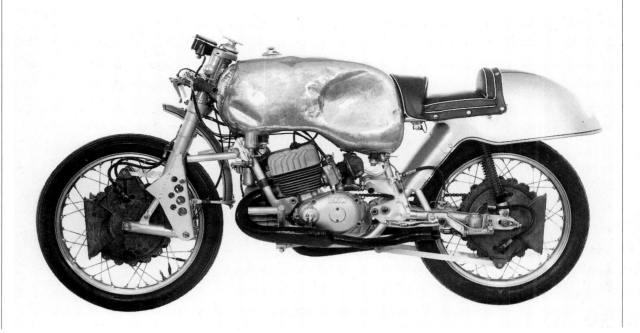

host of changes, including a strengthened crankcase, minus the fins which had previously made a section of it appear almost as an additional cylinder. Another change was a redesigned cylinder liner.

The crankshaft, pressed together from six seperate parts, was a real engineering work of art. To avoid worthless space and to achieve required crankcase compression, there were extremely narrow clearances for the slender, highly polished conrods and full disc flywheels. This arrangement netted a high degree of pumping effect. Wolf had obtained a 48 per cent balance factor, but Georg was able to increase this to 62 per cent.

Both big and small ends had caged needle bearings, and the forged two-ring Mahle pistons were made of Sintal, with American-made steel rings. The depth of these rings was originally 0.75 mm, but Georg increased this to 1 mm. It had been found that ultra-thin rings tended to become caught on the ports and, in addition, had a tendency to vibrate. Also in the Wolf era deflector pistons had been used, but Georg immediately turned to the more or less flat types which have since become the universal wear for 'strokers.

Three Dell'Orto SS1 carburettors supplied the mixture. Those feeding the two vertical cylinders shared a common float chamber, while the horizontal cylinder's carb had its own. In fact, together with the correct shape and length of expansion boxes the positioning of the float chambers was found by Georg to be the most critical of all the engine's performance factors.

During the development stage he also discovered some other interesting details; one of these was that the horizontally mounted cylinder developed less power than either of the two vertical pots. It required considerable redesigning effort before it would yield the same output. This released a substantial amount of extra power compared to the original design. But this was to be only the start of a continuous development trail which took place over the next three seasons.

The first outing for the revised 1954 DKW 350s came at the 17th international Eifelrennen, run over the 14.16 mile Nurburgring on Sunday 23rd May. The 'new' bikes had their maximum rpm reduced from around 12,000 to under 10,500 in order to obtain piston reliability. They had five-speed gearboxes, in place of four, larger 2LS front brakes, and leading link forks, but otherwise externally appeared very little different to the previous 1953 bikes.

Although they took the first three places in the 350 class (Hoffman, Hobl and newcomer Bodmer) and proving faster than Ray Amm's factory Norton, they nonetheless failed to produce a race speed or lap speed to equal that of the 250 NSU Rennmax models which dominated the smaller class. After entering both the French GP and IoM TT, the Ingolstadt team later informed both organisers that they would not be able to compete. On the surface this was a surprising decision, but it was simply that the machines were still not ready for international racing and more development work was needed.

The team reappeared at the Belgian GP on Sunday 4 July, when a considerable number of alterations were revealed. Towards achieving greater weight reduction, the heavy six cylinder car type magneto employed since the machines' original debut was discarded in favour of battery/coil ignition, with a triple contact breaker assembly driven from an extension on the right hand end of the crankshaft. The three carburettors were now fitted with air slides which operated separately through cables from a tiny, triple lever cluster mounted close to the handlebar clutch lever.

The latest leading link front fork assembly was of orthodox construction, with the pivots carried on fabricated lugs welded to the rear of the fork stanchions which enclosed the long compression springs. The slim hydraulic damping units, fitted between the fork links and the stanchions, were longer than they had been on the earlier telescopic fork-equipped machines.

The reduction in engine revolutions was said to have achieved the desired degree of piston reliability without loss of power, though there was now a considerable amount of vibration which had not been apparent previously. However, it might have been due as much to change in frame design as engine tuning. Even with the new frame and forks the roadholding was not yet to the standard which was needed.

For the Belgium GP the DKW team was Wünsche, Hobl and Parry. The race start was faultless for DKW, with Wünsche (who was on the front row) making as *Motor Cycle* put it 'What must rank as the fastest start ever seen in any road race. After Eau Rouge, up the steep climb, he had a clear 100 yard lead.' Wünsche was followed by Hobl, with Quincey (Norton) and Kavanagh (Guzzi) coming next.

Soon, however, the superior speed of Kavanagh's and Anderson's Guzzi singles showed and they relegated Wünsche to third spot, which he held until the end. Hobl held fifth but retired near the end, while Parry had retired earlier without ever featuring on the leader board. The race was marred by the death of new Norton works rider Gordon Laing.

Another feature of the 'Deeks' used at the Belgium GP was an *illegal* form of front number plate-cum-streamlining. The controversial front number plate was the problem. Rather than being essentially flat it was in fact deeply curved. For the Dutch TT the following weekend the team again fitted these, but were not allowed to race with them, though they were used in practice in Holland.

For the Dutch TT, there were four DKW riders – August Hobl, Karl Hofmann, Siegfried Wünsche, and, as in 1953, the Dutchman Piet Knijnenburg. From the start, Hobl on the second row of the grid shot into the lead as soon as the flag fell, making full use of the flashing acceleration of his three cylinder two-stroke. However, soon it was the same old story and by the end of the second lap there was a 1-2-3 Guzzi formation at the front. Hobl retired at mid-race distance with ignition trouble. Later Wünsche and Knijnenburg were also to retire leaving only Hofmann, who came home fifth with an average speed for the course of 92.99 mph.

A couple of weeks later half a million spectators watched the German GP at Solitude. The races were contested beneath a sweltering sun and race and lap records were pulverized in all classes. For once there were DKW entries in both the 125 and 250 events, from two ex-factory bikes. Otto Brueger took his 125 cc single to 21st position while Karl Lottes scored 7th in the 250 race on his 1953 ex-works parallel twin. None of the Ingolstadt team appeared in the 350 race, for reasons officially stated to be 'frame difficulties'. The 'Deeks' were not to be seen in any further classics that season.

The only notable DKW race result for the rest of the year was when privateer Karl Lottes took his twin to the 4th International Scarborough meeting where a crowd of over 30,000 saw a DKW win the 250 race. John Surtees won the 350 and Geoff Duke the 500 (on a Gilera four), this victory was judged significant. *Motor Cycling* described the DKW victory thus; 'Lottes thrilled the crowds with a runaway win on his yowling 250 cc twin cylinder DKW.'

If the year had not been much of a success on the race circuit for DKW, it certainly was in other areas, notably on the production front and off-road. Not only were the factory producing a wide range of motorcycles, but in addition building cars and even exporting engines for use in other manufacturer's machines. These included Nymanbolagan AB (NV) of Sweden.

The Swedish firm not only used the RT125 power unit for their successful 11CL and 11DL roadsters, which featured a de luxe specification, but also bought DKW engines for the highly-rated NV36 Army Six Days trials bike. It gained numerous gold medals in the ISDT and similar prestige events during the 1950s. The NV36 was powered by a version of the RT250 roadster engine mounted in a massive frame equipped with a special hydraulically damped, rear suspension, well tried NV telescopic front forks and sponge rubber dual seat. Among the machine's refinements were a totally-enclosed rear chain, thief-proof steering head lock and rubber-mounted 18-litre fuel tank.

DKW had their own interests in off-road sport to pursue as well. As far back as 1950 the factory had developed a 125 *Geländemaschine* (open country machine) based on the RT125 roadster, with which to compete in the long distance endurance trials. For 1954 a serious attempt was made on this area with the *Geländesmachine* in 125, 175 and 250 versions. All three were based on their roadster counterparts. The

competition bikes featured specially prepared engines with different internal gear ratios and final drive ratios more suitable for their new task; the 125 engine produced 7.2 bhp, the 175 cc 10.8 bhp and the 250 cc 17 bhp. All the machines used plunger rear suspension, high-level exhaust systems, fully-enclosed chains, knobbly tyres, a more comprehensive air filtration system and other off-road features. Later, from 1956 onwards, the 125 was dropped and the 175 and 250 shared a new swinging arm frame, dual seat and stronger, redesigned front forks.

There were also motocross versions in three engine sizes (125, 175 and 350 cc) but these had swinging arm frames from the start. The power outputs in this trim were 8.5 bhp, 12.6 bhp and 20 bhp respectively. All three initially had low-level chromed expansion chambers, but eventually it was found that high level systems were necessary. To compensate for the lack of suspension travel in those days the motocrossers used extensively padded dual seats.

Witness to the rapidly growing interest which was being shown for motocross events in Germany was the country's 1954 Moto Cross Championships which took place at Dusseldorf on 17 October. There were over 20,000 spectators present and German television relayed the events live to an even greater audience. Both major championships went to riders of British machines, but DKW works riders, Gerhard Bodmer and Josef Reiter won the 125 and 175 titles.

Besides the work done on the trials and motocross machines, the other major development project that year appeared in public in September in a blaze of publicity. This was the entry by DKW into the scooter world with a 74 cc (47 × 45 mm) two-stroke single – the Hobby. An innovative design featuring automatic transmission. This provided an infinitely variable drive between top and bottom ratios of 8.33 and 24.4:1 via a system of drive belts.

On the engine shaft was an expanding pulley, operated by a centrifugal governor built into its centre hub, which pulley drove a second, spring-loaded pulley on a countershaft through a vee-belt. From there a helical gear connected the countershaft to a sprocket which provided the final drive to the rear wheel by chain. Any increase in the engine speed, resulting from opening the throttle or meeting a down gradient caused the engine shaft pulley flanges to close up, thus raising the gear ratio, while the spring loading of the countershaft pulley maintained the correct belt tension. Conversely, as the engine speed fell, the gear ratio was automatically lowered to suit the conditions.

Operating a handlebar-mounted lever disengaged the drive by separating the flanges of the engine shaft pulley – effectively acting as a combined clutch and bottom gear. But with a bottom ratio as low as 24.4:1, this was in most cases necessary only for stopping and starting. A neutral position was provided by means of a

In final form, the 350 three-cylinder GP racing engine developed 45 bhp and gave a speed of 140 mph.

lever which disconnected the drive by fully expanding the engine shaft pulley.

To overcome the objection of many scooter users to a motorcycle-type kickstarter, the engine of the Hobby was spun by pulling a cable which rotated the crankshaft through a free-wheel coupling. The operating handle was located within reach of the rider's left hand.

Although it only delivered 3 bhp at 5000 rpm, the Hobby still managed a top speed of almost 40 mph. It also had the advantage of looking like a full size scooter of at least 150 cc capacity, but costing considerably less to purchase and run. Fuel consumption was 139 mpg at a steady 25 mph – test figures obtained by *Motor Cycling*. To simplify matters further for potential owners an automatic petroil mixer was located in the fuel tank. A trend by certain other manufacturers to larger wheels for scooters had been followed by the adoption of 16 inch rims shod with 2.50 section tyres. Front suspension was by a simple form of telescopic fork, while the rear wheel was mounted in a pivoted fork controlled by rubber in compression.

Two versions were marketed – a standard and de luxe specifications. The main difference between the

two models was that the de luxe (Luxus) variant was fitted with a full-width front hub and had a pillion seat, whereas for the standard model this latter item was an optional extra. Finish was also more lavish on the de luxe, with additional chromium-plated parts and wheel grilles together with passenger grab handles on the rear cowling.

Also new at around the same time in the autumn of 1954 were sports versions of the RT175 and RT200, which gained an S at the end of their model numbers to signify Sport. Not only were these more powerful (19 and 11 bhp respectively), but they were also the first DKW roadsters to feature full swinging arm rear suspension. Another new feature was the larger 15-litre fuel tank capacity.

At the same time the new type of front fork used on the RT350 was fitted, not only to the new S models, but the RT250 as well. The RT250 received a face lift at the same time as an increase in power to 15 bhp. However, neither the 250 or 350 were fitted with the new swinging arm frame.

All models were now available with a dualseat as an optional extra, except the 125, which gained plunger rear suspension and full width brake hubs. The RT350 gained full swinging arm rear suspension and became the RT350S, with a larger 17-litre fuel tank, and a larger 26 mm Bing carb, plus an increased 6.5:1 compression ratio giving more power – 18.5 bhp at 5000 rpm.

But perhaps the most important technical innovation for the 1955 DKW line-up was the use of interrupted cylinder barrel finning on all the motorcycle models with the exception of the RT125. This process had been pioneered by Alfred Telves KG, of Frankfurt-am-Main in an endeavour to obtain more effective heat dissipation. In turn this permitted higher engine speeds and, thus, a greater power output. DKW had first used the Telves system in the ISDT – and had been so impressed with the results that they considered it would offer the everyday street rider its worthwhile benefits.

The Telves system was not the exclusive property of DKW in the motorcycle field, but it was by far the most prolific user. The system was based on a process of centrifugal casting which produced bi-metal cylinders combining thin, staggered blade fins made of copper with a cast iron cylinder wall. The centrifugal process in any case made it easier to cast such very thin fins, but it also allowed the cylinders to be made of the two metals chosen. The process exploited the difference in specific gravities. When molten copper (Sg 8.82) and grey iron (Sg 7.20) were poured into a rotating mould, the heavier copper was thrown outwards by centrifugal force to the fin area while the lighter iron built up the inner, or cylinder, wall of the casting.

Advantages claimed were many. Apart from improvement in the rate of heat dissipation due to the copper finning, the construction dampened engine noise and produced a deeper tone which was less offensive to the ear. The German motorcycle industry was becoming increasingly noise conscious. The design also included gaps dividing the fins into short blades which were then staggered. In the case of forced-draught air circulation, for example, industrial stationary engines, the arrangement was invariably that every third blade was on the same horizontal plane as the first. But with 'free air' cooled motorcycle engines a closer pitching of the blades was adopted in order to ensure a better circulation of air to the rear of the cylinder. In this case, the fourth or fifth blade was in the same plane as the first.

DKW's other work and efforts in the field of long distance trials also began to show results. For the first time since the war, DKW machinery was part of an official German team effort in the 1954 ISDT. The Vase B team was comprised solely of *Geländesmaschinen* RT175s, ridden by Bodmer, Finkenzeller and Feser.

The 29th International Six Days Trial got under way

DKW star August Hobl leading World Champion Bill Lomas on a Guzzi at 1956 German Grand Prix. Lomas eventually won this memorable dual by taking the chequered flag a few lengths ahead of Hobl.

from Llandrindod Wells, a small town in the very centre of Wales. The event, organised by the British Auto Cycle Union, set a new record for its international character. Over 14 nations were represented, and more than 300 riders entered.

It proved an excellent test for the nine (including the Vase B team) DKW riders. Not one machine failed through mechanical trouble in the whole six tortuous days. The only retirement was the Vase B team member Finkenzeller. It was not his DKW which was the problem. After missing a checkpoint on the second day he was excluded despite a storm of protest from the German delegation. This effectively killed off the Vase B teams efforts, even though Bodmer gained a gold and Feser a silver medal. Four other DKW riders gained golds, Pellikaan (175), Kampf (175), Klingenschmitt (175) and Sensburg (250), while the remaining two riders both gained bronze medals. It was a highly pleasing result for Ingolstadt's development team.

Until shortly before the event, one of the DKW competitors, gold medal winner Kurt Kampf, was a chief technician at the Ifa (MZ) factory. This was the former DKW plant in Karl Marx Stadt. Many people believe that Ernst Degner, who defected from the factory in the early 1960s, was the first rider/technician to do so, but it was Kampf who pioneered the way West.

On the 20 October 1954, the 250,000th DKW motorcycle to be made since the war left the assembly line of the Ingolstadt plant. During the same period around 122,000 DKW cars had also been produced.

Both the RT250 and recently introduced RT350 twin were proving popular as solos, and also for use with a sidecar. One of the most popular sidecar combinations of the period to be seen on German roads was that of either the RT250 or 350 hitched to a Binder single seat sports chair – a combination which was officially approved by DKW/Auto Union. The Binder was attractive and stylish, with its colour matched livery and DKW/Auto Union badgework, both front and rear, and looked the part with its DKW marriage partner. To allow easy access for a passenger, the whole top front section including the windscreen folded forward, while the rear section aft of the passenger compartment was a large, lockable luggage boot.

A fully tubular steel chassis was employed and this was mounted onto the motorcycle in three places. Both the RT250 and 350 featured frames with sidecar fittings as standard equipment. Weighing in at 65 kg, the Binder had a 19 inch wheel with a 3.50 section tyre under a comprehensive mudguard. There was also a wrap-around chrome front bumper above which was a series of four grille bars.

Over the winter of 1954/55 the race shop controlled by Ing Hellmut Georg was a centre of intense activity. An improved 'three' emerged in 1955 with over 40 bhp being produced for the first time. There was also much modified running gear.

The engine now ran on a compression ratio of 12:1 with effective power available from between 6,800 and 11,000 rpm. In early track testing with the revised engine it had been found that even when changing down with the revs shooting up to 15,000 rpm, nothing fell to pieces. But in any case this was not too important because all the useful power occurred between 8800 and 9500 rpm. In the earlier Wolf motor a 16:1 petroil mixture was used, but Georg was able to bring this ratio down to a safer 25:1, by using a heavier grade oil.

Although the weight of the power unit remained almost the same, the whole bike now weighed about 320 lb without fairing. Despite being considerably heavier than before and heavier than the competition – the equivalent Guzzi weighed 260 lb – the 'new' DKW was well received by its riders. They preferred not only the increased reliability of the power unit, but the fact that the extra weight had removed many of the troubles experienced by the earlier over-lightened models.

Finally, there were now much bigger, stronger and more effective hydraulically operated brakes on both wheels. The earlier, smaller, and lighter units had not only proved borderline in their effectiveness, but prone to cracking. The new brakes were 215 mm in diameter and each wheel had two separate units back to back. These were connected to a master cylinder operated by the foot pedal which applied both brakes and automatically supplied the correct bias to the front and rear wheels. A hand lever enabled the rider to increase braking effect of the front wheel if required. It could be argued that DKW had invented the linked brake system used by Moto Guzzi. Nevertheless it was the Italians who patented a very similar system using disc brakes some two decades later.

Another source of rider discontent which had finally been eliminated was that of high frequency vibration. During 1953 and 1954, the life of a rev counter on one of the racing triples had often been as short as 20 miles! Systematically investigating this problem led Georg to discover that the problem centred around harmonics which were being transmitted from the engine to the frame. He finally solved this by improving the quality of the material use for the crankcase and strengthening the crankshaft. It was also found that the extra weight of machine and modified crankcase supports combined to defeat what had previously been one of the machine's major problems. As might be imagined, few riders would wish to race a two-stroke vibro-massager with a super-narrow power band and no rev counter!

Considerable time was also spent with the Ina bearing company, who came up with stronger needle bearings for both the small and big ends. Georg took this a stage further and from 1955 used needle roller bearings in the swinging arm pivot.

Another problem was crankcase sealing. Much time and effort was spent before a satisfactory solution was finally evolved. This included double-lipped seals in place of the single-lip ones which had originally been specified.

Other changes took in the cylinder heads, porting, timing and most important of all, the expansion chambers. Georg used a flat type of expansion chamber and after many exhaustive bench tests ascertained the optimum length and size. He was able to gain a relatively high increase in the mixture induced at certain engine revolutions – up to an outstanding 80 per cent at certain points.

Then there was streamlining. DKW found, like Moto Guzzi and NSU, that depending upon the circuit, it could add up to 10 mph to the maximum speed. Well over a hundred different types of fairing were tested in a wind tunnel. Unlike the other two factories mentioned above which raced four-strokes, DKW not only had air resistance to worry about, but also the effective cooling of three cylinders to consider.

Georg also built a single-cylinder version of the engine, initially to provide additional data on the behaviour of the horizontal cylinder, but later decided to use it in a 125 class racer. This did not appear until mid-way through the 1955 season, but when it did, it created a sensation by winning its first race at the Sachsenring in East Germany, and breaking the race and lap record speeds in the process.

Before this, the new racing season had got under way for the DKW team at the international Hockenheim meeting in early May. Moto Guzzi works rider Ken Kavanagh won the 350 race, establishing a new lap record at 106 mph. For a time Wünsche on the latest DKW triple seemed to offer a serious challenge, but he was forced to stop twice at the pits for adjustments.

A DKW entry was made in the Lightweight (250) Isle of Man TT by Englishman Arnold Jones, who was rumoured to have the use of a newly built streamlined version of the old parallel twin. But in the event, Jones withdrew and was therefore counted a non-starter.

At the 18th international Eifelrennen run over the 14.16 mile circuit at the end of May, Hobl had given DKW its first race victory of the season in the 350 race. But his team mate Hofmann who finished second set the fastest lap at a speed of 75.29 mph.

The meeting at the Nurburgring also highlighted the merits of streamlining, at a time when some riders still harboured doubts concerning safety in strong cross winds and handling through fast, successive turns. At Nurburgring the DKW team of Hobl, Hofmann and Wünsche held different ideas about the machines available to them. Wünsche decided that he preferred a full view of his front wheel and selected a naked machine, whilst the other two riders took streamliners. Even though the Nurburgring was a circuit full of corners, with hardly a straight in its length, Hobl and Hofmann not only finished first and second, but both consistently lapped faster than fifth placed Wünsche.

Hobl was full of praise for his streamliner, saying that it was less tiring, and provided excellent protection from the rain, with good stability under all conditions. From DKWs point of view, the controversy appeared to be settled.

A month after the Eifelrennen meeting on Sunday 26 June the German Grand Prix was run on the same demanding Nurburgring circuit – the first time since 1931. Laid out in 1927, the Nurburgring was without doubt the pride of German road racing. And justly so, for in the magnificence of its setting and the concentration of hazards the circuit it was unparalleled. It wound and dipped in a confusing sequence of blind bends and undulations over the beautifully wooded slopes of the Eifel mountains. The task of riders in memorizing the circuit's 174 bends was made more difficult by the similarity in appearance of the majority of its curves. Above all, it demanded not only a knowledge of the course, but a rider who could perfect his technique in blending the exit from one curve into the entry of its successor and thus achieve a smooth, fluent style. None of its bends was very slow; few of them were really fast. Nevertheless, the Nurburgring in its original unshortened state ranked equal with the much longer Isle of Man Mountain circuit as the ultimate test in worldwide racing – which makes the designers of today's purpose-built tracks appear timid in comparison.

Ample proof of the rigours of competing on such a demanding track was found in the setting of the 1955 German GP. When race day dawned the higher parts of the circuit were enshrouded in a thick, damp mist. This was in contrast to practice, when the weather had been hot and sunny – with the major problem being molten tar. So while a drop in temperature cured that particular problem, no one relished damp roads. For in addition, the surface had been made extremely tricky by the rubber deposited on it from the spinning tyres of racing cars.

The start was postponed one and a half hours until amost 11 am. By that time the picturesque ruins of the old Nurnburg Castle overlooking the starting line could be seen silhouetted against a steel grey sky.

There were no DKW entries in the first event for 125s, nor the 250 race which followed it. But all this was more than offset by DKW's presence in the 350 event. There were four of the gleaming Ingolstadt triples – all were unstreamlined, which was strange bearing in mind the team's results a month earlier. These naked machines were piloted by Wünsche, Hobl, Hofmann, and Bodmer who was one of the factory's trials team.

As soon as the flag fell two of the snarling three cylinder DKWs leapt to the front of the pack. Norton's John Surtees was hot on the heels of the German pair and moved up to second place during the first lap. Lomas and Sandford too, riding Moto Guzzis, passed Wünsche before the end of the lap, but Hofmann brought the third of the three cylinder two-strokes into sixth position.

During the second lap, Surtees passed the leader Hobl on the curves only to lose the advantage on the final straight. There Lomas passed both men to take the lead. Kavanagh on another Guzzi came through the field to take fifth place, behind Sandford, while Lomas rapidly consolidated his control of the clean air, with Surtees displaying his superb riding to the full in his effort to offset the superior speed of Hobl's DKW.

Towards the end Lomas eased the pace slightly, and even Surtees could do nothing to counter Hobl's better speed and acceleration, so DKW was able to gain its best result to date at world level with the three cylinder 350. It was perhaps even more significant that all four DKW's finished the seven lap, 99.16 mile race. It was proof of the value of Georg's winter spent on experimentation. Hofmann finished sixth, Wünsche seventh and Bodner fourteenth.

Hobl followed this with a duplicate result at the Belgian Grand Prix. DKW newcomer Hans Bartl on the next DKW finished sixth.

A 125 single was evolved by Georg from the DKW triple. It is pictured here in April 1956. Unfortunately, it never achieved the success of its bigger forebear.

A week later the 25th Jubilee *Grote Prijs van Nederland* – the Dutch TT – took place at Assen on Saturday 16 July, the first time the new 4.79 mile Van Drenthe course had been used. With Moto Guzzi riders taking the first three places, the DKW team still showed up well both from a performance and reliability aspect. Hobl was fourth, Hofmann fifth, Bartl sixth and Wünsche eighth.

Another week on, and DKW contested two separate meetings. In Sweden at the Hedemora circuit about 110 miles north-east of Stockholm the non-championship Swedish Grand Prix was nonetheless a popular and well supported event where Hofmann and Bartl had their streamlined threes in action. But Bartl was soon to take an early retirement with engine trouble. After some fierce riding at the front of the field Hofmann settled for fourth place behind the Norton trio of Hartle, Surtees and Brett. These four lapped the remainder of the field at least once during the 25 lap 113.02 mile race.

On the same day, back in Germany, the other half of the DKW team contested at the international race meeting at Solitude. It was attended by 233,000 spectators; a record for a non-Grand Prix event in Germany, possibly for Europe. The 350 race was the best of the day. DKW rider Hobl and Guzzi-mounted Kavanagh took it in turns to dispute the lead and the lap

record, which each broke more than once. At the end, Kavanagh clinched it with a lap speed of 89.67 mph, leaving Hobl as runner-up and team mate Wünsche third.

The following weekend saw Hobl acclaimed as 350 German champion. More than 100,000 supporters of road racing spent an enjoyable day in the sunshine at the Norisring. It was a circuit which ran inside and outside what had been Hitler's pre-war Annual Rally Stadium on the outskirts of North Bavaria's ancient city of Nürnberg. Although Hobl was acclaimed champion, he did not win the race. That honour went to the Italian Enrico Lorenzetti on a Guzzi, with Siegfried Wünsche second and Hobl third.

As in previous years, the DKW team did not make the journey to Northern Ireland for the Ulster GP. But they were at the Italian GP on Sunday 4 September for the 33rd *Gran Premio Motociclistico delle Nazioni*. The Monza course had been shortened from its previous 3.91 mile lap to 3.59 mile.

The biggest surprise was the first appearance in a Grand Prix by two of the new horizontal single cylinder 125 DKWs. Ridden by Hobl and Wünsche, both finished. Hobl was fourth at an average speed of 90.14 mph and Wünsche fifth, albeit a lap adrift. In the 350 event Hobl finished fifth averaging 104.11 mph – only 14.2 seconds behind the winner Dickie Dale on a Guzzi after the 27 lap, 96.41 mile race.

Monza was the last classic that year and Hobl had finished the season with third place in the overall World Championships. At long last the DKW triple was beginning to show its true potential for him in competition.

Following their excellent showing at the 1954 ISDT, three DKW machines were chosen as part of the German Trophy team for the 1955 ISDT held in Gottwaldov, Czechoslovakia. The 30th event of the series which started on 13 September. The complete German Trophy team consisted of a pair of Maico riders and the DKW trio – Abt, Brack and Fezer – all three on 175s. With no marks lost throughout the week, Germany romped home to win the Trophy for the first time since 1935.

DKWs were very popular for ISDT work by this time, several other nations used Ingolstadt machinery for their teams. Belgium's Vase A and Vase B, and Holland's Vase B were two such examples – while DKW *power* was used by the whole Swedish Vase B team on their NV machines. DKW's record for the 1955 ISDT includes four golds and two silvers, but nine retirements. The high level of retirements reflected that unlike earlier years this large number of foreign riders aboard DKW machines were unfamiliar with their bikes.

Two-stroke enthusiasts in Britain had something to talk about in September 1955 when it was formally announced that AFN of Isleworth Middlesex, the BMW importers, would market the DKW range (or part of it) in 1956. Three models were initially mentioned, the RT350 twin and both versions of the variable transmission Hobby scooter. The standard Hobby retailed at £119, the de luxe at £128, while the top of the range RT350 motorcycle went for £280 – which was then as expensive as the majority of home-built 650 vertical four-stroke twins.

In Germany, the 1956 model range was announced at the same time. This consisted of eight models, including the two scooters.

The RT125 continued for what was to be its final year. It had been significantly updated and improved over the years and now had an engine which produced 6.4 bhp at 5600 rpm but retained a three-speed gearbox. Sophisticated features included the fully enclosed rear drive chain, plunger rear suspension, telescopic front forks, full width 150 mm brakes, a 6 volt 35/45 watt headlamp and many other more minor details.

Then came the RT175S which, together with the identically styled RT200S remained unchanged. There was also the RT200 Standard – a budget priced version of the 200S with far less chrome plate and items such as wheel rims and tank sides now painted black. The engine remained in the same state of tune and it was still possible to specify the optional dual seat.

The swinging arm version of the RT350 continued unchanged, but a new model based on the RT200S was introduced. This was the RT250S. It offered improved performance over the earlier versions of the 250 – the RT250 (discontinued at the end of 1954) and the RT250/1 and 250/2, which the new model superseded. With a compression ratio of 6.5:1, 27 mm Bing carburetter and 15 bhp, the 250S delivered, for its day, a decidedly sporty performance. Top speed was a claimed as almost 75 mph, which was nearly as fast as the 350 twin. Many considered the RT250S to be DKW's finest roadster of the 1950s and one which in terms of both looks and performance matched any other German 250 two-stroke roadster single of the period.

For the 1956 road racing season Georg again spent the winter months on painstaking development of both the 350 three cylinder and 125 single. Both machines were similar to the 1955 versions, but with even finer tuning. The 350 ultimately gave a reliable 45 bhp at 9700 rpm, which equated to a road speed of over 140 mph, whilst the 125 gave 17 bhp at 9500 rpm – good for 110 mph.

Early in 1956 the former Moto Guzzi rider and team manager Fergus Anderson tested the 350 DKW triple following a disagreement with the Italian management. Anderson had been full of praise for the German machine, which in his opinion was extremely competitive, but Moto Guzzi happened to have had the best riding talent.

Shortly after the DKW tests Anderson was killed at Floreffe in Belgium on a BMW Rennsport at one of the early season meetings. However, another British rider

Factory brochure rendering of 74 cc Hobby. This scooter had an infinitely variable automatic transmission.

did join the team that year. This was Cecil Sandford, the 1952 125 cc world champion (on an MV Agusta). Sandford had a wide experience, including various MVs. Moto Guzzi and Velocette works bikes. In many ways the Englishman replaced the veteran Siegfried Wünsche, who ended his racing days as a privateer, riding a 125 MV.

The classic season started on the Isle of Man, and although the 1956 DKW team was Sandford, Hobl, Hofmann and Bartl, it was only Sandford who contested the first round of the series. Behind the scenes, the DKW equipe had arrived on the Island with two of its 125 cc six-speed horizontal singles only to find its entries had not been officially made, therefore, they were unable to compete.

Sandford rode his seven lap race to finish fourth in the Junior (350 cc) TT at an average speed of 85.75 mph. Perhaps the most impressive part of DKW's Isle of Man visit was that its three cylinder machine now had complete reliability. According to Sandford, the coupled hydraulic brakes were tricky on wet roads, but apart from that, as he put it; 'She was wonderful and never missed a beat' – a great tribute to the development team headed by Georg back in Ingolstadt.

After the IoM TT came the Dutch TT. Saturday 30 June was blessed with ideal conditions despite rain during practice earlier in the week. DKW made three entries for the 350 class – Hobl, Hofmann and Sandford, while in the 125 they had two – Hobl and Hofmann. Sandford was riding a 125 Mondial in this event.

The 350 race began after the 250 which opened the day's racing. Competition was extremely fierce with MV Agusta fours, Guzzi singles, Jawa twins and a host of privateers on AJS and Norton machinery. But against this opposition DKW showed up well, with Hobl third, Sandford fourth and Hofmann eighth.

In the 125 race which followed Hobl repeated his form with another third. Behind a pair of deep, mellow-sounding MV's ridden by winner Ubbiali and Taveri, the DKW single screamed its war cry ahead of Sandford's Mondial, then came Hofmann, who was ahead of the Czech Bartos on a four-stroke CZ.

Eight days later in Belgium, Sunday 8 July saw all four of the DKWs which entered in the 350 race finish in the first six, although Surtees on an MV four won. The only other non-Ingolstadt machine was another MV four ridden by Masetti which finished fifth. So the 'Deeks' score read: Hobl second, Sandford third, Hofmann fourth and Bartl sixth – all highly impressive, because Spa Francorchamps was the world's fastest circuit. Unfortunately, things did not go so well for Hobl in the 125 race. After a good start his engine seized on the third lap at Stavelot. Hofmann on the other model came home a lonely fifth.

Back to Germany, and the venue for the homeland GP reverted to Solitude, where Hobl repeated his Belgian showing on the 350. But this time it was Lomas on a Guzzi who stood between him and victory. Sandford was fourth and Bartl fifth. Again Hobl managed to head Hofmann, but this time it was in the 125 duel that he finished one place ahead of his team mate.

In search of championship points Hobl made his first visit to Northern Ireland and was rewarded with a seventh place at the Dundrod circuit on Thursday 9 August. He was up against the might of the full Guzzi, Norton and AJS teams. The reason why Hobl had made the visit could not have been more apparent – before the Ulster he was equal on points with Guzzi-mounted Bill Lomas. However, as Lomas won, Guzzi now held a clear advantage. Hobl did not bother to race his 125 'Deek', but he must have wished that he had competed in earlier years to improve his course knowledge.

Some new names appeared amongst the DKW entries for the annual Eifelrennen around the Nurburgring on Sunday 26 August. Among them, Off won the 125 and Bechteler took the 350 for the marque. With the season just drawing to a close, the World Championship circus trail led to the final classic of the year, the Italian GP at Monza on Sunday 9 September.

The 125 race was first on the race card, and it sounded as if a whole wasps nest had been overturned as the 26 bikes came to the line. Gilera twins, desmodromic Ducati singles, MV and Mondial models, plus Montesa and DKW 'strokers – the noise was incredible. Although they were faster than the Montesas, the DKWs of Hobl and Hofmann could not stay with the faster four strokes. Hofmann came home sixth and Hobl eight.

The 350 race was Hobl's last chance to draw equal with Lomas for the championship, but a sixth just was not good enough, even though Lomas did not score any points after crashing out. Hobl was runner up in the 1956 350 World Championships. Again all the DKWs that entered finished; fourth Hofmann, fifth Sandford and seventh Bartl, besides Hobl sixth place.

Nobody knew at the time that this was to prove DKW's classic series swansong. Never again were the screaming threes, or the little horizontal singles, to appear in a Grand Prix. But it was not the team's last appearance. This came later that month at the international Avus road races in Berlin on Sunday 16 September. Hobl went out on a high note giving DKW a victory in the 350 race. He averaged 116.5 mph. It was the final curtain for the post war factory's racing efforts.

With its headquarters at the health and winter sports resort of Garmisch-Partenkirchen in the Bavarian Alps, the 31st International Six Days Trial started on Monday 17 September. DKW again had a trio of riders in the German Trophy team, but this time two of the riders, Abt and Fezer, were on 125s and only Brack was on a 175. They were partnered, as in the past, by a pair of Maicos. DKW also had two official manufacturer's teams.

Controversy raged on the second day when two of the German Trophy team's DKWs were seen with wrong numbers. It later transpired that their original machines had been switched. Both were promptly excluded. This was extremely unfortunate, because all the other nine finishers on DKW machines won gold medals. And one of the DKW manufacturer's teams finished with maximum marks.

But like their road racing brothers, the DKW trials men were to see 1956 as the end of an era. At the Ingolstadt factory, collapse on the production front was quickly to engulf the competition department and ensure its closure.

For DKW, like the majority of the German motorcycle industry, 1956 was a black year. Although a new moped, the Hummel (bumble bee) had been launched in July, things were becoming worse at Ingolstadt. Only the four wheel side kept the company alive. Two reports from the Frankfurt show in October say it all. from Motor Cycling 'Why DKW have done it I can't imagine, but on the models below 250 cc the Ingolstadt people have incorporated a hefty Earles type fork, with pressed steel blades and in-built cowling for the headlamp, which completely spoils the lines of what were originally extremely slick machines'. An official report read 'The DKW position is said to be far from happy. Output has been reduced drastically, many top level executive changes have been made, a new motor cycle with Earles type forks has been introduced, but other models are continued and there is much evidence of mixed thinking.'

Quite simply, the whole lamentable situation arose because the whole industry, not just DKW, had overestimated sales and the management just did not know how best to respond.

Three models designated 'VS', denoting Earles forks, had been launched at the Frankfurt show, the RT175 VS, RT200 VS, and RT250 VS. The first two remained in production for three years, they never proved good sellers, even though their finish and reliability were both high.

The DKW Hobby scooter was taken out of production at Ingolstadt during 1957, but the model had a second life, being manufactured under licence in France by Manurhin. The Manurhin version of the Hobby was made in Paris and had a refined version of the former's variable gears. It was completely automatic.

The French version of the Hobby also had wider tyres, a more powerful engine and modified styling. Because of its self-adjusting belt drive transmission it was known in France as the Beltomatic.

In Britain AFN Ltd remained DKW importers for 1957, and it also sold the Beltomatic in Britain for £143 9s 3d.

But in September 1958 came news that a batch of the Earles forked RT200 VS were to be imported. The selling price was remarkably low at £129 19s 6d. But in place of AFN, the sole distributors would now become Pride and Clarke Ltd of London SW9.

This shake-up was nothing compared to what was just about to happen in the Federal Republic. In November 1958 came news of a massive amalgamation of three major German motorcycle producers. It was masterminded by Franz Flick, controlling shareholder of Mercedes-Benz. On 1 January 1958, Daimler Benz AG gained control by acquiring 88 per cent of Auto Union shares. One of their first decisions was to abandon independent motorcycle production. Up to that point, the Auto Union Group, through DKW had manufactured 519,000 motorcycles since the war.

Called Zweirad Union, the new grouping embraced Victoria, Express and DKW. The Victoria factory at Nurnburg was chosen on the headquarters, although the DKW plant at Ingolstadt was retained. Further, it

was announced that only the RT175 VS, RT200VS and Hummel moped were to be continued.

The Hummel moped was finally imported into Britain from October 1959 onwards by Europa Imports of Reading, Berkshire. Its standard model sold for £84. A de luxe version, with amongst other things, a dual seat and a larger capacity fuel tank, was £97 4s 0d. It continued to sell well into the 1960s, although the final DKW motorcycles were produced at the end of 1959.

In 1966 Zweirad Union joined forces with Sachs-Hercules to form a further concentration of the German motorcycle industry.

Throughout the 1970s it remained the largest German producer in terms of the number of machines built. This story is more fully related in the Hercules chapter.

Effectively, the once proud company formed by Jurgen Skafte Rasmussen after this last amalgamation ceased to exist. Its brilliance, innovation and glories were consigned to the history books.

Earles-forks, swinging arm rear suspension, luxurious dual seat and other items made 1958 RT250 desirable.

Fath

Helmut Fath first sprang to public attention in 1959 when partnered by Alfred Wohlgemuth he finished fifth in the World Sidecar Championship. The following year, again using a BMW Rennsport outfit, the duo totally dominated the World Championship. Winning four out of the five round series with victories in France, the Isle of Man, Belgium and West Germany. Though failing to win the only other meeting, the Dutch TT at Assen, they still managed second.

In 1961, they looked set to repeat this performance and retain the title, after beginning the series with a runaway victory in the first round at Montjuich Park, Barcelona on the 23 April. Here Fath and Wohlgemuth lapped the entire field. Then came tragedy. The following weekend, at the annual international Eifelrennen meeting staged at the 4.81 mile Nurburgring circuit on Sunday 30 April, the World Champions crashed in heavy mist and rain.

In the accident, Wohlgemuth lost his life, and Fath not only lost his passenger but was to be put on the racing sidelines for five long years. At the time, it was reported that he had lost a foot, but this proved to be incorrect. Fath had actually broken his right leg, left ankle and a bone in his hand.

Most men would have retired, but Fath was not most men, and he retained his single-minded love of road racing even during his enforced years away from the circuits.

With the aid of some friends, he designed, built, and tested his own across-the-frame four-cylinder double overhead camshaft racing engine. Fath called it the URS after the village of Ursenbach where he lived.

The URS design was really a pair of side-by-side parallel twins, coupled together by a countershaft driven from the crankshaft between cylinders 1 and 2, then 3 and 4. Firing order was 1-4-2-3, and the engine had a central timing chain. Six main bearings carried the crankshaft, with caged roller big-ends and phosphor-bronze small ends in the titanium con rods. A combined oil cooler and filter was included in the lubrication system. Bore and stroke of the new engine were 60 × 44 mm, and the ultra short-stroke unit developed power between 8000 and 13500 rpm. The URS was a very high revving unit, and it was a remarkable technical achievement to maintain valve control at up to 15000 rpm with a two valves per cylinder layout.

Credit for this went to Fath's partner, Dr Peter Kuhn (formerly a lecturer at Heidelburg University). He had designed the cam profile and valve spring rates to match using special Swedish wire for the springs. The same spring steel was later specified by Fath for use in various other engines.

The valves themselves were large – 34 mm inlet and 30 mm exhaust – and were splayed at 67 degrees. As a result, twin 10 mm sparking plugs were fitted in each cylinder, and unusually, these were mounted vertically. Otherwise there would not have been enough room for the valves.

Fuel was injected directly into the ports by a Bosch injector mounted between the wide angle upper frame tubes above and behind the engine unit. The injector had come from a 1.5-litre Borgward car. A divided cable from the twistgrip moved the single flat throttle plate to regulate the fuel supply. Although contemporary press reports claimed 80 bhp for the engine, Fath laughed at

An engineer of considerable talent, Helmut Fath built this 500 cc racing four at his house in the village of Ursenbach.

this and said his dynamometer had only told him – and he was keeping it a secret.

Fath made his competition comeback in May 1966 at the West German Grand Prix staged at Hockenheim. His reappearance five years after the Nurburgring accident and his new engine created a sensation. Unfortunately, he retired after just three laps when lying sixth. This was just the start of a series of problems its creator discovered with the URS engine during that first season in which Fath hardly finished a race.

At the start of 1967 it appeared to be the same story, with the URS seeming not to have enough power. However, at the West German GP at Hockenheim, Fath took the lead from the start. But despite building up a four second lead over Klaus Enders' BMW, he was forced out near the end with a broken gearbox selector mechanism.

The URS engine was the result of nearly five years work that followed Fath's serious racing accident in 1961. It made its first public outing in May 1966. Notice the fuel injection system and dry clutch.

It was also during this year that the URS engine was first considered for solo use. It was mooted that John Blanchard might race one mounted in a frame built by Colin Seeley. At the time, Blanchard stated, 'I think the engine may be better for a solo than a sidecar, and is now giving good power'. Unlike the sidecar power unit, the solo engine was fitted with carburettors and had magnesium instead of aluminium alloy castings.

By the time of the 1967 IoM TT, Helmut Fath's home-built four-cylinder URS outfit was outspeeding the fastest short-stroke BMWs. And it appeared that if he could achieve reliability and improve handling, he would once again dominate the class.

It was then revealed that although the engine had repeatedly suffered from fracture of the long bolts clamping the crankcase halves to the central driving sprockets, some of Fath's engine failures occurred because the battery and coil ignition system could not cope with the unorthodox crankshaft layout. In light of this, in order to stabilise the ignition, Fath reverted to a magneto.

Difficulties had arisen because of his choice of

John Blanchard testing the Rickman framed URS four-cylinder solo GP racer at Brands Hatch, January 1968.

crankpin spacing. Instead of having all four in one plane (two up, two down), Fath had spaced them like the points of a compass to get smoother running. This resulted in firing intervals of 90, 180, 270 and 360 degrees. However, at the peak power point of 14000 rpm, the 90 degree interval gave the contact breaker precious little time to function. The new system would solve this.

Both Fath and Dr Kuhn spent time in England with John Blanchard at the Seeley works in Belvedere, Kent. Late in July the Seeley-framed Fath four solo racer was completed. Many of the cycle parts – except the full duplex cradle frame – were the same as those used on the production Seeley 7R and G50 ohc single-cylinder racers.

Fath and Blanchard both appeared with their respective fours at the Hutchinson 100 at Brands Hatch on 13 August. And two weeks later, the duo appeared at Scarborough on Saturday 26 August, where Fath and passenger Wolfgang Kalauch scored an impressive win over the world champion Klaus Enders.

Blanchard, however, fell at Mere Hairpin, and put himself out of the running. Blanchard was withdrawn from the Snetterton and Oulton Park meetings which were scheduled for the next two days of the Bank Holiday. This followed a stormy exchange between Seeley and Blanchard at Snetterton over the bike being fitted, without Seeley's permission, with a Lockheed

disc brake before Scarborough. Blanchard was then dropped as development rider and would not be allowed to ride the machine any more that season.

A couple of weeks later, following discussions between Seeley and Fath, the prospects of work continuing on their four-cylinder racer brightened, Fath decided to leave all decisions about the project to Dr Kuhn. The Seeley-Fath co-operation lasted only until the end of the season.

For the future, the Fath team chose to use the Metisse chassis made by the Rickman brothers of New Milton in Hampshire. John Blanchard returned to ride the URS-Metisse solo – and in a supreme irony it was fitted with the very same Lockheed disc brake which had caused the rift between him and Seeley in the first place.

Blanchard gave the machine its first outing at Brands Hatch in January 1968, where he was principally concerned to test the brakes and suspension while being watched by Derek Rickman and Mike Vaughan of Lockheed. Afterwards, all decided they were very happy with the machine's performance, but thought that a little more experimentation was needed to sort out the rear suspension.

More tests were completed before Blanchard and

the URS-Metisse were entered in the season's first classic – the West German GP at the Nurburgring. This was anything but a successful debut, with Blanchard crashing twice. The machine was then offered to John Hartle, who rode it at Hockenheim on 12 May.

But if the solo plans did not proceed as intended, Fath's own racing efforts certainly did. At Nurburgring, he and Wolfgang Kallauch took the chequered flag at the front of the field. Fath's first Grand Prix victory since his win in Spain back in April 1961. And what a sweet taste of success it was for a man who had not only made a successful comeback, but built the engine of his machine into the bargain.

Then came the Isle of Man TT, and a fourth, followed by a fifth in the Dutch TT, a retirement in Belgium and then a couple of victories in Belgium and the final round at Hockenheim. The latter event was to have taken place at the Italian GP at Monza. But as the sidecar event was cancelled by FIM decree, it was run the Federal Republic in conjunction, with the final of the German National Championship in October.

By the time Hockenheim arrived in the calendar, Fath and Georg Auerbacher both had 21 points, while TT winner Siegfried Schauzu was four points astern but still

Helmut Fath and Wolfgang Kalauch on their way to becoming World Champions in 1968. For Fath it was the culmination of a remarkable comeback. He not only overcame injury but also regained the title he had first won in 1960, but this time with his own engine.

in with a chance. With so much at stake, Fath took a desperate gamble after official practising finished. Dissatisfied with his engine, he fitted a completely new short stroke unit which had not been raced before, but which had been showing promising results on the test bed. Would it last the race? Fath commented grimly before the start, 'The only way to find out is to use it'.

The gamble paid off. Before the first corner, Fath and passenger Wolfgang Kalauch already had a tremendous lead, and even the super-fast BMW of ex-world champion Enders was unable to get a tow in the slipstream of the flying URS. A wet and slippery track failed to deter a determined Fath, then 39 years old, and at the end of the second lap, his lead was 6.6 seconds. This doubled in the next two circuits, to take him out of reach of everyone – a lead which was maintained until the end. The 15 lap, 63.15 mile race was won at an average speed of 98.55 mph, with a fastest lap (by Fath) of 100.72 mph. It broke Enders' previous record.

Helmut Fath made history, because up to that time, nobody had ever won a world championship on a home-built machine. Strangely, when defending the title the following year, the results turned out almost in reverse, with wins in France, Holland and Belgium, 3rd in the Isle of Man, and a retirement in Germany. With two rounds to go and leading the championship, he crashed in Finland, preventing him from taking part in the final round in Ulster. Klaus Enders seized the chance to take the title for BMW.

For 1969, Fath built a larger version of his four – initially for British short circuits, where it was popular to

race larger capacity outfits. The 68 × 51.5 mm bore and stroke gave 748 cc against the smaller unit's 60 × 44 mm. Much longer con-rods were used, together with different cylinders and larger valves. The aim was to produce an engine with tremendous low-down punch, rather than power at high revs, and Fath hoped that a four-speed gearbox would be adequate. In this he was proved wrong. The 750 like the 500 proved the need for at least five speeds.

At long last, however, the 500 solo racer began to shine. Ridden by veteran Karl Hoppe, the URS-Metisse dominated many of the early season Continental internationals. Perhaps his finest performance came just a week after his first victory, the Eifelrennen at the end of April. Here Hoppe won the 500 class of the non-championship Austrian GP at Salzburg. Under ideal racing conditions, in front of a crowd of 28,000

Below **Start of the 1968 Dutch Grand Prix sidecar race. Fath URS leads Auerbacher BMW (4), Harris (12), Enders (1), Wakefield (13) and Attenberger (6).**

Right **Karl Hoppe won the Austrian GP in May 1969 on an URS Metisse. The spectators are suicidally close, but this seems not to have worried the victor.**

spectators, none could keep up with Hoppe. He shot away from the start and won as he pleased. Not only was his race speed a record, but he also shaved 0.7 seconds off Giacomo Agostini's lap record set on an MV four in 1967.

Then to prove that his early form was no fluke, Hoppe finished a fine second in the West German GP at Hockenheim behind Agostini's MV. But sadly, Hoppe did not contest the remainder of the classics. This was a great pity. Except for MV, 1969 saw URS emerge as the most serious world championship contender in the 500 cc class.

Although there were several URS engines scattered around Europe, there were still only two machines.

Below right **Fath and Kalauch on their way to a third place in the 1969 Isle of Man sidecar TT.**

Team line-up of 1970 URS riders who were racing under Münch colours. Left to right: Fath, Hoppe, and Kaczor.

Fath's own outfit and the Mettise solo ridden by Hoppe. Fath had also received help from several British companies, including Reynolds Tubes, Automotive Products, Renold Chain, Duckhams Oil (the main sponsors) and Dunlop tyres, who developed a special new 4.00 × 12 tyre for the outfit. Both types of URS engines delivered useful power between 9000 and 13000 rpm, and transmission was via a Norton box with a six-speed Schafleitner cluster.

Bosch fuel injection on the sidecar engine now had twin air intakes insteaa of the single intake previously used. And a solution had been found to beat the ignition problems which had remained despite the adoption of a fully transistorised system. The answer was to fit a separate coil for each cylinder and making a special contact breaker with four sets of points spaced at 45, 90, 135 and 180 degrees. Since each cylinder had two plugs, the coils were double ended in order to furnish pairs of sparks simultaneously.

Things looked bright, but then Fath broke a leg in Finland on 12 August, and while he was recuperating towards the end of the month, news was released that the Fath team had been purchased by Friedl Münch with American backing. The Münch/Fath tie-up was made legally binding in May 1970. And as all his machinery had been taken over, it was not until much later that Fath resumed as a manufacturer. During 1970 and 1971 he was strictly a tuner. Indeed during 1971 he was said to be one of the top Yamaha tuners anywhere. Even the 250 world champion was a customer.

In the middle of 1973 came the first suggestions that Fath, then aged 43, was thinking of a possible comeback. At his forest hideout near Heidelburg, Fath was busy constructing a brand-new four-cylinder outfit. Not only had he plans for a racing return himself, but he hoped to have a spare engine for Billie Nelson to race in solo events.

This time, his design was for a water-cooled, disc valve two-stroke flat four, which many wrongly considered at the time to be a development of the König. In fact, any resemblance to the König began and ended with the flat four-cylinder layout. And in any case, back in the early 1960s, Fath's original scheme had been to build a water-cooled flat four (albeit a four-stroke) before ultimately opting for the across-the-frame layout of the URS. The reason he had not built the original design was said to be the reluctance of BMW to provide certain parts, notably the transmission, on which the design depended.

Unlike the König, Fath's two-stroke had a longitudinal position for the crankshaft, and an integral six-speed gearbox with the clutch at the rear of the crankcase in a similar way to BMW – but with a pair of bevel gears coupling the output shaft to the left hand side-mounted sprocket for the chain final drive, turning it though an angle of 90 degrees. Another departure from König practice was the oil supply to the big-end, which on the Berlin company's engine was by a direct

Mechanical attention to Fath flat four two-stroke engine in 1972.

Billie Nelson on the flat four Fath 500 cc 'stroker leads Veldink's Suzuki at 1974 Dutch TT.

shower of petroil. Fath devised a belt-driven pump controlled by the throttle, which dribbled a supply of straight oil to the big-ends, main bearings and disc bearings. Caged needle rollers were used for both the big and small ends.

With a capacity of 495 cc (56 × 50 mm), the Fath four had aluminium alloy cylinders with Nickasil bores. Originally, Yamaha pistons were used, but these were soon replaced by purpose-built units, carrying only a single ring each.

A unique feature of the Fath design was that each cylinder casting incorporated half the crankcase, so that the crank chambers themselves were also water-cooled. There was no water pump of the type fitted to many water-cooled 'strokers, but as on Bultacos and MZs, a thermosiphon system was used, with water entering the underside of the cylinders and leaving it at the top.

Fuel was supplied by a quartet of separate carburettors – 34 mm Japanese Mikunis. And as Fath used four carburettors, this called for four small disc valves instead of the König's one. Like the König, drive to these was by toothed rubber belt. And again unlike the König, Fath used four separate expansion chambers in an attempt to extract the maximum possible power output – 112 bhp at 12200 rpm. The exhausts exited the top of the engine and curved back under the rider's legs. To prevent him from being burned, they were coated with a baked-on finish, and as Billie Nelson was to remark, 'It's really amazing. You can touch them and

not get burned even after a long race'.

At first, ignition was by a Bosch (flywheel) magneto, with the generator incorporating a pair of ignition coils, two pulse coils and three more for water pump, fuel pump and tachometer. But this system proved too heavy, and thereafter, a battery was installed for current and only a pulse unit was fitted to the front of the crankshaft.

At 44 years old, Helmut Fath was not sure if he would race again, but May 1974 saw Fath's new four in action for the first time, at the West German GP at Hockenheim in solo trim with Billie Nelson as rider. Ready to race, but without fuel, the Fath weighed only 286 lb – some 55 lb less than the comparable Yamaha or Suzuki 500 fours – but there were problems.

The power was exceptional, but not so the handling. The frame had been constructed in only ten days, after the original builder failed to his obligations. Fath, in any case, freely admitted that he was not a frame specialist. The problems centred around the swinging arm, which was whipping so badly at Hockenheim that ultimately it caused Nelson's retirement. There were also early problems with the transmission system.

The IoM TT was allowed to pass, and the machine's next outing was at the international meeting at Raalte in Holland where it again showed a tremendous turn of speed. But trouble with the throttle linkage slowed Nelson in the race although he kept going to finish fourth.

The next race was the Dutch TT at Assen, where in the 350 race Nelson was fourth on his Yamaha. But at the start of the 500 race, the Fath four oiled a plug. By the time it had been changed and Nelson got started, the leaders had already come round to complete one lap. He followed them down the straight and to his amazement caught them up easily. He said afterwards that he could have passed them but for two things. First, he was not 100 per cent confident of the handling on the very fast curve towards the end of the straight, and secondly he himself hated people who indulged in what he called 'dicing with me when I'm lapping them'. The riders whom Billie Nelson was in danger of catching in this way were none other than the trio of Barry Sheene (Suzuki), Giacomo Agostini (Yamaha) and Phil Read (MV Agusta).

Besides evident speed, Nelson was impressed by the smoothness of the engine, describing it as 'just like a big electric motor'. He thought the wide spread of usable power from 8000 to 13000 rpm was particularly impressive. Development continued apace throughout the summer of 1974, with an excellent understanding between builder and rider.

But on Sunday 8 September, all this was shattered. Billie Nelson, the man who had once been known as 'Mr Consistency' on the Grand Prix circuits died after he crashed during the 250 race at Opatija in the Yugoslav Grand Prix. He crashed on a 125 mph left hander at one of the highest points of the closed road circuit which is

on the Adriatic coast. The Yamaha went into the crowd and a spectator was seriously injured, while Nelson suffered severe chest injuries and died after an operation in hospital at nearby Rijeka.

Thirty-three year old Nelson, from Eckington, Derbyshire had begun racing in 1958 and made his continental debut six years later in West Germany. He combined solo racing and riding sidecar passenger for several years. It was a crash while racing as passenger with Fath in 1969 during the Finnish GP which ruined not only Fath's chances of retaining his world title, but also Nelson's hopes of taking the Bill Hannah-sponsored Paton twin to second place in the 500 cc world championship behind Agostini.

Fath and Nelson had been firm friends as well as colleagues, and his death was a cruel blow. Following the accident, Fath decided to make a return to the sidecar scene, and the engine from Nelson's solo was built up into a special three-wheeler for Siegfried Schauzu. However, Fath was far from happy with the outfit (not of his design) and said in May 1975, 'It is far

Siegfried Schauzu with ARO Fath outfit at the 1976 Isle of Man TT.

too big and the width of the sidecar alone loses me between 10–15 bhp'.

Fath had by then almost completed a new engine which he said would produce more horsepower, and hoped that the rest of the outfit would be modified. But early results were far from impressive, with only one placing in the top ten at any of the Grands Prix that year. The ARO-Fath finished fourth at Hockenheim.

For 1976, the sidecar team consisted of two pairings, with Schauzu and Kalauch, plus newcomer Heinz Schilling partnered by passenger Rolf Gundel. In the very first round at Le Mans in France, Schilling managed a third place, and Schauzu came home eighth. At the Salzburgring in Austria, Schauzu came in third, but Schilling had to retire.

Displaying their greatly improved reliability, both crews finished the punishing IoM TT, Schauzu in fourth and Schilling in sixth place. Then in Holland, Schilling was fifth with Schauzu in tenth place, and the following weekend in Belgium the ARO-Fath teams made it third and fourth – Schilling and Schauzu. Neither team competed in the Czech GP at Brno, and the season ended with a ninth for Schauzu at the Nurburgring. As a result, Schauzu and Kalauch came fifth overall in the year's championship table.

In the same year, Alex George, the Scots solo racer, then based in Holland, rode Helmut Fath's four cylinder 'stroker solo in the Czech Grand Prix. George's Suzuki four had been sidelined with a broken idler gear. So, he took over the Fath bike. The chassis had remained untouched since Billie Nelson last raced it. He found the machine to be around 10 mph slower than the all-conquering (but at that time none too reliable) Suzukis, and a match for them on acceleration. He led for most of the first lap, but gradually dropped back and retired when he grounded one of the plug caps.

For 1977, the ARO team was again reorganised. Schauzu left to race his own Yamaha, Schilling was provided with a new ARO-Yamaha. Then, after the season had started, Werner Schwarzel (second in 1976 on a König) was brought into the team with passenger Huber and took over one of the vacant ARO-Fath outfits.

Schwarzel's first finish was a third place at the Dutch TT. He then demonstrated his own superb skill and the potential of the Fath engine to the full by winning the next round at Belgium on the very fast Spa circuit. Schwarzel then retired in Czechoslovakia, but won the final round at Silverstone. This placed him third in the world series. This was an outstanding result when you consider that the team had only finished in three of the seven rounds.

This was to be the pinnacle of achievement for Fath's flat-four, even though it did not appear so at the time. And the man himself was still interested in both the sidecar and solo classes at world level.

At the end of 1977, South African Jon Ekerold, later to be World 350 cc Champion in 1980 on a Bimota-Yamaha, was tipped to be rider of a new machine powered by a Fath flat-four. Fath had been so impressed with Ekerold's riding ability when he saw him in action at the end of the season Nurburgring international that he offered to let him have one of his 500 engines. Fath also volunteered to prepare Ekerold's 250 and 350 Yamaha power units.

Ekerold soon had a Nico Bakker frame with monoshock rear suspension constructed to house the Fath four, but in the end, decided to concentrate on riding his pair of Yamahas. The Bakker-framed Fath four was shelved, and was never to reappear. With the speed and reliability of the new breed of Japanese four cylinder 'strokers, a private effort even with such a gifted tuner as Fath simply could not compete.

In the 1978 world sidecar series, Fath was to suffer yet more disappointment. Schwarzel still proved almost unbeatable, but his two victories at Assen and the Nurburgring, with a second at Mugello in Italy and a sixth in Nogaro, France, were not enough to stop Rolf Biland and passenger Englishman Kenny Williams taking the title with their Yamaha-powered BEO machine. And what a machine – quite simply the most

View of flat four engine showing installation of carbs, exhaust pipes, and gearbox.

Fath flat four engine in Nico Bakker monoshock chassis. Note location of under engine suspension unit.

radical interpretation of the sidecar construction rules that had been seen.

It appeared to be a perfectly natural development of a line that began earlier in the mid 1970s. Parallelogram suspension had appeared when sidecar racing constructors started using sports car suspension and wheels on conventional short-wheelbase outfits. But this line of development, as racing outfits grew steadily more like three-wheeled racing cars, was speedily terminated when Biland produced his BEO tricar. It was so radical that it forced the FIM into creating two world sidecar classes for 1979 – B2A for conventional outfits and B2B for the new breed. Regulations were hastily redrafted to outlaw car suspensions and steering systems. This entailed a total reappraisal by everyone in the three wheel racing fraternity. The result was a new breed of long wheelbase, fully-enclosed racing three wheelers – now commonly referred to as *worms*.

This was the final act for Fath. He had abandoned making a return as competitor but with the split championship in 1979, he decided to call it a day in his bid to be a combination of world champion and one man motorcycle manufacturer.

It was the finale of an era which spanned 20 years. Fath had been world champion in 1960, fought back from serious injury to win the championship in 1969 with his own four-cylinder dohc engine, then had everything taken from him in the Münch deal in 1970 before coming back *again* with a completely new design to join the contest once more.

In the process, some of his closest friends and racing partners had lost their lives through accidents.

It is unlikely that any other man in the history of motorcycle sport has ever suffered such peaks of triumph and depths of despair as Helmut Fath. His character, in overcoming the setbacks can be summed up in one word – fighter.

Hercules

Nürnberger Hercules Werke GmbH was formed on 1 April 1886 by Carl Marschutz. In common with so many other German motorcycle companies, production started with the manufacture of pedal cycles. However, in 1904 the first powered model was introduced – a single cylinder machine.

The engine was mounted according to the contemporary mode in a frame which was almost that of a heavyweight bicycle. Transmission was by direct belt drive to the rear wheel, and the bicycle pedals and chain were retained for assistance on steep hills.

In following years, Hercules used a variety of proprietary engines, including Bark, Columbus, Fafnir, JAP, Ilo, Küchen, Moser, Sachs, Sturmey-Archer and Villiers – and by the 1930s, they were making machines from 73 to 498 cc. The latter model had an ohv single cylinder JAP power unit, and together with a 248 cc JAP-powered single, gained considerable competition success for Hercules. Hans Kahrmann was an outstanding rider for the marque.

Hercules also did well in the long-distance trials of the day, with Carlchen Geffers and Rudi Grenz shining. As war clouds loomed, such events came to a close, but their success was to be mirrored by others in the years after the conflict.

During early 1945, the Hercules factories were heavily damaged by Allied bombing. Repair and reconstruction was not completed until 1948, and motorcycle production was delayed until 1950.

In that year, Hercules displayed two new machines at the Frankfurt Show in March, the 212 and 312. Like all post-war Hercules machines bar one, these had two-stroke engines. The former model was an ultra-lightweight commuter, with a 98 cc (48 × 52 mm) Sachs single cylinder engine and two-speed gearbox. Its unsprung frame was equipped with a pair of blade-type front forks and the machine was primitive in the extreme.

The 312 was much more interesting, with a more powerful engine and more advanced specification, including telescopic front forks – although the rear remained unsprung. The forks were internally sprung, but undamped, and their rubber gaiters concealed nothing more than a steel slider running in phosphor bronze bushes in the base of each leg.

The model's 123 cc (52 × 58 cc) single-cylinder Ilo two-stroke engine was linked to a three-speed gearbox and had a foot operated gearchange. The 312 had twin exhaust ports, like many contemporary German engines, and featured separate exhaust systems running down each side of the machine. Its maximum power of 5.2 bhp at 5000 rpm offered its owner a top speed of 47 mph.

Even though neither model's specifications would seem too exciting today, they proved popular – selling so well that before long Hercules were able to introduce an expansion programme on the strength of their success.

In 1951, three more models appear. These were the 98 cc 316 and 147 cc 313 – both with Sachs engines – and the Ilo-powered 174 cc 314. Both the larger models had four-speed gearboxes, telescopic forks and plunger rear suspension. The plungers were made for Hercules by Jurisch, and were essentially the same components fitted to a variety of other German lightweights.

Continued success in 1952 saw the introduction of a range of larger models. The 315 had a Ilo power unit of 249 cc (65 × 75 mm) which gave 11.4 bhp at 4600 rpm and was channelled through a four-speed gearbox. The 317 had a 197 cc (62 × 66 mm) engine from the same stable, offering 11 bhp at 5000 rpm. This gave the 317 a top speed of over 65 mph. There were several differences from the earlier models, including the appearance of a single exhaust system and full-width brake hubs.

By now Hercules machines were sold throughout continental Europe. Holland, Belgium and Switzerland were the best export markets. In Holland, the full range was on offer, covering 100, 125, 150, 175 and 200 cc machines. Interestingly, at this time, Ilo and Sachs were selling identical power units to manufacturers in all three countries mentioned above, who assembled them into machines which competed directly against imported German marques such as Hercules.

With such a large range, it was assumed that the company would find it difficult to come up with anything new to exhibit at the second international post-war Frankfurt Show in October 1953. But it did – again introducing three newcomers. One was the 320, an improved version of the well-tried 197 cc Ilo-engined 317 which it superseded. The second was the all-new 321 with a 197 cc Sachs engine (57 × 58 mm). This had an enclosed rear sub-frame and swinging arm suspension.

In common with many post-war German manufacturers, Hercules used Sachs engines even in its ultra-lightweights. Pictured is a 220K of late 1950's.

But the star of the range was the first twin-cylinder model, the 318. A luxury tourer with a 247 cc (65 × 75 mm) Ilo twin, this had a maximum speed of 116 kph (72 mph). The engine had cast-iron barrels, alloy cylinder heads, single Bing 1/27/1 carb and delivered 12 bhp at 4750 rpm. Another feature of the model was the way in which the rear sub-frame section was neatly enclosed.

Despite the model's popularity, it was only a short while before the 321 was replaced by the 322 which had a more powerful engine – 15 bhp at 6000 rpm. The 322 also gained full swinging arm rear suspension with twin rear shock absorber units (in place of the Jurisch plungers) oil-damped telescopic forks, and larger full-width alloy brake hubs of 180 mm diameter to replace the 160 mm units used before. The front section of the frame had twin front downtubes instead of the single tube on the earlier models. Improved springing allowed the introduction of another feature for the first time on a Hercules – a foam rubber seat rather than a sprung saddle. Although this was a single seater, it helped to lend the model a more modern appearance – despite it having the same 13.5-litre fuel tank and valanced mudguards as before.

Although these new models were introduced in rapid succession over a few short years, the range then remained the same until 1956. It was a wise decision. With the sudden fall in sales which hit Germany in the mid-1950s, the Nurnberg factory was not vulnerable by being committed to either an expansion programme or the huge cost of developing new models during this critical time. This enabled Hercules to remain afloat when many others were sinking fast. It also meant that with credit at the bank, Hercules were one of the very few German manufacturers able to take advantage of the 1956 Frankfurt Show – the third and last of the series of giant post-war exhibitions held at this venue – and to offer something new.

Hercules two main exhibits were the K100 (no relation whatsoever to BMW's four-cylinder bike of three decades later!) and the K175. Both had Sachs engines, and were replacements for all of the now-ageing Hercules range. The K100 had a 98 cc (48 × 54 mm) engine with a four-speed box, and used 16 inch wheels with an Earles pattern front fork and swinging arm rear suspension.

But most of the interest was reserved for the K175. This was a particularly modern lightweight motorcycle with telescopic forks, swinging arm suspension, 16 inch wheels, and a 173 cc (62 × 58 mm) four-speed Sachs unit. It was this model which formed the basis for the marque's return to motorcycle sport, with entries in endurance trials and even the ISDT.

A prototype K175 was ridden by Walter Bromsamle of the West German Vase 'B' team in the 1956 ISDT. It was staged in the Bavarian Alps at the resort of Garmisch-Partenkirchen during September. Although Bromsamle retired, other Hercules 175 riders did gain medals. Hohn and Huber took silvers, while Scheuenstuhl scored gold. This was the start of some outstanding successes in the event for the Nurnberg marque – particularly in the 1960s and 1970s.

There was another critically important aspect to the 1956 Frankfurt Show. It was the appearance of a co-operative effort between Adler, Triumph (TWN) and Hercules to produce a range of mopeds based on the Triumph Fips model. Triumph and Hercules also co-operated to produce a scooter. Hercules saved the time and the trouble of developing its own model by using the running gear of the Triumph Contessa and a fan-cooled Sachs 191 cc (65 × 68 mm) four-speeder rated at 10.2 bhp at 5250 rpm. The Hercules R200 scooter, as it was called, outlived its Triumph original. It was listed in catalogues until 1960.

Both the Hercules moped and the R200 scooter were imported into Britain. Early in 1957 they were distributed by Cyril Kieff and Co Ltd, and after October by BP Scooters of The Airport, Wolverhampton. In 1958, the importers changed to Industria (London) Ltd of London N7. None of these sold the models under the Hercules brand. The name could not be used in Britain as it was already owned by Raleigh Industries of Nottingham – makers of Raleigh cycles, mopeds and scooters. So under the Kieff regime the range was known under the importers' name, after that it was called Prior.

The 1960s began with Hercules as one of the few survivors of the previous decade's German motorcycle industry collapse. Indeed, the Nurnberg factory had absorbed ailing Rabeneick in 1958. The policy was to concentrate mainly on a range of machines powered by engines of less than 100 cc – although the K175 was still listed and used as the basis of the Hercules' participation in the ISDT.

The 1961 line-up included the 221T/TS, 220 PL/KF and KFX4, K50 and K50S, with the K103S as top of the range. Both 221 models were mopeds with telescopic forks, unsprung frame and two-speed automatic Sachs Saxonette engine giving 2.6 bhp. The 220s were de luxe ultra-lightweights with Earles forks, swinging arm rear suspension and pressed steel chassis. The PL model had pedals, while the KF had a kickstart, but both used the same three-speed, fan-cooled Sachs engine which produced 3.5 bhp. The 220 KFX4 had a 4.3 bhp engine with four speeds, and a larger 13-litre tank.

The K50 and K50S were sporting 50s, with 5.2 bhp and five speeds. The 'S' model was equipped with racing handlebars, exposed suspension springs front and rear, and a red-lined fuel tank instead of the standard K50's white/grey finish.

Top of the Hercules ultra-lightweight range for 1961 came the K103S, with its engine based on the earlier, superseded K100. It still had four speeds, but now developed 8.2 bhp. Running gear was based on the K50 models, sharing their large 130 mm headlight, 115 mm Sachs alloy brake hubs, comprehensive mudguards and two tone grey/cream dualseat. There was a Bosch 35 Watt flywheel magneto in place of the 29 Watt type used on the K50s.

For 1962, Hercules responded to growing sales by offering the largest range of models since the mid-50s. These included the 220, 220L, 220S, 220MK and 220MKL deluxe mopeds, the Model 21 moped, K101, K102 and K103/S. In addition, the K175S was still on offer with a 12.2 bhp engine.

Hercules K175-S was sold in many markets. In Britain the motorcycles were known as Priors.

Hercules offered Ilo powered 5.4 bhp kart in the early 1960's. Power unit was air-cooled.

The motorcycle line-up was completed by a pair of full-blown off-roaders, the GS (Gelände Sport) models. The K50GS had a 49 c (49 × 44 mm) engine with 18 mm carb giving 5 bhp, and the K175GS had a 174 cc (62 × 58 mm) engine with 26 mm carb giving 14 bhp. By 1962, Hercules was able to claim that between them the factory machines had gained 427 gold, 76 silver and 35 bronze medals in competition events in Germany and abroad.

As well as all its two-wheel models Hercules also offered a kart, powered by a 98 cc Ilo engine giving 5.4 bhp at 6000 rpm. The factory claimed it was the first German manufacturer to offer such a vehicle.

In 1963 Hercules and the famous French rider Georges Monneret collaborated to prepare a record-breaking version of the K50S fitted with a custom-made streamlined fairing, called the *Special Monneret*. This attempted to take the world 6 and 12-Hour records and 1000 km record for the standard production machine class, then held by the Italian Guazzoni factory since 1959.

The record breaker had a maximum speed of 76 mph and could rev to 9400 rpm. Team Monneret's challenge took place at Montlhery, near Paris, on the 13/14 September 1963, where the 6-Hour record fell at 71.13

mph; the 12-Hour went at 70.57 mph; and the 1000 km toppled at 70.90 mph.

By 1964 the competition success of the GS models had encouraged Hercules to offer the public not only the K50GS (with five speeds) and the K175GS (now known as the K176GS), but also a new model, the K103 GS with a 97 cc (48 × 54 mm) Sachs engine using a 22 mm carb and giving 8 bhp.

This period was an extremely exciting one for Hercules with a notable endurance feat by a standard K50 which started out in August 1964 and covered 24,941 miles in 22 days, 7 hours and 29 minutes with a team of riders. It was non-stop except for fuel and rider changes. Other successes included the Valli Bergamasche trial held in Bergamo, northern Italy – won for Hercules by Heinz Brinkmann, who went on to become 1965 German Endurance trials champion. Hercules also won 5 gold and 3 bronze medals at the 1965 ISDT staged in the Isle of Man. Much of the design and preparation work for all these successes was the responsibility of Dipl Ing Hutton, the factory's tuning wizard.

In 1966, Hercules joined the Zweirad Union (originally a combination of the DKW, Express and Victoria companies), but this merger made little immediate difference to its output. There were more new models in the standard production range, with the 222TS and 222MF basic mopeds, Roller 50 Scooter (a KTM design built under licence), MK50/1 Super 4 ultra-lightweight motorcycle and the K50 Super Sport.

The latter was one of that year's sensations of the IFMA show at Cologne. The Super Sport featured the five-speed 5.2 bhp Sachs engine and 136 mm full-width alloy brake hubs, but what made it look almost like a totally new bike was its striking red and chrome finish, plus the front forks pioneered on the GS models. The seat was a completely fresh, black racing style unlike the two-tone dualseat on the other K50 models.

In 1967 the 175 was finally dropped, but both the 50 and 125 GS models were considerably improved. The 50 cc bike now had a 19 mm carb and gave 6.25 bhp while the 100 had a 26 mm carb and pumped out 13 bhp through a five-speed gearbox.

In 1969, Zweirad Union was swallowed up by the huge Fichtel Sachs industrial empire. But Hercules was destined to survive even within the corporate giant,

Horst Trinker coaxes his Hercules through special test during 1965 ISDT on Isle of Man.

being the only one of the motorcycle marques which made up Zweirad Union that maintained its own identity throughout all the various management changes and mergers.

Perhaps the most significant event of 1970 was the beginning of the W2000 saga. The machine which was to emerge some four years later was the world's first Wankel-engined production motorcycle. To British enthusiasts it will come as something of a surprise to find this machine in the Hercules chapter, since the model was always sold under the DKW name in the UK – but a Hercules indeed it was.

The Wankel engine was developed by Sachs, the new owners of Hercules. As described in Chapter 12, Dr Felix Wankel's concept of the early 1950s had been developed over the next decade, and this technology now belonged to Sachs. The company had previously used Wankel engines in stationary industrial units or snowmobiles, but never before in a motorcycle.

Often referred to as a 'rotary', the Wankel had nothing in common with the rotary engines used in aircraft, except the process of internal combustion. This takes place in an *epitrochoidal* chamber shaped 'like a fat-waisted figure of eight', as *Motorcycle Enthusiast*

Sachs developed the prototype W2000 Wankel engine from the original NSU patent.

writer John Fernley once put it. Within the chamber revolves a rotor shaped like a curved-sided equilateral triangle. This is connected to a gear attached to one of the side housing and is supported on an eccentric bearing which allows it to rotate while keeping its three tips in contact with the chamber.

To prevent gas leakage through the gaps between the rotor and chamber at the tips of the triangle there are special sealing strips – a feature which gave much trouble during the development stage of the power unit. By the time of the later production Hercules Wankels (such as the Hercules W2000), the rotor seals exploited the advantages of ceramics technology.

The revolving rotor performed all the usual four-stroke cycle of operations – Induction, Compression, Expansion, Exhaust – uncovering various ports as it rotated. In fact each face of the rotor is simultaneously going through part of the operational cycle, with one face in the middle of compression while the next is beginning the exhaust phase and the one behind already beginning the intake of fresh gas – whereas in a piston engine separate phases of action take place sequentially on the piston's top.

In some respects a Wankel engine is closer to a two-stroke. Here the designer has to compromise the port timing to achieve optimum results, but the Wankel has considerable overlap of the functions going on inside its

working chamber at any time. Fresh gas enters at 2 o'clock, compression begins just before 12 and reaches its peak at 9 o'clock, combustion starts at 9 and continues to between 5 and 4 o'clock when the rotor uncovers the exhaust port and the exhaust phase begins. Thus the Wankel is correctly termed a *rotary combustion engine*.

Sach's licence agreement with NSU limited the company's Wankel power units to an output of 30 bhp. This perhaps did not matter much for industrial or snowmobile engines, but was to prove something of a hindrance for a motorcycle.

Hercules' first prototype W2000 Wankel-powered roadster appeared in mid-1970. The engine unit was a Sachs snowmobile engine mated to a BMW gearbox (with sideways acting kickstart) and shaft drive. The engine has often been erroneously described as a *two-stroke* Wankel. Of course it was no such thing as all Wankel designs work on the four-stroke principle. The misconception arose because the prototype and most of the early production machines gained their lubrication from the induction of petroil in a similar manner to contemporary (non-Japanese) two-strokes.

The W2000 breathes this mixture through passages in the main housing. As pre-determined rotor positions are reached, ports in the rotor line up with others in the housing sides (one inboard of each apex) to pass the gas to the transfer ports which direct the charge to the normal intake position. The housing is cooled by an engine driven fan, whilst the rotor is both cooled and lubricated by the constant induction of fresh gas. Passing the gas through the rotor in this way results in some increase in its temperature and a resultant loss in volumetric efficiency – but it makes for a uniform temperature in the housing, thus preventing distortion and promoting better sealing.

Another contentious point is the capacity of the engine. A conventional motorcycle engine's capacity is calculated simply as a total of the displacement of each individual piston. But all sides of the triangular rotor of the W2000 formed a complete working piston surface. So when the rotor turned once there were three power strokes (aiding the exceptionally smooth power delivery). Each side of the rotor displaced 294 cc, so by 'cylinder total' reckoning one turn of the rotor gave a total of 882 cc. However, the crank of a normal motorcycle engine is directly connected to the pistons. The W2000 rotor was geared so that its every turn revolved the 'crankshaft' three times. By 'crank revolution' measurement one turn of the crank only equated to a displacement of 294 cc.

Controversy over this interpretation was to remain a central issue influencing the W2000 throughout its life. Quite simply, as a 300 cc machine its performance was excellent, and it stood up well in the company of 500s.

The Wankel engine cycle in theory.

INTAKE   EXPANSION

COMPRESSION   EXHAUST

Wankel engine was a central feature of display in Cologne, September 1970.

But reckoned as a machine in the 900 class its performance was abysmal although the price tag was competitive – and since hard riding would produce the fuel consumption of a 1000, the performance could be adjudged even poorer.

Even the sport's governing body, the FIM, appeared uncertain what capacity the Hercules Wankel should be. When production was in full swing, the three works-prepared W2000 GS enduro bikes used in the 1975 Isle of Man International Six Days Trial were classified as 'over 500'.

Even though the W2000 took the limelight in the 1970s, the bulk of the company's sales and revenue was derived from the range of single cylinder lightweights powered (of course) by Sachs two-strokes.

These included the introduction of a brand-new machine, the K125BW, specially made for the West German army. This was essentially a detuned, heavier version of the enduro model designed for military use. The five-speed transmission, Sachs engine, braced handlebars, headlamp and engine protection bars, dualseat with rear carrier, knobbly tyres and a host of accessories – including a shovel – provided everything the modern soldier could want by way of robust, practical two-wheel transport. Finish was an overall military drab for everything except the engine and exhaust which were black. The K125BW equipped Germany army units throughout the 1970s and proved popular and reliable in service.

By this time, the GS models had been improved yet again. The K50GS offered 6.75 bhp with a 20 mm carb and had six gears, while the 100 cc model had a 26 mm carb and five speeds. And for factory competition entries, these machines were joined by 75 and 125 cc versions.

West German Army K125BW in 1971 specification with 5-speed gearbox and 12.5 bhp Sachs engine.

In the USA, the 100 and 125 cc models sold well in both enduro and motocross form – and there was also a new 80 cc (46 × 44 mm) version of which only an enduro was sold. The engine produced 7 bhp and the machine featured a five-speed box, 18 mm Bing carb and 6 Volt Bosch flywheel magneto ignition. This model sold in the United States as the Boondocker.

As in Britain, the American Hercules models were not marketed under their own name. In the 1970s the off-road competition bikes (now joined by a series of motocrossers) were first sold in the States as DKWs, later simply under the Sachs name – despite the fact that the importer appointed in 1972 was called Hercules Distributing of Chatsworth, California.

The Nurnberg 'strokers scored an impressive array of wins in such well-known US dirt-bike events as the Baja 500, Elsinore Enduro, Desert Vipers Enduro, and Hare and Hounds Scramble. Works-prepared versions of all three enduro mounts were to compete with a high level of success in endurance trials throughout the world, including gaining many golds in the ISDT.

Late in 1972 a batch of fifty pre-production W2000s was constructed. These had numerous engine modifications, based on information gained from testing the prototype. Otherwise they were largely identical to that machine except for a final drive chain instead of the shaft. At this point an electric starter was added, which became a feature of all the chain-drive W2000s. Smaller differences included frame bracing rails extending rearwards from the front downtubes across the top of the engine, a twin-leading shoe Grimeca drum front brake, silencer on the right instead of the left, and drastically revised styling with a new tank, seat, and side panels with a different decals. The colour scheme was a striking yellow and black.

Of these fifty machines only one was sold outside Germany. This went to North America, where it was tested by two magazines, *Motorcyclist* and *Cycle Canada*.

Launch of a new 125 cc roadster, the K125T (also marketed as the RT125E DKW) came in 1972. This had a Sachs 125 cc engine unit, with six-speed gearbox producing 17 bhp – and offering 75 mph performance it could hold its head up in any company. Dry weight was 238 lb and there was a 13-litre fuel tank. Wheels had 17 inch rims with 160 mm full-width drum brakes and 2.75 inch front and 3.00 inch rear tyres. Unlike the off-roaders and military 125, the roadster had a low-level exhaust on the left. Finish was the same black with yellow tank used for the 1972 pre-production W2000s.

Another newcomer for 1972 was the SB2 Sport Bike. A fun bike with a 49 cc engine and high-level exhaust, five speeds and 12 inch wheels with 3.00 inch section

The pre-production batch of fifty W2000's were released to journalists with a striking colour scheme of yellow.

Sold in some export areas as a DKW RT125E, the 1972 K125T could reach 75 mph.

Hercules provided the whole of the 1974 German Silver Vase team in the ISDT. Eduard Hau rode this neatly presented works Hercules 125.

tyres. Altogether the model was, very similar in concept to the Honda Chaly or Harley-Davidson X90 mini-bikes.

At Cologne's massive IFMA Show in September 1972, Hercules presented 21 models intended to provide a massive sales push in 1973. These ranged from the M1, a basic commuter moped, to the K125BW military machine. In between came such models as the City Bike, Hobby Rider and K50 Sprint — all powered by various Sachs 47 or 49 cc engines.

By 1973, the 125 Moto Cross model was pumping out 20 bhp and proving a popular and successful machine in both Europe and America. But 1974 was an even bigger year for the marque. Not only did the W2000 launch in full production form, but in addition, the updated K125S appeared, with disc front brake, oil injection, direction indicators, rear carrier and new styling.

There was also an updated range of GS models, which had a brand new duplex frame, three-position rear suspension, Ceriani forks, lightweight 140 mm Sachs brake hubs, high tensile steel rims, a 9-litre fuel tank, a new seat with waterproof air filter underneath, Motoplat electronic ignition and plastic mudguards. The 97 cc (48 × 54 mm) engine now gave 15 bhp on a 12.5:1 compression ratio and had six gears like the rest of the range. The 124 cc (54 × 54 mm) engine delivered 19 bhp from a 12.5:1 compression ratio and the 174 cc (60 × 61 mm) gave 24 bhp from a compression ratio of 11.5:1. The West German Silver Vase ISDT team used these machines exclusively, with Hau and Bayer on 125s, Wagner and Grisse on 100s.

On 22 August 1974 several Nurnberg-made models were launched in Britain. These created a lot of interest at the impressive function held in Leicester, despite the absence of the previously-publicised W2000. Hercules' export sales manager Hans Schleibinger explained to a gathering of dealers that the name Hercules had been

dropped in Britain following objections from Raleigh Industries and that all the range would be known as DKWs. British concessionaires Sachs DKW (UK) Ltd was headed by general sales manager Dennis Johnson and joint managing director David Hancock.

Without the W2000, perhaps the most interesting of the machines offered was the AccuBike, a small wheel electric moped powered by two Bosch 12 Volt, 50 Amp/hour batteries. Top speed was quoted at 15 mph and according to circumstances, the range on a single charge was from 20 to 30 miles.

In practice, the Hercules electric moped was to suffer the same fate as other such vehicles at the time including a model built by the Italian moped specialists Garelli. Quite simply, not only was the range poor, but the extra weight of the batteries made the machine a third heavier than a conventional moped — ruling out the lady customers for whom it had been intended in the first place. The price was a hefty £197.24, compared to prices of between £126.51 and £178.44 for the four conventional step-thru mopeds also offered.

The Sport Bike was listed at £241.01, the 49 cc Olympia five-speed sports moped was an expensive £287.93, while the pukka dirt irons came much more pricey — the MC125 motocrosser was £651.02 and the GS125 enduro was £591.10.

When it arrived, the W2000 cost £919 including taxes and delivery charges. Production had just commenced at Nurnberg, when it was launched in September 1974 at London's Hilton Hotel. A blaze of publicity guaranteed much press coverage for the marque, although the normal production two-strokes probably suffered by being overshadowed by the Wankel. Oddly enough, Suzuki chose almost the same time to launch their RE5 rotary at a hotel a short distance away. Both designs were ultimately to suffer a similar fate.

The definitive W2000 began to roll off the Nurnberg lines in October. Compared to the earlier models the main modification was the introduction of a hydraulic disc front brake and a single 'branched' exhaust pipe which split into two under the engine to pass its gases to a pair of very large silencers. The engine (coded Wankelmotor KC24 (also KC27) by Sachs) was essentially unchanged from the pre-production batch of machines, and interestingly, the engine was built by Sachs totally seperately from the rest of the machine which was made of Hercules components and assemblies.

Dual responsibility for making the machine was carried through as far as there being separate spares companies, workshop manuals and even parts books. This is still the case today, with Sachs supplying engine parts and another firm called Sachs-Schreiber of Mannheim stocking the cycle parts for the W2000. The latter company purchased the entire stock for the model from Hercules late in 1986.

The peak power of the production engine was 27 bhp at 6500 rpm on a compression ratio 8.5:1, with maximum torque a useful 3.5 kgm at 4500 rpm. Lubrication was by a 25:1 petroil mixture delivered by a Bing CV (constant vacuum) 64/32/17 carb which took care of ensuring that the engine received both its fuel and oil. Ignition was Bosch, with a 100 Watt (later models had a 123 watt unit) 12 Volt alternator, 15 Amp/hour battery, contact breaker and coil. Cooling was by a ducted fan at the front of the engine, which conveniently (at least in cooler climates) blew warm air onto the rider's feet.

Power was delivered by a six-speed gearbox. Since the crank was in line with the frame, the primary drive was through bevelled pinions with a reduction ratio of 2.76:1 which turned the drive through 90 degrees to use a conventional gearbox and final drive. This was a $\frac{3}{8} \times \frac{5}{8}$ inch (530) chain with a 14 tooth gearbox sprocket and 33 tooth rear wheel sprocket giving a ratio of 2.36:1.

The engine was a solid, if rather ugly, lump, which conferred one side benefit in that it was a useful base onto which to tack the frame. It formed an integral part of the structure, with very short downtubes sweeping from the steering head, to meet the top of the engine. A further pair of tubes curved up from behind the gearbox to meet the top tubes, connecting with the rear swinging arm pivot on the way. A short steel plate on each side acted as a sub-frame for mounting the pillion footrests, with a further tubular section welded on for the silencer mountings. The engine arrangement provided ample ground clearance but left the exhaust pipe somewhat exposed.

Suspension was by a pair of 32 mm Italian Ceriani front forks with 115 mm travel, and rear suspension by twin Betor shock absorbers with five-position adjusters. Wheels were 18 inches front and rear, with Metzeler tyres as standard equipment – a 3.00 inch section front and 3.25 rear. The front brake, a single 300 mm disc, was from Grimeca like the earlier drum front and the single leading shoe drum rear which was the same as before. Both brakes won praise from testers and owners alike for their efficiency.

The W2000 had a particularly neat handlebar layout. The controls and switches were all well placed and gave the rider the impression that the machine had been designed exclusively for him – a feeling which was also conveyed by the design and layout of the footrests, gearchange and brake pedals. A master switch in the instrument housing console controlled both the lights and ignition. The console also included a speedo and tacho made by VDO.

More evidence of concern for rider ergonomics was provided by the seating. The supremely comfortable Denfeld dualseat unlocked and hinged back to reveal the battery and toolkit and space for a small bottle of two-stroke oil. Denfeld also provided the standard-equipment rear carrier, and a windscreen was available either as an optional extra or an aftermarket purchase.

Finish on the Hercules flagship was in the main excellent (except the poor quality of the Italian wheel rims), and smacked of the traditional quality of German engineering. Colour on the production machines was a red and black tank with silver frame and side panels – which was much more conservative than the yellow and black of the pre-production machines, although, like them, there was plenty of chrome work, and polished alloy. Chromed steel was used for the mudguard blades, and the finish was also enhanced by the attention to details like the quality of the castings, rows of Allen screws and the high standard of frame welding (an area often neglected by the Japanese at the

In 1975 a team of works supported riders had specially equipped versions of W2000 GS rotary.

time). Hercules employed both automatic and semi-automatic MIG welders, and the finish was superb.

But what was it like to *ride*? Every tester of the day commented on the engine's uncanny smoothness – at least when under way. *Motor Cycle Mechanics'* tester John Robinson was one of three UK journalists who went to Nurnberg late in 1974 to collect the first production models to be brought into Britain. They were to ride them back, a distance of some 400-odd miles. At the Hercules factory Robinson had a first brief burst in the company's car park where his immediate impressions of the machine were 'small, light and a firm feel'.

His first real ride was through heavy traffic over Nurnberg's mass of cobblestones and tramlines. It was here under stop-start conditions that the W2000's only real vice showed up – the difficulty of selecting neutral. The only reliable way to disengage the gears was to slip into neutral at the last moment while the machine was still rolling.

All the machines had only some 100 miles on their clocks at the time of collection. They were progressively run in for the first few miles, but it soon became clear that one of the identical machines was obviously quicker than the other two. On a fixed half-throttle at around 4500 to 5000 rpm in top, and an indicated cruising speed of 70 to 80 mph (the speedos were 10–12 per cent fast) one would waltz away from the others even on the gentle slopes of the autobahn.

Robinson commented that 'the power comes in smoother than a three cylinder two-stroke and there is no vibration. You can see a clear image in the mirror from tickover right up to maximum revs . . . When you blip the throttle, feed in the clutch and wind it up through the gears there is a pause and smooth surge, like an enormous elastic band being wound up and released. That's what it's like'.

But none of the testers found the motor particularly powerful, although the six-speed box allowed the rider to extract the most out of the 27 available horses. Top speed proved to be just over 90 mph. The W2000 was geared to pull around 100 mph, but because of overgearing it was as fast in fifth as in sixth. Top was well and truly an overdrive. An optimum cruising speed was 70–80 mph, which could be held indefinitely, with fifth coming into its own for hills or rapid overtaking.

Handling also earned praise, and another plus point of the machine was its ability to carry a passenger without sacrificing much in the way of performance. Another tester of the time commented 'This makes the W2000 quite a remarkable touring machine'.

Interestingly, a 250 cc two-stroke roadster twin was reported to be under development in 1974, but this never entered production, although it was later the basis for a larger twin which appeared during 1976. Perhaps the only other models to receive a reasonable

Endurance racing version of W2000 featured a tuned engine, cast alloy wheels, disc brakes and many other special components.

amount of publicity in Britain in those years were the MC and GS models – the GS in particular.

A GS125 was tested in the 30 April 1975 issue of *Motor Cycle News* by Peter Plummer. As an experienced off-road rider, he was mostly impressed with a machine he found as fast as many bikes with double the capacity. A GS Enduro was a no holds barred cross country racer. Plummer summed up its virtues in the following terms; 'Hitting the road with the beastie proved quite an eye opener. Being on scrambles type gearing I did not expect much in performance. Screwing the fancy Magura twistgrip the little bike simply flew. Smart, clutchless changes on the left, up for up pedal soon had the machine around 70 mph'.

He found the engine was super-smooth and that the brakes and suspension were top class. But in his opinion it needed 'better lighting and electrics for peace of mind', and complained that 'the exhaust note is too noisy to be acceptable in the trail riding environment'. He also criticised the high fuel consumption (never better than 27 mpg) and the equally high price tag.

Another test of the W2000 appeared in *Motorcycle Sport* for August 1975. This commented that the engine was not always so smooth as it seemed on the move. 'We already mentioned that the Deek (the W2000 was sold as a DKW in Britain, remember) started with a whirr and a clatter and this din barely abated at tickover. No one could describe the motor as quiet, and at low revs there was a fair amount of mechanical noise which might well have worried us on a conventional motorcycle'.

The *MCS* tester was surprised that the four-stroke machine was lubricated by a petroil mixture. However,

Badge-engineering – a W2000 being ridden for road impressions in Britain where it sold as a DKW.

after around 1200 machines had been produced, the W2000 was fitted with a separate oil pump injection system manufactured by the Japanese Mikuni company.

Despite the cacophony produced at rest, when getting under way, *MCS* commented 'The flat double bark of the silencers merged into one as we pulled away, and what had, when stationary, been an ungainly lump became a smooth, comfortable and very quick motorcycle. It was the perfect transformation of sow's ear into silk purse, and doubts and prejudices that had arisen by merely looking at the DKW, soon evaporated. It was delightful'.

With all this apparently going for it, what was the verdict on the world's first Wankel-engined motorcycle? The test which appeared in *Motor Cycle Mechanics*, asked the question 'Wankel – How practical is it?' going on to say that 'The first production Wankel has been a long time coming, while all the prototypes basked in the rather favourable glow of publicity as each one was announced. Yes, we all mused, the smooth, compact engine is ideal for motorcycles, but isn't it heavy on fuel? And isn't the exhaust too dirty? No, not really, said the manufacturers, and when we've made one, we'll show you'.

In September 1975, Sachs introduced a new seven-speed version of their 125 enduro and motocross engine, with the promise of 175 and 250 seven-speeders later. The original six-speeder with its 'high-headed' radial finned cylinder head could easily be recognised because it was much taller than the later engine.

In that month, too, came news that Sachs DKW (UK) had withdrawn as British distributors for the range of DKW (Hercules) motorcycles, although spares would still be available. The reason? Quite simply, the machines had become too expensive.

On a brighter note, the factory was still pressing ahead in competition, entering seven works-prepared enduro bikes in the ISDT which was staged that year in the Isle of Man during early October. But most noteworthy were the three W2000 Wankels which were making history by being the first rotary engined machines in the ISDT.

This was due to the efforts of the American importer Doug Wilford of Cleveland, Ohio, who had suggested the idea to the factory in 1974 – so it was fitting that Wilford should be one of the team. The others were Fritz Witzel, the German member of the W2000 trio, who had already won 12 gold medals in 12 enduros with the prototype earlier in the year. Ivan Saravasi of Italy was the third member of the squad.

In enduro trim, the Sachs Wankel was certainly a smoker, running on a 10:1 petroil mix, but the exhaust note was the deep boom of a four-stroke twin. The cooling fan was removed, but no overheating problems ensued in tests prior to the event. The model's main

Interesting 350 cc water-cooled twin. Dubbed the CCS, it appeared in prototype form in mid-1976, but it never reached production.

drawback was the FIM's insistence that the capacity of the Hercules W2000 should be rated as 588 cc. Observers pondered how this could be, when anyone else's calculations came up with either the 294 cc total of a single chamber, or three times this due to the triple operating faces of the rotor – but certainly not double it!

As the ISDT got under way, in its Golden Jubilee year, the machines appeared to offer plenty of performance and were well prepared. The big question was how the turbine-like smoothness, an asset in almost every other situation would cope with the slippery, muddy going that was sure to be found over much of the Manxland route.

But it was not to be a fairy tale ending, as all three Wankel engined machines had retired before the trial ended. Of eleven Hercules bikes entered, only three finished, one with a gold medal and two with bronze. All were two-strokes.

The last W2000 was manufactured on 25 November 1975, and although the model sold in Germany, USA, Britain, Canada, South Africa, Australia, France, Spain, Italy, Luxembourg and Belgium, a total of only 1784 (1145 petroil, 639 using oil-injection) were produced. So why did it fail with the motorcycle buying public?

I am pretty certain that John Fernley had the right answer, when he wrote in the May 1986 issue of *Motorcycle Enthusiast*. 'Motorcycle engines are very visible objects. They impose themselves upon the beholder, and we would have it no other way. This is part of the appeal of a purposeful machine. It is said that 30 per cent of the owners of the splendid Mazda RX7 sports car do not even know that the heart of their car is a rotary engine. This reflects the normality and the acceptability of the Wankel, but this could not happen in a motorcycle.'

This, I believe, was the greatest single drawback to the success of the Wankel-powered bike. It simply looked too modern, too advanced and far too different for the tastes of the dyed-in-the-wool motorcycle buyers. With development the W2000 could have been a very fine bike indeed. The handling and roadholding were brilliant, the finish superb, and the performance adequate. The fuel consumption would eventually have been improved, the engine noise would have been refined and the styling would have been brought up to date.

The Wankel, there is no doubt, was seen as the wonder engine of the century, but the 'something for nothing' engine is as ephemeral as the perpetual motion machine; it simply does not exist. And here in this idiosyncratic bike the problems of the Wankel were embodied; the noise, the emissions, the exhaust pipe which glowed cherry red at night because of the high operating temperature, and most of all, the sheer abnormality of the engine in a very conservative field'.

At its simplest, my young son Gary put the problem another way when he spotted a Hercules W2000 on display alongside other classic machinery at the Great Northern Bike Show in April 1987. His comment summed up the machine's whole problem in the sales war; 'Look at that engine dad, it looks like a spin drier!'

The first draft of this chapter was written when the Norton rotary was yet to be launched to the general public. I wrote at the time that Hercules were very brave – even foolhardy – in bringing out their rotary machine in 1974, and said that it was possible that the Wankel might one day make a comeback. But for that to happen the customers were the ones who would have to change. Maybe they have, but so has the machine. Norton is the direct inheritor of Hercules' technology, but aside from technical excellence, Norton's rotary *looks* more like a conventional machine than the W2000 ever did.

Sachs was taken over by GKN (Guest, Keen and Nettlefold) in 1976. The year also saw the introduction of a seven-speed off-road model range – the GS 125, 175 and 250, plus the MC125. These proved popular, with supplies being sent in some numbers to the USA.

Mid-year was the completion point for the new-era enduro range with the 350 model added – actually using a 253 cc (73 × 61 mm) engine produced by over-boring the 245 cc model by 2 mm. This gave 1 bhp more than the 32 bhp of the 250 at the same speed of 8000 revs. All four GS models were imported and distributed in the USA by Doug Wilford's company – Sachs Motors Corporation based in Ohio.

Above **The 1978 50 cc Ultra LC water-cooled sportster engine.**

Below **American importer's brochure offered enduro models in 125, 175, 250 and 350 cc in 1977 model year.**

In August 1976, Hercules (as DKW) machines were imported into Britain once again by Mobyke, a North London wholesaling firm based in Wembley and specialising in importing and exporting motorcycle accessories. At the end of the month, the W2000 and certain other models including the 125 Military and the seven-speed dirt bikes made an appearance at the Earls Court Show in London. Mobyke offered the first 100 W2000s sold before the end of September at a special price of around £1000 – about £250 less than the post-offer price. In the event there were few takers and a year later Mobyke were advertising the W2000 Standard Model (with petroil mix) at £918 and the oil injection version at £1026.

Around this time Hercules developed a road racing version of the W2000. This had a single expansion chamber exhaust, cast alloy wheels, rear disc brake, racing tank and seat, and a full fairing. It was intended for sports machine events rather than as a competitive answer to the then-dominant Yamaha twins.

Hercules also developed a prototype 350 cc watercooled twin roadster based on the experimental 250 of two years before. This was shortly followed at the Cologne Show in September by another prototype dubbed the CCS, which seemed to offer competition to the class-leading Yamaha RD400. The 390 cc watercooled Sachs engine had twin 34 mm Bing carbs, a maximum power of 30 bhp and a six-speed gearbox.

There were six-spoke cast alloy wheels with front and rear Grimeca disc brakes, and suspension was by 35 mm Marzocchi telescopic forks teamed with Spanish-made Betor rear shocks. However, this attractive and exciting machine never went beyond the prototype stage.

Also appearing was the Ultra, a super-sporting 50 much on the same theme as similar machines from rivals Kreidler and Zündapp. As the name implied, an ultimate dream machine for younger riders. Its colour was a striking all-red relieved only by yellow and black graphics. Not only did its colour attract attention, but the 49 cc (38 × 44 mm) Sachs six-speeder offered its aspiring young tarmac champion a meaty 6.25 bhp at 8000 rpm and 53 mph performance potential. When the engine was kicked into life by a starter mounted on the left, close to the gear change pedal, petroil was supplied to the hungry mighty midget from an 11-litre tank via a 19 mm Bing carb.

But it was the running gear which really provided the main sales gimmicks, with Marzocchi forks, exposed-spring rear units, dual hydraulically operated 220 mm front discs with Grimeca calipers and a 160 mm drum rear, 17 inch seven-spoke alloy wheels, matt black exhaust, racing mudguards and seat and a cockpit fairing with matching speedo and tacho, low bars and direction indicators. In fact, it had the works, and the trimmings would have graced a superbike.

By the time of the next Cologne Show two years later in autumn 1978, Hercules was offering not only a watercooled version of the Ultra called the Ultra LC (with white graphics instead of yellow), but also another luxury fifty, called the K50LR LC. In both cases the 'LC' tag denoted that the models were powered by the brand-new liquid-cooled 49 cc (40 × 39.7 mm) Sachs engine. Power output was 6.25 bhp – the same as the earlier air-cooled Ultra, but at lower revs (7100), and the engines were in fact virtually the same as before from the cylinder base downwards. The only exception was the water pump. But the cylinder and head were totally new, as was the very neat miniature radiator which fitted between the cylinder and twin front downtubes of the full duplex cradle frame.

Whereas the Ultra LC had purely sporting appeal, the K50R LC was most definitely a deluxe tourer in the German tradition of high quality and comfort. It still had seven spoke cast-alloy wheels (now painted a more conservative silver), black frame and an attractive metallic green for the side panels and tank had chrome side panels. This green was also used for front fork which was an Earles type of similar design to those on the ISDT machines used by the factory a decade earlier. Gone was the racing style seat, replaced by a far more traditional and comfortable dualseat. There were polished stainless steel mudguards, a rear carrier, and chrome-plated exhaust system. The handlebars had a more touring bend and there was no fairing.

Besides the two LC models, there were also the K50 Sprint and K50 R, both using the 6.25 bhp aircooled Sachs engine. The main difference was that the RL was simply a version of the K50 RLC in a different colour (non-metallic red) and with less chrome on the tank, while the Sprint was the base model, with wire wheels, a blue and silver finish, telescopic forks, painted mudguards and single disc front brake.

For 1979, the Ultra was given a black finish and new graphics, and renamed the Ultra II. To all intents and purposes it was the same machine, and the only other differences were a larger 14-litre tank, chrome exhaust system, polished stainless steel mudguards, and a substantial chrome-plated rear carrier. The facelift gave the machine a far less sporting line, but did successfully project an air of quality.

The balance of the 1979 range was made up by the K50 Sprint, K50 RL, K125 S, K125 Military, and a comprehensive range of commuter mopeds. The GS and MC off-road models were still made, but marketed under the Sachs banner.

No more W2000s could be built even if Sachs had wanted to, because much of the specialist equipment needed for the model's manufacture had been sold to Norton in Britain.

Ultra 80 was introduced in 1981 with five gears, cast alloy wheels and double-disc front brakes.

Line of special racing versions of Ultra 50 used in 1983 Austrian Sachs Cup.

During the next 18 months, the first signs of real problems for the motorcycle industry began to show, brought about largely by the Japanese agencies' adoption of 'sales graph' techniques. In plain language it was a policy of satisfying their masters back in Japan by producing ever-increasing sales regardless of how these were achieved. This left Europe and America reeling from a massive oversell in 1979–82 which threatened the existence of so many of the smaller members of the industry – Hercules included. It could be argued that the only reason for the company's continued survival is that it had the financial might of Sachs (and therefore GKN) behind it at a time when its rivals such as Kriedler, Zündapp, and even Austria's Puch could not muster such support.

Cologne, September 1980 saw a whole new generation of Hercules machines unveiled. These replaced virtually all of the existing models except the military bike and the GS enduro machines – by now renamed Hercules!

This range was made up entirely of lightweight models, centring on the brand-new Ultra 80. In their weighty press release for the show, Nürnberger Hercules-Werke GmbH went overboard in praise of the newcomer, with phrases like; 'The integration of the water-cooled engine into the design make the Ultra 80 an optical delicacy' and 'For a high, exactly dosed brake performance there is the front hydraulic disc brake'.

Heart of the larger LC was the new Sachs 80SW 79.8 cc (46 × 48 mm) engine offering 8.5 bhp at 6000 rpm

Miniature enduro-styled XE9 trail bike with 8.5 bhp on call and five speeds. Launched 1984.

and driving through a five-speed gearbox. Compared with the smaller 49 cc unit, maximum torque had been improved from 6.3 Nm at 7100 rpm to 10 Nm at 6000 rpm.

Much of the machine was based on the Ultra 50 LC II, but the 80 and a further revised smaller model had a number of subtle differences. These included a change in colour scheme to the silver with claret graphics also used on the latest Ultra 50, a enhanced rear section to the dualseat, and a new fairing with rectangular headlamp (now 12 Volt, based on a 130 Watt alternator compared to the 80 Watt job on the 50 cc model, and a 9 Amp/hour battery).

The other new bike was the Supra Enduro using a Sachs 506/4 AKF aircooled 49 cc – 38 × 44 mm – four-speed engine with 3 bhp at 4750 rpm and a 6 Volt flywheel magneto for ignition and lighting. With a top speed of 25 mph, this model was built to comply with the latest German legislation governing *mokicks* – commonly referred to as 'slowpeds'. Even so, it was a fully-equipped trail bike with up-and-over motocross style exhaust, 19 inch front and 17 inch rear steel rims with semi-knobbly tyres and 125 mm full-width alloy brakes, plastic enduro-style mudguards, headlamp/ speedo console, luggage carrier with helmet lock,

spring loaded footrests and direction indicators. Finish was in red or blue.

The balance of the range consisted entirely of step-thru mopeds – the Prima 2N, 4N, 4S, 5N, 5S, S, and 6., Supra 2D, Optima 3S, and Hobby Rider HR2. All used the Sachs 500 series horizontal 47 cc (48 × 42 mm) aircooled engine in various states of tune. There was a choice of one or two speeds – the latter in either manual or automatic form.

Appearance of a brand-new 80 cc model, the RS80 came in 1982. Again based on the Ultra design, it had a full fairing, and a new tank, seat and side panels to give it a far more modern style. Mechanically it was identical to its forerunner, with the same 8.5 bhp engine and running gear underneath the bodywork. New, though, was the 12 Volt ignition system and halogen headlight.

In 1982, Hercules was also involved in a racing series called the Sachs Cup, based on the standard production Ultra 50 II LC. The series, which took place in Austria rather than Germany, used specially-prepared machines built in Nurnberg – definitely not street-legal in their native land! The tuned, watercooled

A 1987 RX9 80 cc roadster, one of several Hercules lightweights that look like continuing into the '90's.

Sachs engines had a special cylinder barrel, carburettor and exhaust system. With full fairing, six-speed gearbox and other modifications, these miniature fliers were capable of over 80 mph.

In 1983, a trail version of the 80 was launched. This had an air-cooled five-speed engine (still producing 8.5 bhp). Compared with the 49 cc model, the XE9, as it was called, was far more of a pukka motorcycle, with proper knobbly tyres, 18 inch rear and 21 inch front steel rims, a square section swinging arm, electronic tacho, square headlamp, and a full enduro styling package.

And so this brings us to today, and the end of the story. The Hercules company continues to survive where so many failed, and remains in the motorcycle business with the backing of Sachs. But production is relegated exclusively to ultra-lightweights. And the days of building machines of over 100 cc are most likely over forever. If, for no other reason than that modern West Germany's high standard of living seems unable to support a volume producer of large machines apart from BMW.

Horex

Friedrich Kleeman was the father of the Horex marque. Together with his son Fritz, Kleeman was involved in several business enterprises in the early 1920s, among which they owned a company in Bad Homburg which made Rex patent containers. Friedrich Kleeman was also the main shareholder of the Columbus Motoren-werke in Oberusel, which manufactured auxiliary engines for bicycles – as well as larger units for motorcycles.

In 1923 the father-and-son team founded another company, with the aim this time of designing and building complete motorcycles. The firm was based at the old Rex manufacturing plant, and the name Horex was coined by taking the first two letters of Homburg and adding them to the Rex brand name. One year later, the first Horex motorcycle appeared.

Perhaps it was only to be expected, but the new company chose a Columbus engine, a 248 cc ohv single, with a hand operated three-speed gearbox driving the rear wheel by chain. The frame was the typical simple steel tubular device of the period, with a flat tank and sprung saddle following standard pre-1930 design fashion. The front fork employed a rocker arm which was suspended on a central spring and incorporated a single friction shock absorber.

Not only did these early Horex machines sell well, but they were raced with considerable success. The interest in motorcycle sport stemmed from the fact that Fritz Kleeman was also a well-known racing driver and motorcyclist. With the new 248 cc ohv single, suitably tuned and stripped for action, he soon had Horex competing in races throughout Germany. There was a team of three riders – Phillip Karrer, Henry Veit – and, of course, Fritz Kleeman.

Horex designs soon proved successful not only in racing but also in long distance trials. Perhaps the greatest success of the original trio came in the first race ever staged over the Nurburgring circuit. Friz Kleeman finished third on a 596 cc Horex with its capacity increased to 675 cc, against the might of experienced works teams including New Imperial, Norton and Harley Davidson.

By 1930, the marque was firmly established and the production tempo had increased so much that some engines even had to be made under a Sturmey-Archer licence. In addition, Columbus engines were being used in increasing numbers by several other leading German marques including AWD, Tornax and Victoria. Eventually Horex and Columbus merged their interests by moving engine production from Oberusel to Bad Homburg, but not before another commercial success was achieved with the Ghom, a 63 cc engine with 'clip-on' attachments for any ordinary bicycle.

The 1930s heralded even more success for Bad Homburg. Horex employed the gifted designer Hermann Reeb, who created a succession of interesting and innovative designs; first 498 and 598 cc sidevalve and overhead valve singles, then 198, 298 and 346 cc models, all with ohv.

Reeb created a sensation in 1932 when he designed a pair of large capacity vertical twins of 598 and 796 cc with chain driven ohc. The drive to the overhead cam was on the right hand side of the engine, enclosed in a large alloy casting which dominated that side of the power unit. This led to the design's one serious drawback. The spark plug for the timing side was obstructed by the vast housing.

There had been vertical twins before, of course, but not like this. Although Triumph and Edward Turner are today universally credited with the conception of the modern vertical trim, perhaps Horex and Hermann Reeb could have argued that they were there some four years earlier?

On the racing front Horex had continued to participate with success. In the late 1920s Franz Islinger and Josef Klein were prominent in the honours on 248 and 498 cc singles. Then at the 1929 German Grand Prix, expatriate Britain Tommy Bullus rode so well on one of the larger machines at the Nurburgring, that only a retirement with just a few miles to go was to rob him and Horex of victory. And in the 1930s Karl Braun used a supercharged version of the ohc twin to win many sidecar events including victory in the 1935 German Sidecar Championship.

By the middle of the 1930s, Horex was challenging not just on the race track, but also for a leading position in the sales war. Not only did it now offer brand new four-valve 500 and 600 cc singles but the ohc parallel twin had had its capacity increased to 980 cc (the size which Braun had used for most of his three wheel wins). At this time Horex' best seller was the ohv 348 cc S35 model which used a Sturmey-Archer engine.

In 1938 and 1939 Horex still continued its development and refinement of new and existing

Following the Columbus pre-war four-stroke tradition, the 342 cc Regina first appeared in the late 1940's. It was to become Horex' most successful model of its entire history. Here it is seen in the version unveiled in 1950.

models, but all these plans had to be shelved during the war years.

After 1945, Horex was doubly lucky to get back into volume production with very little difficulty compared to the rest of the German industry. The Bad Homburg plant had been more fortunate than many of the other major motorcycle factories. Its production facilities remained unscathed. Horex was also the first German motorcycle manufacturer to get permission from the occupying forces to build a machine with a capacity above 250 cc. At the time it was claimed that the Kleeman family had a more than close association with the Americans.

Horex traded under the title Horex-Columbus-Werke KG Fritz Kleeman in the years immediately after the war. From 1953 the Columbus part was removed. And in the late 1940s Horex was authorised to build machines for both the police and other official bodies. These orders allowed Horex to steal a march on the opposition, all of whom were still banned from producing over-250 cc machines until 1950. The Horex machine which was chosen by the various German government departments proved to be the firm's top seller in the immediate post-war years – the 350 cc Regina ohv single.

In many ways this was the most British of all German post-war designs and could well have been conceived in Birmingham rather than Bad Homburg. Much of the Regina's appeal was its rugged engine's reliability, frugal fuel economy and an ease of servicing. Its heart was the new long-stroke 342 cc (69 × 91.5 mm bore and stroke) semi-unit construction thumper. This turned out 15 bhp at a lowly 3500 rpm – but more importantly offered its rider vast amounts of torque with every long-stroke pulse.

Both pushrods were contained in a narrow external tube on the right of the engine, giving it the appearance of an ohc design with shaft and bevels. Inside the cylinder barrel was a three-ring Mahle piston with a compression ratio of 6.8:1, and the gudgeon pin running in a phosphor-bronze small end bush. Both barrel and head were in cast iron, with the large one-piece rocker box in alloy, displaying the marque's pre-war heritage, as did the twin exhaust ports and separate exhaust systems running down each side of the machine.

The crankshaft, with its roller bearing big-end assembly and one piece con-rod had three ball race main bearings. The valve mechanism was totally enclosed in an oil bath and was driven at the bottom end by chain. Valve clearance could easily be adjusted, simply by removing the one-piece rocker cover and slackening the tappet nuts.

Lubrication was dry sump, with a its oil pump housed under the timing cover on the right of the engine unit, while fuel was supplied by a Bing 2/26/23 instrument from a 13-litre fuel tank.

The primary transmission was a duplex sleeve chain which ran in a sealed oil bath, and a rubber cush drive system had been incorporated into the clutch sprocket gear, adding greatly to chain life. Transmission to the rear wheel was by another chain, which was protected from the elements inside a totally enclosed, but not an oil bath, steel chaincase.

A four-speed gearbox operated by a foot pedal on

the right had ratios of 1st, 3.25:1, 2nd, 1.81:1, 3rd, 1.33:1 and 4th 1:1. The overall ratio for solo use was 5.46:1 and for use with a sidecar, could be changed to 6.56:1. In fact there were many sales in these early years to those motorcyclists whose family responsibilities demanded a third wheel. Here, the Regina's excellent pulling power and respectable fuel economy made it a popular choice. In solo form the 350 Horex was good for around 75 mph, dropping to some 56 mph with a chair. Dry weight, solo, was 320 lb and the maximum advisable weight including a sidecar was 695 lb.

If the engines were decidedly pre-war the same could not be said for the chassis. Here all the very latest in motorcycle design practice was employed, using the engine, gearbox and clutch assembly as a stressed member of the frame, with the single front downtube ending at the front of the crankcase and being mounted in two places at the rear. Up front there was a sturdy and well designed pair of oil-damped telescopic forks. While at the rear, suspension was taken care of by a set of plunger units which only required a minimum of maintenance with the grease gun now and then.

The brakes were lovely to look at, and for their day, reasonably efficient. Both were full-width polished alloy units of 160 mm diameter, cable-operated at the front and rod-operated at the rear. These hubs were laced to 19 inch chrome rims which carried 3.25 ribbed (front) and 3.50 block (rear) section tyres.

The earliest post-war civilian Regina models had more brightwork than the majority of German machines, which were usually austere in the extreme, although it still had black silencers with chrome pipes, horn cover, kickstart and other foot levers and in addition to black in the centre of the wheel rims.

The Horex Regina was a high quality machine. One of the factory's brochures for the model explained in its own variety of English; 'Designer as well as the development staff of the Horex Works are old established, enthusiastic motorcyclists which, thus are capable – by means of a continuous and careful consideration of any suggestion being made by the great number of Horex drivers in all the countries – to not only bring the engine up to a top quality but also to – by selecting colours and composing them, by giving the Horex Regina of a pleasing appearance, and by finding a harmony of usefulness is always anew giving pleasure to any owner'.

Horex' motto at that time was a single simple statement; 'Built by motorcyclists for motorcyclists!' But the brochure's descriptive mood continued; 'Chrominium, first class lacquering, and anodized light metal colouring in a pleasing composition satisfy all Horex drivers in their desire to own a vehicle, amongst the multitude of motor cycle models existing nowadays, which excells by an especially, inobtrusive yet convincing characteristic, shape!'

On 30 April 1950 Horex introduced a racing version of the 350 Regina. This closely followed the lines of the production roadsters but had a suitably tuned engine, British Amal TT racing carburettor and a Bosch magneto that replaced the roadster's battery/coil ignition. The magneto was mounted at the rear of the cylinder barrel, which together with the head, now a single exhaust port design was in alloy. Drive for the rev-counter was taken from the end of the camshaft with the drive mounted on the timing cover. Power output was stated to be in the region of 25 bhp at some 5500 rpm and provided a maximum road speed of almost 100 mph.

Chassis and suspension remained the same, but there were now alloy engine plates, lightweight mudguards, alloy wheel rims, alloy fuel tank and larger capacity oil tank. Finishing off the model were clip-ons, rearset foot controls and a massive megaphone exhaust system running down the right side of the bike.

The new model's debut was at the Eilenreide Rennen race meeting at Hanover, but faced with competition from proven ohc racing singles, the race-kitted Regina just did not have enough steam.

The evident shortcomings of the pushrod single cylinder design for this new role led the company to design a new flagship machine both for racing and road use. It was a twin. Dubbed the Imperator, and meaning Emperor or General, the first the public saw of it was in the spring of 1951 when a racing version made its debut at the Waiblinger Dreiechsrennen road races. At the time the factory said that the Imperator was competing solely as part of its development programme and that design work was not complete, nor indeed had the final specification of the machine been decided.

Compared to the pre-war ohc vertical twin, the 1951 version was much wider. But though bulky, its lines were businesslike with the drive to its ohc by chain drive situated between the cylinders – and a lavish use of aluminium for its generously proportioned unit-construction engine kept the weight down.

In comparison to the earlier Horex design, the new unit's symmetrical layout had the advantages of offering more equal cooling for each cylinder and allowing the designer to fit the spark plugs in the normal position. The central camshaft drive also allowed the camshaft itself to be shorter, thus avoiding possible flexing and possible effects upon valve timing.

But on the debit side, the redesign had three factors: First, a four-bearing crankshaft was essential on account of the central timing drive gear. Secondly, the timing chain was more difficult to service and more difficult to assemble. Thirdly, the air passage between the two cylinders was greatly reduced.

Running gear also saw a number of major innovations for Horex. Rather than treating the engine as a stress member of the frame, even though it was full unit-construction, the frame was a full duplex cradle type enclosing the engine. The front forks and full-width alloy brake hubs appeared to be standard production Regina components but the hubs were now 190 mm. However, the rear suspension was a new, full swinging arm system, with twin hydraulically damped suspension units.

There was no oil reservoir as the engine employed wet sump lubrication. A large 20-litre alloy fuel tank, large sponge rubber saddle, hand-beaten alloy tail fairing and a chrome exhaust system with short cobby megaphones slightly rising at the ends completed the specification.

The racing ohc Imperator was clearly a development prototype as the factory claimed, rather than a serious racer – with only 30 bhp and a claimed 95 mph maximum. Towards the end of 1951, the Imperator appeared in roadster form. It closely followed the lines of the racer in its basic power unit and cycle parts.

Horex then revealed that the bore and stroke dimensions were 65 × 75 mm, which added up to a capacity of 497 cc. Suspicions about the power output were confirmed – 30 bhp at 6800 rpm giving a claimed 93.21 mph was very respectable for a sporting roadster, even if it was hardly suitable for a racer. There were twin 26 mm Bing or Amal carbs and ignition was by battery and coil, with a 45/60 watt crankshaft mounted generator. Other technical details included 7:1 compression pistons, a gearbox with four speeds with

This 342 cc ohv racer was developed from the Regina roadster. It made it onto a grid for the first time at the Eilenriede meeting near Hannover, April 1950. It was not competitive.

ratios of 1st, 2.71:1, 2nd, 1.725:1, 3rd, 1.246:1, and 4th, 1:1.

The proportions of the roadster Imperator were . . . generous. Features included a large capacity 20-litre fuel tank, deeply valenced front mudguard and partial rear enclosure. At 386 lb it could hardly be referred to as a lightweight. And although extremely technically advanced for its time, the 497 cc Imperator was destined never to enter series production.

Instead, 1952 witnessed the introduction of a more sporting version of the Regina roadster, the Regina Sport. This was a more highly tuned version – with a higher compression piston, hotter profile camshaft and larger Amal Fischer carburettor. These alterations provided 20 bhp and a 78 mph top end.

The cylinder head was now in alloy, and as on the racing version a single exhaust pipe was employed. The pipe and silencer, both chrome plated, ran up the right hand side of the bike. Other changes included flatter bars, additional chromework, a pillion pad mounted on the rear mudguard and a silver finish which included the frame.

The standard Regina remained almost unchanged, except for the introduction of an alloy head that retained twin exhaust ports and chrome plated silencers. Power output was up to 19 bhp at 6000 rpm. The Regina had a larger capacity fuel tank. It was increased to 18 litres, and enlarged mudguards with more valancing for improved protection completed the picture.

But at the Geneva show in March 1952 a special Regina was displayed with the Teves proprietary

hydraulic rear brake system. Another appeared with almost total enclosure of both the engine and rear wheel. In addition, this machine featured a handlebar fairing and massive front mudguard, but neither of these variants went further than the prototype stage.

At the same event a special two-fifty version of the Regina was shown. It was designed to comply with the most popular Swiss taxation class. This had both bore and stroke reduced, and the revised 65 × 75 cm measurements gave a capacity of 248 cc. Surprisingly, with 17 bhp at 6500 rpm, the power output of the smaller engine was actually more than the original 350's. As on the latest 350, the 250 had an alloy cylinder head. Shortly after this, in mid-April, an improved version of the 500 parallel twin appeared, but this time expressly for competition use.

By now the factory was concentrating its whole energy behind a racing development programme which included not only a dohc five hundred parallel twin but also 250 and 350 singles. Although the singles had full work's backing, they were the inspiration of leading rider Roland Schnell. He was previously renowned for his ingenious Parilla specials.

All three new racers appeared for the first time in public at Germany's early-season Dieburger race meeting on 6 April. Interest was naturally centred around the half-litre twin, two examples were raced by Friedel Schön and Hugo Schmitz. As on the Schnell 250/350 singles, the frames closely resembled the Norton Featherbed design, except that the bracing tubes did not cross over near the steering head.

The bottom end of the twin remained almost the same as the earlier 1951 Imperator sohc engine, with unit construction and four speeds. From the crankcases up however, the engine was far different to the original. Both the cylinders and heads were now alloy with massive finning, and of course, the central chain drove twin overhead camshafts. Two, although some pundits had rumoured four, valves per cylinder were employed, together with exposed hairpin valve springs.

Fuel was now supplied by twin 29 mm Dell'Orto SS1 racing carburettors with a single, remote central float chamber. The carbs themselves were quite steeply inclined at 45 degrees. Ignition was from a twin spark, crankshaft-mounted magneto.

Transmission was now via a clutch which had been modified to a dry type, with a large air scoop. Although the gearbox was housed within the crankcase, the engine was not true unit-construction. In fact, the gearbox was contained in a separate cylindrical casing which was free to rotate within its housing, and as its mainshaft was off centre, turning it to a new position

allowed the duplex primary chain to be adjusted. A similar eccentric gearbox mounting was used in Britain on AMC's lightweight roadster singles of the 1960s.

The cycle parts were largely unchanged from the previous year, except for the frame, but there were subtle improvements. For example, the forks now not only had rubber gaiters, but also a strong front fork brace/mudguard support, while the rider was provided with an additional pair of footrests set further to the rear. These were fitted in such a position on the rear spindle, aft of the rear suspension units, that the rider could lay almost flat, in Fergus Anderson style, along the fast straights. In the days before streamlining this was often worth an additional 5 mph on the maximum speed.

As for the smaller machines, Schnell had certainly waved his magic wand to create a pair of highly interesting Horex 'specials' – even though the 250 and 350 were so alike that one needed to inspect the respective machine closely to see if it had a green or blue number plate. The dominant feature of each model's engine was the casing enclosing the chain drive to the inlet camshaft. It gave them a similar appearance to the works AJS triple knocker. On the left hand side of the camshaft housing there was a further chain drive to the exhaust cam. Again, there were

Roland Schell built these semi-works dohc 250 and 350 cc singles. He raced these with considerable success during the period 1952–54 both in Germany and abroad.

Introduction of higher performance 350 Regina Sport offered riders 20 bhp and 78 mph top end speed.

exposed hairpin valve springs, and two sparking plugs were fitted (one on each side of the head) although quite often only one plug was actually used. Ignition was by magneto and the rev-counter was driven off the exhaust cam.

As with the twin, carburation was via a steeply inclined Dell'Orto SS1 carb. An unusual feature was the very extensive finning on the crankcase. It was not an oil container, because the lubrication was dry sump, with the alloy oil tank fitted below the nose of the racing seat. There was a separate four-speed close ratio gearbox.

The first Classic appearance for the new team was at Berne, for the 1952 Swiss Grand Prix, at the tree-lined 4.5 mile Bremgarten circuit on 18/19 May. Prior to this, in a non-championship race on Sunday 12 May at Hockenheim, Friedl Schön had shown what the new dohc twin could achieve. He took it to a sensational victory in the 500 race at an average speed of 99.73 mph. But in Switzerland things were to be very different.

The whole meeting was staged in brilliant sunny weather and there was a large number of works entries not only from Germany (BMW, DKW and Horex), but also Italy (Moto Guzzi, Gilera MV and Parilla), and Britain (AJS and Norton). In the 250 event a Horex finished eigth (and last) ridden by Hermann Gablenz. In the 350 Schnell himself could finish no higher than sixteenth of twenty finishers and in the 500, the Horex twin retired ignominiously.

Later, at the German GP at Solitude on Sunday 22 July, Horex again tried for Classic honours. They even signed up leading British Continental Circus star Bill Petch in an attempt at glory. However, taking the 500

dohc twin out in practice Petch dropped a valve and was a non-starter in the race. Even so he was reported as having been impressed enough to ride the machine later that season. Before racing got under way, another Horex rider Kurt Mansfeld had badly damaged his back when he fell from his machine.

But in the 250 race Gablenz and Horex had their moment of glory with a magnificent third place behind race winner Felgenheier on a works DKW twin and leading Guzzi privateer Thorn-Prikker. After the Schnell/Horex single, came the veteran Kluge on another works 'Deek' pursued by a pack of Guzzis and Parillas. It should be noted, however, that all the works Guzzis and the NSU twin ridden by Bill Lomax had dropped out, either through accidents or mechanical failures.

At the end of the season, persistent rumours concerning the poor performance and reliability of the dohc 500 twin were finally confirmed, when it was announced in October that it was being scrapped. The following year's 500 would still be a twin, but would be completely redesigned, possibly with gear-driven cams.

If the racing programme had not quite lived up to expectations, there were certainly other things for the Horex management to be pleased about. At the end of the year it was announced that this factory had enjoyed a 32 per cent sales increase for its Regina. And official figures showed that in the first eleven months of 1952 17,000 Reginas had come off the Bad Homburg production lines. It was the highest 350 cc production figure in the world for a similar period. To cope with this volume of business, considerable extension work had already begun to enlarge the Bad Homburg facilities. Horex also revealed that twenty-five per cent of its total production went for export to 50, or more, countries outside Germany. Although Britain was not one of these at the time, *Motor Cycling* journalist John Thorpe was able to sample one of Horex's popular 350 Regina models when two Swedish riders visited London in July 1952 (the other owned a Zundapp K601 flat twin, and Thorpe's riding impression of it are recounted in Chapter 16). The Horex single was owned by Hakan Skioid, and the following is the main burden of *Motor Cycling*'s views of the machine, published in the 24 July 1952 issue of the magazine: 'Hakan's Horex was next scrutinized. A two port, single cylinder, ohv tourer, this model featured unit construction, [*not strictly true*] with rocking pedal gearchange on the right hand side – an unusual feature on a German machine – telescopic front forks and plunger type rear suspension. The rear chain was completely enclosed in an oil bath chaincase.

The lively "350" proved very light in its handling and could be thrown around corners with little effort. Well balanced, the engine was sufficiently flexible to enable the speed in top gear to drop to just under 25 kph – 15 mph – without snatch, and there was only a slight trace of pinking when it was asked to pull away from that gait. Acceleration was marked on both top and third gears, but the bottom and second ratios appeared a trifle low. Over the bumps, the rear suspension worked well, but the action of the front forks indicated that rather hard springs were fitted. As a consequence, the front brake was somewhat spongy in operation. That at the after end, though, was so smooth, positive and progressive in its action that it more than made amends for the relative shortcomings of its "bow end" counterpart.

Common to both machines, was the provision of a soft saddle springing, which insulated the rider from any road shocks which happened to penetrate past the suspension systems.'

The other area beside road racing and roadsters in which Horex made an impact during 1952 was the world of the long distance trials scene. Its highlight came in the ISDT, which that year had its headquarters at Bad Aussee, Austria and was staged from Thursday 18 until Tuesday 23 September.

Although not included in either the Trophy or Vase teams, Horex nonetheless made its debut in the event in dramatic fashion with several medals. Of seven Horex models entered, four riders gained medals, while the remaining trio retired. Golds went to Oelerich (350), Cerny (350), Starkle (350 sidecar) and a bronze to Hurni. Wolf on another 350 retired on the fourth day, Meier retired his 350 Horex and sidecar on day three and Hurni could not even survive day one on his machine.

The success of 1952 on the production side, was reflected the following year when the Regina range was expanded. First, in July 1953 came the Regina 400. This was essentially the successful 350, but with the bore increased to 74.5 mm and the stroke remaining unchanged at 91.5 mm to give a capacity of 399 cc and increase the power to 22 bhp. But perhaps more important, was the improved engine torque and improved power-to-weight ratio, making the 400 even better for either solo or sidecar use. Maximum speed was a claimed 81 mph and with a sidecar 65 mph. The carburettor was a Bing 27.5 mm, but otherwise the bike was unchanged.

Prototype 497 cc Imperator twin appeared in 1952 but was never commissioned for production.

In late September, Horex announced that the 248 cc Regina was to go into full production for the German home market and general export. The decision was taken after a test marketing period in the Swiss market for which it was specifically made. From a graph supplied by Horex to the public it was possible to see that the smallest Regina peaked at 17 bhp at some 6600 rpm with power coming in nicely once 3500 rpm had been attained, though below that the curve was somewhat flatter. The fuel consumption curve showed that, at 60 mph, a figure of approximately 60 mpg could be expected.

On the 250, a Bing 2/26/21 carburettor was fitted, and the model had a single exhaust port, with one exhaust pipe/silencer on the left. But the rest of the machine was identical to its larger brother and even the internal gearbox ratios were the same. So with the range of 250, 350 and 400 Regina models, Horex were in the fortunate position of having three capacities to sell, but only needing one stock of spare parts.

Further proof of the Regina's rugged reliability came with a round-the-world marathon undertaken by a pair of enthusiasts. Eduard Edilitzberger and Norbert Wittasek completed 29,558 miles between 2 April 1953 and 6 November 1954. Their epic journey was carried out with a 350 Regina and heavily-laden sidecar, which carried almost everything except the workshop walls.

In racing, although the Schnell singles were virtually unchanged from the 1952 models, this certainly did not apply to the larger bore parallel twin. As promised, the

Part of the successful Horex team which competed in the 1952 ISDT that was staged in Austria.

engine had seen a considerable amount of extra tuning although it still retained chain drive to the overhead cams.

However, the gearbox and clutch were completely redesigned, and repositioned too. The clutch had been transferred to the rear righthand side of the engine, the position formerly held by the gearbox, which in turn had been fitted in a more conventional position within the centre of the crankcase. The gearchange pedal was now on the right.

A revised, much smaller housing was fitted in front of the exposed clutch in place of the crankshaft generator assembly, which had been replaced by a simpler total loss battery/coil system. The carburettors had been mounted on much longer induction manifolds which carried them up virtually underneath the seat.

The frame, front forks and wheels remained unchanged, but the rear tail fairing had been discarded and a new seat, deeply scalloped alloy fuel tank and fairing assembly were fitted. Finally a new black exhaust system with shallow taper megaphone, and rear suspension units with exposed springs completed the package.

Although they took part in the German national championships the Horex team's main test in 1953 was in the classics. These started in June, with the Isle of Man TT, but for this event no Horex machinery was entered. Then came the Dutch TT at Assen where Horex joined the fray but none of their machines finished.

Next was the Belgium GP – 'The Fastest ever Grand Prix' – as the headline in *Motor Cycling*'s claimed for their 9 July 1953 issue. The highest-placed of Horex' entries was way down in seventeenth place in the 350

Above **Schnell-Horex 500 cc single appeared at Hockenheim, May 1954, with Earles forks and 'bird beak' streamlining.**

race by one of the Schnell singles ridden by Fritz Klager.

Two weeks later the German GP was staged at Schotten. But there were problems in store for the organisers, when the majority of the foreign works teams – AJS, Norton, Gilera and Moto Guzzi – decided not to compete, in protest against the slippery state of the circuit.

With the competition much weaker than normal, Klager did well in the opening stages of the 350 race, holding fifth position before finally retiring. In the 250 race which followed, the other Schnell/Horex dohc single came home ninth ridden by Georg Braun. It was a good result, because in this event some of the works Guzzis and all the NSU and DKW factory riders were out in force.

For the 500 race, Horex had its new signing Müller (later to be the 1955 250 World Champion on an NSU Sportmax) riding not the re-vamped parallel twin, but a larger version of the dohc single. At the end of the first lap Walter Zeller on a factory BMW Rennsport led, but Müller was second. With another two works BMWs in

Front fork designed and constructed by Roland Schnell and Hermann Gablenz in 1953. Intended for Schnell-Horex racers but was used on a few Horex roadsters.

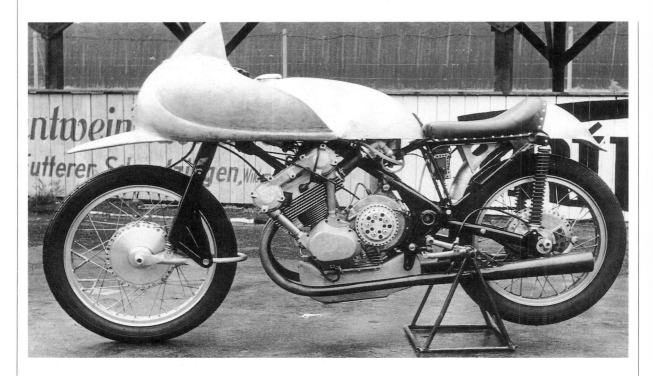

the race – ridden by Hans Baltisberger and Hans Meier – Müller's third place at the finish was an excellent performance.

After the Schotten meeting, the FIM finally decided that its results would not count for champion points, so the next opportunity for real GP glory came at the French Grand Prix in early August. Held at Rouen, the only Horex entry was the 500 twin, piloted by Friedl Schön. And only one machine failed to complete the first lap in the 500 race. Schön's Horex had got oil in the contact breaker housing and had run out of sparks.

Then on Sunday 23 August came the Swiss GP at Berne. A most depressing place in the rain, and there was a lot of it during the practice period. But on race day morning, the Bremgarten Forest, on the outskirts of Berne, presented a colourful scene in clear, brilliant sunshine.

There were no Horex entries in the 250, but in the 350 event Horex riders Schnell and Müller lined up against an array of talent from the world's leading manufacturers. The order at half distance was Anderson, Lorenzetti and Kavanagh (Guzzis), Coleman (AJS), Brett (Norton), Farrant (AJS), Hofmann and Wünsche (DKWs) and then the Horex pair of Schnell and Müller – ahead of Hollaus and Storr (Nortons). The final results were Müller seventh and Schnell twelfth.

In the 500 race Müller, again aboard one of the singles, this time with a full fairing, lined up amongst a field which included six Gilera fours, two factory entries from both AJS and Norton and three BMW works flat twins. As the first lap was completed Müller was eighth

– a superb showing. But this was not to last, when he Müller retired at quarter distance with engine trouble.

For the next round, the Italian GP at Monza, Müller was loaned an MV four and he obliged by finishing sixth. The first eight home were all on Italian fours. But in the 350 race Müller rode the Horex single, finishing seventh and at one stage looking as though he could grab fourth. Another excellent performance when one considers that the might of both the DKW and Moto Guzzi teams.

And so the classic racing season came to a close, with once again the more expensive and larger parallel twin hardly finishing a race. In contrast, the Schnell-developed singles had proved competitive even at world level.

Schnell also had a hand in some of the developments on the production roadsters. The Frankfurt Show in September 1953 was the debut for the brand-new 400 Imperator twin. One of this machine's most distinctive features was its front fork assembly, which had been devised by Schnell and fellow racer Hermann Gablenz at their workshops in Karlsruhe. It was similar to an Earles-type fork. Originally only planned for racing machines, the fork design soon proved to have such an advantage over the standard Horex telescopics that the firm's bosses authorised mass production.

The Schnell fork was based on a pair of conventional telescopic forks, but immediately below the lower fork yoke each stanchion was angled back to form a strut pointing almost vertically downwards. On each side, these struts termininated in fabricated pivot points, the

A 350 prototype racing twin of July 1954 with bevel gear driven dohc and leading-link front forks.

rigidity of which was assured by a welded, horizintal loop carried behind the wheel to join the two struts and also form a mudguard support. The wheel was carried in two separate wheel links pivoting from these points and were suspended by hydraulic dampers which were raked at the same angle as a normal stanchion, thus giving the fork a fairly conventional appearance. One of the major advantages claimed, at least for roadster use, that a 30–40 per cent increase in the life of the front tyre could be expected.

The 1954 production range comprised the 1953 trio of Regina singles, plus the 400 Imperator. And in the company's publicity leaflets, the advantages of the four-stroke engine were pushed to the full.

Presented very much as a flagship model for 1954, the new Imperator shared virtually nothing with the old, ill-fated, 497 cc prototype of 1951. It is interesting to note that the reason Horex favoured the 400 rather than the more popular 500 class for both their largest Regina single and the new Imperator twin was that road taxation and third party insurance premiums were the same for 350 and 400 cc machines, whereas the cost was 25 per cent higher for a 500.

The 1954 400 Imperator was, in my opinion, the most advanced German motorcycle of its era. It would not have looked out of place some twenty years on when the Japanese produced and sold countless near-replicas of the Imperator concept of a 400 cc middleweight powered by a single overhead cam, unit-construction parallel twin. In fact its only real difference from the later Japanese twins of the mid-1970s was its long-stroke 61.5 × 66 mm bore and stroke measurements and four-speed gearbox.

With a capacity of 392 cc, 7.25:1 compression pistons, and a single Bing 24 mm carb it still managed to let the efficient engine design turn out 26 bhp at 6500 rpm. Internal gearbox ratios were: 1st: 2.541:1, 2nd: 1.56:1, 3rd:1.14:1, 4th: 0.917, and the overall ratio was 5.7:1 solo or 6.45:1 with a sidecar. Maximum speed was a claimed 84 mph and dry weight with a 17-litre fuel tank was 386 lb.

Following modern trends, 18 inch Weinmann alloy rims were built onto the 190 mm diameter full width alloy hubs, with 3.25 (front) and 3.50 (rear) section tyres. The rear mudguard hinged upwards at the back to allow easy access to the wheel. A choice of either Schnell-type, or telescopic front forks was offered to customers. Incidentally, both types used the same yokes.

In racing, 1954 was to begin with a win at the beginning of May for Georg Braun on a 250 Horex single at the Grand Prix of the Saar. It was run over the 2 mile St Wendel road circuit. Braun's average race winning speed was 57.6 mph. Australian Keith Campbell's 500 cc race winning average of 60.6 mph in the twisty, around-the-houses event.

The next week, on Sunday 9 May Fritz Klager scored a magnificent third place against first class opposition in the 350 cc race at the star-studded international Hockenheim meeting. By now Muller was a full time works rider for the NSU team, so for 1954 Klager and

Production of 392 cc chain driven sohc Imperator sports/touring twin began in 1954. In many ways it was a forerunner to the concepts used by the Japanese two decades later.

Schnell were the two main Horex team members. Schnell rode the latest version of the 500 dohc single, which for 1954 sported streamlining based very closely on the 'bird-beak' type employed by Moto Guzzi on its 1953 works machines. Like the Italian bikes, this was hand-beaten polished alloy, with the front mudguard and fairing seen very much as an integral unit. The Horex 500 also sported Schnell's special front forks.

Later that month, at the 17th international Eifelrennen, run by the ADAC on the twists and turns of the 14.16 mile Nurburgring, Georg Braun created a minor sensation by taking second place in the 500 race on the single. Amazingly, the combination of Braun and the Horex proved faster than not only all the other singles except Ray Amm's race winning factory Norton, but the entire works BMW team as well. It must be said, however, that BMW were without team leader Walter Zeller, who had been sidelined after a practice spill. In the 350 race, Klager had to be content to finish fifth behind four DKW threes but ahead of sixth place man Ray Amm on his smaller Manx model.

However, at the beginning of July, Horex was again in the news when a most interesting machine made its public bow in training for the Belgian Grand Prix. Ridden by Georg Braun, the newcomer was yet another parallel twin, but this time a 350, having absolutely nothing in common with any of the earlier Horex road or racing twins. Although it was not actually ridden in the race because of a minor fault in the lubrication system, it nonetheless put up some fast practice laps.

Designed by the Austrian Ludwig Apfelbeck, the impressive-looking dohc engine appeared to follow a similar path to some NSU twins with separate shafts on the left for each camshaft. The power unit carried its oil in a massive alloy sump tank under the engine's crankcase, and was nearly square with 60 mm bore and 61.6 mm stroke dimensions giving a capacity of 349 cc. Some 38 bhp at 9000 rpm indicated its potential. Drive to the rev counter was provided from a take-off point on the right hand end of the exhaust cam.

There were hairpin valve springs and large diameter valves, both were made in a special material. Fuel was supplied by twin Dell'Orto carbs mounted on long rubber manifolds, which meant that as the carbs were already steeply inclined by the position of the engine in the frame and angled from the cylinder head they were almost hidden away from sight underneath the large capacity alloy fuel tank. Ignition was a Bosch battery and coil system.

The gearbox was built in unit with the engine with the pedal on the right. It had five speeds, and with long, shallow-taper megaphones plus the high rpm available, this meant that coming down to the La Source hairpin and accelerating away again, rider Braun was able to play a magic tune.

The frame was a backbone type with the engine assembly hanging underneath, and no front downtube.

The rear section formed the pivot point for the swinging arm, and the rear suspension units were angled, with the top connection tilted rearwards. The front forks were a leading link type, and completely different to any previous Horex, as was much of the machine. Finishing off the cycle parts, the tank was built for maximum wind cheating effect as a unit with the handlebar fairing and front mudguard.

After the Belgian GP came the German at Solitude, watched by a massive half-a-million crowd. In the 350 race, Braun brought the new twin to the line for its first race, and came home in sixth place, averaging 80.73 mph for the 24 lap, 99.57 mile race. Klager on the single finished way back in seventeenth position, a lap behind.

Sadly this was to prove the last occasion when official works-supported Horex machines competed in the classics, as the money and time devoted to the new production models now began to make difficulties in other areas. Another factor was, that for the first time since production began again after the war, Horex began to experience flattening demand. At the time this was thought to be due to the customer wanting a more up-to-date machine than the long running and previously successful Regina series, therefore, the company went to a lot of trouble and expense to provide a suitable modern replacement. In reality, the market was changing and the customer for the larger, heavier four-stroke models was fast moving away from two wheels to three or four and a roof over his or her head.

Imperator 400 cc power unit. Compare it with XS400 Yamaha unit of late 1970's.

Another sign of clear desperation at Horex was the introduction of a cheaper 250 Regina in September 1954. This was the 250V with an 'austerity' finish selling for DM 1,850. But the new single which Horex hoped would recapture its sales impetus appeared in June 1955. It was clearly stated at the time that it was intended to supersede the long-running Regina. This was the Resident, which used a brand new 349.24 cc (77 × 75 mm) short-stroke, full unit-construction ohc single.

The Resident's cast-iron cylinder barrel had the pushrod tube cast into it, and the alloy cylinder head used coil valve springs. As on the Regina, tappet adjustment was carried out by removing a one piece rocker box cover. Finning on both head and barrel were more generous than the earlier single and the finning was continued down the front of the shapely crankcases and along the oil-bearing sump. Claimed peak power was 24 bhp; with a sustained output of 22 bhp at 6250 rpm.

An unusual feature of the engine design was that the duplex $\frac{3}{8}$ inch primary chain was inboard of the timing gear. The crankshaft timing gear pinion was located immediately outboard of the engine sprocket, and since the sprocket was carried close in to the substantial roller main bearing, and an outrigger ball bearing was fitted outboard of the timing pinion, chain pull was very well resisted. Oil thrown off the primary chain lubricated both the camshaft and the lower section of the valve operating gear.

The multiplate clutch ran in the oil of the primary drive compartment. The overall ratios of the four speed gearbox (solo) were 5.68, 7.89, 11.36 and 18.45:1. Internal ratios were 3.25, 2.00, 1.39 and 1:1 from 1st to 4th respectively. With a sidecar, the overall top gear ratio went to 6.59:1. The rear drive chain, as on other Horex roadster models, was totally enclosed.

A full duplex type frame closely resembling the 400 Imperator's was used. The Imperator's rear sub-frame was bolted but the Resident's was welded. The Schnell-type forks were standardised. There was no option of teles as on the Imperator twin. Once again, 18 inch wheels were fitted.

Like the Regina, the Resident employed a twin port head with separate exhaust pipes and silencers. This can really have only added cost and certainly did nothing for performance. Horex claimed 81 mph, and a specific power output of 65 bhp per litre. The company's PR department had by then become more colourful in their descriptive phrases of which the following is just a sample: 'Coupled with the almost incredible power/weight ratio of about 15.5 lbs/hp, give, the Resident the acceleration of a racing sports car.'

But the Resident did manage to accelerate from rest to 62.5 mph in 10.5 seconds. It also had the advantage over much of its two stroke opposition in being able to accelerate cleanly and without snatch in top gear from

Horex press office photograph of 350 cc Resident twin port single. The model was a replacement for the top selling Regina. It entered full production in 1955 but was never to achieve the same sales as its predecessor.

as low as 25 mph. It also achieved frugal fuel economy.

Horex also stated that the Resident promised to be a worthy successor to its famous sister the Regina. The management also hoped it would carry on the family tradition of being manufactured in greater numbers than any other 350 cc motorcycle in the world. However, the reality was very different. Quite simply, although Horex was armed with a couple of excellent modern designs in the Imperator twin and the Resident single, Horex sales took a nose dive.

At a high point in 1953 of 18,500, sales for 1955 were down to around 5,000 units. With this alarming drop, Horex decided that although it had always proclaimed itself as the marque for the real motorcycle enthusiast, what they really needed now was a scooter!

But the problem was that not only had Horex no experience of scooter production, or its potential new customers, but they also committed the cardinal sin of building a scooter to motorcycle design priorities. In fairness, just about every other motorcycle producer who tried to build scooters fell into the same trap.

The result in Horex's case was the Rebell. The name meant 'rebel' and in retrospect this just about summed the Horex scooter up perfectly. As the 12 January 1956 issue of *Motor Cycle* put it: 'A job which seems to follow the design theory of such models as the Guzzi Galletto and Maico Mobil in being a motorcycle/scooter hybrid'.

The Rebell was powered by a highly-innovative 249 cc ohc engine, of the horizontal aircooled type, which offered 16 bhp, with a four-speed, foot operated gearchange. Even its frame and suspension employed motorcycle practices. With its 16 inch disc-type cast alloy wheels, motorcycle type swinging-fork front and rear suspension, enclosed final drive chain and even motorcycle type exhaust system, it was as *Motor Cycling* summed it up; 'probably the nearest approach yet made to marrying the weather protection of a runabout with the performance and handling of the medium weight motorcycle. It will be in interesting to see how the experiment turns out.'

The result of the experiment was to prove an embarrassment for everyone connected with the Horex scooter project. Despite a huge amount of time and money being spent, not one single machine was actually sold!

Meanwhile, although a smaller 250 version of the Resident single had been introduced, 1956 was a disastrous year for Horex. A total of only 2,600 machines of all types being manufactured.

The smaller-capacity Resident was basically a shorter-stroke 350 model, using the same 2/27.5 Bing carb, battery/coil ignition and a 6 volt Noris generator. It used the same 77 mm bore as the 350, but had its stroke reduced to 53.4 mm, giving 248 cc. On a 7:1 compression ratio, maximum power output was 18.5 bhp and its specific output per litre was up to 74 bhp. Maximum speed was 75 mph and acceleration to 62.5 mph from a standing start was 13.5 seconds.

Horex even tried tempting the potential buyer with both racing (RS) and enduro (GS) versions of its 350 and 400 Imperator models as well as enduro variants of the Resident single. Top of the line was the 400 RS Imperator for which the factory claimed 37 bhp at 8200 rpm and a maximum speed of 105.4 mph. But even though these competition models were smart and purposeful machines. Although they sold in small numbers it was too little to stem the ebbing sales tide. Indeed, no variants of the smaller twin were ever built.

At the Frankfurt Show in September 1956 Horex was reduced to a tiny stand in the corner of one of the vast halls. There was no spare money for a larger display after its sales campaign that year had been left in tatters. Too late, the company realised in the latter part of 1956 that it had to change direction completely if it was to survive.

This led eventually to the decision to build small capacity two strokes and to diversify altogether into areas outside motorcycling. New ventures included not only offering a fan cooled version of the Imperator twin engine for use by other manufacturers in their mini cars, but also a contract to build parts for Mercedes Benz.

Rebell scooter – it was an abortive and costly project. Power came from an innovative 249 cc horizontal ohc single.

Consequently, Horex was able to continue in business.

For the 1957 season, Horex offered its familiar range of four-stroke singles and twins – the 400 Imperator twin, 250 and 350 Resident singles. But there were also two new lightweight 'strokers, both powered by bought-in Sachs units. These were the Rebell 100 and Rebell Moped in two and three-speed versions.

The Rebell 100 was a full lightweight motorcycle, with its 97 cc three-speed engine producing 5.2 bhp at 5250 rpm, housed in a pressed steel frame with leading link forks and swinging arm rear suspension. Electrics were provided by a Bosch 6 Volt flywheel magneto. The wheels had 120 mm full-width brakes, with 16 inch steel rims and 3.00 section tyres. The 9.5-litre fuel tank had a reserve capacity of 1.5 litres, and a distinctive feature of the bike was its two-tone dualseat. The Rebell Moped followed very similar lines, except it was obviously smaller and less powerful – in fact 'spindly' would be a more accurate description.

Both the two-strokes hardly matched the idea of what the Horex reputation had been built up on. Consequently sales were few and far between, plunging the already ailing motorcycle manufacturing side of the business into crisis. The picture, however, was not uniformly depressing.

One lifeline was a continued strong presence in its export markets of the world. In January 1958, it was announced that the Horex range of motorcycles was to be handled, for the first time in Britain, by Buyers' Agents (WA) Ltd of High St, Andover, Hampshire. This organisation stated it intended bringing over the full range of models from the 50 cc moped to the 400 cc overhead cam vertical twin. In addition the sporting fraternity was not forgotten. Both racing and scrambling machines, the RS and GS variants were also to be landed. And it was thought that three-wheeler manufacturers would doubtless be interested in the fan cooled vertical twin cylinder power unit.

All this was to mean very little as it is unlikely that any Horex products were ever imported into Britain. Almost simultaneously, the Bad Homburg plant closed.

Several enthusiasts throughout Germany continued to keep the Horex name alive, even into the sixties, by building machines from spares or rebuilding older machines. One of these was Friedl Münch. He was later to win worldwide fame, if not fortune, with his Münch Mammoth motorcycles. This is more fully related in Chapter 11.

Another enthusiast who kept the Horex flag flying was Alfred Petith. He built a home-brewed 700 cc vee twin by grafting two 350 Resident cylinders and heads into a common crankcase to create a superb looking special. This vee twin Horex-based bike was the star of the show at the 1965 Elephant Rally, held at the Nürburgring in January.

Then in the late 1970s Münch built an amazing turbocharged version of his Mammoth, which he called the Horex 1400 TT. This time, it was more than just the product of one enthusiast, however, but a genuine attempt at a rebirth of the marque.

Project Horex centred around Fritz Roth, who was then the German Ducati and Laverda importer. Roth, who had earlier acquired the rights to the Horex name, had run the Suzuki and Moto Guzzi concessions in Germany but was brave enough to ditch the Japanese Suzuki factory at a time when their unreasonable and dictatorial sell-sell-sell-at-all-costs demands went contrary to Roth's own principles and knowledge of the German market. He was later proved right when Suzuki's German sales plummeted during the early 1980s. Roth also abandoned the Moto Guzzi side of his business. After giving up an annual turnover of 30 million Deutschmarks (about £8 million pounds sterling at the time) he was forced to rebuild the empire. This he did partly by taking on Ducati and Laverda concessions. In less than two years these were built up into a business with an annual turnover of £1.36 million.

Münch and Roth were joined by Klaus Ibsen in the attempted renaissance of Horex. Ibsen, not short of business acumen, was responsible for setting up the entire network for the massive Castrol oil brand in Germany. His eight years as the lubricant company's front man brought him into business contact with Roth. Ibsen was so confident of Project Horex that he moved his family from Hamburg, 350 miles away, to Roth's headquarters at Hammelbach, south of Frankfurt.

In essence, Project Horex gave Münch the role of design engineer. Roth was the financial organiser and Ibsen was the marketing wizard. The Horex 1400 TI was intended as a publicity tool. It is not difficult to see why. The 143 bhp monster was an exercise in superlatives. A 1400 cc (80 × 66.5 mm) chain-driven sohc engine, like the rest of the Münch Mammoth designs based upon the NSU Prinz car unit, was mounted in a massively strong frame.

Nevertheless, the 1400 TI was also a viable street machine. Münch spent over two years from early 1977 developing it in readiness for limited production by mid-1979. In the end, it was only prevented from going on sale in Germany in 1979, after appearing the previous September at the biennial Cologne Show, by the German motorcycle industry's self-imposed ban limiting power output to 100 bhp.

The proposed production range was much more down to earth. Back in early 1978 the dream was that a range of 80-750 cc models, all with single cylinder engines, would be on sale in Europe by 1980. Münch even had drawings of a proposed 750 with four valves and it was hoped to display the full model spectrum at the Milan Show in November 1979. The new Horex range was expected to use as many common parts as possible, thus keeping design time and production costs to a minimum. The business plan also foresaw the use of an already-established manufacturing plant in Italy. It was argued that building and tooling up a brand-new factory in Germany was neither practical nor economic.

The first of the new Horex breed was scheduled to appear in December 1978, when Roth expected to deliver 600 trial and motocross machines. But when these appeared they were not four-strokes and not even 80 cc models. Instead they were mere two-stroke 50s!

Powered by Italian Minarelli engines, although they had Horex on the tank, they were in fact purely badge-engineered Testi models from a factory in Bologna. These were followed by other Horex-Testi models including the Rebell Sport (Testi Champion Special) Rebell Enduro (Testi Monocross), and Biber 40 (Testi Militar).

By 1982, the association with Münch was over, and still no four-stroke singles had appeared. Problems at the Testi factory then forced Roth to seek another line of supply. This led to co-operation with the Portugese SIS firm, and thereafter, both 50 and 80 cc Sachs-engined SIS models were imported by Roth. They were sold under the Horex banner.

But Roth had not given up entirely on his plan to market larger-capacity four stroke models. Although no Münch-inspired models ever appeared, the Horex big thumper did stage a mini-comeback in 1985.

Rebell 100 was a full-size lightweight motorcycle with a bought-in Sachs 97 cc two-stroke engine.

Above **In 1985 the Roth organisation offered a Horex-HRD 500 cc cafe racer with Rotax power. A pure racing machine and an off-roader were also marketed by Roth.**

These models were specially built for Roth by HRD in Italy. Like many small-volume productions of around this time they used an Austrian Rotax engine. It was a short-stroke, 89 × 81 mm, 503.91 cc (also available as 562 cc – 94 × 81 mm) powerhouse which could be ordered with various specifications, and gave power output figures up to around 60 bhp. The Horex-HRD machines were built in three guises – trail, cafe racer and road racer. All three had beautiful lines, but few had been built before HRD failed in 1986.

The next move for Roth, and the final chapter as far as Horex was concerned, followed the closure of the HRD factory. Roth entered into a joint venture with the Indian Bajaj company. Bajaj held a licence to produce Vespa scooters, and to expand into a European operation together with Roth they set up a company in Hammelbach called *Fritz Roth Jr – Bajaj Motor Fahrzeuge – Vertriebsges für Europa GmbH.*

Even though there were problems with the parent Piaggio company in Italy, the venture prospered.

Fritz Roth at this point seemed finally to have given up the rebirth of the new Horex. And so today Horex, once one of Germany's premier enthusiast marques, seems to have died once again.

Right and above right **Friedl Münch revived Horex marque in the late 1970's with 143 bhp 1400 cc turbocharged version of the Mammoth design.**

König

Early in 1969, Dieter König, factory boss and chief engineer of the König factory, decided to build a 500 cc class solo road racing motorcycle for Rolf Braun.

Based in West Berlin, the König factory had built a solid reputation during the 1960s, but not for motorcycles. The company made a successful range of multi-cylinder two-stroke engines for power boat racing. It was one of these modified production boat engines, a horizontally opposed, water cooled four cylinder two-stroke, which formed the basis of the bike engine.

Despite lack of experience at the new game, König was not content to start at club or even national level. The new machine first appeared in the West German Grand Prix at Hockenheim on 11 May 1969. And even on paper, the König engine showed promise. Together with a Manx Norton racing gearbox and clutch, it weighed 110 lb. This was less than a Norton engine *without* its gearbox. Usable power was available from 7000 rpm, and its peak power of 68 bhp was produced at 9000.

In effect, the engine comprised a pair of flat twins mounted side by side in the common crankcase. The pressed up, three bearing single crankshaft ran across the frame. Bore and stroke measurements of the four cylinders were classic 'stroker, 54 × 54 mm, while the Mahle pistons each had a single Dykes-type ring. A belt-driven pump circulated water through a small radiator and a reservoir under the engine.

For bike racing, the boat engine had been equipped with a pair of East German BVF carburettors to improve acceleration. Each of these supplied petroil mixture to one pair of 'fore and aft' cylinders which fired at the same time. Induction was controlled by a single disc valve situated on top of the crankcase. Exhausts pipes from the front and rear pairs of cylinders were siamesed and ran into a massive expansion chamber over the gearbox.

But the first prototype was very much a development vehicle rather than a developed racing unit, and Dieter König fully expected to encounter teething problems. His main fear concerned the cooling system, which he correctly considered would need a radiator of larger capacity. Essentially, 1969 was a series of problem-solving exercises, rather than a real racing programme. But 1970 saw a giant leap forward with the addition to the team of Australian Johnny Dodds as rider and New Zealander Kim Newcombe as development engineer.

By the time the König was raced seriously in the Dutch TT at Assen that year, power was up to around 75 bhp. The gearbox was a six-speeder comprising a Norton shell and Austrian Schafleitner internals. A Krober electronic tachometer was fitted, and a major revision to the breathing arrangements came with the use of a pair of high-level expansion chambers.

Although the machine was fitted with an extra-large radiator, it was a non-finisher due to problems which again centred on ineffective cooling. Despite this, the two-stroke four had impressed with its straight-line speed and acceleration. The next move was to fit a

Designer and company head Dieter König with his prototype solo motorcycle early in 1969.

Another view of the König prototype. it is difficult to imagine that this highly original unit had started as a racing outboard engine for powerboats.

Right **Australian Johnny Dodds campaigned a König in the Continental Circus round during the mid-1970's. By this time the engine was reliably delivering 75 bhp.**

smaller radiator, and more attention was paid to forced air flow. The smaller radiator also permitted a much narrower fairing which helped the racer's penetration at higher speeds.

A new frame was promised once the engine was perfected, but for the present, it had remained much as in the original 1969 design. However, the bottom frame rails were omitted and a square-section swinging arm was used in place of the old round-tube one. Front forks were Ceriani, with Girling rear shocks, and the König used racing Fontana brakes.

Also on the sidelines was a larger capacity version, rumoured at the time to be of 800 cc, but with similar external dimensions. This had already been used successfully on the other side of the Atlantic. In the USA, König-powered midget racing cars were producing a claimed 120 bhp on alcohol fuel. In June 1970, Newcombe stated that 'On petrol, the figure should be around the 90 bhp mark'.

Dodds continued as König development rider through 1971, prompted as much as anything not just by the engine's potential, but also by the earlier, and expensive, failure of the Italian Linto four-stroke twin which he and the other European Circus riders had purchased. However, during the season, the Australian's only placing within a GP top ten was a tenth at Hockenheim for the 1971 German GP.

Over the following winter, a major redesign was completed. For the first time, the original square engine dimensions were replaced by four cylinders with the stroke of 50 mm in a 56 mm bore giving 492.6 cc. The crank was re-engined, with two main bearings on the drive side, one at the opposite end, and a fourth in the middle. Lubrication was still by petroil at a ratio of 16:1, because the mixture was directed straight at the caged roller big ends, there was no need for the usual two-stroke slots in the con rod eyes. This provided additional strength. The small ends were uncaged needle rollers.

Another major change was a switch to a 45 mm twin choke Solex carburettor. But it was still controlled by a single inlet disc. The drive to this from the right hand end of the crankshaft looked impossibly weak. Not only did the toothed belt have to change direction from the vertical to horizontal, as it circled the pulleys, but the two rollers which effected these changes required the belt to twist through 90 degrees each time to offer the smooth side of the belt to the rollers. In practice, however, the arrangement proved quite adequate, as did the similarly flimsy-looking pair of synthetic rubber bands which drove the water impeller.

Another feature which caused problems was the exclusive use of chains in the transmission system. The difficulty centred around the fact that the König unit was still really only an engine which its constructors had fitted with a gearbox and a clutch from another source. This usually meant the use not only of the secondary drive chain but as many as three triplex chains in the primary transmission. Later this was to prove an embarrassment.

The revised power unit made its classic race debut at the 1972 West German GP. The event was staged around the twists and turns of the difficult Nurburgring. By now, Dodds had left the team and was replaced by Newcombe, who was doing his own riding, and German Ernst Hiller.

The race line-up was formidable. A pair of MV Agustas were ridden by world champion Giacomo Agostini and Alberto Pagani; works Kawasaki threes with Dave Simmonds and the Japanese rider Araoka, together with a factory Swedish Husqvarna ridden by Bo Granath. These were supported up by a swarm of leading privateers that included Jack Findlay and Billie Nelson.

Amazingly, the race proved not only that Newcombe's winter development had been spot on, but also that his riding talent was something special. The New Zealander was only headed by the pair of super-fast Italian multis and scored a brilliant third place ahead of Simmonds' Kawasaki. Then came Hillier on the second König, with a sixth.

More development work meant that the team did not appear at every round. But Newcombe took another third at the Sachsenring, East Germany, behind Agostini and Rod Gould on a Yamaha. A fifth at Anderstorp, Sweden, and a tenth in the French GP at Clermont Ferrand then followed. The Swedish result was extraordinary as *Motor Cycle News* reported in its 26 July 1972 issue under the headline 'Impressive Kim'.

Newcombe in exciting, crowd pleasing action at the Dutch TT, 23 June 1973.

New Zealander Kim Newcombe made the König into a competive racer. He was gifted both as a rider and as an engineer. Seen here at the Dutch TT, 23 June 1973.

As the article reported, 'after the New Zealander had come through to fifth place after being last on the first lap, Newcombe said "I had to push to the first corner before it would fire, and then the clutch cable broke on the third lap and I was getting into slides on every corner"'. The machine's performance proved that air vents he had styled into the fairing seemed to have solved previous overheating problems'.

A newcomer, Paul Eickelburg, had joined the team mid-season, gaining a third place in the Yugoslav GP and an eighth at the Dutch TT. He was also responsible for several points scores in non-championship Continental internationals in which Königs performed even better.

Typical was the 500 race at Chimay, Belgium on Sunday 9 July. Here Kawasaki team leader Dave Simmonds had looked certain of victory until the Englishman's engine seized after three laps. Hiller on another Kawasaki took over. But with three laps to go, slow starting König rider Eickelburg got by to take the flag 35 seconds ahead of Hiller, followed by yet another König rider.

Perhaps the most impressive König performance of 1972 was when Eickelburg won the 500 race at an international meeting held at the Hengelo circuit in Holland on 27 August. In the process he set a new

outright lap record for the 3 mile course at 91.28 mph – 3 mph faster than the legendary Jarno Saarinen had done in the earlier 350 race on his works Yamaha. Dave Simmonds had taken the lead from the start and was pursued by 350 Yamaha mounted Chas Mortimer. Then Simmonds had to pit stop to wire up a loose expansion chamber, which allowed Mortimer to take over. But he could not match the speed of Eickelburg, who had made another slow start but now passed him.

In the same year came the introduction of a 680 cc version of the König four, and the debut of both 500 and 680 units in sidecar events. Here, both Rolf Steinhausen, with a fifth in France and a fourth in Austria, and the British Boret brothers Gerry and Nick (with a brilliant third in the Isle of Man) proved the potential of the König for sidecar use at the highest level. And as 1973 dawned, the König horizontally opposed four was poised to challenge BMW's long supremacy in sidecar Grand Prix racing.

Its attractions for the sidecar class were both technical and economic. Spares for the BMW Rennsport engine were becoming ever more scarce and therefore expensive. A complete machine demanded a price almost no-one could afford. In contrast, the Berlin outboard-based engine units were available at a reasonable price and perhaps more important with readily available spares at a fraction of what was being asked for BMW components.

But there were also problems with the König. Besides the transmission weakness mentioned earlier, the sidecar constructor also had the difficulty that the König had almost a total lack of engine braking compared to the BMW twin. So an outfit needed powerful brakes. Massive drums were most common, but front discs were beginning to win favour.

The first Grand Prix of 1973, which was staged at Le Castellet, France, König machines took honours in both the two and three-wheel categories. In the solo class, Newcombe gained a fifth at the start of what was to be a year both of sweet success and bitter tragedy.

But it was the chair men who really flew the Berlin company's flag that day. Three of the first six outfits home were Königs. Although world champions Klaus Enders and Rolf Engelhardt kept their works BMW ahead, they were hard pressed for most of the race by the König pair Jeff Gawley and Peter Sales ahead of Schwarzel and Kleis on another König. Steinhausen and Scheurer on yet another came home fifth.

Gawley again showed his form with a repeat performance behind Enders at the next round, the Austrian GP at the Salzburgring. Following these early successes, many observers were tipping him as a future world champion. Sadly, lack of funds and mechanical

problems meant that his championship thrust was all but over. Gawley's only other top six placing was another second, this time in Belgium during mid-season. The Englishman final y finished fifth in the world series.

But another König pair came through to second in the World Championship. This was the team of Schwarzel and Kleis, who besides their fifth in the opener in France, scored in almost every round. Their greatest moment of glory was a second place at Hockenheim. Although König failed to win a single sidecar GP, another second from the Boret brothers in Holland, their only GP finish that year, meant that the flat four 'strokers had mounted a serious challenge to BMW's crown.

This was confirmed by the speed trap figures carried out during the IoM TT, where the fastest 500 sidecar was the Boret's König at 130 mph. In the 750 class Gawley's 680 König was fastest, screaming through the electronic eye at 136 mph. This was a record for chairs.

The Boret brothers on the Renwick Developments' König powered wedge at Snetterton, April 1974.

Engine installation of Renwick König.

It beat the previous best of 134.8 mph, set by Helmut Fath with his four-cylinder 500 Münch URS in 1969.

In the solo class, König reached its development peak in 1973. Only Kim Newcombe achieved world class results. The Kiwi not only scored the marque's only solo Grand Prix victory, but also gained the runner-up position in the World Championships. In the process he split the MV Agusta pair of Phil Read and Giacomo Agostini. Disaster came after this excellent result. The New Zealander was tragically killed on 12 August while competing at Silverstone in the penultimate round of the World Championship before the Spanish GP.

Prior to this, his fifth place in the season's opener in France, Newcombe had taken a third in Austria, victory in Yugoslavia, second in Holland, fourth in Belgium, third in Sweden and finally fourth in Finland. But it was his Yugoslavian win at the Opatija circuit on 17 June which created the headlines. 'Newcombe takes the lead with first Grand Prix win' *Motor Cycle News* reported. And Newcombe summed it up like this 'I just can't believe I have won. We have been trying for so long to get the König over the line first and now all the effort seems worthwhile'.

After the New Zealander's death much of the momentum seemed to go out of the König race effort. Certainly, in the solo class there were virtually no successes in 1974. A König finished fourth in the 500 West German GP at the Nurburgring that year, but this was an empty result as there were only four finishers because the race was spoilt by a mass withdrawal of star riders. They cited safety grounds as the reason for their grievance.

On three wheels it was a totally different story. Königs scored three classic victories and secured second (Schwarzel) and fifth (Steinhausen) in the title

chase. Add to this four seconds, including George O'Dell and Barry Boldison's runner-up spot in the IoM TT, and it soon became apparent that Königs were now real championship material for 1975.

The chances of victory in the coming season had been greatly reinforced by two factors. The first was the engine's greatly enhanced reliability. The second was the withdrawal of König's major competitor. Many had said that the 1974 championship had only been retained for BMW by the highly skilled riding of the victors, Klaus Enders and passenger Rolf Engelhardt. They took their sixth and fifth world titles respectively. Accustomed to winning easily, that year they had seen ever-increasing competition from König, and kept the title in dispute until the very last round. It may have been this close shave which influenced the BMW team's decision to retire at the end of the season.

Ender's sponsor and tuner Dieter Busch transferred his allegiance to Steinhausen and König for 1975. This faith was repaid in full when Steinhausen and Huber took the world championship on the Busch/König by winning three of the seven rounds staged. An eighth, scheduled for Imola in Italy, was not run because of insurmountable organizational difficulties.

Except for the West German event, which Rolf Biland won on a Yamaha, every round went to a König. Schwarzel and Huber won two rounds and Schmidt and Matile another. As a result, König also took second and fourth places in the Championship that year.

Also at the start of the 1975 season, the success of the König engine prompted the Austrian gearbox specialist Michael Schafleitner to build a batch of 20 special six-speed gear clusters for use in König-powered sidecar outfits. He commented at the time; 'A closer set of ratios are needed than any of my previous designs, to make full use of the König's power output.' This was a statement of the obvious. Although a solo König could make use of power from as low as 4–5000 rpm, the extra demands (and weight) of a racing sidecar outfit greatly reduced this ability. On an outfit the engine had to be kept spinning above 8000 rpm to produce its maximum output and torque. The Busch-tuned König was rumoured to produce well over 90 bhp, which was substantially up on the 1975/76 production racing engine that developed a claimed 85 bhp at 10000 rpm.

The final year in which works-supported Königs were raced in the solo class was 1975. Early in the year, Frenchman Christian Leon, dropped by the French Kawasaki team, signed up to race the Königs used by the late Kim Newcombe. In February, he had tested both 500 and 680 Königs at the Paul Ricard circuit near Toulon. He was reported to have been very impressed. On standard engines, he lapped in 1 minute 15.6 seconds, four-fifths of a second outside the circuit record held by the late Jarno Saarinen. Leon had two 500s, with two spare engines and one 680 plus a spare engine. The 1975 version of the solo 500 was tuned to allow the exhaust system to run under the seat, while the 680 sported magnesium wheels, triple Brembo discs and Marzocchi front forks.

The Leon deal was part of what was termed at the time 'a major factory effort'. Other Königs were scheduled to be raced in solo events that year by Horst Lahfield, former West German junior champion. But in the world championships the team was dogged by a series of retirements. Only three finishes in the top ten were made all season. Lahfield took a fine fifth at the Salzburgring in the Austrian GP and notched a sixth in the Finnish GP at Imatra. Leon's only placing was a seventh at Hockenheim.

In 1976, the solo effort was over. But Steinhausen retained his world title, with victories in Austria, the Isle of Man and Belgium. And Schwarzel won at the Nuburgring. Many other results for the record book were gained by König-powered outfits at all levels from club events to Grands Prix.

But this reign at the top was to be all too brief, for other, more suitable engines were starting to appear from Yamaha and Fath. Both of these power units featured an integral gearbox and clutch, something which the König never had. And so, in 1977 all König's top contenders for championship honours defected to other engines.

Steinhausen had a Busch-tuned Yamaha, while Schwarzel went with ATO-Fath power. The result was inevitable. Except for the previously unknown partnership of Venus and Bittermann, who took second slot at Hockenheim, the highest-placed König outfit in the 1977 World series was Steinhausen's Busch-König at the same event with sixth place. This was just before the

Rolf Steinhauser's Busch-König was the top three-wheeler at the Isle of Man TT, June 1975.

Steinhauser and Huber, World Champions and TT winners for the second time in 1976.

team switched to Yamaha. The challenge from the tiny Berlin factory was over.

A few 680 Königs were raced solo at private level, and two of these were British efforts. One was the Crossier Special, ridden by Scotsman Bob Steel, and the other was owned by Roy Baldwin and ridden by Jerry Lancaster.

But from 1977 on, virtually nothing was heard of König. The remaining machinery, both solo and sidecar, disappeared from the scene very quickly.

Though König was at the top for a few short years, it nonetheless scored some excellent results at the highest level. The Berlin factory earned a prominent place in the history of motorcycle road racing, despite never building a roadster or venturing into the lower branches of the sport.

Kreidler

In 1982, when the Swiss rider Stefan Dörflinger piloted his midget racer to win his class for the season, the list of Kreidler's world titles rose to six. An impressive tally in just over a decade. And what makes the company's achievement even more remarkable is that it chose to compete with just one type of machine – the 'humble' 50 cc ultra-lightweight.

Kreidler's half-dozen titles set a record which now looks never to be broken. The smallest world racing class has been increased to 80 cc.

In itself this was an outstanding record for any factory. But how many people today realise that at one time Kreidler was also the largest volume producer of motorcycles in Germany? It enjoyed sales of over half the domestic market.

To trace the origins of this extraordinary marque, we have to travel back to 1951. There was a sprawling factory complex in Kornwestheim just north of Stuttgart. This was the home of Kreidler Fahrzeugbau, where motorcycles were very much a sideline to the real profit earner, which was supplying semi-finished metals to German industry.

Kreidler's expertise was in complex alloys, tubing and special mixtures, but its first venture into motorcycle manufacture was not in the least special. The K50, like virtually every other bike to leave the factory gates was essentially no more than a moped. Right from the start, Kreidler seemed to adopt a policy of 'small is beautiful' and its determination to concentrate on the very smallest machines was to prove outstandingly successful. At the very least, it ensured that Kreidler was to survive longer than most of its rivals.

The K50's 49 cc (38 × 44 mm) piston-ported two-stroke, two-speed engine was basic, but of an excellent quality as befitted a company with Kreidler's background in specialist metals. The rest of the machine followed conventional principles, with a U-shaped 'step-thru' frame, miniature telescopic forks, a motorcycle-type exhaust system, 100 mm full-width brakes, 2.00 × 26 tyres, cycle-type saddle, luggage carrier above the rear mudguard and a 7-litre fuel tank on the front section of the frame. Dry weight was 99 lb.

The success of this first moped led to the introduction of the de luxe K51, which used the same basic engine assembly and wheels but had a more luxurious and stylish appearance. This effect was aided by various metal panels covering the centre of the

machine above and behind the engine unit. Both machines had an identical 34 mph performance. For a commuter moped, in countries where their speed is unrestricted this pace would be acceptable even today.

The K50 and K51 remained unaltered until 1955, when in October new speed restrictions were placed on all mopeds. This was the result of a resolution passed in July 1955 by the VFM (Union of Bicycle and Motorcycle Industry). From then on, mopeds in Germany were limited a maximum speed of 24.8 mph. The regulation had been agreed in principle in May the previous year. As soon as the decision was announced, Kreidler started research into power output restriction. At the same time it also tested a light-alloy cylinder with hard-chrome plated bore. It was introduced late in 1955 on both the K50 and K51, as well as on the new R50 scooterette.

The R50 used the same 49 cc engine with two-speed gear controlled by a twistgrip, but unlike the earlier models, featured full enclosure of the engine and partial enclosure of the rear wheel. Leg shields and a pillion saddle were also provided. Other major changes were

Even the early Kreidler models, including this K51 moped of the mid-1950's used a horizontal two-stroke single cylinder engine. This was later to become the hallmark of this widely acclaimed Stuttgart marque.

the use of smaller wheels, with 2.25 × 19 tyres, and relocation of the fuel tank below the dualseat. Unrestricted export R50s gave 2.3 bhp at 5500 rpm.

Motor Imports of London SW9 were appointed British importers and in September 1956 a R50 sold for £99 14s 3d. The 27 December 1956 issue of *Motor Cycling* commented favourably on the Stuttgart-made model in the following terms; 'A lightweight scooter having many pleasant features and excellent looks'. But the big news came the following year with the introduction of the model which was to mould Kreidler's whole future, the Florett. The name means 'foil' in the sense of a weapon used in fencing.

The heart of this newcomer was its brand-new, horizontal 49 cc (40 × 39.5 mm) piston-ported, three-speed engine. To escape the moped speed restrictions, the Florett was marketed right from the start as a motorcycle, albeit one of flyweight proportions. Its power output was 3 bhp at 5500 rpm, enough to propel the 165 lb machine along at speeds up to 41 mph.

Not since the unorthodox 98 cc Imme, which was in manufacture until 1951, had a German manufacturer used an engine with a flat single configuration. In common with other Kreidler models, the bore was

Manufacture of Kreidler R50 scooter started in 1956. It was the first of the marque to be imported into UK.

hard-chrome plated directly onto the alloy cylinder, and it was fitted with an 8.5:1 Mahle piston. The gearbox was still operated by twistgrip control.

Another notable feature was the Florett's pressed steel frame, which together with the deeply-valanced mudguards, fully-enclosed chain and partly-covered engine gave the Florett a completely different look from any other moped-cum-motorcycle of the era. Although the frame was still an open 'U' type, the 8.4-litre tank and comfortable saddle only had a small gap between them. Completing the picture was a full motorcycle-style suspension, with swinging arm at the rear and Earles-type forks at the front. Full-width 100 × 20 mm alloy brake hubs were laced onto 23 inch chrome rims with 2.50 section tyres.

The Florett was an exceptionally modern-looking machine, and one which was to prove both popular and long-lasting. So long-lasting in fact that the factory presented owners who had completed 100,000 kilometres (62,500 miles) with a solid gold tie pin bearing the Kreidler emblem. This was a tradition that was carried through well into the 1970s.

In the late 1950s Kreidler was one of the few success stories in a German motorcycle industry. At the time, many of the largest within its ranks switched to the manufacture of other products or simply went out of business. In many ways, the success of Kreidler against

Race equipped ultra-lightweight Floretts made their initial racing forays with factory blessing in 1959.

this background was like that in Spain a couple of decades later when the Derbi factory boomed while producers of conventional larger motorcycles failed. The fuller story of Spanish experience in this field is given in my book *Spanish Postwar Road and Racing Motorcycles* (Osprey).

With the Florett, Kreidler was able to exploit a virtually untapped market for the cheap and reliable '50' which looked like a full grown motorcycle but at a fraction of the normal costs in terms of both buying and running.

Soon, many of its new owners were subjecting their purchase to various forms of motorcycle sport. At first, these were purely off-road. However, it soon became clear that the Kreidler engine with its high level of reliability was also eminently tunable. This was discovered just at the time when the new 50 cc road racing class was gaining its initial foothold in motorcycle sport. The first Kreidler road racing machine appeared in 1959. In essence, it was simply a stripped and tuned standard Florett, even retaining its original engine side panels, tank, seat and rear mudguard. Besides the layers of foam rubber piled on the tank top the only other giveaways that this was really a racer were clip-on handlebars and 19 in alloy wheel rims.

It was at this time that Kreidler's name was first linked with Hans Georg Anscheidt. A man who was to become one of its biggest stars.

Anscheidt started his motorcycling career in cross-country competitions, winning 25 gold medals from 1954–56. An urge to go faster led to grass, cinder and sand races. From 1957–59 he won some 21 races out of 40. Then in 1960 he joined Kreidler and worked in its research and development department. It was the year

he became a works road racer and won the Hockenheim Motor Cup for his factory. It was a prelude to Kreidler's full-blown racing attempt the following year.

But the first real honours for the factory came in endurance cross country events, where Anscheidt won his and his factory's first gold medal in the 1960 ISDT. He gained another 'gold' the next year as a member of the West German Vase B Team when the event was staged in Wales. In addition, the Swiss Vase team used two Kreidlers ridden by Haller and Steiner. Both gained top awards. Additional golds were taken by other Kreidler-mounted competitors including Dittrich and Lehner from West Germany and Kappelli from Switzerland.

This success ensured that for several years afterward Kreidler's 50s were a feature of the ISDT and often took gold awards. But it was on the 'hard stuff' that the factory was to find the most glory. As the 'tiddler' class grew in stature, so the machines began to be taken more seriously as real racing irons rather than overgrown bicycles.

The turning point was in 1961 when the FIM instigated the Coupe d'Europe as a series of international races with a minimum duration requirement. Eight race organisers agreed to run Coupe d'Europe events – three in Belgium, two in Germany, and one each for Yugoslavia, Holland and Spain. Rather surprisingly, neither Italy or Britain showed much interest, although 50 cc machines had been racing on a firm basis in both countries.

The first of the Coupe d'Europe events was held at

Renn Florett ridden by Hans Georg Anscheidt in 1961.

had no need to worry when his Kreidler team-mate Wolfgang Gedlich won the seventh round. It was held at the then-new Heysel circuit near Brussels and Gedlich averaged a speed of 56 mph. The Coupe's eight and final round at Zaragosa, Spain, but it was not contested by Kreidler. There was no need to come to the grid because the factory had already won the Championship, with Anscheidt first and Gedlich second.

Kreidler's 1961 machine, the Renn Florett, was in reality little more than a standard production engine fitted with a Dell'Orto SS1 carb. The piston-ported cylinder remained at Florett's original bore and stroke measurements. This power unit developed 8 bhp at 12,000 rpm and was good enough for around 75 mph, although the frame, forks, suspension and brakes were clearly based on the roadster.

Full world status for the tiddler class in road racing came in 1962. The 50 cc World Championship was staged over ten rounds. Kreidler responded to the challenge by announcing a full works' team in February that year. Three riders would contest the series – Anscheidt (as team leader), Wolfgang Gedlich and Rudolf Kunz.

Mouseron in Belgium and the winner was a local rider on an Italian Itom. No Kreidlers were entered. The second outing for the series contenders was the Saar Grand Prix over the demanding and hilly 'round-the-houses' circuit at St Wendel. At this event Kreidler machines made their debut with a couple of works entries from the Stuttgart factory.

This event saw Anscheidt display some of the skill which was to make him a world champion in the future. He won at an average speed of 51.17 mph which compared well to Ernst Degner's winning 125 cc race average of 62.63 mph on a works MZ.

The third round was a landmark, being run as part of the German Grand Prix and staged at Hockenheim. With the flat-out Hockenheim circuit boasting only two corners, it could have been expected that the slower speeds of the racing 50s would make a boring spectacle. But this was not so, as the race turned out to be one of the best that day. Anscheidt on his Kreidler battled the Yugoslavian Tomos team for honours. Kreidler was just beaten by Miro Zelnik who was first across the line at an average of just over 70 mph.

Next round for the Coupe was at Zolder in Belgium, where Anscheidt scored his second win and gave himself and Kreidler a commanding lead in the series. The fifth round was at Opatija in Yugoslavia. Again Anscheidt won, as he did at the next round over the Zandvoort circuit in the Netherlands.

With four victories Anscheidt was by then in a commanding position in the Championship table, so he

A 1961 works engine with twin Dell'Orto UBF carbs.

Interestingly, Kreidler management declared it was a condition of the honour of riding for the marque that it was open only to people already working at the factory. That year although Kreidler committed considerable resources to the development of new racing machinery, the firm survived without a specific racing department. Chief engineer, other mechanics and riders came from the research office and returned there on Monday morning (travelling arrangements permitting).

Kreidler had realised that the piston-port racing two-stroke developed from the roadster was at the end of its power line, so during June 1961 the team had begun work with a rotary valve engine. It continued perfecting it through the winter. It was this design which formed the mainstay of the Stuttgart factory's 1962 World Championship bid, and like its forerunner, the new engine was a horizontal single. But to arrive at the maximum permissible 49.9 cc Kreidler used a bore of 40 mm and lengthened the stroke to 39.7 mm. Amazingly the crankshaft was taken from the roadster, which said something for the production model's reliability. The alloy cylinder barrel was finished with a 'pin-pricked' hard-chrome surface with a forged Mahle racing piston. Several of the engine castings were in magnesium alloy to cut down on weight. Finning of the head and barrel were a square-section rib pattern rather than the 1961 machine's rounded radial finning.

For carburettors Kreidler abandoned the Dell'Ortos used in 1961 and chose two special Bings (one for each rotary valve) made to their own specifications. This pair of carburettors cost as much as a complete standard Florett roadster.

The 10 bhp power output was routed via a four-speed foot change gearbox, which gave twelve ratios thanks to an external three-speed overdrive controlled by a twistgrip on the handlebars. Even Kreidler thought this was really too many, but because the effective power band only existed between 9500–11000 rpm it was necessary to provide a wide range of ratios. In the German hill climb championships the wide gear selection had its uses, although only eight were ever used because of the more or less constant gradients and similar curves. Perhaps Kreidler opted for a policy of 'be prepared' which was valid in the light of the problems suffered by Honda in the 1962 GP series. The Japanese company started the season with four gears and were soon forced up to provide eight.

With twelve gears it was, in theory, possible to pick a ratio for every corner on the circuit, subject to the rider's weight and his knowledge of the course. But in practice, although upwards changes presented no problem, the difficulty came with changing down and remembering exactly which gear you were in. It was an almost impossible task, according to Anscheidt at the time.

The 1962 Renn Florett frame was made from aircraft-quality chrome moly-tubing. For that season Kreidler had developed a design based on something approximating to a pair of parallel ovals, where the two main tubes were both continuous loops, running from the steering headstock down and back to support the engine unit, then around and up to the headstock again. The tubes were cross-braced not quite halfway back, and a triangular steel pressing fitted at the rear of the twin loop system made up the main engine mounting point, the front pivot for the swinging arm and also the platform for the 6 volt battery.

As in 1961, the Earles forks used adjustable spring legs. Experience had shown the factory that attention to suspension details on these flyweight racers was worth at least as much as, if not more than, an additional 1 bhp from engine tuning. A major problem was actually keeping the 121 lb machine on the ground. The FIM had introduced a rule that riders had to weigh a minimum of 132 lb, this meant the rider was heavier than the motorcycle.

The fairing itself took almost as much time to design as the rest of the machine. Using a Stuttgart wind tunnel, Kreidler plumped Anscheidt in the racing crouch position and went to work – day after day. A wire mesh grid was covered with flexible plastic and bent in small increments until an absolutely perfect form was found. Anscheidt considered the wind tunnel testing session harder than actually racing, but experimentally Kreidler found that this attention to detail gave a significant improvement.

Braking was uprated for 1962, with larger drums cast in elektron, so that they were no heavier than the earlier type, but much more powerful.

The first Grand Prix ever to count for 50 cc World Championship points was the Spanish, held in May 1962. At the twisting Montjuich Park circuit in Barcelona, Anscheidt led the pack to take a solid victory for the Stuttgart team. Second was Derbi rider Jose Busquet and third Honda team member Luigi Taveri from Switzerland. Gedlich came home fourth. Ulsterman Tommy Robb, was fifth, and in sixth spot Kunimitsu Takahashi from Japan. Both men were on Hondas.

The next round was the French GP at Cleremont Ferrand. Here Anscheidt retired, but Dutchman Jan Huberts took his Kreidler to victory ahead of three Honda and a pair of Suzuki ridden by Japanese riders. Next came the IoM TT. Here the Japanese speed of technical development began to show. Anscheidt's was the first Kreidler across the line and he had to be content with fourth spot behind race winner East German Ernst Degner's Suzuki and Robb and Taveri's Hondas.

One of the pair of factory Kreidler Floretts used in 1961 ISDT. Both machines proved they were good for gold medals in the rugged Welsh mountain terrain.

The Dutch TT at Assen saw local rider Huberts bring his Kreidler in second, behind Ernst Degner. Anscheidt was third and Gedlich sixth. Next came the Belgium GP at Spa, which again Degner won, with Anscheidt second, Gedlich fifth and Huberts sixth.

At the important German GP at Solitude, Degner won yet again, with Anscheidt second; no other Kreidler finished in the top six. The Grand Prix circuit then moved behind the Iron Curtain to the East German GP at the Sachsenring. A crowd of 250,000 spectators who saw a Kreidler grasp victory. Huberts crossed the line ahead of a herd of screaming Suzukis and Hondas. Englishman Dan Shorey having his first ride on one of the Stuttgart flyweights managed a creditable sixth place.

Kreidler won again at Monza, where in the Italian GP Anscheidt finished ahead of Itoh (Suzuki), Huberts, New Zealander Hugh Anderson (Suzuki), Morishita (Suzuki) and Taveri (Honda). This penultimate round of the world series was staged in Finland at the Tampere circuit. With their Hondas now equipped with eight speeds, Taveri and Robb finished first and second. Anscheidt was third, one place ahead of his main rival for the championship, Degner.

So the title went to the final round in far-off Buenos Aires, Argentina. Even though Kreidler sent a full team, including new boy Gunter Beer, this could not stop a Suzuki one-two. Degner rode to a second place that day and was assured of the world crown. Anscheidt came home a dejected third – and second in the Championship table. Huberts, who finished fifth in Argentina, was fourth in the championship.

Although the Stuttgart factory had failed in their world title attempt, 1962 was still an excellent year for the marque. In 1961 Kreidler had produced 35 per cent of the powered two wheelers sold in Germany, and in 1962 this figure had risen to over 50 per cent. In effect, Kreidler built more machines that year than all the other German manufacturers together.

There were four main models, the Florett 3.4 HP motorcycle and 3.4 HP moped. (They were identical except for methods of starting – kickstarter or pedals). Florett 4.2 HP motorcycle and Florett Super. It is worth noting that in Germany the moped speed restrictions still applied.

Not only was Kreidler extremely successful in the home market, it was also enjoying something of a boom in Continental Europe. The Netherlands and Switzerland were particularly lucrative. For example in 1960, 21.25 per cent of all purchasers of lightweight motorcycles in Switzerland had chosen the Florett. In 1961 this figure had risen to 45.81 per cent and in 1962 the proportion of the Swiss market held by Kreidler went up to 64 per cent.

All four Florett models used the same basic 49.9 cc (40 × 39.7 mm) piston-ported horizontal single cylinder power unit. But the 4.2 HP and Super had a four-speed, foot pedal gearchange in place of the earlier three-speed twistgrip-operated system which was still used on the cheaper basic Florett machines.

The Florett 4.2 HP and Super models' four-speed engine gave 4.2 bhp at 7000 rpm, which provided a maximum speed of 47 mph. The Super featured as standard a luggage carrier, mirror, white-walled tyres and a black ivory finish.

In early 1963 *Motor Cycle* journalist Peter Fraser visited the factory and met chief designer Johann Hilber. He found that a lot of effort was being expended on developing the racing machines. What was of particular interest was the underground test shop with three dynamometers for measuring power output. It was an obvious sign that Kreidler was taking their crack at the 50 cc world championship very seriously indeed.

While at the factory, Fraser was able to borrow one of the works ISDT mounts for an afternoon. He found that the performance was outstanding for such a small engine. Reputed to produced about 5 bhp, the ISDT Kreidler would accelerate to its 50 mph maximum with astonishing rapidity. Fraser found that even steep banks could be climbed without footing thanks to the 52:1 (yes, 52 to 1) bottom gear. He also commented that the engine seemed virtually unburstable. Furthermore, the model's brakes and suspension were so good that the power could be left 'all on', over the most uninviting going.

In Britain the import concession for Kreidler machines had lapsed at the end of the 1950s, but in April 1963 Hans Motors of South Norwood, London (already the importers of Heinkel scooters) announced it would bring in the Stuttgart flyweights. Hans Motors concentrated its efforts on the top-of-the-range model, the Florett Super, which sold for £137 8s 9d.

Motorcycle Mechanics tested one in the September 1963 issue and was highly impressed both by the quality and performance. The first paragraph of the test summed up the case; 'If anybody had said ten years ago that 50 cc motorcycles would be capable of carrying two people at a cruising speed of 45 miles an hour, they would have been considered as rather eccentric. But the Florett Super did just that'.

Although the production roadsters never made any real impact on the British market, privately-owned Kreidler racers certainly did. The popularity of 50 cc racing in the 1960s was high, inevitably several competitors turned their attention to the German 'strokers. At first they were seen as an alternative to the machine which dominated the flyweight class in the mid-1960s, the Honda CR110, but they later took over the position of the Japanese machine completely. One of the earliest Kreidler exponents was ace two-stroke tuner Brian Woolley. He campaigned a tuned Florett in 1962 on British short circuits. This machine was the first Kreidler Florett seen in Britain and finished 13th in the 1962 50 cc TT (the first such event). It was ridden by Horace 'Crasher' Crowder. Another Kreidler enthusiast of the time was Terry Keen.

On the Grand Prix racing trail in 1963 the machinery

Works racer modified for record breaking, November 1964.

improved still further. The engines now delivered 12 bhp. Once more Anscheidt was Kreidler's number one, with wins in Spain, France and Finland. But again, it was not enough to contain the strength of the ever mightier Japanese works teams. Anscheidt and Kreidler fought right down to the final GP. But Suzuki and Hugh Anderson won the day and with it the second world championship.

Determined for better things in 1964 Kreidler spared nothing and built an almost totally new machine. The underslung horizontal engine had been subjected to a considerable amount of development during the winter months. It now sported a cylinder barrel and head with more copious finning, a new expansion chamber exhaust system, and an air-cooled clutch. The layout of its twelve gears had been changed so that there were six in the engine coupled to a two-speed, cable operated overdrive.

The newly designed chassis was a vast improvement on the old loop-type. It was a reversion to an underslung arrangement which held the new 100 mph, 12.5 bhp engine under a lattice work of tubing. Up front, a pair of 30 mm leading-axle telescopic forks replaced the previous Earles-type. Narrow and extremely light, the new Renn Florett and Anscheidt were ready to do battle with the Japanese – or so the Stuttgarters thought.

The first Grand Prix of the season was the US, at Daytona. Here, Suzuki's latest weapon, the rear exhaust RM64, outsped everyone, Kreidler included, to take the first three places. Anscheidt was fourth, with new team-mate Frenchman Beltoise fifth.

Although Anscheidt won in Spain, this was his only Grand Prix win that season. At the season's end, Anderson had again taken the title, with late-starting Ralph Bryans on a Honda second, and Anscheidt in third.

At the London Earls Court Show, in November 1964, Hans Motors displayed various versions of the Florett. Cheapest was the standard model at £136 15s 11d, while at the top end the Super now cost £166 6s 3d.

The snag with being a tiddler ace, as Anscheidt had discovered, was that unless employed by one of the Japanese factories there was precious little racing. Even including practice sessions there was little time in the saddle. To ease this problem Kreidler's star rider had found a way to put in more track hours by racing a 125 Bultaco during 1963 and 64.

However, for the 1965 season he went one better by squeezing a 125 air-cooled rotary valve MZ engine into a spare Kreidler chassis. The frame used was of the full loop type used in 1963 before the factory returned to underslung engine mounting, but the forks and wheels were from a 1964 machine. The most fantastic aspect of this hybrid is that even with a fairing and larger section tyres, it only weighed 147 lbs including a gallon of fuel.

There were several alterations to the 50 cc Kreidler power unit for the 1965 World Championships, though basically it still remained a horizontal single with two rotary discs. But there was the adoption of positive lubrication to the crankshaft by a pump drawing oil

from a reservoir under the fuel tank. Secondary compression was up to 20:1 and peak power was a claimed 14 bhp at 14,000 rpm.

Transmission modifications included a strengthened clutch, and gear clusters giving 12 or 18 speeds. These were now alternative six- and nine-speed main clusters (foot operated) and a two-speed, hand-operated overdrive. As *Motor Cycle* stated at the time; 'There must be a job going for a genius who can appreciably broaden the power band!'

Then at Hockenheim on Sunday 11 April 1965, riding one of the earlier machines with a specially-tuned engine producing 15 bhp at 14,000 rpm, Anscheidt broke the world 50, 75 and 100 cc standing start kilometre records with a speed of 68.88 mph. The record-breaking machine weighed 101 lb. To save weight, the front brake plate complete with brake shoes was removed, leaving only the rear stopper operable.

But on the Grand Prix trail it was a dismal year for Kreidler and Anscheidt. Their best placing all year was in the final round staged at Suzuka in Japan, when Anscheidt took fourth place. Even at Barcelona the German rider could only finish fifth. Following these less

Anscheidt flat out around Abbey Curve at Silverstone during 1965 Hutchinson 100.

Supercharged 49 cc streamliner ridden by Rudolf Kunz at Bonneville salt flats in autumn 1965.

than satisfactory results, Anscheidt left Kreidler and signed up with the Japanese Suzuki team for the 1966 season. Straight away he proved the value of this decision by becoming World Champion.

Anscheidt's move had been brought about by the presence in the 1965 title race of such machines as the twin cylinder water-cooled RK65 Suzuki, whose 32.5 × 30 mm engine gave 15 bhp at 16,500 rpm. And even this was not enough to win that year. The title went to Ulsterman Ralph Bryans and Honda's jewel-like twin cylinder RC114. Its 33 × 29 mm dohc engine developed 15 bhp at 20,000 rpm.

With its air-cooled single Kreidler had no hope of meeting the Japanese on equal terms. But what most upset Anscheidt was that over two years previously the Stuttgart factory had designed a racing 50 cc twin but then not built it because of disagreement at boardroom level. This centred around the apparent conflict of racing twins and marketing singles. A powerful grouping of the company's directors could not reconcile themselves to what was demanded by the logic of the situation.

The view of the racing team, and Anscheidt in particular, was that this was ridiculous. And as 1965 was to prove, had that engine been built it could have led the class, or at least given Kreidler's riders an equal chance against the Japanese twins.

A final blow came when the non-racing rival Zündapp factory team arrived at Monza, Italy in May 1965 and snatched away Kreidler's world speed records. This promoted a renewed bid to regain lost prestige by planning a supercharged fifty to contest the 50 cc world standing and flying start records.

The Spring Congress of the FIM in Moscow that year agreed to recognise standing quarter records from 31 May 1965 onwards. At the same time the mile was reinstated as a record distance for both the standing and flying starts, after a lapse of nearly nine years.

Kreidler meant to take full advantage of this and a team from the factory left for the Bonneville Salt Flats, Utah, USA in early October. The rider chosen for the attempts was Rudolf Kunz. He established the first world record for the standing start quarter mile. Using a specially prepared streamliner he clocked a mean time of 19.586 seconds, which gave an average of 45.96 mph.

Kunz also took the standing start mile record with a mean time of 53.506 seconds or 67.28 mph. He handsomely beat Massimo Pasolini's 1956 Aermacchi average of 51.5 mph. However, the flying mile record of 122 mph by Hermann Müller with a fully enclosed Baumm-NSU in the same year was beyond the Kreidler's reach.

Another bonus for Kreidler's pride, and perhaps more important for its future, was the continuing success of the standard production models. These still continued to sell well. The top export market was now Holland, which was to prove a significant factor in the future of the marque.

A *four* cylinder Kreidler made its racing debut in 1965. However, this was not a factory effort, but an extremely workmanlike device created by the German constructor, Karl Reese. Reese had taken four standard production Kreidler alloy cylinders and barrels, fitted oversize 40 mm pistons, built up a crankshaft and cast a light alloy crankcase. Presto! A 208 cc four cylinder racing engine which Reese called the KRD.

In reality, things were not quite that simple. Reese had started work on his special way back in 1959. But the result of his six years' work was well rewarded. The

Karl Reese built this 208 cc Kreidler four about 1965.

KRD was an equal to contemporary race-kitted Honda twins and Ducati singles. The KRD had its first race outing at a Junior meeting at Hockenheim in September 1965 where it was ridden by Koichi Shimado, a Japanese living in Hamburg.

As well as the other changes, the cylinder heads had been modified to give a compression ratio of 11:1. Carburation was by four Bing instruments operated by a transverse shaft with a single throttle cable. Fuel feed was from two remotely mounted float chambers. Battery ignition was used, with one coil for each cylinder, and the battery was mounted at the rear of the main downtube above the swinging arm.

The KRD's power unit produced 26 bhp at 10,800 rpm, although its builder was confident that the safe limit was in fact considerably higher at 12,500 rpm. A four-speed gear cluster was carried in a bolted on housing at the rear of the crankcase. The primary drive was by gear, and there was an exposed, air-cooled, dry clutch. The home-made frame had twin front downtubes and was fitted with front forks from a Horex. The front brake was also Horex, and the wheels carried 3.00 × 18 front and 3.25 × 18 rear racing tyres mounted on alloy rims.

In 1966, being without Anscheidt, Kreidler limited their racing effort. At the West German GP at Hockenheim Otto Dittrich was fifth and Dutchman Cees Van Dongen sixth. Later at Monza, the Italian rider Roth came home sixth. A growing Dutch influence on

Factory race kit transformed humble roadster into a 9.5 bhp flyer capable of over 80 mph.

the Kreidler racing effort was apparent by 1967. Alt Toersen of the Netherlands gained fifth places in both Holland and Belgium against strong opposition.

A race kit for the new five-speed Florett was launched in September 1967. It contained head, barrel, gaskets, piston, Dell'Orto SS1 25D racing carb with remote float chamber, 13 and 14 tooth gearbox sprockets, an expansion chamber exhaust system and various smaller items including racing sparking plug, cables and brackets. Together these transformed the humble roadster engine into a 9.5 bhp flyer. Testing for the its development was completed at Hockenheim by Ernst Degner, formerly world champion with Suzuki. Degner had suffered from a bad fall during the Japanese Grand Prix in 1963 while riding one of the infamous 250 Suzuki square fours. He had been seriously burned. Degner never really found his form again, and had officially retired at the end of the 1965 season.

Anscheidt, Kreidler's former team leader, had his final racing season in 1968. He went out for Suzuki as he had come in, by taking the world title. It was his third in a row. After this triumph, he spent part of 1969 on four wheels in BMW Formula Sports. Subsequently, Anscheidt devoted himself to his business at Leomberg near Stuttgart.

But 1968 was also a year which gave Kreidler

Florett sports lightweight in 1968 model year trim.

supporters something to cheer about. In the first GP of the season, the West German at the Nurburgring, Anscheidt was victorious on his Suzuki, but Kreidlers filled the next four places. There was almost a repeat performance at Assen in Holland, where in the Dutch TT Alt Toerson came third, followed by three other Kreidlers. All the machines were sponsored by the Dutch Kreidler importer, Van Veen of Amsterdam.

This was the start of a long and fruitful association between Van Veen and Kreidler. The Dutch company made a considerable impact not only on the Grand Prix scene, but also in the world of speed records. During the summer of 1968, a Van Veen/Kreidler made a 400 metre standing start run in 16.01 seconds – 2 seconds quicker than the official record then held by the Italian Minarelli company.

The record machine was one of a group originally bought from the parent Stuttgart race shop and modified for record breaking or sprinting. The remainder of the batch were used in World Championship road racing events. In charge of the Van Veen team was manager Jan Leferink. He directed that the special sprinter should be fitted with a 24 mm Bing carb and allowed to rev to over 14,000 rpm.

The rider of this special machine was Alt Toerson, and in early October he took the Van Veen/Kreidler sprinter to Elvington in North Yorkshire in an attempt on several speed records. Toerson's performances were

shattering. He took three world records, among them the standing start mile with over 9 seconds off the figures set by Rudi Kunz riding the factory Kreidler at Bonneville in 1965.

The tiny twosome won the hearts of riders, officials and spectators alike and his performances won him a coveted Chandy Trophy. Other world records gained by Toerson were the 50 cc standing start quarter mile in 15.569 seconds (57.8 mph), and the 50 cc standing start kilometre in 30.319 seconds (73.781 mph).

The first water-cooled Kreidler was introduced in 1969, although the majority of the team still used the air cooled engine. The water-cooled prototype was ridden by Jan Schurgers. He rode it that year to become Dutch champion.

The 1969 world series developed into a battle royal between Toerson – who won the first three rounds (in Spain, France and West Germany) – fellow Dutchman Paul Lodewijkx who won in Yugoslavia, Italy and Czechoslovakia. And Spaniard Angel Nieto on a Derbi was also in contention.

The title went to the fiery Spaniard. Toersen and Nieto tied on points but the judges gave priority points to Nieto despite Toersen winning more races.

But perhaps the most important event of 1969 was the decision by FIM to impose further restrictive racing regulations on the class. These permitted a maximum of six speeds, one cylinder and a minimum machine weight of 60 kg. This not only provided firms like Kreidler with more chance of success at an inter-manufacturer level of competition, but the new rules also helped the chances of the privateer.

Kreidler introduced a series of cash prizes for privateer riders for the 1969 season. These covered not only the World Championship and German national championship events, but junior racing and even events behind the 'curtain' in East Germany.

At the Belgian Grand Prix a most interesting entry appeared in the list for the 125 class. This was the Belgian rider Francois Moisson's V-twin Kreidler. A 45-year-old shoe shop owner with a preference for specials, Moisson had started with a standard five-speed Kreidler, plus another engine and, after cutting off the gearbox, bolted the rest into the frame above the first unit. The engines were also tuned using parts from the Florett factory approved race kit.

Van Veen supported Dutch rider Alt Toerson who took three world records at Elvington, Yorkshire, in October 1968.

Moisson connected the two engines with a large helical gear which meshed with others on the two crankshafts. The coupling gears were housed in a light alloy case made by the constructor. Unfortunately, the connecting gear stripped teeth in practice and the machine was a non-starter. The V-twin was ridden several times before development was finally abandoned, and while it kept going, the Kreidler special proved faster than both the Bultaco and Honda production racers of the period.

A turning point for Kreidler in Britain also occurred in 1969, when Roy Baldwin motorcycles of Rochester, Kent imported a simple piston-ported, Mohr tuned production-based Florett 'moped' engine. Anton Mohr was based at Koblenz, and he built a formidable reputation amongst his knowledgeable customers.

With the high numbers of Kreidler roadsters sold over the years, Mohr had no shortage of work. Whereas the factory Florett 'race kit' produced 9.5 bhp, Mohr, using road components could coax up to 14 bhp from his tuning. And it was one of these units that Roy Baldwin put to such good use.

In 1970 Toerson left for the rival Jamathi team. Jan Huberts took over as Van Veen/Kreidler team manager. Rudi Kunz now raced a Kreidler prepared in Stuttgart. He gained some excellent results. Kunz finished in the top ten at every one of the ten rounds in the series. Even though Henk Van Kessel came third overall, and Jan De Vries came fifth, Kreidler machinery only won one round, the Italian GP at Monza. So, in 1970 the Championship again went to Nieto and Derbi.

Gold medal presented to Kreidler owners who had ridden their Floretts for over 100,000 kilometers.

Local rider Francois Moisson appeared in the 1969 Belgian GP with 100 cc Kreidler twin 125 race.

Meanwhile, on the standard production front, Kreidler remained faithful to the long-running Florett-based design. The 1971 model range consisted of two automatic two-speed, step-thru commuter models and three Floretts – the standard, TM and RS. The latter was the top-of-the-line sports model, which in standard trim turned out 6.25 bhp at 8500 rpm, had five speeds and a maximum speed 56.25 mph. It was available in either orange and chrome or red and chrome. The 100,000th model produced for sale in Holland came down the line in 1971, and the Netherlands remained the principal export market.

The strength of the Dutch interest was underlined by the Van Veen team building a brand new Kreidler 50 cc Grand Prix racer for 1971. Developed by West German two-stroke wizard Jorg Moller, the machine had a new frame and sported a revised water-cooled motor that could produce 17.5 bhp.

So dramatic was this advance in development, that the metallic green flyer caught champions Angel Nieto and the Spanish Derbi factory completely flat-footed. Jan de Vries, the likeable, diminutive Dutchman, and Kreidler with five GP wins snatched the 1971 World title from Derbi's grasp. Finally the Stuttgart factory's name was engraved on the World Championship trophy.

Amongst the riders drafted into the Van Veen team mid-season were Britain's Barry Sheene and the Flying Finn, Jarno Saarinen. Sheene won in Czechoslovakia and was fourth in Sweden, Saarinen sixth at Monza.

Kreidler's roadster range swelled in 1972 by the introduction of the Florett LF and LH three-speed tourers, plus the four-speed RM. All these were very much economy models. Besides the sofer engine tune, fewer gears and less chrome plate, they had 120 mm brakes in place of the larger 160 mm stoppers on the TM and RS.

On the 1972 Grand Prix circuit, De Vries and Nieto went neck-and-neck with three wins each. The Dutch Van Veen/Kreidler star winning at Nurburgring, Imola and Anderstorp. Ultimately the title was decided by the two riders' times for the total race distance in Germany, Italy, Holland, Belgium and Spain. Nieto's time came out at 2 hours 27 minutes 26.29 seconds and De Vries' 2 hours 27 minutes 47.61 seconds. No other world title has seen a closer finish, not even the Toerson/Nieto encounter of 1969. Derbi's final Grand Prix year was 1972, but many would like to have seen a Kreidler victory, if only because this was not a true factory effort, but a very well-organised private team.

By 1972, increasing numbers of race-kitted Kreidlers

Left **By 1970 race development had been taken over by Van Veen, Kreidler's importer in the Netherlands, Jan Schurgers is pictured at the 1970 Ulster Grand Prix.**

were finding their way onto British circuits. It was only the ex-works Jamathi and a few other bikes which prevented a total Kreidler whitewash. I can well remember from personal experience just how competitive were these 'tuned' Kreidlers. During the 1972 50 cc Enduro 4 hour race at Lydden Hill, Kent, on the 27 May, I was sixth on the first non-Kreidler home. I was riding a Honda in my last competitive race.

However, in 1973 Terry Keen intensified the race for 50 cc power by bringing over a Kreidler with a Van Veen cylinder which developed 16 bhp. From this point onwards, very few other marques even scented victory. But with this thrust for even more power came in a most unwelcome side effect – unreliability. Revving to over 16000 rpm the tiny machines were now expensive to run for a privateer. In Britain this meant that, in contrast to the £150 Roy Baldwin had paid for his new five-speed Mohr tuned piston-ported engine, it was now common to be asked of £25 for a piston, and £150 for a cylinder. These components often needed replacement every half dozen races. But if you wanted to stay up front you had to swallow hard and pay what was demanded.

On the world scene, without the Derbi team, Kreidler only had Jamathi as a serious rival in 1973. At the season's end Kreidler won not only the Championship but also had its riders in all but one of the top six places. Even at the first round in Hockenheim, although Kreidler factory did not win, eight of the top ten berths went to the marque. A star of the future, Henk Van Kessel first showed his potential by taking second place and leading all the other Kreidler riders home. Jan

The 100,000th Kreidler for the Netherlands came off the end of the production line in 1971.

Works Van Veen racer developed 17.5 bhp at 16,000 rpm. The 26 mm Bing carburettor was reliable, and with a dry weight of only 126 lb the machine could reach 125 mph.

Huberts, Bruno Kneubuhler and another champion of the future, Stefan Dörflinger all rode Kreider that year. By the end of the season, De Vries, with no Nieto or Derbi in contention, easily won the title. He scored five victories (Italy, Yugoslavia, Belgium, Sweden and Spain) in the seven-round series.

In 1974 Van Kessel, who had made fifth place in the 1973 world series, grabbed the crown at last. The road to fame, if not fortune, had been a tough one for him, and a much longer one than the World Championship story would suggest. In his native Netherlands, Van Kessel had been at the top in 50 cc racing for some considerable time but the top laurels had eluded him no matter how hard he rode.

Contrary to popular belief, his world championship bike was not backed by Van Veen, but was a stock Van Veen/Kreidler production racer, tuned by two-stroke expert, Dutchman Jorg Moller. It was reputed to produce 21 bhp (measured at the crankshaft) at 14,000 rpm. And at the 1974 Belgium GP, Van Kessel's machine was timed at 125.5 mph on the quickest part of the Francorchamps circuit. Apart from Moller's tuning, there was nothing special about the Kessel machine, which featured Marzocchi suspension, a spine frame and Fontana brakes.

Van Kessel competed in all ten rounds scoring six wins, two seconds, one retirement and was a non-starter at the Nurburgring. The highlight was no doubt at Francorchamps where he broke the lap record formerly held by Jan De Vries. He raised the average lap speed from 100.74 mph to 101.07 mph.

All top six riders in the 1974 Championship were Kreidler-mounted. This run of Kreidler success was all too much for former tiddler king Angel Nieto, with the result that in a bid to get his championship back, the Spaniard joined the Kreidler camp for the 1975 season. He made the right choice too, taking the title with wins

Right **A pair of magnificent racing Kreidlers that were sponsored and prepared by Van Veen.**

at six out of the eight rounds staged that year.

Nieto chose Kreidler for the simple reason that at the time it was the best machine. In view of this the governing Spanish motorcycle authority allowed Nieto to ride a foreign machine. This was exceptional. At the time Spain's race-ruling body would not usually allow a Spanish rider to ride anything other than a Spanish bike.

Kreidler Concessionaires of Ferndown, Dorset was appointed in 1974. It was headed by Cliff Holden, who had previously backed Ossa UK.

At the Amsterdam Show in 1975, a highly interesting machine appeared. This was the superbly-made three cylinder PDS Kreidler 150. It featured a neatly crafted frame in which the engine formed part of the stressed members, being 'hung' from the twin front down tubes and which were braced near the steering head. At the rear a massive central tube then took a shortcut forward and upwards to the steering head in addition to its power unit carrying duties. It also had a three-into-one exhaust, three carbs, electronic ignition, 17 inch wheels, full-width drum brakes, clip-on handlebars and stainless steel mudguards.

But this unique machine remained a prototype. Kreidler management would not budge from its established 50 cc formula for production models.

Conditions were not so rigid in respect of the race track. By the mid-1970s, development of the 125 mph Kreidler had more than paid off. The water-cooled rotary-disc induction power unit relentlessly found more power and at the same time improved torque figures. Even 0.1 bhp could often be the difference between first and second places for the combatants on a race circuit.

However, there was another competitive machine in the 1975 series. This was the lone Italian Piovaticci ridden by Eugenio Lazzarini. This had shown its potential with several top placings throughout the season, including a win at Anderstorp in Sweden. But Piovaticci ran into financial trouble and its race team was sold to Bultaco in Spain. Nieto played a leading role in the marriage. Nieto then quit Kreidler and rode for Bultaco, with the result that in 1976 Nieto won yet another Championship. However, this time he was mounted on a Piovaticci which had been further improved and now sported Bultaco tank decals. Bultaco and Nieto retained the title in 1977 and Ricardo Tormo took it again for Bultaco in 1978. But Kreidler came back to win in 1979 with Lazzarini taking the championship. The game of 50 cc racing musical chairs was now complete.

The 1977 production range again concentrated on

A 1974 roadster brochure highlights Jan de Vries and his World Championship victories.

Superbly engineered PDS 150 cc three-cylinder Kreidler special was on display at 1975 Amsterdam Show.

the Florett. It was considerably updated, with the RS-GS now in a striking green and chrome finish and sporting electronic ignition, cast alloy wheels, 208 mm disc front brake, plus a matching electronic speedo and tacho. Standard equipment included a choice of low or high handlebars, front crashbar, rear carrier, fully-enclosed rear chain, direction indicators dual racing-style saddle, large 160 mm headlamp and five-speed gearbox.

Former World Champion Henk Van Kessel and a new Dutch team headed by Piet Plompen make a successful attempt on the 50 cc land speed record in 1977. The record attempt had originally been planned for the early morning of 6 September when the weather conditions were close to ideal. But much to everyone's annoyance the electronic timekeeping at the Apeldoorn, Holland location failed and the team was forced into hours of frustrating delay.

In the late afternoon of the same day everything was finally ready, but again the attempt was postponed. This time strong winds were the problem. Finally, at 7 o'clock in the evening, 12 hours after the scheduled run, Dr Helmut Bonsch, FIM delegate at the record attempt gave Van Kessel official permission to practice.

The streamliner, called Black Arrow, averaged a speed of 132.31 mph over the flying kilometre with the wind straight on the nose. Then turning to collect a tail wind, Black Arrow shot through the timing lights at 136.89 mph – a mean average of 134.6 mph, and a new world record captured by accident.

Next morning the team had another try. At 8.30 am they made the first attempt. The target was the outright speed record held by Rudolf Kunz at 139.5 mph. This had been set 12 years before in 1965 at Bonneville Salt Flats in the USA, by the specially prepared factory-backed machine described earlier.

Even though 'steering was nearly impossible' as he said later, Van Kessel and the Black Arrow went out and set a new world 50 cc speed record of 141.7 mph. A mean speed of 137.38 mph ensured a new flying kilometre record into the bargain.

These record attempts were not the brainchild of Van Kessel, but the initiative of Piet Plompen. At the time, Plompen was running a team of Kreidler racers but with no help from the Dutch Kreidler importer, Van Veen.

Plompen constructed the Black Arrow in his Rotterdam garage with assistance from Leo de Ridder and Andre de Grave. Because of his skill and knowledge of Kreidlers, Van Kessel, the former road racing champion, had been asked to pilot the projectile.

Surprisingly, the team used no wind tunnel facilities

for the streamlining, but received some aerodynamic advice from engineers in the Royal Netherlands Air Force. 'The influence of the streamlining was tremendous' reported Van Kessel afterwards, and he went on to add, 'Without streamlining the machine would only pull fourth gear, but it really went like an arrow with the complete streamlining, including the tail and the shield above my back and head fitted'.

The record breaker was fitted with a rear wheel sprocket that had slightly fewer teeth than the highest gearing Van Kessel had ever fitted at Francorchamps. And still the rev counter rocketed past the red line at 16000 rpm. The engine was tuned by Plompen, and the carburation was set up by the rider. The team ran the Black Arrow on normal petroil mix and power output was estimated at between 20 and 21 bhp – estimated because no bench testing was carried out.

The engine was slung under a monocoque light alloy frame made up of a cage of light tubes. The streamlining was constructed of glass fibre. Fully fuelled and with water, the machine weighed only 138 lb.

Meanwhile, Van Veen had formed a branch in Germany called Kreidler-Van Veen Sport GmbH at Duderstadt. Initially it concentrated upon limited production of the Van Veen 50 cc production racer. This was a supposed replica of the team's latest GP hardware. The company claimed 19 bhp at 16000 rpm, but in reality its power output was 16.5 bhp. Other details included water-cooled head and barrel, dry

Dutch 'Black Arrow' Kreidler-powered streamliner ridden by Henk Van Kessel and tuned by Piet Plompen averaged a speed of 134.6 mph for the flying kilometre in 1977.

clutch, six speeds, space-frame, cast alloy wheels, 2.00 × 18 front and 2.25 × 18 rear tyres and 210 mm front and 190 mm rear drilled discs with Scarab calipers. The machine was supplied complete with fairing, paddock stand and spares kit.

At the Cologne Motor Cycle Show in September 1978 Van Veen Sport displayed the Geländesport, which had a tuned roadster engine that was claimed to produce 12 bhp. A full range of off-road clothes was also unveiled. Except for the engine the newcomer owed nothing to the standard production Kreidler flyweights. Although blessed with superb looks, *Which Bike?* made the following observation in its show report issue; 'Naturally there were a host of small capacity machines on show for the first time at Cologne, many of them obvious gimmicks designed exclusively to attract the stares of a gullible public. Not the least of these was a space-framed 50 cc Kreidler Geländesport enduro . . . one big rock and your engine goes for a burton!'

The Geländesport, now called the GS50, was updated in 1980 with the addition of a pukka enduro headlamp surround and number plate unit, revised rear mudguard, side panels and seat. The exhaust system (now a garish orange/yellow) had been changed for what appeared to be a more restrictive TUV-approved type. Formerly the exhaust had been almost a racing-type expansion chamber in black. With these changes came a change to the claimed power output. It was more soberly stated to be 8 bhp at 10000 rpm – with a 10:1 compression ratio and classic Kreidler 40 × 39.7 mm bore and stroke measurements.

In its standard form the machine was supplied with five-gear box. At an extra cost a customer could specify

Left **Van Veen Sports company, based in Germany, offered GS50 Geländesport enduro 1978–1981.**

a six-speed cluster as part of a performance package which also featured a new cylinder/piston, head, carb, selection of jets and sprockets, and unrestricted exhaust system. Van Veen Sport claimed 14 bhp at 13800 rpm for a GS50 fitted with this kit.

The general specification of the GS50 enduro (in standard form) included 28 mm Bing carb, Motoplat electronic ignition, Betor 30 mm front forks, Grimeca conical brake hubs, (120 mm diameter at the front and 116 mm rear) and Akront alloy wheel rims, with 2.50 × 21 front and 3.00 × 18 Metzeler Enduro-Cross tyres. Dry weight was 158.4 lb.

Another product of the Van Veen Sport team was

the KVV schoolboy motocrosser. It used the GS motor in a smaller chassis.

In early 1981 the GS50 was offered for sale in Britain for £925 by CK Consultants (Plastics) Ltd of Hertford. This company's managing director was British 50 cc racing enthusiast Mike Cook.

Back in the world championship road racing arena Kreidler's 1979 champion Lazzarini had defected to the tiny Iprem team, but by winning the first two rounds in 1980 and then finishing in the other four rounds with two seconds and two thirds, he became Champion again. However, Stefan Dörflinger with two victories at the final GPs of the season established himself as the leading Kreidler runner. Dörflinger took second place in the series.

Tormo and Bultaco came back to take the title in 1981, but Dorflinger was out for half the season. But he

Below left **By 1982 Kreidler was in financial difficulties but was still able to produce the 80 Mustang trail bike.**

Below **World Champion Stefan Dörflinger leading the Dutch TT, Assen, June 1982 on Krauser sponsored Kreidler.**

did win the first round at Hockenheim, followed by three second places in the next three rounds.

Dörflinger came back into the fray with a vengeance in 1981. Now sponsored by Michael Krauser, the leading German accessory manufacturer, he took his Krauser/Kreidler (still tuned by Van Veen) to a well-deserved world title. Dörflinger was victorious in Spain, Italy and Holland, with second place in the other three events that contributed towards the Championship that year.

Although Kreidler still featured strongly on racing score sheets the situation on the commercial front in 1981 was a depressing contrast. Sales had plummeted to an all-time low, and in a last-ditch effort the factory introduced a whole string of new models during 1981 and 1982. These models included the 24 mph three-speed Sport-Mofa-Flott (Fast Sport Moped). It had a tubular spine frame, bolted-up Honda Comstar-type wheels and the familiar horizontal engine with revised square engine castings. There was also a range of 80 cc (actually 79.8 cc from 46 × 48 mm) lightweight motorcycles, the Florett 80, 80E and 80L, and the Mustang 80 trail bike. All these shared the same engine with vertical cylinder which delivered 8.5 bhp at 6000 rpm.

The Florett 80L (Luxus), although attractive and well-made, failed like the other new models to save the company. An attempt was made with a concept machine called the Joker (surely an inappropriate name). Essentially it was a styling exercise by Target Design. This is the company which created the Suzuki's Katana. However, the Joker project did not progress beyond the prototype stage. Kreidler finally went into liquidation in the summer of 1982.

The sad end of the once-proud market leader of the 1960s was even more bitter when it is considered that unlike the majority of German motorcycle manufacturers who had not seen out the 1950s, Kreidler had not only weathered this storm, but gone on to dominate the market (at least in terms of production figures) in the following decade. Even in the 1970s Kreidler had quietly maintained a leading brand position.

Perhaps, in retrospect, if the company had put more into research and development of its standard production models during the boom years it might well have survived the sales depression which confronted European motorcycle manufacturers in the early 1980s. But by the time it launched its new models it was already too late.

Even after its death the factory was credited with more success in the World Championship. Dörflinger retained his title in 1983.

Although it was now called a Krauser, the machine was essentially pure Kreidler. If Dörflinger's victory is taken into consideration, Kreidler actually won more world 50 cc road racing championships than any other marque in the history of the sport. Today, these seven World Championships are probably how Kreidler is remembered best. But it also deserves wider recognition for its 30 year record as one of the world's major producers of quality lightweight machines for the masses.

Maico

Maico is acknowledged as one of the most famous in the field of off-road motorcycle sport. But it was also once almost as well-respected for its range of often highly original roadsters, scooters and cars.

The marque's history can be traced to 1926 and the formation of Ulrich Maisch & Co in Poltringen, near Stuttgart. But it was not until 1931 that the Maico story had its first real two-wheel connection. It was then the two young sons of the founder began building bicycles in a small workshop at the rear of the factory. They bought-in some parts but welded their own frames.

The success of the bicycle venture led the two brothers, Otto and Wilhelm Maisch, to think about manufacturing powered two-wheel transport. In 1933 they adopted Maico as a marque name by forming a natural contraction of Maisch & Co. From its inception to its end, the Maisch family was always committed to the company.

Maico's first real motorcycle was built in 1935 and designated MP 120. It was a neat looking lightweight using a 118 cc Ilo single cylinder two-stroke power unit. The MP 120 was soon to be followed by several other similar machines, including the popular 143 cc Konsul.

All Maico motorcycles prior to 1939 used Ilo engines but that year, the company introduced the Maico-Sachsonette. It was an autocycle with a 50 cc Sachs engine.

The encouraging sales of the various models produced in the 1930s allowed the brothers not only to expand into new and larger purpose-built premises at nearby Pfaffingen, but also to lay down plans for a new machine incorporating their own ideas. These included the first engine to be designed and built by Maico.

Production was scheduled for 1940, however, by that time Maico was sucked into the war effort. It concentrated upon manufacturing aircraft parts for the Luftwaffe. Maico motorcycles were not needed by the military because BMW, DKW and Zündapp provided machines for the German armed services.

As was so often the case with companies working on military contracts, production was impossible beyond the end of the war. To add to Maico's misfortunes, the factory was almost totally dismantled by Allied occupation forces. Moreover, manufacture of aircraft parts was banned by the French military authorities who controlled the zone around Pfaffingen.

The decision was quickly taken to restart production of motorcycles at a factory about 8 miles away in Herrenburg. Herrenburg was in the American sector. Not only were the controls less strict, but there was a real possibility of purchasing much-needed machine tools and new materials.

The brothers bought secondhand machinery, some of which was then transferred back to Pfaffingen.

There was plenty of local labour available, which helped overcome the great difficulties facing the enterprise when it relaunched in 1947. And with hard work and energy, a year later the company's first postwar machine was not only in production, but being offered for sale. This was the M125, which at last fulfilled the Maisch brothers' dream of an all-Maico motorcycle.

At the heart of the newcomer was a 123 cc (52 × 58 mm) piston-ported single cylinder two-stroke with three speeds, unit-construction and vertically split crankcases. The 5.5 bhp power output at 5200 rpm gave a maximum speed of 48.5 mph. Like many of its competitors in a Germany trying to rebuild itself after the war, the M125 was essentially a cheap, basic form of transport.

Even so, it managed to include undamped telescopic front forks, plunger rear suspension, twin chrome-plated exhaust pipes and a battery in its specification. When it went on sale the price of 951 Deutschmarks

Early M150 single at 1950 Frankfurt Show.

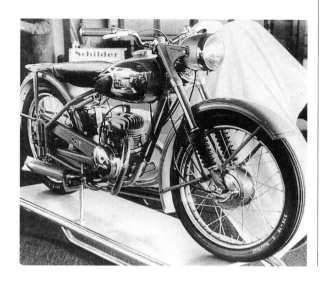

was comparable with many other post-war German 125s. But the majority of the other motorcycles still had girder forks and a rigid frames. In contrast, the Maico with its teles and plunger suspension offered an almost de luxe ride.

Success of this first all-Maico machine meant that a larger model was introduced in early 1949. This was the M150 and its quick development was no more than the smaller machine bored out to take a 57 mm piston and give a capacity of 148 cc. Otherwise it was totally unchanged.

Later, a more innovative design was commissioned. Launched as a prototype at the Reulingen show in June 1950, the Mobil, or Maico-Mobil as it came to be called, was one of the stranger devices created by the post-war German two wheel industry. Looking like an overgrown scooter, it featured truly cavernous bodywork accommodating the engine assembly, a spare wheel and enough room for a considerable amount of luggage. At the front was an equally massive built-in fairing and screen. But scooter it was not, for beneath its bodywork, the Mobil was virtually a fully-enclosed motorcycle, with a full duplex frame and telescopic forks.

Maico was aware of the image it created and in one sales brochure clearly stated it to be; 'not a scooter but a motorcycle with a body giving a high degree of protection against the weather.' The company saw the Mobil as 'The Auto on Two Wheels' and claimed that it was quite possible to travel 300 miles a day without any strain on the rider. It was certainly true that when complete with screen the Mobil allowed an owner to ride in very bad weather conditions wearing only light clothing.

The potential of 300 miles in one day falls into perspective when it is realised that the power unit was a conventional, aircooled 148 cc two-stroke single. This was a development of the twin-port engine used in the M150 motorcycle but with a three-speed, hand operated gearchange. The engine was mounted so that it almost sat on the swinging arm, which pivoted on a pair of coil springs mounted in a similar position to the monoshock unit found on one of the latest hi-tech Japanese race-replicas of today.

Power output was a claimed 6.5 bhp at 4800 rpm (the same as the M150 motorcycle), but with a dry weight of around 275 lb this was simply not enough for a serious touring machine. But the Mobil had been envisaged as such. By the time it entered production in 1951, the Mobil had a larger power unit. Again a single cylinder two-stroke was used, but now fan-cooled, and with new bore and stroke measurements of 61 × 59.5 mm adding up to a capacity of 174 cc. With a single port iron cylinder and alloy head it developed 9 bhp at 5300 rpm.

Air for the forced-draught cooling was drawn around the cowled cylinder by a multi-bladed cast alloy fan. It was driven by rubber V-belt from a pulley on an extension of the left hand end of the crankshaft. In unit with the engine, the three-speed hand operated gearbox had internal ratios of 3.3, 1.9, 1.34 and 1:1. The final drive chain was partially enclosed in a pressed steel cover. As before, the whole assembly pivoted on the swinging arm sub-frame.

Car-type interchangeable alloy wheels were 14 inches in diameter with 3 inch section tyres were bolted into alloy hubs incorporating 130 mm brakes. Other standard refinements included trafficators mounted on the outer section of the front fairing panels. Both fairing and trafficators were of alloy construction.

When *Motor Cycling* tested an example of the Maico Mobil they were particularly impressed with its weather protection, commenting; 'A 115 mile journey was undertaken at the outset, and on arrival at the destination the rider had only superficial water splashes (it had been raining continuously) on the shoulders and head. A pedestrian walking 400 yards would have suffered more'. Maximum speed was found to be almost 60 mph, a noticeable improvement over the earlier prototype. And pulling power was definitely improved, although as *Motor Cycling* discovered, 'it was desirable to drop to third when climbing long main road hills'.

At the time of the test (December 1953), the Maico Mobil was not officially imported into Britain. A single example was brought over especially for E. O. 'Blackie' Blacknell, who was the proprietor of the well-known Nottingham sidecar manufacturing company.

The next real milestone in the company's history came in late 1951 when the 1952 model line was announced. This included the M151 (an improved version of the M150) and the all-new M175. The latter model used an engine based on that of the latest Mobil. The M175 shared with it the same engine dimensions, but had an additional 1 bhp and foot pedal gearchange. Unlike later versions of the same design, the original 175 motorcycle used undamped front telescopic forks and plunger rear suspension. Full production began during the spring of 1952.

Almost immediately the model gained a considerable amount of success, not only in sales to the roadgoing motorcyclist, but also in sporing events. It was the machine that won the first of many gold medals for the factory in the tough world of the long distance trials.

Maico's involvement in this sport had grown from modest beginnings. It is often observed that not too many designers believe in taking the personal risk of putting their theories to practical test, but Maico technician Ulrich Pohl had made a single entry in the *Konstrukteur* (manufacturers team) for the 1951 ISDT. But the fame of the 175 Maico spread so rapidly that by the summer of 1952, the German Federation announced that works-prepared machines would represent their country in that year's ISDT. It was staged in Austria.

Maico chief designer and rider of some enthusiasm, Ulrich Pohl (right) with team mate Karl Westphal after the 1953 ADAC Three Day Trial. The motorcycle is a factory supported ISDT machine.

Tubingen. This factory was responsible for frame fabrication, painting and assembly. During his visit, Holliday tested several of the company's machines. He had a spin on the new M200. He reported that the model handled well, and he was especially taken by the excellent suspension front and rear, the comfortable dual seat, the smoothness of the oversquare two-stroke 'power egg' and the positive short travel of the gear lever. Brakes too were of 'above average efficiency', and the maximum speed was 63 mph from 11 bhp at 5000 rpm.

Also in 1953 globe-trotting Dutch journalist Wim Dussel covered 50,000 miles on a heavily-laden 175 Maico-Mobil.

As the 1953 ISDT in Czechoslovakia had shown, not only were the latest 175 cc machines beautifully designed and built, but they were also reliable. Maico provided three machines for the official German effort (Pohl and Westphal in the Trophy, Aukthun in the Vase). In addition, Maico had for the first time entered a manufacturer's team with the same trio as riders. Both Trophy entrants were among eight 175 cc Maico riders to gain a gold medal that year. Unfortunately, Vase team man Aukthun was forced out on the fifth day after being unable to restart at a check point.

October 1953 was dominated for Maico by the second of Germany's monster exhibitions for two wheels. Staged at the giant Fair and Exhibition centre in Frankfurt there were 387 stands in eight halls. It was even bigger than the original 1950 event.

The most startlingly unorthodox of all the new models on display was, as *Motor Cycle* stated; 'The fantastically sleek 350 cc Maico Taifun (Typhoon)'. A 400 cc version was also displayed, and as the magazine reported, Maico had gone from strength-to-strength since its introduction of new models and ISDT successes.

But the new Taifun roadster far overshadowed all the marque's previous achievements. The parallel-twin 348 cc (61 × 59.5 mm) two-stroke engine itself was a fairly conventional unit with twin (later changed to single for production machines) 26 mm Bing carburettors concealed within the rear frame pressing. But the transmission was by helical gear drive to a four-speed gearbox in unit with a unique free-wheel device (dropped on production machines) and an automatic clutch. A highly innovative feature of the Taifun design was the duplex rear drive chain. It was housed in a totally enclosed cast aluminium oil bath chaincase, which acted as the left side of the swinging arm. As the gearbox sprocket was in-line with the swinging arm pivot, chain tension was constant.

As a result, when the Trophy team was announced in August, it was found that, contrary to many popular opinion, Germany was not relying upon BMW flat twins, but 175 Maicos and ohv NSU Foxes. Pohl joined Hans Danger to make up the Maico part of the official Trophy team that year.

Germany managed only fifth place in the Trophy league. It was not the fault of the Maico pair. Both gained golds, but the poor showing of the NSU trio held the team back. Of the six 175 Maicos to start, all achieved gold. A truly remarkable result for a factory new to the rigours of the world's toughest dirt bike test. This particular success was the foundation stone of Maico's later off-road achievements.

The 125 and 150 models disappeared at the end of 1952. New roadsters, the Fanal (Signal) – a more highly tuned M175 with 9.2 bhp at 5300 rpm – and the M200 were introduced in 1953. The latter was obviously the most interesting, featuring not only a larger 197 cc (65 × 59.5 mm) four-speed engine. But, for the first time on any Maico motorcycle (if you discount the Mobil), there was a full swinging arm rear suspension and oil damped front forks.

In the summer of 1953, *Motor Cycling's* assistant editor Bob Holliday went on a vacation to Germany. While he was there he paid a visit to the Maico plants at Herrenburg, which was devoted solely to the manufacture of engines, and to the other at Pfaffingen-

Changes to the bore size for the 400 cc version gave it a capacity of 394 cc (65 × 59.6 mm). It was more oversquare than the smaller twin. Performance was claimed to be quicker by 3 mph than the 350's 78 mph and with the bonus of improved torque.

The Taifun's frame design, ingenious though it was, had the added advantage of being utterly simple. From the steering head, a single front down tube picked up the front of the streamlined crankcase casting to which it was secured by four Allen screws. The rear end of the top frame mated with a large light alloy casting which blended into the lines of a deep, inverted U-shaped steel pressing which extended rearwards to form the rear mudguard, tool box and dual seat mounting. Line blended into line, giving a supremely clean external image. The 16-litre tank had chrome plated sides and rubber knee grips. Both exhaust pipes were joined by a common expansion box which was situated below the crankcase, but recessed into it so that an unbroken line resulted. The expansion box was later dropped on production machines. Pillion footrests, when not in use, fitted snugly into recesses provided for them in the rear frame pressings.

An orthodox telescopic front fork was fitted to the prototype displayed at Frankfurt. But all production models used a specially designed Earles-type fork, which was so cleverly camouflaged by a deep-section mudguard and light alloy fairings that it could have almost passed as a shortened pair of teles. The rear suspension had twin springs on each side, set inside the comprehensive rear mudguard. An external lever allowed selection of either single or double springs. Maico claimed that the layout was cheaper than combined units. Large-diameter, 200 mm full-width alloy brake drums carried 18 inch wheel rims with 3.50 section tyres. Dry weight was lighter than expected at 322 lbs, because of the relatively wide use of alloys in construction.

Riding impressions of the Taifun generally reported

Detail of Taifun rear suspension.

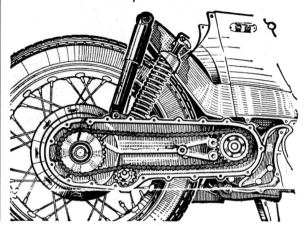

that it was very smooth with superb handling and a comfortable ride. Indeed, it was well above the normal early 1950s standards. This applied both with and without a passenger. Acceleration was excellent when driven hard, but the engine needed to be revved to get the most out of it because there was not as much low down torque as expected. Possibly this was due to small crankshaft flywheels and oversquare engine dimensions. The gearbox was slightly notchy engaging first, but from then on, other gears selected smoothly. There was a pronounced whine in intermediates, but very quiet cruising in top. More noise at tickover was attributed to the straight-cut spur gears with overlarge teeth. However, the final reduction within the gearbox enabled a small diameter rear wheel sprocket to be used.

The French magazine *Motocycles* tested a 400 Taifun in July 1955 around the Montlhery circuit. An average speed for one lap was made at 84 mph prone, whilst upright the figure dropped to 78 mph. Overall fuel consumption including the speed testing averaged 60 mpg.

Besides the Taifun, the only other really notable exhibit on the Maico stand at Frankfurt was a version of the Mobil with a radio fitted to the dashboard. There were, however, a whole family of variations of the popular 175 and 200 singles – the M175S, M175T, Passat 175, M200S and M200T, which replaced the M175, Fanal and M200. These went on sale early in 1954. The Mobil was given a power boost for 1954 with the 200 cc four-speed foot change engine, and went over from alloy to steel pressings for the wheels, inside dash and wrap-over centre section.

For Maico, 1954 was a good year. Indeed, the whole German motorcycle industry was revitalised. Sales were the best ever. In the sporting world, the factory again provided machines for the ISDT in Wales that September and once more gained a whole string of golds. But not for Pohl, who on the third day was in collision with a local motorcyclist on a narrow secondary road. The unfortunate Pohl broke a wrist and went to hospital. Germany was virtually out of the running for the Trophy because of his accident.

Shortly afterwards on 17 October, Maico factory rider Kurt Wustenhagen won the 250 German motocross championship at Dusseldorf. And January 1955 heralded the debut of two new models which made full use of the technical development work which had gone into the German championship bike.

The first, surprisingly, was a totally new Maico, the Maicoletta scooter. The Brussels Show report in *Motor Cycle* dated 20 January 1955 mentioned that its 247 cc fan cooled engine was similar to 'one of the Maico motorcycles'. In fact, what this really meant was that the new roadster used a detuned version of the motocross engine.

The other machine was the Blizzard 250, styled on

Maico Mobil – motorcycle handling with scooter protection.

the lines of the 175 Supersport, and like this machine it was available in two versions. The first came with telescopic front forks and later the Earles-type. More oddly, it was also available with either right hand exhaust (S/1) or left hand exhaust (S/11). With a power output of 14.5 bhp at 5050 rpm, the Blizzard was very much the touring partner for the smaller 175 Super Sport. But it was capable of a genuine 70 mph maximum.

Both the Blizzard and Maicoletta scooter (in 250 form) shared a very similar engine specification that included a bore and stroke of 67 × 70 mm. But while the motorcycle followed earlier Maico practices, the

Taifun (Typhoon) twin cylinder 'stroker with many unusual features was produced in 350 and 400 cc versions.

new Maicoletta certainly did not. It combined the comfort and weather protection of scooter panelling with the performance of a motorcycle. It soon won a strong following and maintained it for several years. Later in 1955, the model was offered in both 250 cc and 175 cc versions.

Even more progress was made in off-road sport that year, although the factory suffered a serious setback when Dieter Haas was killed. Only 17, Haas won 31 races for Maico during the 1955 season. Many felt he could have been a World Champion had he survived his crash that occurred during a motocross heat at Leichlingen.

But for the first time during this period Maico began to notice – the first signs of the mid-1950's depression in two-wheel sales. To offset this, and to join the growing trend for four wheels, the company bought out the ailing Champion car factory in June 1955. A new four wheeler in Maico livery made its bow at the Frankfurt Automobile show that September.

Powered by a 400 cc Heinkel watercooled two-stroke twin, it was very much a straight reproduction of the Champion-designed original. Maico had done little more than some simple badge engineering. Relatively

Maico acquired the ailing Champion car company in 1955. Now badged as a Maico, the little cycle-car continued to be manufactured until late into 1957.

large numbers (around 6000) of a successor model, the MC 500/4, with a 500 cc version of the Heinkel engine were manufactured by Maico before production was halted in December 1957. There was also a very limited run of an estate car version. Maico's final fling with four wheels came with the 500 Sport Coupe. Only four were actually produced.

Financially, the car making business was not a success. Rather than helping, as vehicle assembly had for BMW and NSU, at Maico the car side was just an extra drain on vital capital.

Meanwhile, Maico two wheelers were first exported to Britain during August 1956. Maico Distributors (GB) Ltd was established at 23 Astwood Mews, Courtfield Road, London, SW7. The first model landed was the Mobil, now with 197 cc engine and costing £198. It was followed a month later by the 247 cc Maicoletta.

One of the scooters was soon taken on a road impressions run by *Motor Cycling*.

Tester John Griffiths was truly impressed. On every single point, save operation of the centre stand, the test machine was praised lavishly. Eye appeal, quality, handling, performances, braking were all of the highest order. And certainly this was one scooter which really seemed to have benefitted positively from its motorcycle parentage.

But it was the final paragaph in which Griffiths managed to highlight just what an impact the machine

An example of the limited run of 354 cc machines built in 1965. Mostly used for ISDT and similar events.

had caused while in his care; 'Riding the Maicoletta was almost an embarrassment. On numerous occasions motorcyclists – particularly those of the enthusiastic clubman type – surprised by its turn of speed, came up alongside for a second look. And at a standstill it proved a magnet to all kinds of people, attracted by its unusually good looks and pleasing finish of light blue and grey with red trimming'.

Across the other side of the Atlantic ocean the Maico name was thrust forcefully into a large number of homes across North America. Full page advertising appeared during 1956. It was part of the strategy of Whizzer International Inc of 350 South Sanford Street, Ponitiac, Michigan. As American importers, Whizzer offered Americans the M200S, Maicoletta, Blizzard scrambler and 400 Taifun. Other companies superseded Whizzer, but it was the Ponitiac go-getters who established the marque in the USA.

In Europe, at the same time, the motorcycling press was running headlines of which the following is typical: 'The International Six Day Trial – Germany wins the Trophy on 175 cc and 250 cc Two-strokes'. Together with a trio of 175 DKWs, Maico made up the balance of the victorious Trophy-team. It mounted the first successful challenge by Germany since 1935. Then the Germans had won on home soil at Oberstdorf. With no marks lost in 1956, the Germans were clear winners.

Czechoslovakia, the host nation, was second with 29 marks lost, Britain was third with 329 and Austria was a lowly fourth 1147 marks adrift.

Not only did the pair of Trophy riders, Deike and Von Zitzewitz, gain golds, but so did another two competitors – one on a 150 and the other 175 mounted. Others, riding privately entered Maicos gained a silver and two bronze awards. But there were casualties. Two Maico privateers were non-starters and one was forced to retire.

After the Trophy result all the other problems of poor sales and tight financial restrictions were forgotten for a short while by the German industry as a whole. But while others foundered, Maico introduced two new models. At the Frankfurt Show in 1956 were a moped, and a tuned version of the 175 roadster, the M175 Supersport.

The new 175 was a prototype to test public reaction and its engine used much of the technology embodied in the successful ISDT machines. With 15.5 bhp available it was the most powerful German machine in its class. It entered production in early 1957 and became one of the company's most popular roadster motorcycles over the next few years. It had sparkling performance, 75 mph was within its reach, good handling plus a high level of reliability.

Meanwhile, in December 1956 both versions of the Taifun were imported into Britain for the first time. A 350 sold for £281 6s and the 400 at £291 8s. Also, to special order, enthusiasts could buy a genuine motocross Scrambler model. However it is worth noting that only about forty 400 Typhoons (as they were known in Britain and the USA) were actually imported, and the smaller twin's sales were even more modest.

Although Germany hosted the 1956 ISDT in Bavaria it was unable to match the previous year's outstanding result. In the Trophy team von Zitzewtiz and Wellahofer rode 250 machines based upon the Maico Blizzard roadster. Ernst Deike competed on a Maico 175. In support were two manufacturers' teams. In all, ten golds and one bronze were balanced by two retirements.

Throughout 1957 sales continued to fall. Even so Maico, together with Zündapp, again provided machines for the German effort to regain the International Trophy award which they had lost to the Czechs in the 1956 ISDT. Arguably, the 1957 ISDT at Spindleruv Mlyn, Czechoslovakia was the toughest ever. However, the German team, with consistent and carefully calculated riding, survived the week without losing a single mark. This exemplary performance compared well with the second placed Czech team with 700, Italy with 1613 and Russia in fourth spot with 2,208 marks lost. Three Maicos were part of this outstanding German team – Aukthun (175), Kamper (250) and von Zitzewitz with a new 277 model.

Although never used on a production motorcycle, the 277 cc capacity engine was available on the Maicoletta scooter from autumn 1957. A 4 mm increase in bore size to 71 × 70 mm was the only difference from the unit which powered the 250 (and smaller 175) version. All three Maicolettas had long-skirt pistons. They were also all fitted with electric starters, rather than kickstarters as on the motorcycles.

When the 1958 model range was announced by the British importers in October 1957, it was largely an unchanged line-up. However, the Maicoletta was offered in both 248 and 277 cc engine sizes, while the Mobil, 400 version of the Typhoon and the Scrambler remained as before.

In Germany and export markets the latest version of the 175, 250 Blizzard and 175 Maicoletta were widely sold. Even so, by mid-1958 Maico was under severe financial pressure. In July the German press widely reported that Maico had been forced to suspend payment to its creditors. However, this crisis was averted, due mainly to the sales performance of Maico's off-road machinery and popular Maicoletta scooter. Improved manufacturing efficiency also made its contribution. Simultaneously, the model range was reviewed, with the result that the remaining 400

Typhoon was discontinued. It had become too expensive to manufacture for the small numbers sold.

The factory was fast becoming feared in Continental Europe for motocross. There was a series of race victories that only the Czech Jawa and British Greeves could challenge in the 250 category. The introduction of the European Championship in 1957 gave the class a new importance, and Maico responded by taking the new title in its first year with works rider Fritz Betzelbacher. The whole story of the Maico motocross effort is outside the scope of this title. In any case, it could justify a book to itself due to the company's long involvement with the sport. Maico is still continuing with motocross today. It is enough to say that without motocross sales it is unlikely that Maico would have survived into the 1960s.

One major event which helped them on the way was the 1958 ISDT. Garmisch-Partenkirchen, Bavaria, was the German choice as a base. Again, Maico provided three of the six machines for the German ISDT Trophy team. The same three riders as before were selected, but Kamper switched to 175, Aukthun took a 250 and von Zitzewitz retained his 277 berth. The German national team seemed likely to carry off another flawless win but were robbed by the retirement of Zündapp-mounted Richard Hessler. The Germans had to be content with third spot and a total of 38 marks lost.

When the British Maico importers announced the model line in November 1958 it appeared that at long last the Blizzard was available. Its price was £199 12s. Top of the line, the 277 Maicoletta was now £247 0s 1d. Others in the range were the 247 Maicoletta, Mobil and Scrambler.

At the end of the year on 22 and 23 December, in appalling weather conditions – rain, hail, sleet, cloudbursts and particularly poor visibility, for thick mist covered Snaefell from the Guthrie Memorial to Creg-ny-Baa – a 247 cc Maicoletta was put through torture on the Isle of Man TT Circuit. It successfully completed its twin missions – continuously lapping for a distance of 1000 miles and carrying on the ordeal for a full 24-hours.

Co-riders in the venture were both former Manx Grand Prix competitors. Maico GB's northern representative David Gallagher was joined by Harold Rowell, the IoM's Maico agent. Exploratory tests had taken place a week prior to the attempt. On Sunday, 21 December, Gallagher flew over to the Island and decided to set off on the Maicoletta at noon on the following day. After contending with the vile conditions and the winter cold, at the end of the 24-hours the Maicoletta had covered 1062 miles (over 28 laps of the circuit) at an average of 44.26 mph. A fastest lap of 44

Rotary valve MD125 Sport made its exhibition bow at the Cologne Show, September 1966.

min 0.6 sec (51.45 mph) was a creditable performance when account is taken that the weather was appalling and that unlike race periods the roads were open to normal traffic.

Over the years it was the Maicoletta above all Maico's other roadsters which won the most praise from the press and others alike. It was also, unusually, liked by both motorcyclists and scooterists. This was no doubt due to its superior handling which gave none of the normal skittish cornering antics of the conventional scooter. Imperceptibly the Maicoletta became surrounded by an aura of respect which was almost uncanny. Owners of other scooters made envious comments, while riders even of large capacity motorcycles took the machine seriously. Everyone appreciated its air of quality. Added to this was its sporting success, for example, a Maicoletta 277 won the very first scooter race staged in Britain. It was at the Crystal Palace circuit in 1961 that John Gamble stood atop the podium for Maico.

By the end of 1959 seven separate models were being offered by Maico GB; the 247 Maicoletta in standard or de luxe trim, a 277 de luxe version, the 197 Mobil, 247 Blizzard in standard and Supersport versions and the 247 Moto Cross.

Production versions of the 247 cc Geländesport ISDT model were marketed by 1960, under the prefix GS 250, while works versions still continued to give excellent results for the German national team.

It was an award of a substantial military contract which ensured the marque's recovery. The order for specially converted models caused 10,000 to be built. The German armed services started taking delivery of the M250-M in 1961.

During 1961 sales of the roadsters dropped drastically and most of the model range was discontinued. Only the two versions of the Maicoletta were still offered in Britain. In the same year Maico GB became a concessionaire for Honda. It was the success of the oriental newcomers, rather than anything which originated in Germany, which the British company increasingly relied upon for profits. By the end of 1962 Maico GB had ceased importing Maicos. Ironically, it was not long before the rate of expansion meant that Honda established its own import dealership and this resulted in the commercial death of the original British importer.

Back in Germany, production of the Maicoletta and Blizzard models continued. In 1962 they were joined by the Maicolino, an ultra-lightweight motorcycle with the choice of either an Ilo 49 cc or Sachs 47 cc engine unit. Both with three-speed gearboxes; the Ilo was foot-operated, and the Sachs by twistgrip. Both featured kickstarters rather than moped-style pedals and were mounted in a neat spine frame. In appearance they were not dissimilar to the works Kreidler racers of the period. Telescopic oil damped forks with 90 mm of travel, combined with oil-damped rear suspension units, ensured a comfortable ride. Flat, narrow handlebars, together with an Italian-style 11-litre tank

and dualseat gave the tiny Maico an undeniably sporting line. However, against competition from similar machines from Kreidler, Hercules and Zündapp, the Maicolino failed to sell in large numbers.

It was then that management decided that brand-new machinery was needed for the 50 and 125 cc classes. Not coincidentally this was the only buoyant part of the German motorcycling scene. The results of this policy were the MD 50 and MD 125, both featuring a totally new rotary valve, five-speed unit-construction engine. By the end of 1963 they were ready to enter production. The Maico stable now contained the Maicoletta available only in 248 cc form, Blizzard, M250/B, ISDT replica GS 250/360s and the pure dirt bike racing motocross MC 250/360s.

The smaller MD had a capacity of 49 cc (38 × 44 mm) with a compression ratio of 10:1 and an alloy cylinder, with reborable cast iron liner, 19 mm Bing carb, giving up to 5.5 bhp at 7500 rpm. The larger unit featured square engine dimensions of 54 × 54 mm, giving 123.5 cc. On the same compression ratio, alloy cylinder and 22 mm carb, 11 bhp at 7200 rpm was available and providing a speed of almost 70 mph – compared with around 56 mph for the smaller machine.

Both shared many common parts, including the duplex frame and 13.5-litre tank, but obviously such items as forks and brakes were different. The brakes on both models were full-width polished alloy hubs built into 16 inch alloy rims bought-in from the Italian Grimeca, 125 mm (MD50) or 136 mm (MD125) front and rear. Forks also came from Italy, as did the 130 mm Aprilia headlamp common to both models. Mudguards on the larger model were polished stainless steel, painted steel on the '50'. A choice of flat or wider, braced handlebars was available.

In 1964 the Blizzard was renamed the Super Sport, but was otherwise little changed. By early 1965 rumours were circulating that the long running Maicoletta had been taken out of production, but the British magazine

Amor Special, a 125 race tuned roadster by Anton Mohr may well have given Maico the inspiration to produce the 125RS racer in the winter of 1967/68.

Scooter World for August that year was able to confirm that its journalists had recently seen the Maicoletta assembly line still functioning.

An unsuspected reason for Maico's survival was revealed by Maico's export manager Hans Kresen. He stated that at the time, two wheel production occupied approximately 25 per cent of Maico's capacity. So, how was the company sustained? Quite unexpectedly, one of the main lines was a special watering can for thirsty pigs, together with double feeding containers. Maico also made farm machinery, including agricultural loaders which could be powered either by a small motor, or coupled to a tractor. Another section of the factory made disc brakes under sub-contract for Volkswagen.

But to return to motorcycles. Although it is generally known that Maico roadsters were imported in significant numbers to North America in the late 1950s and the dirt bikes sold even better in a later period there was a parallel business. Another roadster (the MD125 five-speed) was offered in 1966 for sale in the USA by Gray International of 4461 West Jefferson Avenue, Detroit, Michigan.

Also during that year the GS range of enduro bikes was increased to four models – 175, 250, 350 and 360. Except for minor modifications, additional lighting equipment and a large chainguard, the GS models by then were virtually the same as the motocross dirt racers. The smallest pumped out 16 bhp at 6200 rpm, the 250 gave 25 bhp at the same revs, the 350 (actually 345 cc – 77 × 74 mm) 28 bhp at 5800 rpm and finally the 360 (354 cc – 77 × 76 mm) 29 bhp at 6000 rpm. A full range of sprockets was available so an owner could gear the machine of his or her choice. Gearbox sprockets ranged from 13 to 17 teeth, rear wheel from 46 to 65 teeth.

By this time, Ing Pohl who had designed the Blizzard engine had left Maico to join BMW.

Although Maico did not provide machinery for the official German ISDT team that year, 1966 saw the American Silver Vase contenders entered on Maicos. Sweden provided the venue for the event held from 30 August to 4 September. The team was composed of Bud Ekins, his brother Dave Ekins, Charlie Hockey, and Jack Chrivman. Originally the Americans had chosen to ride Triumph twins, however, the American Maico importer arranged for the factory to supply two 350s and two 360s to the start line.

The team was additionally sponsored by CBS Television. A unit was sent to Sweden to make a half hour colour film of their progress. The footage was shown on CBS' *Wide World of Sport* programme. Seven Maico riders gained gold medals that year, but none were American. At the last moment the US riders had changed once again, this time to a variety of machinery including Zündapp and Husqvarna.

At the IFMA biennial show at Cologne in September

1966, the only really noteworthy addition was the MD 125 Sport. Its tuned engine now had claimed 14 bhp at 6900 rpm. This had a larger, 15-litre fuel tank which was totally chrome-plated and direction indicators at the end of the handlebars.

The model was to form the basis for Maico's entry into road racing. The notion was first suggested by the Amor Special, a private project developed by Anton Mohr (a leading two-stroke tuner of the era), during the winter of 1967/68. This very neat little bike used the bottom end of the five-speed engine, but with a special heavily finned alloy cylinder and head, housed in the duplex frame and front forks of the roadster. Other special parts were an Oldani two-leading shoe racing front brake and an exhaust system which exited at the rear of the barrel and had a massive high level expansion chamber running down the nearside of the machine. Details included a long, slim fibreglass tank and suede-covered racing seat, 18 inch Dunlop triangular tyres and Girling rear suspension units. The Amor special was claimed to be good for over 110 mph.

In autumn 1968 the factory announced its own version, the 125 RS production racer. This was similar to the Amor machine, but had a forward-facing exhaust port, low slung expansion chamber, Ceriani forks and Maico's own front brake. The 124 cc engine shared the same square dimensions of the roadster, but now gave a claimed 21 bhp at 11,000 rpm, using a 32 mm Bing carburettor. The gearbox had six ratios – 1st: 3.07, 2nd: 2.35, 3rd: 1.85, 4th: 1.59, 5th: 1.41 and 6th: 1.32. Complete with fairing the 150 lb flyer was capable of over 115 mph.

Prior to the racer being announced the factory began

Maico's 1969 version of the 125RS production racer was competitive even at a Grand Prix level.

offering a more highly-tuned version of the MD125 Sport. It was designated the Super Sport with 14.5 bhp being available at 7200 rpm. It used a 26 mm Bing carb and 10:1 compression ratio. Except for a more rounded 15-litre tank (still chrome plated) a partially black exhaust system, low handlebars (not clip-ons) and enclosed rear units it was unchanged from the earlier model. Finish was black and red.

From this machine was developed the GS125 enduro that replaced the 175 model when it was dropped. Another change was that the Pohl Blizzard-type engine had been replaced that year by a new radial-finned assembly used for motocross machines and the two larger surviving 250 and 360 GS models. These competition engines were the work of new development engineer Gunther Schier. Unlike the road racer, the GS125 used only five gears while the GS250/360 four.

The majority of the off-road exports by this time went to the giant American market. A decade long boom in US off-road sport was just beginning.

In Britain during 1969 a major row erupted between the Bolton, Lancs dealer Tom Jones, Maico's importer since 1965 and Peter Bennett, another dealer. Bennett had opened a Maico sales business at Crawley, Sussex importing Maico motocross and roadster machines. The storm ended with a court hearing at the factory's headquarters at Tubingen. Jones failed in his bid to retain exclusive British import rights and Bennett was allowed to continue landing the machines.

In reality, however, nobody gained. Bennett was restricted in the number of machines he could bring in – threatening that if necessary 'I shall go to Belgium to get machines from the importer there.' Jones felt extremely unhappy after four years hard work establishing the marque in a depressed market. And Maico eventually lost when both men decided shortly afterwards to cease handling the company's products.

Eventually Doug Hacking of Bolton purchased the remaining spares when Jones decided to pull out at the end of 1969. This was shortly after Bennett had finally decided to pursue other interests. Early in 1970 former motocross star Bryan (Badger) Goss became the new importer but concentrated almost exclusively on the dirt bikes.

More happily, the factory gained much needed publicity when the Swedish rider Kent Anderson scored an impressive second place at the opening classic of the new season. Jarama was that year's setting for the Spanish Grand Prix and the event was the official racing debut of the 1969 RS125. The same rider then went on to finish second at the Dutch TT, and fourth in Belgium. These results were good enough to enable the Swede, and Maico, to gain fourth spot in the World Championship table.

But even better was to follow. For 1970 Maico signed up another Swedish rider Borge Jansson to contest the World series. He was teamed with the German rider Gruber.

The first round was on home soil, over the twists and turns of the Nurburgring. Gruber was fourth. Then at the next round, the French GP staged at Le Mans, Jansson proved his ability by scorching to a superb second place behind winner Dieter Braun on a works Suzuki twin. Gruber finished fourth in France, then came the Yugoslavian GP at Opatija, where Jansson finished fourth again.

Next came the Isle of Man TT. Jansson had a skillful ride and came home second behind Braun. But at the Dutch TT Gruber was fifth, and Jansson slipped back to sixth. However, the following weekend, the Swede made amends by reversing positions with Gruber. The Maico pair finished third and fourth. Another third was gained by Jansson at the Sachsenring in East Germany, and a fifth at Brno, Czechoslavakia. At Monza in Italy and Imatra in Finland the Maico team leader failed to score. But at the final round in Spain, Jansson rode the race of his life to finish third, one place ahead of Braun, in a race won by local hero Angel Nieto on a Derbi twin, from Suzuki star Barry Sheene.

Dieter Braun emerged at the season's end as the 1970 125 cc World Champion. In the 1971 season he began a new association with Maico by taking a fourth place at the Austrian GP over the Salzburgring on a factory machine. Another newcomer to the team was fellow German Georg Bender who came fifth in Austria. Maico's trio was completed by Jansson's membership.

English rider Chas Mortimer pilots his 125RS during the Czech Grand Prix at Brno, July 1971.

Also receiving limited support was the 1970 team man Gruber.

In the West German GP at Hockenheim that year, Gruber came fourth, Bender fifth. And in the Isle of Man, Jansson was his runner up again. English privateer Carl Ward on a production RS125 came sixth. Jansson and Braun fought back hard at Assen, where in the Dutch TT they finished third and fourth respectively, with Gruber sixth. Even better results came in Belgium. Bender scored his best-ever Grand Prix result, second behind race winner Barry Sheene on a Suzuki. Braun was third.

Jansson put up another excellent showing in East Germany, where at the Sachsenring he came third. This time he was behind Nieto and Sheene, but ahead of fourth place man Braun. Confirming his challenge for a top placing in the world ratings, Jansson then put up a terrific fight to keep both Sheene and Kawasaki team leader Dave Simmonds at bay to finish second behind Angel Nieto's flying Derbi in the Czech GP at Brno. At Anderstorp for the Swedish GP, Jansson again turned in a top class performance with another second, this time behind Sheene, but beating Anderson (now Yamaha mounted) Braun, Simmonds and Gruber.

In Finland Sheene again won, but this time the second place was taken by Braun, with Bender third. Jansson was well up in the early stages but was forced to retire. Only two rounds then remained, Italy and

Spain. The first of these was at Monza, where the surprise winner was the Italian Gilberto Parlotti on a Morbidelli, with Nieto second, then Sheene, followed by Jansson. At the last round at Jarama, the only Maico to finish in the top ten was Bender in seventh. The final placings in the 1971 championship race showed Jansson again in third spot behind now champion Nieto, and Sheene. Maico team-mate Braun was fourth.

In 1972, it was Jansson who gave the Maico factory its first Grand Prix victory when he won the 125 race at the East German GP. He won again at Brno, Czechoslovakia. Even though he was also second in the Dutch TT, but at the year's end he was only fourth in the Championship. In 1973 he was fourth again. This was the year he won the Swedish GP in front of a partisan crowd. It was Maico's last classic victory, except for a hollow win by the local rider Reitmaier at the 1974 West German GP. This was achieved almost by default, because most of the leading riders boycotted the event at the Nurburgring. The international stars claimed

safety measures were inadequate. Of the nine finishers all but one were Maico mounted.

The last top ten placings for Maico came in 1976. The German rider Walter Koschine was second at the Nurburgring. Other noteworthy Maico riders of that year were the Swiss rider Tschannen, Kinnunen of Finland and the Frenchman Cecchini.

By this time, many of the RS125s were watercooled. A conversion which was achieved by machining the fins off the head and barrel and fitting a cast alloy sleeve, various plumbing pipes and a radiator. Even today the sight of one of these Maico-based machines in the 125 cc class at German club meetings is not unusual.

However, besides the mass of 125 singles there was another Grand Prix racing Maico. It was a narrow angle 250 V-twin 'stroker ridden by Dieter Braun. Although it was called the SMC, this machine used many Maico components. It was conceived during the winter of 1971/72 by three other Germans, Alfous Sender, Josef Franz Schlogl and Anton Mang. From the start the SMC was watercooled and although fast never achieved the level of reliability required for a serious stab at GP honours. It was a frequent retirer during the 1972 season, and never finished a single Grand Prix.

Braun in action on amazing 250 cc water-cooled V-twin at the Austrian Grand Prix, 14 May 1972.

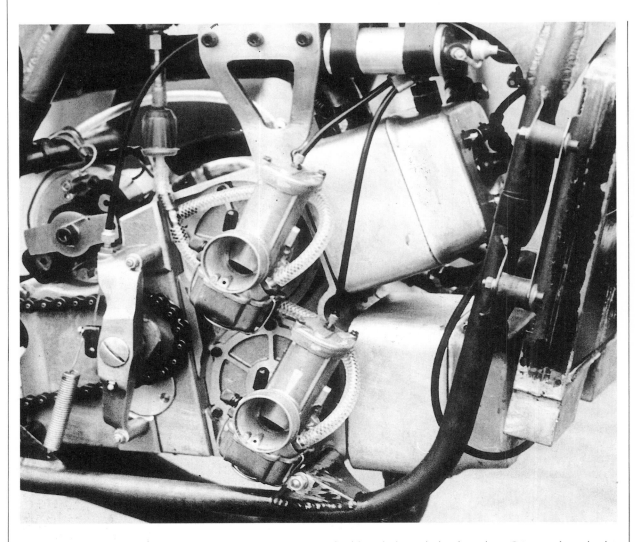

Narrow angle, Maico-based, V-twin 250 cc racing engine built by three enthusiasts for Dieter Braun, winter 1971/72.

Eventually tiring of the project, Braun purchased his own private Yamaha and it was with one of the Japanese twins that he became 250 World Champion in 1973. His racing career came to an end at the Nurburgring in August 1976, when he was involved in a serious accident after which his doctors advised against competing again.

The early 1970s saw Maico strengthen its position as a major force in off-road sport with enduro and motocross machinery in 125, 250, 350, 400 and 440 capacities.

For roadsters, 1971 had seen the introduction of a new 245 cc (76 × 54 mm) rotary valve six-speed single. At first styled very much as a larger version of the 50/125 rotary valve single, the MD250 gave way in 1974 to a completely revised version with many Italian cycle parts. These included 32 mm Marzocchi forks, 180 mm

double sided, single-leading shoe Grimeca front brake and 160 mm single sided single leading shoe rear, plus CEV lighting equipment with direction indicators.

By 1974 the MD250 with twin silencers, 12 volt Krober ignition system, 12:1 Mahle piston and massively finned alloy cylinder barrel and radial-fin head, was delivering 27 bhp at 7800 rpm. This was sufficient for 93 mph, and its speed, combined with excellent handling from the Italian suspension and full duplex frame ensured that the MD250 was to be seen occasionally taking part in sports machine races. Fred Launchbury rode one in the 1974 Isle of Man Production TT.

The same year also saw a proper racing version appear. Developed by Rolf Minhoff, it had the official backing of Maico through chief designer Dipl Ing

Above right **MD50 of 1974 had rotary valve and developed over 5 bhp.**

Right **By 1974 MD250 incorporated many Italian cycle parts, including forks, wheels and lighting equipment.**

Schier. Mounted in a much lower frame (still a duplex design), the tuned motor gave a reputed 43 bhp and around 136 mph. Although quick for a single it was no match for the then dominant Yamaha TD 3 twins.

The factory was also successful in gaining another contract to supply military motorcycles. The latest drab green machine was the M250 Militar, which unlike the MD250 roadster, relied on the dirt-bike inspired, piston-ported 247 cc (67 × 70 mm) five-speed engine. This gave 17 bhp at 6000 rpm and breathed through a 26 mm Bing carb. Hardly the most attractive of motorcycles, the M250 was nonetheless an important asset for the company's financial health through the 1970s. Several thousand were produced for the German military services and also the police.

By the Cologne Show of 1978, the MD250 was the only remaining Maico roadster but it had received an update for the 1979 season. This was very comprehensive, for the new machine, the MD250 WK, was not only completely restyled, but the 245 cc engine unit was watercooled. Peak power output was still 27 bhp as before, but at a lower 7000 rpm. The bottom end of the engine remained much as on the air-cooled version, but with modified porting.

In appearance the MD250 WK had similar lines to the final aircooled Yamaha RD250. The roll call of major components included front and rear 260 mm discs, cast

Throughout the 1970's Maico was underwritten by a contract for thousands of military specification M250s.

wheels, a tail section in the dual seat and tilted twin silencers which looked considerably different from the earlier air-cooled MD250. Detail improvements included a change to Bosch electrics.

Motor Cycle News tested one of the water-cooled Maicos for its 1 August 1979 issue. The magazine's journalist recorded a best maximum of 94.6 mph, but

MD250 WK – only a small batch were constructed in 1983.

remarked that during the speed testing 'it was impossible to hold the bike flat out for more than a few minutes at a time because of the pain'. This 'pain' was the high level of engine vibration! At the time British importer Bryan Goss said that the factory had a new crankshaft design in the pipeline which 'subdues the vibration' and were thinking of adding a head steady.

From the start, a run of piston problems plagued the bike, but by 1983 when a more highly-tuned, fully-faired version in red and yellow was introduced this had largely been cured. But 1983 also heralded the first of the financial problems which were to cripple the company in the mid-1980s. Only a rescue package with the help of the American importer saved the marque from extinction.

Following this, no further roadsters were produced, and with the last of the military contract completed some years before, the name Maico now meant only dirt bikes – in 125, 250 and 500 capacities. Monoshock rear suspension was an innovation for Maico bikes in 1983. In Britain, following the factory's financial problems, Bryan Goss quit to become KTM con-

cessionaire, and the new importer from September 1983 was Bill Brown of Whitehaven, Cumbria.

By 1985 all the dirt bikes were water-cooled and Maico's fortunes were heavily dependent on the export markets. In November 1986 the strain proved too much and Maico hit the financial headlines again. By early 1987 all but ten of the workforce, including Wilhelm Maisch Jnr, had been dismissed.

However, contrary to rumours at the time, this was not to be the end of Maico. In April 1987 British importer Brown claimed that he had 'spent £120,000 on spares alone since the factory went bust and they are still continuing production. They have a buyer from Munich who is interested in taking over and it's likely that the factory will be moved from its present site'.

This claim became a reality in the summer of 1987 when it was disclosed that the liquidator had sold the company to Laurence Merkle. It was his intention to transfer the plant to a new location in Bavaria and restart production. Over half a century of motorcycle construction in the little town of Pfaffingen near Stuttgart came to an end with Merkle's fortunate intervention. The name Maico, however, has survived to continue the struggle – not only on the motocross circuits of the world, but as one of the very last survivors of the once-prolific German motorcycle industry.

By 1985 all Maico motorcycles were based on dirt bike principles. They normally were water-cooled and had monoshock rear suspension like this GM500 enduro.

Münch

Since the age of six, when he first rode a miniature motorcycle built for him by his father, Friedl Münch has been deeply in love with two wheels. Münch has had an exceptional career spanning many decades of the German motorcycle industry. His wide reputation is justly based on the unique NSU-based Mammoths. These extraordinary bikes were a force for two decades. But there is much more to Münch's story than the Mammoths.

Münch became interested in engineering after his war service with the Luftwaffe as a mechanic. He later developed this interest in the Horex racing department during the 1950s. Here he built 250 and 350 singles in addition to the dohc Grand Prix parallel twins. Münch might have remained with Horex had the factory not closed in 1959.

His association with Horex really started at the end of the 1940's when he prepared and tuned his own pre-war machine. Unfortunately, racing ended after an accident seriously damaged his liver and other critical organs. At this point, he turned his attention to tuning other riders' machines. His first project transformed a standard ohv single cylinder Horex Regina roadster, which had a rev limit of 5000 rpm, into a highly competitive racer with a dohc cylinder head, capable of revving to around 7000 rpm. From this outstanding start he built a flourishing reputation.

Friedl Münch's four-cylinder dohc racing engine, 1963/64.

Münch's enthusiasm led him to sponsor the up-and-coming Klaus Enders on a Norton solo and a parallel twin Horex with twin-choke Weber carbs. But the Horex was getting old and eventually Enders took the chance of racing a BMW Rennsport outfit. In 1966 Enders took his first World Championship points with a fourth place in the Isle of Man TT, and won the first of his six world titles the following year.

During the early 1960s Münch turned to the design and construction of his own racing front brake. It was widely used by many of the top international privateers. This potent equipment was fitted to both solo and sidecar machines. The commitment of the brake project to volume production signalled that Friedl Münch had taken his first step to becoming a motorcycle manufacturer.

The next pace forward was with a four cylinder 500 cc racing engine which was completed early in 1964. This dohc unit was an extremely neat piece of engineering and proved that Münch could build more than just cycle parts.

During the late summer of 1965 Münch was operating from a cramped workshop at 6361 Nieder-Florstadt, Friedburg, when he was approached by Jean Murit, a Frenchman based in Paris. Murit was an ex-sidecar racer and record-breaker on BMW machinery, who knew of Friedl Munch's engineering expertise through his German contacts. Murit wanted a motorcycle which was faster, stronger and more powerful than any machine then available from an established manufacturer. He made a simple request to Münch – 'The right bike regardless of cost.' Münch considered the options but from the beginning was aware that his major problem was the choice of power unit. Eventually, after he had dismissed many possible engines he found what he was seeking.

NSU, who had until a short time before had been a motorcycle manufacturer, had just released a new car, the Prinz 1000. This was available in two versions, the standard 1000 and the 1000 TT. Both used a 996 cc (69 × 66.6 mm) aircooled four-cylinder ohc engine, and even though it powered a four wheel vehicle, Münch realised that the NSU four owed a lot of its design techniques to the motorcycling.

It took Münch eighteen weeks to build Murit's machine, which he called the *Mammut* (Mammoth). This name had to be dropped later because it was found that it infringed a pedal cycle manufacture's copyright. This first bike used the more highly-tuned Prinz 1000 TT engine as a base. In standard trim this produced 55 bhp at 5800 rpm (against the more sedate Prinz 1000s 43 bhp at 5500 rpm). But with Münch's tuning, Murit's machine had well over 60 bhp on tap. Primary drive was by gear to a four-speed gear cluster housed in a shell cast from elektron. Elektron is a form of magnesium alloy widely used by Münch to keep weight down.

As well as the gearbox Münch also provided his own clutch, cams and high compression pistons. He also paid special attention to polishing the cylinder heads and blending in the exhaust and inlet ports. The clutch and gearbox were built up for Münch by Kurt Hurt. As a leading German specialist Hurt earned his main living making Porsche gearboxes. Electrical power was provided by a six volt 400 watt Bosch generator from a BMW 1800TT car.

The frame was a near copy of the legendary Norton Featherbed. Münch constructed the front fork and oil-bath rear drive chain casing from elektron. The brake hubs were of his own design and again they were cast in elektron, and built up with 18 inch alloy rims using 3.50 front and 4.00 rear section tyres. However, on later bikes the rear wheel design was changed for a thick-spoked car type wheel in elektron alloy. The change was made because after 500 kilometres the original rear wheel spokes on the prototype distorted.

As well as his extensive use of elektron, Münch used other light alloys wherever possible. For example, an aluminium panel provided the raw material for the hand-crafted 25-litre fuel tank. As a result, while the bare engine weighed 104 lb, the completed prototype weighed in at 433 lb dry.

The Mammoth's development was closely monitored by NSU, even though they were no longer producing motorcycles. Indeed, all the Neckarsulm top brass turned out for the Münch Mammoth's first test in late February 1966. This included NSU boss Dr Stieler von Heydekampf who told Münch 'Bring us orders from governments, and NSU builds the Mammoth'. Dr Froede, the famous NSU designer and Ewald Praxl, the former racing team manager were also present.

To record this event was arch-enthusiast and journalist Ernst Leverkus, father of the famous Elephant Rally. It was Leverkus then working for *Das Motorrad* who really told the world about the Friedl Münch creation. Almost every other motorcycle magazine reproduced the story not only because Leverkus himself had been captivated by the Mammoth, but because the world's press saw it as a supremely newsworthy story.

After insistent requests from the journalist Münch allowed him to have a test ride. Leverkus eulogised not only about the 125 mph maximum speed (confirmed at Hockenheim race circuit) but also the Münch giant's

Münch (right) and Dr Stieler von Heydekampf, director general of NSU, in early 1966 with the prototype Mammoth. It used a NSU Prinz car engine as a foundation.

ability to sit all day on the autobahn at 110 mph with a level of comfort and sheer muscle that easily surpassed any other bike in the world at that time. At the other end of the scale, the Mammoth would waffle along at 20 mph in top and then accelerate cleanly all the way through to its two-miles-a-minute maximum in a completely fuss-free manner.

The memory of the ride later prompted Leverkus to write to Münch asking if he was prepared to build more machines like Jean Murit's machine? Incidentally, the original Mammoth had cost the Frenchman 7500DM. Munch told Leverkus that he would be prepared to build more bikes. The floodgates swung open, within less than two months of the first article appearing in the press he had 18 firm orders from all over Europe and the USA.

The price was between 6–7000 DM depending upon the exact specifications. Each machine was hand-built. Initially, Münch was helped by Werner Sauter, who was four times a German champion in endurance trials and winner of ISDT Gold Medals on NSU machinery. In hindsight the customer was perhaps given too much of a choice because every early Mammoth was different.

At the IFMA Cologne Show in September 1966 Münch had a small stand to display his wares. These included his massive drum brakes and the latest Mammoth. The bike now had a new rear wheel, one piece seat and rear mudguard (again in elektron), a

Four times German enduro champion, Werner Sauter (left) with Friedl Münch and journalist Ernst Leverkus. The engine is being started for its first ever run, March 1966.

Opposite top **Friedl Münch is just visible in the background at the 1966 Cologne Show. On display is an example of the production Mammoth TT.**

massive headlight/instrument casing, side panels and various other more minor changes. The capacity was increased to 1085 cc and power to a claimed 70 bhp offering a maximum speed of almost 140 mph. But the cost had escalated to 8500 DM.

Around this time the first of Munch's several business partners appeared. This was the American publisher and millionaire, Floyd Clymer, who initially undertook the world distributorship of the Münch Mammoth. Clymer was 70 years old, but still retained a flair for business and a great passion for motorcycles.

The Los Angeles-based publisher soon discovered Münch's shortcomings as a businessman, even though he was a brilliant engineer. Without intervention from Clymer it is likely that the Münch enterprise would not have lasted very much longer. There was no management control plus too many orders. Inevitably this led to dissatisfied customers because machines failed to arrive on time. When Friedl Münch built the first bike these problems were never envisaged, simply because he could not see beyond the machine he was

building at that time. But once launched into the competitive, commercial world, business discipline was essential. And although he was never at a loss to solve a mechanical problem, however tough, Münch could not cope with the demands involved in increasing the production tempo.

Münch urgently needed someone with the ability to assume command of the commercial and financial side of the business. Quite naturally, he wanted to devote himself entirely to the engineering side. Clymer chose to visit Münch just at the right time, and as soon as he viewed the overcrowded chaos of the workshops he decided to get totally involved. Very soon Münch was able to move from his cramped stable-like premises to a brand new factory facility at Ossenheim. It opened in September 1967.

Opposite bottom **On the far left is American publisher and businessman Floyd Clymer, Münch is in the centre with engineer Egon Wegmann at Indian/Mammoth factory in 1967.**

The Mammoths remained largely unchanged except for the adoption of twin headlamp units mounted in a cast alloy housing. About 50 workers were recruited to build them, including Egon Wegmann, a former engineer with Maico. In the early stages there was another side to the factory. Four ex-Indian engineers from America along with Dick Gross, a well-known Indian tuner appeared at Ossenheim. These men were sent by Clymer to Germany to relaunch the Indian marque.

Clymer, a former Indian works rider, purchased the manufacturing rights for the Indian marque when the original factory went out of production in 1953. And now, part of the Clymer/Münch factory was tooled up for the manufacture of five Indian motorcycles a week. The output was intended for the US market. The machines were 50 bhp, 750 cc side valve V-twins with four-speed gearboxes and electric starters, housed in a frame which was very similar to the Mammoth Featherbed-type with Ceriani forks and Münch brakes. But for once Clymer had acted on sentiment, rather than commercial logic. Perhaps, at his age he thought for once he could afford the luxury to do this, but for whatever cause, the reborn Indian V-twin was a dismal failure.

During 1968 both Münch and Clymer worked long and hard on making the Münch a success. At the 1968 Cologne Show they unveiled some of their combined craft. The centrepiece was a 500 cc dohc parallel twin designed and built by Münch, which the pair hoped would be battling out the European Grand Prix circus the following season. Also on display was a sohc version which was designed to compete under the rules of the American Motorcycle Association (AMA) in national racing.

The GP parallel twin, which was not based on Münch's 1964 racing four, had a bore and stroke of 71.5 × 62 mm. Its dohc valve gear was driven by a chain which ran up the middle of the engine. There were four valves and a central spark plug for each cylinder. The crankcase was cast in magnesium, while the heads and barrels were of a new high strength ultra-lightweight aluminium alloy.

Designed in unit with the engine was a five-speed close-ratio gearbox. Underneath the crankcase was a deeply-finned wet sump which contained six pints of oil, but the gearbox and engine oil were separate – unlike the single overhead cam production engine. Primary drive was by straight cut gears, with a dry six-plate clutch.

Münch tried several types of carburettor, including Amal, Dell'Orto and Weber, with choke sizes ranging from 35 to 40 mm. The show engine, however, was fitted with Amal GPs. Test results confirmed a power output of over 60 bhp at 10,000 rpm as the ultimate target. If the engine achieved this goal, it was planned to offer it for sale to selected top international riders.

It was stated that the company was planning a thorough test programme throughout the winter months, and the complete machine was scheduled for race testing later in 1969. A twin loop cradle frame had already been designed to house the Grand Prix engine. But as a precaution, Münch was also seeking the help of established frame specialists. Among these were the British Rickman brothers, who were famed for their Metisse chassis. Brand new telescopic front forks designed by Münch had 148 cc of damping oil and a travel of 5.9 inches. The familiar Münch front stopper was to be used, together with an Italian Fontana rear brake.

The other Münch project – the sohc twin – was intended to power the bulk of a new range of Indian middleweight machines. Clymer still had a dream of seeing the old marque re-established, even though the 750 V-twin project had by now been aborted.

In many ways the sohc twin owed a debt to the Horex Imperator of the 1950s, which was an extremely modern design for its day. Münch used his knowledge of the Horex to the full. Many could say that it was really a Horex rather than a Münch. Ironically, in April 1969 a Metisse-framed prototype roadster actually had an Imperator unit fitted, with 'Horex' still proudly displayed on the clutch cover.

Münch's original plan called for the single cam production engine to be made in 450, 500, 600 and 750 cc capacities. All models of the engine were planned to be oversquare, with the 600 being typical at 76 × 60 mm. In the three smaller versions, the camshaft was driven by a chain in the same way as the racing unit and the two-piece crankshaft ran on four roller bearings – two in the centre and one on each side. The crank was splined together for ease of maintenance, but a useful side effect was that the engine firing order could either be 180 or 360 degrees. Primary drive was by helical gears, with the sump now holding 5 pints of oil for both the gearbox and engine.

The 450, 500 and 600 engines had, it was claimed, already been extensively tested. Their power outputs were 42, 50 and 56 bhp respectively.

Meanwhile, Münch was reported still to 'be busy on the 750, as the bores on this are too big to allow the camshaft drive chain to run up between the cylinders'. He intended resolving this problem by running the chain up the outside of the engine. Though this powerplant was still in the early development stages, Münch was confident it would produce around 65 bhp when finalised. All the quoted power figures were for standard production versions of the engine. It was planned to offer tuning kits to raise this significantly for

In 1969 a Münch 500 cc ohc twin based upon an earlier Horex design was mounted in a British Rickman frame. The project went no further than the prototype stage.

racing. These would include new cams, high compression pistons, and stronger valve springs.

On display at Cologne were complete machines with the Münch's parallel twin engines housed in special frames built for Münch-Indian by the Italian Italjet factory whose head was Leo Tartarini. The firm also planned to offer machines powered by the 500 Velocette single cylinder motor. A limited number of these were built. Pride of place in the display was the latest version of the Mammoth with its NSU engine now based on a 1177 cc TT Sport engine. By using heads from the latest of the NSU cars the 'lump' was reputed to develop 90 bhp.

Despite its outstanding technical promise, the whole Clymer/Münch/Indian partnership was in trouble. The problems centred on Floyd Clymer's health which deteriorated sharply and caused him to retire at the end of May 1969. It was a well-founded rumour at the time that he had sold his entire interest in the factory to an unidentified source represented by the Chase Manhattan Bank of Frankfurt.

It later transpired that the mystery backer was George Bell. This American millionaire's son was a Münch Mammoth owner. Clymer's wife had sold the shares while her husband was very ill . He died in the spring of 1970. Bell immediately reduced the price of a Mammoth by over a third from the US $4,000 which Clymer had set as the American price for the machines. In the year to April 1969, about 100 various Clymer/Münch motorcycles had been produced – and very little else, even though there had been a lot of money and time spent on various developments.

Bell also instructed Friedl Münch to increase production. Permission, however, was given to continue with the other projects including the dohc racing parallel twin. It may have appeared brisk and efficient but in reality Bell was far too interested in racing rather than the task of producing more roadsters. This was highlighted by the shock headlines on the front pages of the motorcycling press that September. Typical was *The Motor Cycle* which claimed, 'Fath-Münch Tie-Up!'

The story centred around links between Helmut Fath, 1960 and 1968 world sidecar champion, and creator of the four cylinder URS – and Friedl Münch, maker of the world's most expensive motorcycle. These two joined forces to produce racing and record-breaking machines. It was a concept born through Bell's desire to get quick results in the competition world. He saw Münch as able to build a record breaker and Fath a Grand Prix

road racer. Bell, by this time, had already written off the dohc parallel twin as not being likely to win.

In the first phase of collaboration with Bell and Münch, Fath and his partner Dr Peter Kuhn would continue to operate from their existing premises. But a brand new factory, scheduled for completion the following spring, was being built at Altenstadt near the Münch works at Ossenheim. When this was completed, all Münch and Fath interests would be concentrated there, and both men would co-operate on roadster and racing projects.

The first project was completed during the winter of 1969–70. A larger capacity version of the Mammoth was rolled out for an attack on the world one hour speed record. Mike Hailwood on a 500 MV four in 1965 had achieved around 145 miles for sixty minutes. Constructed in the short space of six weeks, the new machine was intended to net valuable publicity for the Münch roadsters. And as Bell was an American from Florida, what better place to flaunt this machine and

boost his ego than Daytona? So the Daytona Bomb was born.

The engine from a 1177 cc 1200TTS road bike was bored out to 1370 cc, and produced 125 bhp at 8600 rpm. Specially cast alloy cylinders replaced the original's cast iron ones. Drive to the camshaft was, as on the standard engine, by duplex chain up the left of the engine. The use of 13:1 pistons necessitated the use of a set of powered rollers to start the brute. Carburation was taken care of by four 35 mm Dell'Orto SS1 racing instruments, with each pair sharing a remotely fitted float chamber.

Lubrication was by a semi-dry sump system as the crank was not submerged in oil. To cope with such extra demands, a larger capacity system was employed where the oil was contained in a separate magnesium sump bolted to the underside of the engine. The flywheel was removed and which left the five-bearing crankshaft to be dynamically balanced after the primary drive pinion was fitted. This was driven by specially made helical gears on the left of the engine, which in turn, drove the standard Münch four-speed gearbox via a 12-plate dry clutch. In order to cope with the vastly greater power than the roadsters the clutch was considerably enlarged.

An additional 10 mm spark plug was provided for each cylinder. The original 14 mm plugs were activated by a Volkswagen distributor which sat at the front of the engine and was driven by a single row chain with a tensioner pulley on the right hand end of the crankshaft. The second set of spark plugs had their own distributor. It was mounted on the right hand end of the camshaft with 38 degrees advance being employed.

The frame was fitted with the Rickman heavyweight front forks of a type formerly employed on Metisse scramblers. These were the only units available at the time strong enough for the purposes for which the machine was intended. Münch's own 250 mm elektron drum brakes were fitted, with a four leading shoe pattern at the front and a twin leading shoe at the rear.

Surprisingly, in view of the earlier problems with the original Murit Münch Mammoth prototype, the rear wheel was not cast, as were the ones used on the production roadsters, but a conventional wire spoke type with an 18 inch alloy rim. However, it was not the wheels which were to prove the machine's downfall,

but tyre problems which doomed the record breaking project.

Interestingly, it was Ernst Leverkus again, who fed the news media with details of the Daytona Bomb prior to the team's arrival in the United States. Prior to leaving for the USA rider Ferdinand Kaczor said 'No rider is able to use all power of the engine!' after he had road tested the monster.

After waiting for the end of the annual Cycle Week at Daytona International Speedway in March 1970, the team (including Friedl Münch, Kaczor and Helmut Fath) were then further delayed by poor weather. Initial runs finally started in the last week of the month. When the record runs began the machine proved very fast. It rocketed through the electronic eye at 178 mph at the Daytona speed bowl. But it could not sustain this performance for more than three laps (around nine miles) before the rear tyre tread began to disintegrate. Kaczor claimed he went through premature ageing process when rubber chunks began to litter the track. Even changing tyres for other types did not solve the problem. There was nothing left to do but return to Germany and attempt to persuade tyre manufacturers to back the project by developing tyres capable of standing up to the 1400 cc Behemoth.

The 'Daytona Bomb' was built for an ill-fated record attempt in 1970. Although it was capable of tremendous speeds, the rear tyre technology of the time was not able to match the power of the engine. Riders expected most tyres to have shredded within three laps of Daytona's Speed Bowl.

The machine stayed in Florida waiting for the team to return. Unfortunately, no other record attempt was made by Münch at Daytona. For eleven years the bike was stored in a Miami warehouse. Finally a court awarded it to one of the American backers in lieu of payments owed.

The Daytona Bomb finally made a reappearance in 1981, when it was purchased by well-known American road racer John Long, and his business partner Richard Evans. Evans surprised the road racing fraternity by appearing with the machine at the 1982 Daytona Vintage Classic race. After enlisting the help of the American Honda racing team's rollers to get the monster fired up, Evans completed a handful of sedate laps. The Münch was voted the best sounding machine at Daytona that week. What a superb tone was emitted from that chamber orchestra of four giant megaphones!

Evans has since invested a considerable amount of time studying with Friedl Münch in Germany and learning about the machine. Although the engine was barely run in, Evans has had it rebuilt. This paid off with an unexpected win at the West Palm Beach raceway. This not only proved that the original project was viable, but also shows how tyre technology has improved since 1970.

Ferdinand Kaczor was one of the two-man Münch GP solo racing team that competed at Hockenheim in May 1970.

In Germany Münch, Fath and Kaczor faced other problems, as was revealed in *Motor Cycle News* on 15 April 1970 with the headline, 'No URS four!' Helmut Fath, despite an all-out effort hindered by the record attempt, had been unable to complete work on the two Munch-URS solos that 47 year old veteran Karl Hoppe and Kaczor were due to race at Le Mans. This race was intended as a warm up for the following month's West German GP. *MCN* went on to say that Fath hoped to have the new fours ready for the Austrian GP at Salzburg when they would be fitted with carburettors and not the fuel injection system originally intended.

True to his promise, 29 April saw the Münch fours in action in Austria. The race was a real test of endurance. The 20 laps (more than 50 miles) were completed in driving rain and snow. Gerhard Henkeroff on Renzo Pasolini's 1969 works Benelli four streaked into an early lead. Behind him came the Münch machines with Australian Johnny Dodds on an Italian Linto twin and New Zealander Ginger Molloy on a bored-out 350 Bultaco growling at the leaders' heels.

Dodds crept ahead of the pack until the fourth lap when Kaczor settled into the task of handling his new machine and swept by on the long home straight. He was never headed again. Dodds gradually slowed with a niggling misfire and Molloy replaced him in second spot for several laps. Behind the leaders, Hoppe played a strategic game, and overtook the works Bultaco to join his team mate with five laps to go. Fastest lap went to Kaczor at 87.68 mph.

Horst Owesle, World Sidecar Champion in 1971, was the engineering brain behind the URS Münch racing team.

In early May the West German GP was staged at Hockenheim. Here Hoppe took a solid fourth place, and on the surface all might have appeared perfect. But in reality, almost the reverse was the case.

Perhaps it was too much to expect two such gifted and self-made men to work amicably at all times. Conflict became open hostility at Hockenheim during practice. Münch insisted that Fath (who was then still an active competitor) should race the latest low-line Münch-URS sidecar outfit. However, Fath objected to this, wanting instead to use his own non-Münch machine. When Münch disagreed with him, Fath decided to quite the team altogether. Complicating matters still further, Ferdinand Kaczor moved to Fath's house at Ursenbach to race a 350 Yamaha TZ2 and a 500 BMW Rennsport prepared by Fath. Fath commented at the time, 'I think he is a very good rider but he needs more experience. I want to see how he performs on British short circuits and I hope he will be accepted for internationals at Brands Hatch and Mallory Park in the near future.

Kaczor had his last ride with the Münch team at the French GP at Le Mans two weeks later on the 17 May. Here his four seized during his second practice lap and

he was unable to race. Team-mate Hoppe held twelfth spot for much of the race, but stopped three laps from the end with engine trouble.

At Le Mans a stunning new 40 foot long Mercedes transporter which serviced the Münch racing team made its first GP appearance. Weighing 18 tons unladen, the vehicle had a workshop fitted with a lathe, milling machine and a series of machine tools, a rest room and kitchen. And this really sums up the George Bell way of doing things – if you paid enough money, you could buy success. The lavish transporter was the best ever seen in a race paddock.

The Munch-Fath quarrel had another twist. When Fath originally agreed to join the team, Bell had in effect bought out Fath's own racing team. This meant that even though Fath had not moved all his machines and equipment to the Münch factory at Ossenheim, he was no longer the owner of the remaining hardware. Not unnaturally, this resulted in more ill feeling 'I was cleared out' stated an annoyed Helmuth Fath afterwards when he was left with an empty workshop after he left the Münch organisation. 'They came with a pantechnicon and cleared out every engine I had.'

Even though Fath had left, Horst Owesle and Dr Peter Kuhn, who had both previously worked with Fath before the Münch link-up, stayed with Münch. Although the new partnership had no significant success in the 500 cc solo class once Fath left, Kuhn did develop a 750 racing four, and gained some good results on three wheels.

The 750 was publicly mooted in September 1970, but its appearance was delayed until mid-1971. The rider was Yorkshireman Tony Jefferies, then a TT winner. He was without his works Triumph following the withdrawal from racing of the BSA-Triumph Group. Jefferies tried the Münch 750 for the first time at Snetterton on Thursday 26 August, prior to racing it at Norfolk Circuit's Race of Aces international meeting the following Sunday.

Commendably light for a 750, it weighed only 350 lb. The frame was a much-modified unit from a 500 Münch-Fath GP racer, with forks and double disc brake from Paul Dunstall. Power output of the engine on the Münch test bed was 105 bhp using fuel injection. Plans to convert to carburettors caused problems. At Snetterton Jefferies retired with wet plugs.

In sidecars, Horst Owesle, Junior German national sidecar champion on 1969 on a BMW, and former Fath employee, created something of a sensation by carrying off the World sidecar crown for the Münch team in 1971. He used one of the original four cylinder engines inherited from Helmut Fath. For the first three GPs Owesle and his partner Kremer only managed one placing – fifth in the first round, the Austrian GP at Salzburg. Then Owesle teamed with the Englishman Peter Rutherford. But following this partnership of Owesle/Rutherford scored three wins in Holland,

URS Münch 750 cc solo being prepared for Tony Jefferies' ride at Snetterton, 29 August 1971.

Finland and Ulster, plus a second in Belgium. A further second came with John Blanchard as passenger. Blanchard had been a successful solo racer whose career included riding the Fath four. He was now the Münch team manager. Owesle and Rutherford both retired from racing at the end of the season.

Some interesting information came to light when speaking to Tony Jefferies in 1987 regarding the Münch racing team. For a start, even though Blanchard was the team manager, partly backed by Duckhams Oils, it was Owesle the mechanical wizard who wrote the terms of the deal. Jefferies also revealed that although he also rode the 500 four, the 750 was much more difficult to ride with a narrow power band which lay between 10–12000 rpm (compared to the 500's 11500 – 14000 rpm). Below 10,000 rpm the 750's engine would die, to quote Jefferies, 'just as surely as if the rider had flicked a light switch, whereas the 500 was a truly superb motor'. Running-up both the 500 and 750 Münch fours from cold was difficult. The only way to be sure all eight plugs were firing was to check each exhaust pipe for temperature.

The 1971 championship-winning engine was bench tested at 86 bhp, using four Keihan carburettors, higher lift camshaft and dry sump lubrication. But Jefferies believed that the Münch fours were much better in sidecar use because their power characteristics were suited to being driven hard. Jefferies also felt that the handling of the solo machines was; 'Very reminiscent of the Manx Norton era, rather than the Yamaha or Triumph Tridents I was used to. Whereas these latter machines had more flexible frames which allowed the rider to adopt a 'hanging on-and-off the bike' style of riding, the Münch required a fixed position in the older style – something I was not used to.' To sum up, Jefferies commented 'The engines never broke down when I was racing the machines and although not in my opinion fully devloped the 500 engine was superb.'

Racing was to prove the centre of Münch's problems. Despite warnings from the German engineer, Bell had sunk over half a million Deutschmarks into the 1971 racing campaign, and although Owesle was World Sidecar Champion, the factory was in severe financial difficulties. With creditors arriving almost hourly, Bell left the scene. Friedl Münch was once again abandoned to solve his own problems.

Luckily a commercial 'White Knight' was waiting for

Bell's departure. The board of directors of a local enterprise, Hassia GmbH, a packaging company with branches throughout Germany and the rest of western Europe rescued the Münch plant. Hassia believed that with its mangerial expertise it could turn Münch into a profitable enterprise. Its view was largely based on the positive trend of motorcycle sales in Germany. Given this background, Hessia appointed one of its brightest young senior managers to re-shape the business. Friedl Münch was instructed to go back to his forte – engineering – and all assets not required were sold in order to maximise the company's capital base.

Hassia established an expansion programme for Münch roadsters. This embraced producing larger numbers of the Mammoth and developing a new three cylinder two-stroke. The latter was a 660 cc aircooled unit with seprarate vertical cylinders and heads set across the frame. Several components came from a Sachs snowmobile unit. About the only thing the bike shared with its bigger brother was the front brake, otherwise everything was new. The frame was a neat full double cradle with exposed Ceriani-style front forks plus rear shocks with exposed chrome springs. The large 20-litre tank had the legend 'Münch 3' emblazoned upon its sides. At the biennial Cologne show, in September 1972, the company not only displayed the new three cylinder model in public for the

At the Cologne Show, September 1972, the Mammoth 1200 TTS was a major magnet for the crowds.

first time, but also showed a sports version of the TTS1200 with low handlebars and four black megaphone silencers.

To benefit from increased production and the possibility of an expanding range, Hassia-Münch's management team was enlarged to include a home sales manager and another for export markets. At the same time a number of dealerships were established throughout Germany. Following a car franchise network model Münch quickly built a powerful marketing machine. In return for an exclusive territory dealers agreed to stock a specified number of machines; maintain an inventory of spare parts and send mechanics for specialised training at the Münch factory.

Friedl Münch was relieved of all responsibility for administration and financial tasks. He welcomed the instruction to concentrate upon further improvement of the four cylinder Mammoth and to develop the new three cylinder model. Unfortunately, the latter was never to reach the production stage.

But what the new management had not reckoned with was the fundamental rationale for customers to want a Münch. Two powerful reasons for ownership were interwoven. A Münch was a low volume production bike that had the prestige of being hand-built. To own one was to be served personally by Friedl Münch. The new organisational methods meant that both sales advantages ceased to exist.

To potential customers it seemed that the company

planned to mass-produce the machines and to prevent Friedl Münch himself from dealing with customers. Their reaction to this soon became apparent in extremely poor sales through the dealer network. Consequently, a large surplus stock of unsold motorcycles rapidly built up at the factory. Compounded with this, the three cylinder two-stroke proved unsuccessful in trials and was abandoned.

Surprisingly, after the problems of the Bell era, racing was continued by the new owners, albeit in a restricted form for the 1972 season. Blanchard was retained as team manager and the retired Owesle was replaced by British charioteer Chris Vincent. But Vincent did not make his debut in the GPs until the fifth round at Assen in Holland, where he and passenger Peter Cassey scored a brilliant second place behind Klaus Enders/Rolf Engelhardt on a factory BMW.

At the Belgian GP a week later the Münch team came home fourth, followed by another second in Czechoslovakia. Finally, at the last round at Imatra, Finland, came victory. The Münch outfit beat the new World Championship pair of Enders and Engelhardt. Even though they had only contested half of the rounds the Münch team still scooped fourth position in the World series.

Disaster for the Hassia-Münch enterprise came in 1973. In May *Motor Cycle* alleged that a British sidecar enthusiast John Bailey had had his bid of £10,000 for the whole racing team turned down. Blanchard denied this hotly, but Bailey stated that his aim was to be able to continue Vincent's sponsorship with a British-owned team. Sadly, the team was eventually disbanded with no sale.

Commercially, the company was in a terminal condition. Not only had the Hassia management totally failed to appreciate what was needed to make a success from a hand-built, ultra-expensive superbike, but worse still, its own packaging empire was crumbling. The first winds of recession were devastating the industry. The final result was that at the end of 1973 the whole Hassia organisation went bankrupt.

As if waiting for a stage direction, Heinz Henke presented himself to Hassia's management. Henke was not only a successful businessman but also a Münch owner and irrepressible enthusiast. He had made his name through milk products and electrical transformers. Diverse businesses which provided him with a large amount of excess capital. But perhaps more importantly, both were now established and running well with their own management teams. So well, in fact,

The 1972 700 cc three-cylinder Münch two-stroke was ill-fated. Although popular at that year's Cologne Show, few realised a Sachs' snowmobile unit was the engine's origin.

that Henke found for the first time in several years that he had spare time on his hands. While visiting the Münch plant at Friedburg to have his own Münch TTS1200 serviced, Henke realised that the company was in financial trouble. And when it went into liquidation he purchased the remains from the receiver.

Friedl Münch could have used the opportunity to sever his connection with the business, but agreed to join Henke for the simple reason that his whole life was centred around his beloved Mammoth. The great advantage of the Henke-Münch alliance was that for the first time the business had a backer who completely understood what made a Münch motorcycle buyer tick. And Henke was neither a playboy, nor a non-motorcycling businessman.

Henke quickly disbanded the ill-fated dealer franchise system. He correctly reasoned that while it was a good system for mass-market manufacturers, like the Japanese big four, it was not suitable for Münch. Henke re-established the personal contact so that once again Münch enthusiasts could deal directly with their hero. Henke also saw the importance of making full use of the hours when the expensive engineering facilities were not operating fully. He therefore embarked on a programme of diversification, with the Münch plant producing parts for his transformer factory.

The new company's name was Heinz W Henke, and it was based in a small, but modern factory unit at Waldsiedlung a few miles northeast of Altenstadt. When production restarted in the spring of 1974, it was concentrated at first on two models, both of which used the 1177 cc NSU-based four-cylinder engine with a bore and stroke of 75 × 66.6 mm. The top of the line 4TTS/E had a compression ratio of 8.5:1 and produced 104 bhp at 7500 rpm with Bosch fuel injection. The cheaper 4TTS had twin Weber carbs and a lower power output of 88 bhp at 7000 rpm.

The only immediate visible difference between the two models was the seating. The 4TTS/E came with a single racing-type saddle, whilst the 4TTS featured a dualseat. And both models had several factors in common. These included gear ratios – 1st 2.53:1, 2nd 1.55:1, 3rd 1.14:1, 4th 1:1 – the $\frac{5}{8} \times \frac{3}{8}$ (530) heavy-duty drive chain, fuel tank with a capacity of 34-litres, and 12 volt electrics including a 180 watt alternator. The weight had risen to 656 lb.

October 1974 was the debut of the Münch Dolomites Rally. The inspiring force was Henke. This was to be held annually at a site in northern Italy, and the instigators believed that Münch owners would travel long distances to attend. They were correct. At the inaugural event Henke and Münch were on hand to mingle with the owners of the machines, when both could be perceived as true enthusiasts.

Just at the point in the mid-1970s when the rightness of Henke's policies were beginning to be vindicated with a period of stability for the firm, Friedl Münch

himself discovered that Henke's good business sense was actually working to restrict his own creative flair for new developments.

So, in early 1977, Friedl Münch and the company Heinz W. Henke Münch Motorrader went their separate ways. Henke continued producing the TTS/TTSE until the early 1980s, and Münch continued developing the Mammoth concept. Part of this was the introduction of big-bore kits for existing Münch models giving either 1400 or 1600 cc capacity. From 1979 until well into the 1980s Münch was involved with the design of the Horex 1400TT (Turbo Injection) in co-operation with Fritz Roth.

However, just to prove that one can never be sure what Münch will do next, in the autumn of 1986 at the age of 59 he once again stunned the motorcycling world by producing another Mammoth-based monster – the Titan. Its capacity was almost 1800 cc. The massive 1786 cc motor with a bore and stroke of 85.5 × 76 mm was purpose-built by Münch for a wealthy American enthusiast, Californian Paul Watts, at a cost of 60,000 DM (£20,700). The supercharged lump was alleged to kick out 160 bhp. This was even more than the Horex 1400 TI. A chassis very similar to the original Mammoth of twenty years before was fabricated to house the engine. Münch's Titan weighed in at a staggering 704 lb.

Münch said he planned to build a further ten such machines, but with a more sophisticated set of cycle parts, for the Titan still sported the famous Münch 250 mm drum brakes and many other familiar components.

With such an extraordinary history it is safe to conclude that Friedl Münch will make his mark many more times in the future.

A specially prepared Mammoth engine revealed its mechanical details at the Amsterdam Show, February 1973.

NSU

production models

NSU as a marque began in 1873, when Heinrich Stoll and Christian Schmidt set up a modest workshop at the small town of Riedlingen which is built on an island in the channel of the river Danube. The company's business was the manufacture and repair of *Strickmaschinen* (knitting machines).

Despite the humble start, business quickly prospered. At the time, most garments were knitted purely by hand, but the newly-introduced mechanisation meant that knitwear manufacturers were able to turn out cheaper clothing of excellent and consistent quality. This led to a sudden boom in knitwear sales and Stoll and Schmidt's fledgling enterprise was soon very well capitalised.

As a result, they moved north the next year, in 1874, to new premises at Reutlingen. Here the business was expanded and consolidated steadily for the next six years. But then the partnership divided. Schmidt left Stoll and moved further north to Neckarsulm, a small town near Heilbronn. Neckarsulm is the confluence of Neckar and another river.

Christian Schmidt had always an ambition to manufacture bicycles. He did nothing practical, however, in terms of manufacturing two wheelers. Instead, Schmidt concentrated upon his knitting machines. The new company was called Neckarsulm Strickmaschinen Union. In Schmidt's first year of command he employed nine people. Four years later he died at the age of 39, with his ambition unfulfilled and leaving a now well-established business to his brother-in-law Gottlob Banzhaf.

Banzhaf quickly assumed control. Within five years he had not only enlarged the company's profitable turnover, but had also realised Schmidt's dreams of building bicycles. In 1889, Neckarsulm Strickmaschinen Union assembled two hundred 'bone shakers' and in 1892, the company changed its name to Neckarsulmer Fahradwerke (bicycle works). Production of the firm's first pedal cranks began in the same year. This aspect of NSU's business was to continue almost unbroken until 1960.

The first use of the letters NSU, as an abbreviation of the old knitting machine company name, came at this time. The stamps and medallions used as the maker's mark read 'NSU im Hirschorn'. 'Hirschorn' was a reference to the arms of Wurtemberg, in which a deer's antler was embodied.

Banzhaf was both inventive and energetic. In 1892 he ordered the knitting machine manufacturer to be phased out as the boom had passed. The success of his bicycles, and even more so of associated proprietary fittings, encouraged him towards applying the then new internal combustion engine to a powered bicycle.

A series of experiments progressed steadily and well. In 1900 the first pre-production prototype appeared at NSU. When it went into full scale manufacture a year later, the NSU became Germany's first motorcycle (in the accepted sense of the word) to be marketed commercially.

Although it was a sturdy affair, the machine was to modern eyes extremely crude. A Swiss-made ZL (Zedel) clip-on engine was mounted at an incline in the centre of the frame. Engine power was transmitted through a direct belt drive, and a conventional bicycle pedal crank and chain were retained to allow the machine to be used if the engine was not functioning. Under favourable conditions, the engine, which was fed by a drip-feed carburettor, would produce around 1.25 bhp. A speed of 24 mph was attainable on the flat.

This model remained in production until 1903. NSU, however, had made its British debut as cycle component makers in 1901 at the Stanley Show which was held in the Crystal Palace in London. By 1902, the NSU had become a 'real' motorcycle. The Zedel engine (now giving 1.75 bhp) was mounted vertically in separate engine plates within a redesigned frame.

It was at about this time that Karl Schmidt, son of the late founder, joined NSU. Schmidt had received his engineering training from the great Gottlieb Daimler. As technical director of NSU, the young Schmidt was determined to design his own engine. In 1903 the first motorcycle totally built by NSU was ready for the showrooms.

Schmidt's machine had a single cylinder engine of 329 cc (75 × 75 mm) unit which produced 2.5 bhp and gave a top speed of 41 mph. Most importantly, it proved to be a good seller – 2,228 machines were sold between 1903 and 1905.

From this point the company grew ever stronger in the motorcycle market. A 804 cc V-twin, followed by several singles were introduced in 1904. Then came the company's first competition motorcycle – the 402 cc *Renn maschine* (racing machine) of 1905 which had a top speed of 50 mph and a 5 bhp engine. In 1905, the

Sulmobil took NSU onto three wheels, and in the following year, the Motorwagen became the company's first four-wheeled vehicle.

Karl Schmidt gave up his post as technical director in 1910 to start his own company *Deutsche Oelverbrennungswerke zu Heilbronn am Neckar* (German Oil Burner Factory of Heilbronn on the Neckar). The business was relocated in Neckarsulm during 1917 to produce non-ferrous castings and later an iron foundry was established. The name was then changed to Karl Schmidt GmbH. It went on to produce motor components, especially pistons and friction bearings, as well as pressure die castings and Alfin cylinder barrels. Today the company is one of the world's largest engine component manufacturers.

NSU recognised the value of export markets. As early as 1905 an NSU company was registered in Britain and offices were opened in London. Sales exceeded even the most optimistic forecasts. British riders purchased almost a quarter of Germany's total motorcycle exports by 1906. Naturally the United Kingdom was the mainstay of NSU's foreign sales.

The export market collapsed with the outbreak of the Great War. NSU converted to the manufacture of munitions. After the Armistice, the company rapidly returned to the business it understood – motorcycles. By 1922, production was at full capacity and over 3,000 people were employed.

The Neckarsulm factory pioneered 'production-line' techniques for the German industry. In 1929, the leading British designer, Walter Moore left Norton and joined NSU. The move aroused bitter controversy. Moore is generally credited as the creator of Norton's overhead camshaft racing singles. These followed the introduction of his works racer in 1927. For the commercial market it was transformed into production model CS1 (Camshaft 1) in 1928.

When Wall Street crashed on 'Black Friday' 24 October 1929, the effect on a still weakened German economy was almost immediate. Then as now, when America sneezed, the poor men of Europe were likely to catch pneumonia. The decline of NSU was almost as sudden, and it was only solved by an arrangement with the Italian industrial giant Fiat. It was agreed the Turin management would take over NSU's car manufacturing facility at Heilbron. The blow was doubly hard because this plant had only just been completed at the cost of virtually all of NSU's available capital.

Freed from a major financial drain, NSU turned to the production of cheap, practical two-wheel transport. The only exception to this came in 1934 when it was commissioned to build prototypes of what was later to become the Volkswagen 'Beetle'. NSU was prevented from going into production of Dr Ferdinand Porsche's Type 32 light car (as it was officially known at the time) by the terms of the agreement with Fiat. Baron Fritz von Falkenhayn, then the NSU chief, was initially keen to produce the new car. But NSU received an unequivocal

Introduced in 1951, the Fox 2 had a 123 cc two-stroke engine. This replaced the earlier 98 cc ohv unit of the Fox 4.

note from Fiat which reminded von Falkenhayn that NSU could not re-enter the car market. NSU stuck to the letter and spirit of the contract until the 1950's when, with Fiat's blessing, it returned to the four-wheel sector.

NSU's forced concentration upon two-wheelers and the need for cheap transport were instrumental in creating the first long line of mopeds. Mopeds were commonly known at the time as autocycles. Called the Motosulm, this 63 cc machine first appeared in 1931. Its two-stroke engine was mounted over the front wheel, to which power was transmitted via a clutch and chain drive. There were successes with larger machines. Here Walter Moore's contribution to his new employers could be detected. Other popular four-stroke singles of the era included the 501/601 TS, 351 OS, 351/501 OSL, 201/251 OSL, 351 OT and 601 OSL models. The numbering system did not necessarily refer to their exact capacities.

However, all these were eclipsed by Walter Moore's first miniature two-stroke design, the 98 cc (49×52 mm) Quick. Between 1936 and 1953 235,411 were manufactured. It was NSU's most successful machine of all time bar the post-war Quickly moped. Both ladies' and gentlemens' frames were offered (*Damenrad* and *Herrenrad*). The choice of model name came from a suggestion made by Fraulein Schröder while she was secretary to Baron von Falkenhayn.

The peak of post-World War 1 output at NSU came in 1938 with a record number of motorcycles being produced – 62,619 – a figure which was not to be bettered until 1950.

With the declaration of war in 1939 the Nazi Party instructed NSU to build motorcycles for the military. In counterpoint to the popular image of Germany's military motorcycle transport being made up entirely of heavyweight sidecar outfits, NSU produced 28,000 lightweights – 18,000 ohv 250s and 10,000 two-stroke 125s. In addition NSU also built 60,000 bicycles for civilian use and 3,000 for the army. Express of Bremerhaven made the majority of bicycles for the Wehrmacht, therefore, NSU's contract for the armed forces was comparatively small.

War time production for NSU also included the manufacture of aircraft components, and one of the oddest vehicles of the entire conflict the Kettenrad (chaintrack motorcycle). This was a small, tracked personnel carrier which had the steering and front wheel of a motorcycle ahead of a body which carried tracks on both sides. Open seating was perched above. Power came from a four-cylinder, water-cooled Opel car engine of 1478 cc (80×74 mm) giving 36 bhp at 3,400 rpm. There were three forward and one reverse gears plus a two-speed conversion box giving the driver a choice of six forward and two reverse gears. Thus equipped, a Kettenrad was suitable for both on and off-road use.

NSU was also heavily involved in the wartime production of aero engine starters. The factory made a standardised design consisting of a horizontally-opposed, twin-cylinder, aircooled two-stroke which had to be able to sustain 10,000 rpm and achieve its load peak at 7,000 rpm. The same unit was also manufactured by Ardie and Victoria.

After Field Marshal Montgomery accepted the German surrender on Luneburg Heath it was agreed by the Allies that German heavy industry should be dismantled. It is, therefore, rather mysterious that the NSU factory nevertheless manufactured 98 Quick motorcycles, 75 Kettenrads and 8,822 bicycles before the close of 1945. In addition, a small number of 250 ohv 'war office' models were assembled from existing parts for civilian use.

It may seem odd that the factory should produce the obviously militaristic Kettenrad in those first few months of peace. But this came about because in war-ravaged Germany, there was an urgent need for a vehicle which could go almost anywhere and transport almost anything. Furthermore, NSU was extremely fortunate, for unlike DKW and others whose production facilities were in the Soviet sector, Neckarsulm was under the liberal American regime. The Kettenrad remained in production until 1948. A total of 550 was produced in the post-war years. The American Forestry Commission alone bought 200 machines.

By 1946 NSU was busier than Vulcan's forge in a country where millions endured starvation in enforced idleness. A hundred Kettenrads came down the production line, followed by 566 Quicks, a mountain of ancillary equipment, 12,893 cycle cranks; 6,085 bicycles and a complete new range of lawn mowers.

By 1948 recovery was further accelerated by the factory acting as a repair centre for the US Army. During that year almost 300,000 pedal cranks were produced together with over 58,000 bicycles and various other items including a new stationary engine. Motorcycle production was also returning to its former strength. From January until December over 9,260 units were sent into the market. These were made up by just three models. The 125 ZDB and 251 OSL had been reintroduced in very small numbers the previous year, but in 1948 a total of 2,358 ZDBs and 667 OSLs were assembled. Even so, the sheet anchor of production was the ever-popular Quick of which 6,245 were made.

Walter Moore had left NSU at the beginning of the war, and had been succeeded as chief designer in 1947 by Albert Roder. Under his leadership NSU now updated their production machines. In 1948, Roder made the first of a number of important changes to the production machine line-up. He designed a 98 cc (50×50 mm) ohv engine which gave 5.2 bhp at 6,500 rpm. This was mounted in a pressed-steel chassis with forks which were patented by Roder. These were to feature in many of the factory's roadsters. The new lightweight

Konsol II 501 OS-T, with 498 cc engine. The motorcycle was available 1951–54. A comprehensive racing kit supplied by the factory put 100 mph almost within reach.

was called the Fox 4 and was the forerunner of a whole new decade long line of NSU singles.

It entered production in 1949. Before New Year's Eve of that year 6,636 units were manufactured. Very shortly after, a racing version, the Sportfox, appeared. There had been no plans to sell the model, but the project was modified vastly in the wake of the 1950 Frankfurt Show. Here, orders were said to have been taken by beleaugered stand staff for some *five to six hundred* of the Sportfox.

But the really big news on the NSU stand at the show was the NSU-Lambretta scooter. This came about as the result of an agreement between NSU and the Innocenti factory in Milan. Essentially the model which appeared was identical to the Italian edition. For the German market, however, the metalwork was made by Volkswagen. The power unit, of course, was supplied direct from Innocenti. NSU then undertook only assembly and sales distribution, although it was later proposed that it should manufacture the engine at Neckarsulm.

In Italy, the model was referred to as the Type C Lambretta. It had a piston-ported single cylinder two-stroke engine giving 4.5 bhp at 4,500 rpm. Transmission was through a twistgrip-controlled 3-speed gearbox. With a dry weight of 365 lb, it was capable of quite respectable performances.

In the first year of manufacture, 1950, the total production of NSU-Lambrettas was 743, but it was the motorcycles which stole the limelight as far as volume was concerned. The total figure for the year was 67,804 units, of which more than half (38,060 machines) was once again made up by the Quick. The production

figures also included the only 'new' motorcycle model that year – the re-introduced 351 OSL. Like the companion 251 OSL it was hardly changed from the original pre-war design. The most significant alteration to both was the adoption of telescopic forks which finally replaced the old girder type.

Next year, 1951, both the 125 ZDB and the 351 OT were retired. Only 455 of the latter had been built since the war – 150 of them in that last year. Sales of the 125 ZDB were, however, much better, with 5,700 made in 1951 out of a total of 34,589 in its ten-year life span. Scooter sales were well up at 8,105, out of a buoyant total of 73,639 machines.

The most significant developments were the launches of four new models – the Fox 2, Konsul I and Konsul II, and the Lux 201 ZB. In that first year 8,847 of the new Fox 2 were made. It was essentially a redesigned Fox 4, but in place of the 98 cc ohv unit was a piston-ported 123 cc (52 × 58 mm) two-stroke engine giving 5.4 bhp at 5,000 rpm. At 185 lb dry, it was 2 lb lighter than the smaller unit and was a shade faster at 52 mph. Both Konsuls were based on pre-war designs, at least in the engine room department. The Konsul I was a development of the 349 cc (75 × 79 mm) 351 OS-T, while the 498 cc (80 × 99 mm) Konsul II was derived from the old 501 OS-T.

Compared with the new NSU four-strokes which were to appear shortly, the Konsuls were obsolescent even as they entered production. A limited power output – 17.4 and 21 bhp respectively – married to overweight running gear giving dry weights of 418 and 430 lb led to a decidedly docile performance. The heavyweight frames were full-cradle designs with a single front down-tube and plunger rear suspension, matched to a pair of oil-damped telescopic forks up front. Braking was by single-sided 180 mm diameter cast-iron drums, laced into 19 inch chromed rims with 3.50 section tyres. Other details common to both machines were twin-port cylinder heads with separate exhaust pipes and silencers with fishtail ends, 14.5-litre fuel tanks, single sprung saddles, and a parcel carrier mounted over the rear mudguard. The electrical equipment consisted of a 6 volt 45/60 watt Noris generator and 7 amp/hour battery.

The only 'all-new' model for 1951 was a much more trend-setting design. The Lux was a 198 cc (62 × 66 mm) two-stroke of exceptionally clean lines, with many of its cycle parts being used on later NSU machines. Its piston-ported engine gave 8.6 bhp at 5,250 rpm with a 6:1 compression ratio. A Bing 2/22/16 carburettor with integral metal box-type air filter was used, and the chromed exhaust pipe led to a silencer with a fishtail end. This power unit was housed in a backbone frame made up from steel pressings that also formed the forward section of the rear mudguard. The rear suspension (by duplex coil springs and a hydraulic damper unit) was entirely enclosed by the frame pressings. Front suspension was by leading link forks and both wheels were 19 inch with 3.00 section tyres. The finish was an austere black overall, and that included the wheel rims.

In 1952, announcement was made in September of a new and very unorthodox 247 cc (69 × 66 mm) Max model. In frame and fork design, there was plenty of evidence of the debts it owed to the Fox and Lux models, but the overhead cam engine was all-new and featured a type of valve gear unique amongst motorcycle power units. Called the *Ultramax* system, it was patented by its designer Albert Roder. As he received a royalty on every one produced, it may account for its popularity in many of his designs, including the Max, Maxi, Sportmax and Superfox and Prinz cars.

In the Ultramax system the drive to the overhead valve gear was by long connecting rods or levers housed in a tunnel cast integrally on the left of the cylinder barrel. At their ends, these rods carried an eye encircling counterbalanced eccentric discs connected to the half-time pinion and the overhead camshaft. As the engine revolved, so the eccentrics imparted a reciprocating motion which was transferred to the valve gear. Hairpin valve springs were used and the entire mechanism was enclosed.

The Ultramax system could be seen to owe a debt to similar valve gear designs which had been pioneered in the car world as early as 1919 by Pomeroy on a Vauxhall

NSU had the Max with 247 cc engine in production 1952–56. It was different to later Supermax in many ways, but perhaps the most obvious was the rear suspension.

and standardised on six cylinder Bentleys from 1924–30. But one of the problems which Pomeroy and Bentley never overcame was that of the differential expansion of the materials used. Which with the rigid link formed by the eccentrics could throw the whole timing out. Roder overcame this with his novel 'floating' camshaft arrangement, which was rigidly held in position by a tie-rod between the half-time pinion and the camshaft housing. Another of Roder's designs of the period was a similar device for rear wheel drive. However, unlike the Ultramax valve gear this never entered production.

Only 62 of the new Max models were produced in 1952, but this was largely because 1952 was the final year of the 251 OSL. The Neckarsulm lines assembled 2,879 in the closing twelve months. In total, 67,442 units were despatched between 1934 and 1952. It was also the year which saw the first public television transmission in Germany. The initial programmes went out on Christmas Day. Three days later, a 45 minute programme on motorcycling included a feature on NSU works riders Otto Daiker and Werner Haas. Both men appeared with their machines in the Hamburg studios.

The year also saw the first of a number of post-war co-operative Italian-NSU projects. Vittoria (not to be confused with the German Victoria marque) displayed a scooter powered by a 125 NSU two stroke engine at the Milan Show at the end of November 1952. This was put into limited production in 1953.

With 1953 came many new developments, including the end of the long-running Quick model, with some 16,000 having been built in its final year. A total of 235,441 Quicks were built since its inception way back in 1936. Another model axed was the Konsul I. It had never sold well, and lived in the shadow of the larger

Above **The Italian Caproni-Vizzola company was just one of many firms throughout Europe to use NSU engines. An example of typical Germano–Italian liason was on view at the 1953 Milan Show.**

capacity Konsul II. The Neckarsulm factory raised invoices for 8,247 Konsul II between 1951 and 1953. Production of the new Max hit stride with 24,403 being built, but top sales went to the NSU-Lambretta at 29,004 units.

Excitement was caused in the German two-wheel fraternity when early in the year the factory offered a speed kit for the 500 Konsul II. It could be used for either fast road work or clubman's racing events. This transformed NSU's previously mundane 22 bhp machine into a sportster which, while it might not yet be up to BSA Gold Star or Gilera Saturno standards, still had the legs to see off most of the half-litre roadsters of the day.

Left **NSU Quickly was the company's most successful design for a two-wheeler. It first appeared in 1953 and over the course of a decade a total of 1,111,744 units were sold in Germany and scores of export markets.**

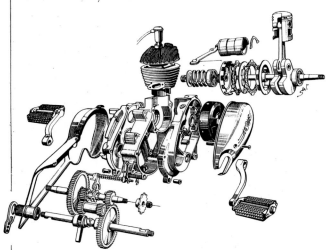

Factory illustration of the Quickly engine.

The kit was extremely comprehensive and included a new cylinder head and barrel in light alloy with more comprehensive finning, forged slipper 7.5:1 piston, larger valves (44.5 mm exhaust, 45.5 mm inlet), new pushrods and tube, plus rockers and high lift cams. Unlike the standard engine, the hairpin valve springs were left exposed. Other new parts included an Amal 32R carb and inlet stub, a single exhaust pipe and the choice of a new silencer (for road use) or a racing megaphone. A tacho was fitted and there were alterations to cables, gaskets and various smaller items.

Obviously there were other considerations including the need for a hotter spark plug and revised gearing, but the result of fitting the kit raised the power output to 30 bhp if a silencer was used or 33 bhp with a megaphone. Both output peaks occurred at 6000 rpm. Modified, a Konsul II became very much a wolf in sheep's clothing. Its new maximum speed rose to 91 mph with silencer and almost 100 mph with megaphone.

The Lux was also updated for 1953 with a new cylinder head, a Bing 2/22/20 carb with air filtered placed through the frame, and generator output increased to 60 watt.

In the summer of 1953, another Italian-German 'mystery' model appeared to baffle the world's press, at least for a short time before its identity was revealed. It emerged that this was the product of a tie-up between NSU and the Italian company Aero Caproni of Trento – better known as Capriolo. The machine was powered by a Lux motor, but all the running gear was purely Latin, including a pair of Earles-type front forks and full swinging arm rear suspension. Later a similar machine appeared under the Moto Muller banner. There was also a Max powered-model built by Caproni-Visola. The company was another of the former Caproni aviation factories and was located just north of Milan. A further area of Italian-NSU co-operation was the evolution of a four wheel delivery vehicle, called the 'Maxmobil'. Not very original in concept it was similar to the typical Vespa-Lambretta wine delivery trucks which abounded in Mediterranean countries.

International co-operation went even further in the second half of 1953. In November agreement was reached after six months of negotiations for an Anglo-German range of machines. The new motorcycles would be badged as NSU-Vincent. Vincent Engineers of Stevenage, Herts were already world-famous for the 500 Comet single and 1000 Rapide V-twin models.

Philip Vincent, the managing director, explained to the press that Anglicized versions of NSU machines would be built at Stevenage for sale in Great Britain and the Commonwealth. With him were executives of the Layford Trading & Shipping Company Limited of London SW1, who as the British and Commonwealth concessionaires for NSU were signatories to the agreement with Vincent.

In theory, the alliance made Vincent one of the most versatile motorcycle manufacturers in the world because it would offer a vast range of machinery from the 50 cc Firefly cycle-motor right through to the legendary 1000 cc V-twins. Four NSU-Vincents were to complete this range: the Max, Lux and both versions of the Fox. The plan was for NSU to ship to Stevenage the engine units, frames and forks. All the remaining equipment was supposed to be of British manufacture. Vincent claimed at the press conference that the 'local content' would be of 'over 50% of British material'. This was in any case necessary to comply with the Commonwealth Preferential Tariff agreement and then allow Layford to market the machines in the British Commonwealth at a more competitive price than would have been possible otherwise. It was claimed that this customs advantage was the prime reason for the tri-partite agreement. Unfortunately, the master blueprint was to fall well short of what each company had hoped for.

In fact, it was a dismal failure. The sole achievements were the production and sale of a dismal 160 examples of the Fox two-stroke, and completion of a Max prototype. None of the proposed Lux models were made (although a partly completed machine existed). The reason given later by Philip Vincent in his book *Vincent – Fifty Years of the Marque* for the Max never entering production was the 'high cost of the German components'. But the more likely cause of problems centred around the cost of the 51% British content. It can only be wondered why each project was not fully costed before the press announcement in November 1953.

Behind the scenes, there may well have been another motive for the Vincent tie-up. It is a matter of speculation, but perhaps the NSU management, aware of the Quickly moped's sales potential, needed access to the enormous Commonwealth markets. But without a British partner, the tariff barriers were unbreachable.

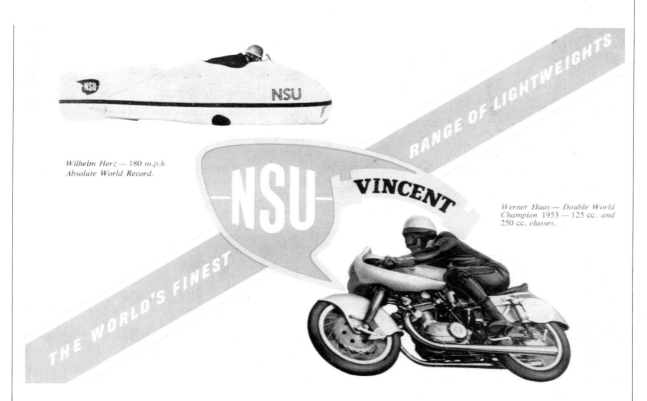

Wilhelm Herz — 180 m.p.h.
Absolute World Record.

Werner Haas — Double World
Champion 1953 — 125 cc. and
250 cc. classes.

Brochure announcing the alliance in November 1953 with NSU's British partners Vincent. It was not successful.

The first model, the Quickly N was built in 1953 and 9,120 were produced in Neckarsulm. The following year production rocketed to 123,671 and peaked in 1955 at 228,135 units. When production ceased in 1962 a total of 539,793 Quickly Ns had been manufactured and if this figure is added to the other Quickly variants an amazing 1,111,744 total is revealed. This 49 cc (40 × 39 mm) piston ported single was very much *the* moped, until the arrival of the Honda Cub. Its success lay in the combination of style, quality and price. A formula which in its day could not be matched by any manufacturer in the world. This unglamorous machine, nevertheless, dominated NSU's fortunes for most of the remainder of the company's history.

Designed by Roder, the Quickly entered the market at a time when sales were still on a upward curve. The Quickly is fully deserving of the title 'Father of the modern moped' – even though when it appeared the term had not been invented and it was still referred to as an 'autocycle'.

The Quickly was just that – a powered bicycle. An elegant, spindly affair it had 26 inch wheels carrying narrow 2.00 inch tyres, a pressed steel spine frame, pedalling gear and leading link front suspension. All-up weight was a mere 80 lb and it carried 2.8 litres of fuel. The engine's 1.4 bhp maximum power was developed at 5,200 rpm and there was a two-speed (15.99 and

30.06:1) twistgrip-operated gearbox and helical gear-driven clutch. There were good, if tiny drum brakes, and the machine was complete with full lighting equipment, luggage rack and centre stand.

In Britain Vincent distributed the Quickly. It went on sale in November 1954 and approximately 12,000 units were sold. This no doubt helped Vincent's cash flow, but it alone could not prevent the cessation of motorcycle production at the Stevenage works. The last Vincent motorcycle came off the production line on 16 December 1955, although a few other machines were later built up from spare parts.

NSU in 1954 made great strides in the sphere of competition. This was the final year of both Fox variants, and also the end for the Konsul II. NSU also gained an American West Coast distributor. The Flanders Company of Pasadena, California, augmented its network of main US agents. Butler & Smith Trading Corporation of New York continued its domination of the Eastern Seaboard.

In September, the 1955 model programme was announced. The Superfox replaced the two Fox machines. The Superfox featured a 123 cc (52 × 58) ohv engine, which turned out 8.8 bhp at 6500 rpm, and had a compression ratio of 7.8:1. Carburation was by a Bing 2/20/16. The newcomer very much followed the lines of the successful Lux and Max duo, but used 19 inch wheels with 2.75 section tyres. Its four speed engine gave a respectable 59.25 mph for a dry weight of 253 lb and a 10.8-litre tank ensured a good range.

Another newcomer for 1955 was the Superlux. Developed from the already well established Lux, which was to be discontinued, its 197 cc engine had a revised cylinder head and barrel. Power output was raised to 11 bhp at 5250 rpm and with it the top speed went up to 68.75 mph. Also new were the full-width 180 × 40 mm alloy brake drums, larger 14-litre tank and generally more pleasing lines. These were assisted by additional chrome plate and a black or 'Christiana' blue overall finish.

For 1955 the Max received similar treatment, with the same new full-width brakes and larger tank as on the Superlux. The name was also changed to Special Max.

A larger capacity for the well established and popular NSU-Lambretta was announced for 1955. The model had its 123 cc engine changed for a new 146 cc (57 × 58 mm) unit with an increase in power to 6.2 bhp at 5200 rpm at 52.6 mph top speed. Otherwise the machine remained unchanged.

Karl Schmidt died at the end of 1954 at the age of 78. Yet he was content in the knowledge that his father's creation had grown to become one of the largest companies of its kind in the world. It employed well over 6,000 workers, including more than 1,000 refugees from various countries. In the mid-1950's, barely ten years on from the end of a war which left the country shattered, NSU were very much at the vanguard of what was to be later called *das Wirtschaftswunder* – the economic miracle of post-war Germany.

At the Vienna Spring Fair in March 1955 NSU displayed a new, larger capacity Max. Here it was shown in *four* different colour schemes. But all production models were finished in steel blue. The new machine was known as the *Osterrich* Max 301 OSB and was only sold in Austria. The reason for the model's restriction to this country was Austria's customs tariffs which protected Puch by penalising foreign manufacturers of motorcycles with a capacity of 250 cc, or lower. The regulations that affected NSU in 1955 are essentially the same as those in force today. It was only on sale in 1955/6 during which time 2,756 were produced. It was virtually identical to a Supermax but with a 297 cc engine (72 × 73 mm) using a Bing 2/27.5/5 carb and giving 21 bhp at 6500 rpm.

There was plenty more evidence of NSU's international interests at around this time. In Scandinavia, Monark of Sweden offered a Max engine mounted in a standard Monark rolling chassis. And in Spain, the Lube factory bought NSU engines from the mid to late-1950s. Ultimately a decline in motorcycle production by NSU, prompted Luis Bojarano, as head of the Lube marque, to develop his own power units based upon an NSU design.

Meanwhile in Britain, a highly publicised 880 mile test was successfully completed by Tim Wood. He set off on a Quickly N moped from Lands End towards John O'Groats at 8.39 am on Saturday 16 May. The Quickly covered the first 10 miles at an average of 22 mph. It continued on its journey during that day and Sunday. Arrival at Crawford in Scotland at 6.00 am on Monday morning for the final leg of the journey to John O'Groats was slightly ahead of schedule. The journey was completed at midday on Tuesday. The route (before any motorways were built) was via Bodmin, Bridgewater, Gloucester, Worcester, Wellington, Warrington, Kendal, Penrith, Lanark, Airdrie, Stirling, Inverness and Wick to John O'Groats. The total time was 37 hours 51 minutes at an average speed of 23.29 mph. Total fuel consumption was 28.35 litres. *138 m Pg!*

From 31 August 1955, all service, spares and distribution of NSU machines in Britain passed from Vincent Engineers Limited to NSU Distributors (Great Britain) Limited of Ealing London W3. Some interpreted this as a forewarning of Vincent's imminent demise.

The same month there was a full road test of the Special Max in *Motor Cycling* published 18 August. The headline left little to be said; 'A Luxurious German Touring 250 with Unorthodox Cam-drive and 350 cc Performance'. In fact, the highest one-way speed recorded was 76 mph, and except for the low-geared twistgrip throttle action and a couple of very minor points, the NSU was highly praised. The article summed up the Special Max in the following terms: 'Nobody has yet produced the perfect touring motorcycle, but the NSU Max comes very close to it and is certainly a very remarkable – and likeable – machine'. Finish of the test machine was pastel blue, with white lining and chromium plated tank side panels. The Denfeld dual seat was finished in a cherry red. And the whole bike was yours for £235 6s 1d.

NSU powered two-wheeler production hit its peak in 1955. The only new models introduced that year were the Superfox and Max 300, together with the Quickly S moped. But these models were only a fraction of the 298.583 units made by the factory. Of this 1955 total, 228,135 machines were Quickly N machines. Exports of Quickly N's which went to 102 countries and accounted for 73,460 units.

It was also a year of technical innovation. One of the most interesting developments by any motorcycle manufacturer during 1955 was NSU's *rotary valve* engine. Dr Froede's objective as project leader was to prove the effectiveness of the head and barrel joint seal. His data was to have an important role in the development of the Wankel engine.

The rotary valve principal had been known since the turn of the century. In fact, the first British petrol engine used in a motorcycle (designed in 1887 by Edward

Right **Three-times World Champion Werner Haas demonstrates that 'wheelies' were not the sole perogative of riders in the 1970's. The machine is a 123 Superfox and it went on sale in 1955, the year of this photograph.**

Butler) had used a conically-shaped rotary valve. For lack of metallurgical research, however, none of the earlier attempts were truly successful. The central problem which Butler and other pioneers experienced was that although the valve sealed effectively, it wore at an unacceptable rate.

Rotary instead of conventional poppet-type valves theoretically allow a designer to select much higher compression ratios *and* engine revolutions than would otherwise have been possible.

Dr Froede, then the chief research engineer with NSU, experimented with rotary valves. Among Froede's many advances was a working prototype which could be developed alongside the existing Max production engine. This work was of considerable value, because it enabled direct comparisons to be made with the Max. Not only were the engines of the same capacity, but the rotary valve engine used a bottom end from the Max unit. Employing the same compression ratio and the same fuel, the Froede rotary valve engine in its original development state showed a performance increase through the entire speed range. At its maximum, the rotary valve engine was 18 per cent better than the conventional 'lump'.

Besides the Wankel connection there was another very good reason why Froede was interested in rotary valves. At one time it had been considered that they offered a benefit to the factory's race programme. Simplicity, alone, was enough to make them attractive. The conventional valve mechanism of the twin cylinder 250 Rennmax engine consisted of 240 parts, the prototype single cylinder rotary valve engine employed only 62.

Froede's NSU rotary valve engine employed a horizontally rotating valve above the cylinder. It consisted of a large diameter disc, toothed around its circumference and directly driven by the timing shaft. Primarily located by a large diameter ball bearing in the sparsely finned cylinder head, it was pressure lubricated by a standard Max oil pump with slightly increased capacity. Larger displacement was necessary because oil flow for lubricating the rotary valve also served for cooling. This oil-cooling system acted as a barrier between the inlet and exhaust ports with the valve disc. Maximum protection against heat transfer from the exhaust port to the inlet was ensured. Conversely, the cooling effect thereby obtained was sufficient to prevent the rotary valve being damaged by heat distortion.

An important feature of the NSU single cylinder rotary valve prototype engine was the location of the carburettor. This was at the very top, rearwards, of the cylinder head, and effectively lowered the mixture's temperature. For the prototype the carburettor was otherwise conventionally positioned, but for racing purposes Froede considered that a down-draught type should have been used.

This advertisement appeared in Motor Cycle, **16 February 1956, it shows the then new Prima D scooter which was a development of a joint NSU–Lambretta design project.**

He also found the detail design of the valve mechanism was not a problem. But the old metallurgical bogey was still encountered, even though modern technology had greatly assisted in finally solving most of the difficulties. Perhaps the most interesting lesson of Dr Froede's research was that a rotary valve two-stroke engine was possible. In time, it was postulated the conventional method of piston-ported intake and exhaust control would become obsolete.

This was largely to become a reality in many 'strokers of the future. However, this avenue was not fully explored by NSU and the Froede Rotary Valve engine never entered series production. What it did do was to lay the groundwork for a practical Wankel rotary engine.

It was long anticipated by NSU that 1956 would be a decisive year. Most important was the expiry of the agreement with Lambretta. A total of 117,045 NSU-Lambrettas were produced from 1950–56. But the partnership ended in December 1955, by which time it was known that NSU would produce its own scooter. This was launched at the 39th Brussels Show in January 1956. At first glance the new machine, the Prima, seemed so like the original Lambretta that it was unofficially whispered at Brussels that the machine exhibited was no more than a stop-gap and that the *real* NSU model would not be ready for several months. The pundits said with a wink what it would appear at the Frankfurt Show in November.

This was untrue. NSU's scooter was in fact considerably different to a Lambretta. Various improvements and alterations brought the machine up to the standards and luxury by then expected by customers in Germany and abroad. These qualities were soon to make the Prima one of the top selling scooters, not just in Germany, but in several export markets. In Britain it was sold as the Prima D. When the Prima D went on sale in Britain during the spring of 1956 it was priced at £198 6s 9d.

Although the engine, gearbox and transmission were all but the same as its predecessors – with identical capacity, bore, stroke and power output figures – there were considerable differences in its rolling chassis. The Prima D, for example, had pressed steel front forks in place of the tubular type of its Italian progenitor, and plunger-type seat springing was used. The Prima's headlamp nacelle, front mudguard, and side panels all had grilles which would not have been out of place on an American automobile. Unlike the NSU-Lambretta, the handlebars had pressed covers which enclosed all the control cables, a VDO triangular car type speedo, flanked on the left by a knob linked by a cable to both air control and carburettor tickler. On the right side there was a matching, push-pull ignition switch, the key of which could be withdrawn and used to open or close the petrol tap through an aperture on the engine shield.

Like the early Lambrettas and NSU-Lambretta design the engine-gear unit did not pivot with the rear wheel assembly. Instead, the rear wheel was separately sprung, pivoting on a separate casting above a bearing at the rear of the shaft drive housing. The gearbox was still only a three-speeder, but there was now an electric starter with 12 volt electrics. A pair of 6 volt batteries in-series were housed in a compartment behind the weathershield and the arrangement was patented by NSU. The exhaust system was one of the largest (and most effective) ones of the period. The 4.00 × 8 wheels were interchangeable and a spare, together with a large chrome rear carrier were provided as standard equipment.

Although not fast, with a maximum of just over 50 mph, the Prima D was a supremely reliable and luxurious machine, giving owners years of troublefree service. During 1956 a total of 37,062 Prima D's went out to the agent and dealer network. Without these substantial sales 1956 would have been even more traumatic for the Necksarsulm marque.

Following 1955's record number of sales it became apparent at the beginning of July that 1956 was not continuing the trend. NSU announced that 640 workers were to be dismissed over the following two months because sales were lower than expected.

What was happening to NSU was experienced in all areas of the economy. The press started to carry headlines along the lines of; 'German Industry Slowing'. With this background, from the 1 September NSU decreased manufacturing down to a 36 hour working week because of slackening trade. This following so quickly upon the large dismissal of workers in July was a certain warning that the company was in a mortal condition.

Despite the gloom an improved version of the Special Max was announced. Named the Supermax it was ironically to prove the definitive variant of the Max roadster line. Compared to its forerunners, the Supermax differed both in engine tune and chassis details.

The biggest change was the adoption of twin shock, swinging arm rear suspension, of the type used on the Geländemax model from 1953. In the engine department power output was up one bhp to 18 at 6500 rpm. Weight had increased to 383 lb and a maximum speed of 78.5 mph was claimed. Although, when tested by *Motor Cycling*, a best one way speed of only 74.7 mph

Final development of the Max – the Supermax. It came onto the market in 1956 and incorporated many improvements compared to the more basic package offered earlier.

was achieved at the Motor Industry Research Association (MIRA) test circuit near Nuneaton, Warwickshire.

Like earlier Max models, the Supermax built a fine reputation for a long reliable life and an excellent finish. Its virtues are summed up by a letter the author received as editor of *Motor Cycle Enthusiast* magazine in June 1986 from a Mr Henderson of Addingham, West Yorkshire who wrote amongst other things; 'I have been fortunate enough to have owned and ridden most of the modern "classics" but must rate the NSU Super Max as one of, if not *the* most superbly made and finished motorcycles ever produced. It made even a contemporary BMW seem tacky. The paintwork was like black glass and the chrome was so deep you could swim in it. Mechanically it was totally silent, the exhaust being a barely audible thud, thud from the gigantic silencer. Weighing some 375 lbs, acceleration was somewhat sedate, but it would build to its maximum speed and sit there all day, with no oil leaks and no temperament. Handling and roadholding were first class, indeed on a twisting road it could stay ahead of modern machinery of twice its performance as I proved on more than one occasion.'

Motor Cycling concluded its test in similar terms by saying that; 'the Supermax, then, is a fast and docile mount, uncannily quiet, reliable and running for long periods with minimal maintenance and well worthy of consideration for utilisation and pleasure purposes'.

Another version of the Max theme was the Max Scrambler. This was a model built specifically for the American market as a 'street scrambler'. It featured modified front and rear suspension. The front had additional external suspension units, the rear being of the Geländemax/Supermax type. A cut'n'shut Superfox front mudguard, Superfox headlight and fuel tank, plus a Denfeld duo-tone dual seat, and a BMW-type rear light on a specially shortened rear mudguard were fitted. No centre stand was provided, just the standard spring loaded propstand. Neither was a tool box nor a battery box fitted. The battery was instead mounted on a bracket on the offside of the frame; this imitated Geländemax/Sportmax practice.

The remainder of the motorcycle was essentially standard production Special Max/Supermax, but the engine was rumoured to have some tuning goodies, possibly including some genuine Sportmax components. The latter was to enable it to 'compete' in those desert races which American riders of the day referred to as 'scramblers'.

The production Scrambler Max did not appear in Britain. There was, however, another machine with a very similar name – Max Scrambler – which did. This was not a factory-produced machine but the work of Englishman Brian Stonebridge. He was well known for an outstanding run of success in both motocross and trials with Greeves.

Technical illustration of Supermax which revealed many of the details vital to the motorcycle buying public.

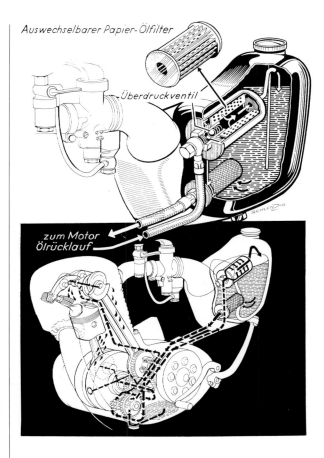

Auswechselbarer Papier-Ölfilter

Überdruckventil

zum Motor
Ölrücklauf

Lubrication system of Supermax including filtration.

The Stonebridge Max Scrambler first appeared in early 1959, and was a tuned production Max power unit grafted into a Greeves scrambler chassis. The frame normally held a Villiers two-stroke engine. Even though Stonebridge was the factory's number one rider at the time, boss Bert Greeves turned a 'blind eye' to the Stonebridge NSU project because, in his opinion, the extra weight of the Max unit would give the chassis additional valuable testing. Moreover, Greeves at that time made no engines of its own.

The tuned Max engine was mounted within a steel box girder, which joined the traditional Greeves alloy front down member to the tubular sub-frame and carried the lower engine mounting. Its creator found that the NSU power unit provided an excellent torque curve, with power available at both ends of the scale. Engine tuning included a Hepolite 10:1 piston, Amal Monobloc carb, racing-type valves and springs. Surprisingly, the camshaft remained standard.

Development of the project was only shelved following the success of the standard Villiers-powered motocrosser which Stonebridge rode to second place in the European Championships that year. The original Stonebridge/NSU survives today.

Show season 1956 opened with first Paris in early October, followed by Frankfurt later that month. Although NSU exhibited at both, the introduction of new models was reserved for the larger home event. Frankfurt 1956 was very much a shop window of an industry with the severe over-production problems. Even so, most manufacturers, NSU included, put a brave face on things and combined to make it the largest-ever motorcycle show up to that time anywhere in the world.

The Neckarsulm factory had a hall to themselves at Frankfurt. Special display items were the Baumm II and Delphin III record breakers covered elsewhere. As *Motor Cycling* reported 'the former so small that it looks, at first glance, almost like a model of itself!'

Pride of place was afforded the recently introduced Supermax, but the new Quickly L was no doubt the most important new exhibit for NSU – perhaps even in the whole show. It was a de luxe version of their best seller. It had partial enclosure of the rear wheel, a deeply valanced front mudguard, leg shields, scooter type handlebars/headlamp layout and swinging arm rear suspension. Engine specification remained unchanged. Although only 116 were produced in 1956, 55,651 left Neckersulm the following year. But it never achieved the success of the Quickly N.

A show surprise was the Maxi, a brand new model which was to replace both the 125 Superfox and 200 Lux when production started in early 1957. The exhibition models and the very first production version were virtually a 175 engined Superfox with a more

A Supermax' filler cap was considered by many to be a work of art. It was cast in alloy and proudly stated that NSU riders had won the World Championship in 1953, 1954 and 1955. Competitors could only be jealous.

NSU's ohv 174 cc Maxi appeared in 1957. Its 62 × 58 mm engine produced a very useful 12.5 bhp.

deeply valanced front mudguard. The main production model had a Superfox main frame, but the rear sub frame now sported external Supermax type twin hydraulic shock absorbers. The early version also had Superfox pressed steel handlebar, while later versions had Supermax tubular bends. The 175 cc (62 × 58 mm) ohv engine gave 12.5 bhp at 6500 rpm with maximum safe revs of 7000 rpm. It used a Bing 2/22 carb and four-speed gearbox, and with a dry weight of 284 lb would reach 68.75 mph. Electrics were Bosch 6v 45w and other details included 3.25 × 18 front and rear tyres and wheels with 140 mm diameter full-width alloy hubs. Fuel tank capacity was 10.8-litres.

With motorcycle and moped sales falling while demand for small cars was growing, a decision was made in 1956 to re-enter the car market after a break of over 35 years. However, this only came after Fiat had agreed to release NSU from the two companies' agreement of 1930, which had until then effectively banned NSU from car manufacture.

Throughout the following months considerable effort was put into getting NSU ready for its break back into four wheels. This was realised in September 1957 when the Prinz I was announced. Powered by an air cooled twin cylinder four-stroke, the drive to its ohc was by Roder Ultramax valve gear.

Series production of both the Prinz I and II did not commence until 1958, but thereafter NSU was to place increasing reliance in four rather than two wheels.

The Prinz car did, however, have more than its Ultramax valve operation to connect it to its two-wheel cousins. The engine was later used in several motorcycles. Most important of these was the Münch Mammoth, but in addition to this limited-production superbike many Prinz engines finished up in both solo and sidecar specials, for both road and racing use.

Production figures in 1957 took an even bigger knock with 148,420 mopeds, 31,938 scooters and only 8,971 motorcycles being produced by NSU. The motorcycle production total was broken down into 1,408 Superfoxes (making a total of 15,530 produced from 1955 to spring 1957), 2,563 Supermaxes and 5,000 of the new Maxi.

Three significant new models were announced during 1957, the Quickly-Cavallino and two new Prima scooters, the III and the V.

The first of these, the Quickly-Cavallino was made in relatively small volumes (a total of 21,584) between 1957–60. Its styling was decidedly Italian, but although having a far more sporting appearance than any other Quickly model, the Cavallina was a sales failure. The 49 cc (40 × 39 mm) engine gave a maximum output of 1.7 bhp on a compression ratio of 5.5:1. With a three-speed gearbox, weight of 118 lb and 2.25 × 19 inch tyres, it had a top speed of 25 mph. The model's UK price in August 1958 was £99 19s 11d.

Of the two Prima scooters, first came the Prima V (also known as the Five Star) which was introduced mid-way through 1957. Although bearing a family resemblance to the original Prima D, the basic concept was very different. Other than the obvious styling changes, the Prima V had a completely new frame and a larger capacity 174 cc engine – again of new design. Still a single cylinder two stroke, it had a bore and stroke of 62 × 57.5 mm adding up to 174 cc and producing 9.5 bhp at 5100 rpm, with a compression ratio of 6.35:1.

Pivot-mounted to the frame, the cast iron cylinder was set horizontally and transversely on the right of the machine. This left the dynamo flywheel facing forward, although the same forced-air cooling system, by means of fan blades on the dynamo flywheel, was employed as on the original Prima. There was no primary transmission and the engine drove a single dry plate clutch coupled to a four-speed, foot operated gearbox in unit with the engine. Where the earlier machine had

employed a drive shaft, this was replaced with a series of spiral bevel gears, thus, the secondary drive was transmitted directly to the rear wheel.

Maximum speed was increased to 56 mph. But the biggest improvement area was the machine's ability to cope with a pillion passenger. Suspension and ride of the Prima V were adjudged to be excellent. This was in no small way due to the combination of pivoted engine suspended by a compression spring with telescopic hydraulic shock absorber between the rear casing and the frame. The front suspension had also been altered. A swinging arm principle was adopted, together with a single hydraulic damper unit mounted on the left-hand side arm. Tyre size had been increased to 3.50 × 10 to improve both the general ride and handling.

Standard equipment for the Prima V included 12 volt electrics. A Dynastart starter unit, a mudguard mounted fog lamp, larger fuel tank, spare wheel and carrier were also factory fitted.

The Prima V, was, from all aspects considerably better than the earlier NSU scooters. Indeed, it was often said that its handling improved when a passenger was carried. Usually the reverse was true with scooters. The close to silent two-stroke engine coped admirably with any tasks it was asked to perform.

Shortly after the introduction of the Prima V, an

Quickly-Cavallino, although it was sporting in styling it never sold in high volume compared with other Quickly models. The factory last made Quickly-Cavallinos in 1960.

economy version appeared. The Prima III had a 146 cc capacity, achieved by sleeving the original cylinder and fitting a 57 mm piston. The electric starter was replaced by a kick starter and the fog lamp and expensive facia that included a clock on the Prima V was deleted.

NSU's Engineering Department, secure in having patented its Ultramax rotary valve system announced details of further developments. Whilst retaining the eccentrically operated driving rod, NSU incorporated cranking so that the rise and fall of this rod caused the overhead camshaft to oscillate instead of rotating. There were at least three applications. In one the inlet and exhaust camshafts were co-axial but each operated by a separate rod. A third rod, referred to as a radius rod, served to control the distance between the operating shaft and the camshaft, thus compensating for changes of head shape and position through thermal action.

The next option was the same concept taken a stage further, with a dohc engine, dispensing with rockers using the same principle. The third possibility was a refinement in which the cam wheels were carried on trunnions pivoted concentrically with the mainshaft pinion. The attitude of these trunnions was controlled solely by the length of the radius rods. This was clearly desirable, as it meant that all distortion was automatically compensated for, instead, as in the first two types, of only having its effect reduced to an acceptable minimum and which could be accommodated by the shaft supports.

Yet again, in 1958 production at NSU fell. With the Prinz cars coming on stream the consequences were not as acute as they might have been for a manufacturer whose sole business was motorcycles. Car production accounted for 13,022 sales against 94,256 Quickly models and a total of just 3,546 motorcycles (Maxi 1,189, Supermax 2,357). All two-wheeler production was, therefore, down to 123,973 machines. It was fortunate for the company that another new line – the Agria – sold well. The Agria was a Quickly engined rotavator and a total of 79,752 of these were produced between 1958 and 1965.

In October, the British importers NSU (GB) Ltd announced that eight models would be available for the 1959 season. These were the Quickly N, S and L, the Quickly Cavallino, the Prima D, III and V and the Supermax. The Supermax had a price tag of £262 11s 7d. At the Earls Court show in November 1958 the highlight of the NSU stand was a revolving turntable on which were mounted three Prima III scooters in distinctive colour schemes. One combined turquoise and cream, the second tangerine and cream and the third black and lime green. Also shown was a single Supermax and five Quicklys, one of which was resplendent with all available optional extras.

NSU in 1959 reported increased turnover in all departments, except motorcycles and scooters. These

Right **The Quickly S, built 1961–63, was one of the final variations on NSU's profitable theme.**

showed yet another small drop. Car sales accounted for 33,376 out of a total of 162,450 units, while Quicklys made up 102,544 of the rest, Prima scooters contributed 23,273, and motorcycles a mere 3,257 made up of 1,854 Maxis and 1,403 Supermaxes.

Technically, however, the company was as buoyant as ever. At the end of the year had come the first public reports of, as *Motor Cycling* put it, a 'Revolutionary NSU engine'. This referred to Felix Wankel's engine and the development had been undertaken over the last six years at the NSU plant.

Wankel's design could not be described as completely new because details of a similar unit had appeared as the British Beaumont as far back as 1938. Although with the onset of war, development of this particular project was shelved. And if you call the NSU-Wankel a *Drehkolbenmotor* (revolving piston engine) a *rotary* engine, then several others existed as prototypes as early as 1886. However, whatever the arguments, Wankel achieved the first commercial application of the concept. And, therefore, occupies an important place in automotive history.

NSU's first contact with Felix Wankel came in 1951, when Dr Froede first began research into his own rotary valve project, and needed information on sealing technology. As Wankel had been engaged in this area during the war, specifically on rotary disc valves for German Navy torpedo engines, it was not unnatural that the two soon found themselves exchanging ideas.

The agreement into which Wankel, Froede and NSU entered into was originally confined to rotary valves. And it was not until around late 1953 that Wankel discovered that the four-stroke engine cycle could be contained by an epitrochoidal bore containing an equilateral rotor. But there is evidence of later co-operation in 1956 because NSU used a compressor based on Wankel's design principles to propel its 49 cc two-stroke powered Baumm II record-breaker.

A year on, Froede with Wankel's help, succeeded in turning the inner and outer sections of this machine inside out, and so created what was to emerge as the Wankel engine. As development continued throughout the late 1950's, unknown to the world, NSU and Wankel's project became imperceptibly interwoven.

Following official announcement of the Wankel engine's existence the concept was to dictate the company's future as it entered the new decade. For 1960, however, the trend towards the Wankel development and four wheels was not reflected in an unchanged selection of NSU two wheelers for the British market. The range topping Supermax available at £253 17s 11d. This was the only 'real' motorcycle available, the balance of this range being made up by Quickly mopeds and Prima scooters.

In fact, during the 1960s the only new NSU motorcycle was the Quick 50 introduced in 1962. The Quick 50 has often been described as 'just another Quickly'. This is not accurate. It had its own four-speed engine unit and did not share any of the Quickly moped engine components.

The cycle parts had been used on a previous model known as the Quickly TT and TTK (which were produced from 1959–63 and 1960–61 respectively. Both the TT and TTK employed three-speed Quickly engines and had pedals, so unlike the Quick 50, which had a kickstart, they were true mopeds rather than motorcycles.

The Quick 50 had Earles-type front forks, swinging arm twin shock rear suspension and a pressed steel space frame. The Continental 2.50 × 23 tyres were mounted on chromed steel rims, with full width alloy brake hubs on both wheels. Dry weight was 176 lb.

The 50 cc (40 × 39.5 mm) power unit was like the Quickly's in layout, a single piston port 'stroker, and had a 9:1 compression ratio, while running on a petrol/oil mixture of 25:1. The four-speed gearbox was in unit with the engine, and foot-operated by a pedal on the left. Primary drive was by helical gear, with the final drive

chain protected by a pressed steel fully-enclosed case.

The Quick's price when it was launched on the British market in October 1962 was £119 17s 6d, which by March 1964 had risen to £127 15s 0d. When tested by *Motor Cycle* in their 26 March 1964 issue the Quick 50 was found to have a maximum speed of 45 mph and fuel consumption of 120 mpg. Suspension was felt to be on the soft side, although this was not detrimental to roadholding. With its large two-tone dual seat, it was as capable of carrying two adults as any machine of a similar capacity had ever been.

By the summer of 1963, reports begun circulating that NSU was to discontinue production of motorcycles and mopeds. This brought an angry denial from both the factory and its British importers NSU (Great Britain) Limited. The latter's Sales Manager Peter Bolton, later head of Puch in Britain, made a statement to the British press. Bolton explained that he had only just returned from Germany where he had been discussing production schedules of the Quick 50 and Quickly moped for 1964–65. While he was at the factory he had taken the opportunity of looking over the new production lines and assembly shops, which he stated 'were the most modern in Europe'.

For one rider this was the ultimate NSU. It appeared at the Amsterdam Show in 1974 and had a Prinz car engine in a Norton frame. It is interesting to note that this superbike was built nearly ten years after NSU made its last two-wheeler.

Bolton also pointed out that, in a company report, Dr Gerd Stieler von Heydekampf (NSU chief from 1953 to 1969) had stated that because of labour shortages at Neckarsulm arising from meeting increasing demand, it was necessary to find additional capacity.

What of course this statement did not reveal was that the 'increased demand' was for cars, not two-wheelers. In many ways the press rumours were not far short of the mark.

Indeed, the last Supermax rolled off the production line in 1963. Compared with Max and Special Max, production figures for the Supermax were low. Only 15,473 machines were produced between 1956 and 1963. NSU's span of 74 years of bicycle making also came to an end in 1963. Overall, the company had built 1,742,838 muscle-powered two-wheelers. The Prima scooters went the following year, together with the Maxi motorcycle, while the final batch of 2,500 Quick 50s was produced in 1965. The total number for Quick 50s was only 9,323.

The last NSU two wheelers on sale in Britain were three Quickly models offered at prices between £76 15s 4d and £105 11s 1d in November 1966 by Layford (Automotive) Limited of Harbour Way, Shoreham-by-Sea, Sussex.

Without a doubt, throughout the early 1960's NSU management appeared to be totally preoccupied with its range of rear-engined Prinz cars and the marketing of licences for the Wankel engine. By 1964 the company could boast total production of the various Prinz models for the year at 88,292 units. Licences for the Wankel engine, apparently, going well. Automotive application were buttressed by marine and domestic power unit products.

But it was the award-winning Ro80 car introduced in 1967 which was ironically to prove the Neckarsulm company's final, and fatal, move. When launched, the new coupe was hailed as a truly exciting technical achievement which broke much new ground. And, at first at least, it sold well. In Britain, Octav Bottnar, now better known as the driving force behind Nissan in the UK, came from Germany to revitalize the NSU franchise. Bottnar very successfully raised market penetration from 350 units a year to 10,000 in the four years from 1966.

The Ro80 combined a silky smooth 115 bhp Wankel twin rotor power unit, front wheel drive, an electric clutch controlled by a knob on the gear lever and an aerodynamically streamlined body shell that would not have looked out of place twenty years later.

Unfortunately for the Ro80, and most of all for NSU, the car was hampered with problems. Heavy fuel consumption and rapid wear of the rotor tips were the two most cited causes of complaint.

The company was forced into massive over-spending of its planned budget in an attempt to solve these failings and in the end the problems beat them. Quite simply NSU had *guaranteed* that the Ro80 was unburstable. When customers managed to blow them up NSU replaced the engine for free under warranty. Just fitting a simple rev limiter could well have avoided this expensive exercise.

By early 1969 NSU were in deep financial trouble, the first time since their crisis of 1930, and an injection of capital was needed to survive. On 10 March that year the once-great company ceased to exist as an independent body. Audi NSU Auto Union AG was officially integrated into the Volkswagen Group to become Germany's largest automobile manufacturing complex. Today, Audi's advertising slogan *Vorsprung durch Technik* (Progress through Technology) could well have applied equally to at least one of the present company's direct ancestors – NSU.

A rare bird, at least in Britain. A 1951 Konsol II with Steib sidecar which was photographed at the 1983 Vintage Motor Cycle Club Coventry to Brighton run. Today, NSU's are steadily acquiring value as more collectors and restorers hunt for examples to return to splendour.

NSU

the racing machines

Almost from its beginning, NSU recognised the importance of motorcycle sport as a proving ground for its technology and a marketing tool for its products. As early as 1905 it offered a purpose built competition motorcycle 50 mph 402 cc *Rennmaschine* (racing machine).

There is no doubt the NSU marque's success in the British market in the early 1900s was a major reason why the German company took part in the very first Isle of Man TT races in 1907. Martin Geiger, NSU's manager in Britain, rode his Neckarsulm machine to come home fifth in the single cylinder class.

There were other sporting interests, too, from a very early stage in the company history. In 1908, realising the importance of record-breaking in capturing the public imagination, NSU rider Liese achieved a two-way speed of 68 mph. It was claimed as a world record – even though no official records were maintained at the time. The following year, Lingenfielders clocked 77.5 mph just outside Los Angeles to claim another record. His success propelled NSU into the lucrative North American market. These early attempts established that NSU could see the importance of being able to lay claim to the 'world's fastest' title. It was to become even more significant in the light of later, post-World War Two events.

The next major phase in sporting development came some years after World War I, when NSU 'bought in' the expertise of Norton's leading designer Walter Moore in 1929. Moore claimed the Norton overhead camshaft racing singles design as his own on the grounds that it

had been done in his own time. And as a result, Moore's new 1930 NSU Renn Maschine's 494 and 592 cc engines although using a four-speed gearbox looked so much like a 1928 works Norton that they were laughingly dubbed 'Norton Spares Used'. Even so, they were good enough to remain in the NSU line-up until 1935.

The technically advanced 348 cc (56 × 70.5 mm) supercharged dohc parallel twin (also raced in 248 cc form that year) ridden by Heiner Fleischmann, Karl Bodmer, 'Crasher' White and Wilhelm Herz appeared in 1938. But Germany and NSU were then very rapidly caught up in a conflict which put paid to sporting plans for almost the next decade. Walter Moore left the company at the beginning of the War. It was not until he had been succeeded as chief designer in 1947 by Albert Roder than NSU had the management leadership to return to racing.

Roder first produced an unblown version of the pre-war supercharged 350 parallel twin racer. Its double overhead cams were arranged in 'Y' formation. He had also been instrumental in the development of the production lightweight, the Fox 4, and a year later a racing version, the Sportfox appeared. The power unit was basically a tuned roadster engine which gave 7.5 bhp at 7,000 rpm, and was mounted in a stripped-down standard chassis. The factory had originally intended making thirty of these under-100 cc racers for loan to promising youngsters in order to encourage fresh blood to gain racing experience and fulfill its potential. A laudable aim, but commercial reality intervened and the machines were offered for public sale after enormous interest had been shown at the Frankfurt Show in March 1950. It was probably this event which was to set in motion NSU's huge Grand Prix effort with the 125 singles and 250 twins over the next few years.

NSU's early post-war racing programme was centred firmly around the pre-war 348 cc parallel twin – now code-named RK1 – in both the original supercharged and unblown forms. These were joined in 1949 by a 499 cc (63 × 80 mm) version, also called RK1, which gave 85 bhp at 8,000 rpm with a supercharger fitted. As Germany was then excluded from the FIM it continued

NSU's sidecar pairing of Hermann Böhm (left) and passenger Fuchs in 1949. The lady is Inge Lowenstein, who was then 'Miss Germany'. This dohc 500 cc parallel twin was a much improved version of a pre-war design.

to develop supercharged machines even though the FIM had banned them from competition in 1946.

By 1950, with 98 bhp on tap, the supercharged 500 twin was a highly potent machine for its time, even though it weighed 484 lbs and was unstreamlined. One ridden by Heiner Fleischmann sped through the electronic timing eye at 143.75 mph during a race at Hockenheim in May 1950. But Fleischmann, and the other NSU stars Wilhelm Herz and Walter Zeller were brave men to pilot these machines when one considers that their phenomenal power output was matched to far from perfect handling and braking. For example, at the front were pre-war girder forks and at the rear an early form of plunger controlled damping. It could not have been easy to control all that power.

Perhaps the best performances which the parallel twins put up was in record breaking. On the Munich-Ingolstadt autobahn on 12 April 1951 Wilhelm Herz broke the world speed record by achieving 180.17 mph using one of the blown 500 parallel twin motors mounted in a streamlined shell. This was followed just a few hours later by Hermann Böhm on the same machine, but equipped with a third wheel 'outrigger', who set a new sidecar record at 154 mph.

Even though he had achieved over 180 mph, Herz said at the time that had a more suitable course been available an even higher speed would have been obtained. The reason was that the part of the autobahn which was available to the team was not long enough. There were also problems associated with the effect two bridges across the autobahn had on the steering of the streamlined machine. So great was the sideways thrust at these two points, even on a calm day, that the distance of the run had to be shorter than what was actually needed. An unusual facet of the record attempt was that narrow ribbed 19 inch tyres were used on both wheels.

A little later a 348 cc supercharged engine in the solo record breaker set a new world record at 172.5 mph in the 350 cc category for the flying kilometre. On this run the engine was accidentally over-revved to the extent that valve float caused indentations in the piston crowns over a depth of nearly 2 mm.

Shortly after the successful record spree, on 29 April, came the first public appearance of a brand NSU racing machine. The four cylinder model was put on display at the Eilenriede-Rennen, Hanover National Championship race meeting.

The story of the 500 four racer project really began in July 1949, when NSU's new chief designer Albert Roder completed an Alpine publicity tour aboard the newly introduced 98 cc ohc Fox roadster. In Switzerland he made a point of staying in Berne in order to watch the

Supercharged battle of the giants, Heiner Fleischmann (11) chases BMW's Georg Meier at Hockenheim, May 1950.

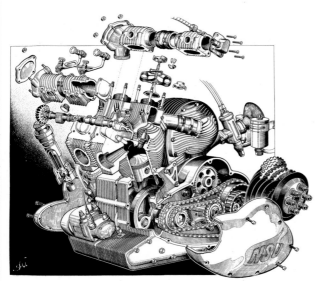

Cutaway drawing of a blown 499 cc parallel dohc racing engine circa 1950. This unit was used for both circuit contests and record breaking.

Swiss Grand Prix at the Bremgarten circuit. For the first time since the war, Roder had the opportunity to study non-German racing machinery at close quarters. Without question the machine which held his attention the most was the four-cylinder Gilera, and on his return to Neckarsulm, Roder devoted himself intensively to the job of producing a similar machine. Within the incredibly short period of four months he formulated a complete design and produced a set of drawings for his potential world beater.

With German racers still using compressors, he drafted two versions – a supercharged machine with the chance of producing 125 bhp at 10,000 rpm, and an atmospheric induction model capable of around 60 bhp at the same engine revolutions. Both versions shared the same 55 × 54 mm bore and stroke dimensions, which gave an exact capacity of 494.68 cc. Fortunately, both design options were favourably received by the company's senior management. It was unanimously agreed by the Board that to gain world prestige through racing was excellent publicity for the sale of standard production machines. Furthermore, because of Germany's impending entry back into the FIM fold, authority was given to produce and develop the unblown version.

By the end of 1950, the European motorcycle racing community was abuzz with rumours that believed NSU had produced a really novel machine incorporating much new thinking and technical innovation. The machine, now given the code name R54, was finally unveiled at the Eilenriede-Rennen race meeting. The prototype displayed a great turn of speed, but was put out of the running in the race on the fifth lap by a broken petrol pipe. However, its performance attracted

considerable press coverage. It was reported in *Motor Cycle*, 17 May 1951; 'to show great promise'. It also proved that the Neckarsulm company was not afraid of venturing into completely new territory.

Externally the engine appeared, at first sight, to be a fairly conventional across-the-frame four cylinder, with dohc. The two camshafts were driven by a train of gears from a crankshaft mounted pinion in a housing between the second and third cylinders. And there was a secondary take-off from the crankshaft pinion to the four-speed gearbox and oil pump. This pinion also powered two twin spark Bosch magnetos which were situated immediately behind the cylinders above the gearbox. The heavily finned crankcase casting was in two halves, split horizontally, and carrying a heavily finned separate sump. There were four separate alloy cylinders with horizontal finning, and four massively finned aluminium alloy cylinder heads. These had different finning around the exhaust ports, into which four slender exhaust pipes were retained by screwed-in finned clamps. The exhaust pipes themselves terminated in short shallow, chrome plated reverse cone megaphones. Carburation was via four clip fitting 20 mm Amal remote needle instruments with synchronised throttle slide operation from an inlet cambox mounted linkage. Two independent, rubber mounted, float chambers were housed between each pair of carburettors.

The outside of the engine might have appeared conventional, but inside it was a completely different story. The massive nickel-chrome steel crankshaft assembly was fully machined and highly polished all over. A truly magnificent piece of engineering in its own right. And it was built up using Hirth couplings, brought together by differentially threaded bolts. A Hirth coupling consists of a series of radial serrations machined on two mating faces formed at 90 degrees to the shaft axis. A different pitch is used for the internal thread in each of the mating parts so that tightening the double-ended bolt which engages the threads and clamps them securely together. This unique method of construction results in an extremely rigid assembly and permits accurate assembly of the various components and also allows roller bearing big-ends to be used with one-piece connecting rods.

In the NSU design the crank had two bobweights per cylinder. Eight main bearings were used to support the crankshaft, of which six were mounted in special housings independent of the crankcase castings. From these housings were mounted six pairs of long slender studs which were used to retain the upper half of the crankcase, the cylinder barrels and cylinder heads. This unconventional method of construction resulted in an immensely strong bottom end and the elimination of crankshaft 'whip' at the high revolutions. The bottom half of the crankcase casting was bolted to the upper half by a series of studs and was totally unstressed.

NSU took great care to ensure adequate lubrication, even to the extent that the SAE 20 vegetable racing oil was pre-heated to about 90°C by NSU technicians before the engine was started. The oil pump was of a complex design and extremely well made. It was situated within the heavily finned sump and was driven by the gear pinion in the centre of the crankshaft at one quarter engine speed. Oil was fed constantly to the big-end bearings by four 2.2 mm diameter nozzles squirting directly on to the bearing surfaces. Lubrication to other parts of the engine unit was controlled by ten 1.2 mm phased jets, while the supply to the overhead cam gear was via external pipework running alongside the camshaft drive housing. From the camboxes oil was gravity fed to the cylinder head and drained down through external pipework back to the crankcase and sump.

The dry multi-plate clutch had fabric friction inserts and lay in a ventilated housing on the left of the machine. Drive was transmitted through a conventional four-speed close ratio gearbox to the main drive sprocket on the right. Final transmission was by chain.

The engine/gearbox unit was housed in a duplex tubular cradle frame of all-welded construction, in which the widely-splayed front downtubes connected with the crankcase assembly via a separate linkage. Rear suspension was controlled through a triangulated swinging fork pivoting on the frame at a point immediately behind the gearbox final drive sprocket. The swinging fork engaged a large, moulded rubber suspension damper mounted to the frame at a point beneath the nose of the saddle. Rebound damping was controlled by adjustable friction dampers mounted on each side of the frame.

A rubber-in-torsion rear suspension may have been quite revolutionary, but the front suspension was also ahead of its time. It had two curved legs extending forwards and above the front wheel spindle. These were rigidly held together by heavy top and bottom lugs at the steering head. At the foot of each fork member was a steel pressing containing a rubber suspension unit and individual cast aluminium trailing links. The trailing links retained a short operating arm which engaged with the rubber suspension unit. Rebound damping was controlled by a large, wing-nut operated friction damper situated at the trailing link pivot.

Braking was by built-up full width hubs constructed in light alloy, containing twin leading shoes at the front and single leading shoes at the rear.

The dry weight was considerably more than the contemporary Gilera and MV Agusta four. The machine became much heavier still when fuel was added to the hand-beaten 27-litre alloy fuel tank.

The R54 was entered in numerous German events during the 1951 season and ridden by NSU development riders Herz and Fleischmann. In addition an R54 engine assembly, mounted on a girder fork, plunger sprung frame was used in sidecar events by the German national champions, Hermann Böhm and Karl Fuchs.

In spite of intense development the design only achieved moderate success. At its inception engine output was 53 bhp, which was promising enough, but it was hobbled by many mechanical problems. No doubt, given time, these could have been solved, but an edict by NSU management shelved the machine before this could happen.

The policy decision was based on the fact that although in 1951 NSU was producing a range of roadsters from 98 to 500 cc, the company's long term aim was to rationalise the range to four engine sizes: 125, 200, 250 and 300 cc – plus a complementary range of mopeds and scooters. If NSU was to concentrate sales on smaller capacity machines it made sense to strive for racing success in the ultra-lightweight and lightweight (125 and 250 cc) classes.

And so, from the ashes of the short lived 500 four project there sprang up a series of single and twin cylinder NSU lightweight racing machines.

The lessons learned in the development of their larger brother were quickly and effectively put to use in the new challenge for honours.

June 1951 saw the first apperance of a brand new 125

Heiner Fleischmann with the 1951 four-cylinder R54 500 cc Grand Prix racer.

cc racer. The R11 Rennfox was one of the first machines which benefitted from technology gained from the abortive four cylinder project. Like the 500, it used square 54 × 54 mm bore and stroke dimensions, which gave a capacity of 123.67 cc. Power output of the dohc single was 12 bhp at 10,500 rpm, with a forged three-ring piston that worked at 9.8:1 compression ratio, and Amal RN9 26 mm carb. The engine was an extremely neat piece of work with full unit construction, and a huge cambox. A mass of gears on the right of the unit had power transmitted to it by bevel shaft. There was also another gear assembly with a conventional pressed-up crankshaft and one piece con-rod with roller bearing big-end. Integral with the crankcase was a massive oil chamber for the wet sump lubrication system. External plumbing for the pump was stainless steel braided hoses. A large oil filler cap protruded from the engine alongside the forward-mounted magneto drive pinion. The cylinder head and barrel were inclined 12 degrees from vertical.

The engine unit was mounted on a pressed steel chassis, based on the road-going Fox, with leading-link front forks of a different design to the 500 four. These were controlled by an external damper, while at the rear was a form of monoshock rear suspension without

Hermann Böhm aboard the record breaking version of the supercharged 500 cc parallel twin. For the attempt it was equipped with a third wheel 'outrigger'. Unorthodox, perhaps, but it snatched the world sidecar record in April 1951.

rebound damping. Brakes were aluminium alloy full-width drums front and rear which carried flanges secured by rivets for the alloy wheel rims. The machine's appearance was dominated by the exhaust system. Its long, shallow-taper megaphone ran back on the right, almost as far as the extreme rear of the machine, while a neatly crafted 14-litre alloy tank proclaiming 'Fox NSU' really set the little bike off. Weight was 198 lb and top speed was 93.75 mph.

An interesting sideline to the sporting programme in 1951 was the Renn-Lambretta racing scooter. However, very little of this machine bore much more than a passing resemblance to the then-current range of production NSU-Lambretta scooters. Its tuned engine produced 9 bhp at 8,000 rpm and had a top speed of almost 80 mph. A special frame was used, plus larger 3.00 × 12 inch wheels, conventional motorcycle-type fuel tank and a front mudguard-cum-fairing. Both the latter components were made in hand-beaten alloy.

A notable rider of the Renn-Lambretta was the Italian Romolo Ferri. He later raced works Gilera and Ducati machines. Ferri was one of a threesome with Ambrosini and Rizzi who had been entered by Innocenti for a speed record attempt on 5 October 1950 at Monthlery, in France. On a supercharged 125 Lambretta streamliner they shattered the world's 125 cc records for the 1,000 km, 6-hours and 12-hours, with speeds of 82.34, 82.59 and 82.34 mph respectively. During 1951 the same machine captured the 50 km at 100 mph, 100 miles at 98.5 mph, and the 1 hour at 98.2 mph.

But the most magnificent of the whole series of records came at an attempt where Ferri alone was the rider. On the 8 August 1951 he took NSU's blown 'stroker (claimed to develop 13.5 bhp at 9,000 rpm) out onto the Munich-Ingoldstadt autobahn. He then recorded the outstanding speeds of 124.8 and 125.442 mph over the flying kilometre and mile distances.

Towards the end of the year talk in GP pit lanes began to hint that NSU had built a 250 twin racer and speculation grew that 1952 would see the factory extend its racing activities.

For 1952, the 125 Rennfox was reported as 'considerably improved'. But by studying the 1952 model, it was evident that essentially it was an enhanced 1951 bike, rather than a new design. Major changes which were visible included the dry clutch and front suspension with new-style leading links and internal hydraulic spring/damper units, plus revised brakes with the operating lever on the left. Other engine changes encompassed a shallower sump and vertically-mounted oil pump whose delivery was via a cast-in feed to flexible hoses on top of the righthand casting, plus a four-stud fixing blanking plate covered the magneto drive pinion. Less evident was the engine tuning, with power was now up to 14 bhp at 11,000 rpm. During the 1952 season, there were more suspension developments. The rear fork was now controlled by twin external spring hydraulically-damped suspension units.

Motor Cycling 10 April 1952 reported that NSU had recently advertised throughout Germany for riders willing to compete for a place in the factory team. In the first week alone there were 274 applications. At the same time, although the 250 twin project was spoken of, it was still reported to be on the secret list.

The debut of the new team was at Germany's first major event of the year, the international *Rhine Cup* at Hockenheim on 11 May. In the 125 race four NSU machines were entered and ridden by Romolo Ferri, Wilhelm Hofmann, Hubert Luttenberger and Walter Reichert. With a great show of reliability the four riders came home, third, fourth, fifth and sixth respectively. However, the Rennfox at this time clearly could not match the speed of the FB Mondials which finished in front of them and ridden by race winner Ubbiali and second placed Müller. Ubbiali made fastest lap at 85.69 mph.

But it was the 250 race which really attracted attention. Here there were works entries from Moto Guzzi, DKW and NSU. The latter pair of marques drew the following comment in the 15 May 1952 issue of *Motor Cycling*; 'Among the several interesting designs entered for last Sunday's international Hockenheim meeting in Germany were two which may materially help to put that country back into a position of serious

rivalry to British and Italian factories'.

How right that forecast was to prove, especially in relation to NSU. For the three machines entered were the first of what was to prove the definitive NSU racing motorcycle, the 250 R22 Rennmax dohc parallel twin.

Unlike the 125 Rennfox, the twin was the work of Dr Walter Froede. Contrary to popular belief, this initial Rennmax was not based on a projected road-going twin cylinder model, but was completely purpose-built. The 1952 Rennmax shared the square 56 × 56 mm dimensions of both the 125 single and 500 four, giving a capacity of 247.34 cc. Initially the power was 25 bhp at 9,000 rpm, improving to 29 bhp at 9,800 rpm by the season's end.

The engine was again full unit-construction with primary drive by enclosed chain to a four-speed close ratio gear cluster. It featured a pressed-up crankshaft assembly supported by three roller bearings. Early failure of light alloy big-end cages at high engine speeds was overcome by the use of an improved alloy and by anodizing the friction surfaces. There was an Alfin cylinder barrel, with an aluminium alloy head. The twin overhead camshafts were driven on the offside of the engine by separate 'Y' bevel shafts in the same manner as the earlier 350/500 parallel twins. A feature of the early 250 was the use of torsion bar valve springs, but

A 1952 Rennfox 125 cc double knocker single.

Otto Daiker, Roberto Colombo and Wilhelm Hofmann – NSU's 1952 racing team. Hofmann (129) is astride the original prototype Rennmax, the other machines are later 125 Rennfoxes. The team members were treated as celebrities.

after initial problems these were changed to hairpin springs which remained thereafter on all the later Rennmax models.

Two single float chamber 24 mm (later 25 mm) Amal RN carburettors were fitted, inclined at 30 degrees downdraught. As on the smaller machine, both megaphones were of the long shallow taper type. Ignition was by battery and coil but with no generator. Two 6-volt 7 amp/hour batteries wired in parallel were housed in a light alloy pressing beneath the seat. The use of coil ignition on the twin was not due to any desire to save the small amount of power absorbed by a magneto, but was dictated by repeated magneto problems encountered in the early stages of development with the 125 Rennfox. A distributor, housing the points and condenser was mounted in the timing chest and driven by a skew gear from the lower bevel for the inlet camshaft drive coupling.

A full cradle, twin downtube, tubular frame was employed with twin shock swinging arm suspension and telescopic front forks. It was the only NSU racer to use them. An aluminium alloy fuel tank and full width single leading shoe brake hubs built into 18 inch alloy wheel rims were indicative of the bike's character. Dry

weight was 253 lb. On some of these early Rennmax machines a large hand beaten alloy tail shell was employed, but on many other machines the rear end was left naked.

Neckarsulm's competitions department concentrated throughout 1952 on development work and preparation in anticipation of the 1953 World Championship for 125 and 250 classes. In the classics the factory's best result in 1952 was that of new boy Werner Haas. In his first big race for the marque at the German GP at Solitude, he displayed the hallmarks of a future world champion by winning the 125 race. Haas had taken on and beaten the Mondial of Carlo Ubbiali and the MV Agusta of World Champion-elect Cecil Sandford. Haas had served his racing apprenticeship on a home-built Puch split single. Coincidentally, this man who was born in Augsberg in 1927 had chosen an NSU 501 OSL as his first motorcycle.

Other positions gained by NSU riders that year in the 125 class was a fifth at Solitude by Luttenberger and a sixth by the same rider at the final GP at Monza. It was also at Monza that the 250 showed its form in the World series. Haas finished in second place, behind race winner Lorenzetti's factory Guzzi. Roberto Columbo on another Rennmax came home fifth. A warning of what to expect in future was plainly displayed.

As if the advances on the production and racing fronts were not enough for NSU that year, the company also launched into the gruelling world of the ISDT. For this type of off-road event NSU gave all its machines the prefix *Gelände* (open country) in front of the model name – Fox, Max etc., became Geländefox; Geländemax etc.

That year the ISDT was staged 18–23 September in Austria, with Bad Aussee as 'base camp'. The trial was staged in appallingly bad weather. Constant rain gave way to snow in many places. High mountain passes, muddy tracks and treacherously slippery tarred main roads were just some of the practical hazards along the 1,250 mile course.

NSU's entry into ISDT events was spectacular. The company provided half the German Trophy team. Dollmann, Reinhardt and Kollmar were all mounted on 98 cc ohc Geländefox machines prepared in the factory's competitions department. The complement of the Trophy team was made up by the Maico pairing of Dänger and Pohl. One of the little NSU Geländefoxes ridden by Fischer was in the first pair of riders to get the trial under way.

Besides the official team five other factory prepared NSUs were entered. Three more Foxes, a 500 Konsul II and most unexpectedly, a genuine Rennfox road racer lightly modified for off-road use. It was ridden by Wilhelm Hofmann. A typical press comment at the time was 'Hofmann was attempting the seemingly impossible by using a works Rennfox road racer

Prototype 250 Rennmax during testing, summer 1952.

through the trial – he was seen jockeying his rorty midget around with considerable zest – and noise!'

At the end of the first day's run the NSU ranks were depleted. Three of the five who had set out on 98 Fox models failed to come in, one of them was Robert Dollmann. A member of the national Trophy team Dollmann's machine came off worst in a collision with a dog. The other two Fox retirements were Werner and Fischer. In addition the 247 Max of Ullmar also expired.

Things hardly got better, with the Fox of Reinhardt retiring on day two, followed on day four by the last remaining Fox ridden by Kollmar and Hofmann's the road-racer-cum-dirt-iron Rennfox. Only one NSU survived the week, this was the Konsul II ridden by Pfeiffer. He gained a Bronze medal.

It was not a week to relish, but the Neckarsulm team soon overcame its disappointment and rededicated itself to building more competitive machinery and improving its technique.

In December, Englishman Bill Lomas signed to race 125 and 250 NSUs for the 1953 season. His fellow countryman Cecil Sandford, although originally considered for a place in the team, finally elected to ride Italian MV machinery in the 125 and 500 cc classes. The official factory race team for 1953 announced at the end of January was Lomas, Daiker, Haas and Luttenberger.

Evidence of NSU's meticulous approach is witnessed by Lomas and Haas being sent to the Isle of Man ten weeks before the 1953 TT began. At the majority of meetings machines were warmed by a system in which heated air was directed at the engines through large diameter flexible pipes from a hot air pump. The oil was also pre-heated. Ducati used a similar system for its 1958–60 works bikes.

The primary purpose of the IoM trip, in retrospect, was that the experienced TT rider Lomas should pass his valuable course knowledge on to his fellow team member. Haas arrived with no outline in his mind about the course. But after Lomas' instructions, and only two days covering the ground, he could recite from memory all the bends from the start to the Glen Helen section. A drill was devised by the two men that divided the circuit into eight sections and a day was spent on each memorising all the details of this exceedingly tricky 37.73 mile circuit. Incidentally, Haas' first impression was that the TT was 'less difficult than the Nurburgring'. Both teacher and pupil for these sessions used standard Max roadsters.

The first international race meeting of 1953 was the popular annual Belgium event, around the 13.6 kilometre Floreffe course. This usually acted as a reliable pointer to form for the forthcoming GP season.

In the 250 race, Fergus Anderson came to the line with his new four-valve, twin carb Guzzi single. In practice it was Anderson who was fastest. His nearest rival was Bill Lomas (the only NSU entered) enjoying his first competitive outing on Neckarsulm raceware. From the start, Anderson opened a large gap between himself and the NSU rider. And it looked as if Lomas had resigned himself to runner-up spot, when on lap 5, the Rennmax came past the start/finish line in first position with a very long lead. News soon filtered through to the effect that the Guzzi had retired with a blown-up motor. Lomas sped on to win and the German national anthem and God Save The Queen rang out across Floreffe's sun-dappled woodlands.

In appearance the latest Rennmax was considerably different from its 1952 predecessor. A brand new pressed steel chassis, leading link front forks, wrap around 'bikini' aluminium fairing and fuel tank were just some of the more apparent advances. The compression ratio was increased to 9.8:1, larger 25.4 mm Amal RN9 carbs were used, and hotter cam profiles resulted in power output being bumped up to 32 bhp at 10,000 rpm. Much of this tuning was a result of closed-season testing.

A fortnight after Floreffe, at Hockenheim, Lomas again led the 250 race before retiring. Haas then completed a NSU double for he had earlier won the 125 event on a 1953 specification Rennfox which had been completely revised for the new season.

The new machines' engines were smaller externally and of a different appearance to the original type. The vertical coupling (bevel shaft) to the ohc was on the left hand side of the cylinder instead of the right as on the earlier model. And the old Rennfox's 'square' style engine finning had been replaced by a new round-look head and barrel with the new dimensions of 58 × 47.3 mm. Another notable change was that coil ignition was selected as on the 250s, and the contact breaker was driven by a worm gear from the camshaft coupling. The frame on these machines was a composite of pressed-steel and tubular steel. It was completed by hydraulically-damped front and rear suspension. The Hockenheim version of the 1953 Rennfox had a single overhead cam, but later machines used a dohc version after an extensive development programme. Engine cooling arrangements, brakes, suspension and stream-lining were also modified as the season unwound.

Following Hockenheim came the IoM TT. NSU entered Lomas and Haas for both the 125 and 250 events. The 250 was billed as a duel between NSU and the Moto Guzzi trio of Fergus Anderson, Enrico Lorenzetti and Bruno Ruffo. In the smaller class MV Agusta was the challenger. Les Graham, Cecil Sandford and Carlo Ubbiali presented formidable opposition to Neckarsulm.

Things warmed up early. A practice spill put out Ruffo with a broken arm. Haas came off during a 125 practice ride, but was uninjured. Then in the final session the pride of the NSU stable Lomas, first put himself on the leader board in the 250 cc class with a standing start lap and then did the same thing in the 125 cc category. But on his third lap things went wrong and he crashed at Sulby Bridge. Although at the time it was reported that he was uninjured, when race day for the Lightweight (250 cc) TT on 10 June dawned the Derbyshire rider was a non-starter. It later transpired that he had damaged a hand and it had to be set in plaster. This set back not only kept him out of racing for some time, but ended his association with NSU. The unfortunate Lomas was later to class himself as, 'NSU's favourite, unluckiest rider'. In both races Haas had to be content with finishing second – in the 250 behind Anderson and in the 125 behind Graham.

The dohc 125 engine had first been seen during practice for the TT. These new machines were first raced at the Dutch TT, at Assen. Here Irishman Reg Armstrong supplemented the team in the larger class while Dickie Dale took out another 125.

The 250 race came first. Though Fergus Anderson had not been unduly pressed by Werner Haas in the Isle of Man, the brilliant young German's performance on the difficult and unfamiliar Manx circuit had suggested that the latest Rennmax would be extremely formidable on the majority of European tracks. So it was to prove.

As the traffic light starting signals blinked from red and amber to green, Haas streaked into the lead on his high-pitched, screaming Neckarsulm twin. His heeling round the De Haar curves, which are close to the start, was a superb sight. In the end, in addition to setting the fastest lap at 92.36 mph, the German rider won. But only just, as the wily Scottish Guzzi team leader steadily pulled back so that towards the finish Haas and Anderson were neck-and-neck.

However, on the last half lap, Haas pulled out all the stops and the Guzzi had to accept second spot. New boy Armstrong finished a creditable third on his debut ride.

This set the scene for the rest of the season. Haas won the World title with victories in Germany, Ulster and Switzerland and the Netherlands. His second place in the Italian GP at Monza sealed the title for the man who was the first German to carry off a World Championship. Just to prove that this was not a fluke, Haas and NSU also took the 125 title. Following his second place in the Isle of Man, Haas went on to score first in Holland, second in Germany, first in Ulster and finally another win in Italy.

Armstrong came second in the 250 World Championships with wins in Ulster and Switzerland, and a fourth in Italy, to add to his third in the Dutch TT. Originally the Assen race had been a 'one-off ride' as a stand-in for the injured Lomas. But Armstrong's excellent showing, and Lomas being injured for much longer than expected, meant he was made a full member of the NSU team.

But it was very much Haas' year. Not only was he double World Champion, but became double German champion as well. In December, Haas was voted Germany's 'Sportsman of the Year' for 1953. Among those at the NSU factory when Haas was presented with a new Mercedes car by the management was Tommy Bullus, the Englishman who rode for NSU before the war.

It was not just on the race circuits where NSU shone in 1953. The ISDT that year, the 28th in the series, was held around Gottwaldov, Czechoslavakia from 15–20 September. The competitors had to complete a course with a total distance of 1470 miles.

Following its disastrous showing in 1952, not surprisingly NSU was not invited to supply any of the official German Trophy or Vase team machines. However, this did not deter the marque from taking an active interest and entering an official manufacturer's team. And at Gottwaldov was the debut of what was to prove the definitive NSU ISDT bike, the 247 Geländemax. It was based on the standard production Max model.

All these purpose-built machines were assembled in the competition department and used a twin-shock swinging arm chassis, which was the forerunner for the production Supermax roadster that followed in 1956. The 247 cc engine was built on the Max roadster of the period, but with power increased to 19.5 bhp at 6,500

Above **Besides its winning ways as a solo machine in the International Six Days Trial, the Geländermax was also a victorious sidecar powerhouse.**

Below **Werner Haas was a successful NSU mounted ISDT rider in the early 1950's. Later, and again aboard NSU machinery he was World Champion three times.**

rpm. There were a large number of detail changes from the production roadsters including knobbly tyres, sump shield, number plates, tyre inflator, emergency ignition, system map case, and larger tool kit.

Testimony that the preparation of the Geländemax was to a very high standard is the fact that NSU machinery suffered only one retirement that year. This was on the first day when Luxembourg's sole representative, Nennig burnt out his clutch in heavy sand. He repaired the damage, then set fire to the machine with a backfire when restarting and ruined the motor with the sand he threw at it in an attempt to put out the flames.

Gold medals were secured by Frey, Otto Haas (Werner's brother), Staab, Stecher, Ullmar and Sautter – all six Geländemax mounted. Silver medals were gained by a pair of Geländemax models equipped with sidecars and piloted by Kollmar and Hoffmann. With only one retirement, NSU not only retrieved its pride, but proved that its machines could be ultra-reliable in the world's most demanding motorcycling event.

March 1954 brought news that the entire works racing team for the coming GP season, except Reg

Armstrong, was on the Isle of Man for course instruction. Werner Haas acted as the professor of the bends. The team was Hans Baltisburger (at one time a team mate of Walter Zeller at BMW before joining NSU in 1954), Hermann Müller and Austrian Ruppert Hollous. All of them flew into Ronaldsway airport with race manager Ernst-Gustaf Germer. Their course learning machinery arrived the same day by sea. The bikes were Max roadsters, except for the team leader's whose mount was a Geländemax. The double World Champion was allowed to indulge in a spot of off-road riding when time allowed.

Later the same month press reports confirmed that Wilhelm Hertz, holder of the 'world's fastest' title, was to make a return to road racing. He was reputed to have been entered for Hockenheim on 9 May as well as other German events. In reality nothing happened, and the reports seemed to have been based on rumour only.

If the Herz affair fizzled, it was soon forgotten. Shortly after dawn on Tuesday 21 April, a commercial artist named Gustav Adolf Baumm gained world wide publicity for himself and NSU, by breaking a total of eleven small-capacity world speed records with NSU powered streamliners designed by himself and built by the Neckarsulm company. The most unusual aspect was that Baumm lay horizontal with his feet forward, which, as *Motor Cycling* reported in the 29 April 1954

issue; 'could scarcely have been ideal for the gusty conditions which prevailed'.

In both machines the engine unit lay behind the rider and transmission was through a four-speed gearbox with drive to the rear wheel by chain. For the smaller classes the engine was based on the 49 cc Quickly unit with a 13:1 compression ratio and was said to produce 3.4 bhp at 7,000 rpm. The larger power unit was one from an ohv 98 cc Sportfox with a 10.8:1 compression ratio which provided 7.5 bhp at 7,000 rpm. Both ran on alcohol fuel, but the main reason for the increased speed was the effectiveness of the alloy fish-like steamlining.

These miniature projectiles had disc-type 16 inch wheels and the suspension, both front and rear, was by rubber bands on the Quickly powered machine and pneumatic damping on the larger bike. On each machine both wheels were fitted with brakes. Steering was effected by two levers, one on each side of the reclining rider. The other controls were fixed to the appropriate levers.

Baumm had originally conceived the idea for his 'Flying Hammock' record breaker in 1950, when a draughtsman at the NSU factory. At first, his concept was accepted by only one man, Dr Froede, but after designing the Rennmax, Froede had passed its development onto Ewald Praxl. This allowed Baumm's design to be fabricated in Dr Froede's department.

A quartet of works Rennmax models in the warm-up area at the French Grand Prix in May 1954. This superb period photograph evokes the full tone and flavour of the Continental Circus of the mid-1950's.

Baumm originally visualised his layout as a basis for both touring and racing machines of the future, although he acknowledged the difficulty of accommodating two people on one machine.

The record venue was once again a section of the Munich-Ingoldstadt autobahn, but this time nearer Munich itself. The weather, it was claimed, meant that the speeds obtained with the smaller engine were lower than had been anticipated.

The records broken were as follows; 50 cc: flying kilometre 79.7 mph; flying mile 79.4 mph; 5 kilometre 78.3 mph; 75 cc: flying mile 74.4 mph; 5 kilometres 78.6 mph; 100 cc: flying kilometre 110.8 mph; Flying Mile 111.2 mph; 5 Kilometre, 106.2 mph; 5 mile, 102.7 mph.

But overshadowing these events was the belief that an attempt was shortly be made to raise the world's fastest record to 200 mph using the Baumm shell and one of the latest Rennmax racing twin engine units.

The 1954 international road racing season got under way with what was proclaimed as the *Grand Prix Dress Rehearsal*. This was the 21st Circuit de Floreffe, near Namur, Belgium on 2 May. And so far as the entry was concerned it lived up to its name, with the Norton, Guzzi, MV and NSU factories all using it as a testing ground for the models to be raced during the classics that summer. The widsom of so doing was proved by the number of teething problems revealed. Furthermore, the gusty conditions in racing and practice gave

Left **Irishman Reg Armstrong at Italian Grand Prix with a Rennmax twin, Monza September 1953.**

each team a realistic idea of how their exaggerated streamlining would perform on the mountain sections of the Isle of Man TT.

For NSU it was the public unveiling of the latest version of the Rennmax which had received a major redesign during the winter. In spite of appearing larger, the 1954 Rennmax was 8.5 lb lighter than the 1953 version, weighing in at 258 lb. The most noticeable difference between the new twin cylinder engine and its predecessor was that the former separate shafts and bevel overhead cam drives, which were on the right of the engine, had been replaced by a single shaft on the other side at the rear of the cylinder. In turn this drove the inlet camshaft and was driven from the intermediate gear of the primary train. Spur gears transmitted the drive from the inlet camshaft to the exhaust camshaft. In addition the tacho-drive was taken from the exhaust cam.

The new power unit was appreciably shorter in height than the earlier motor. This showed up in the bore and stroke measurements which were now over-square at 55.9 × 50.8. The engine was also narrower due to the elimination of the bevel drives from the right hand side of the crankcase. The new camshaft drive allowed a shallower casting. Battery and coil ignition was retained. Power output at the time being stated as

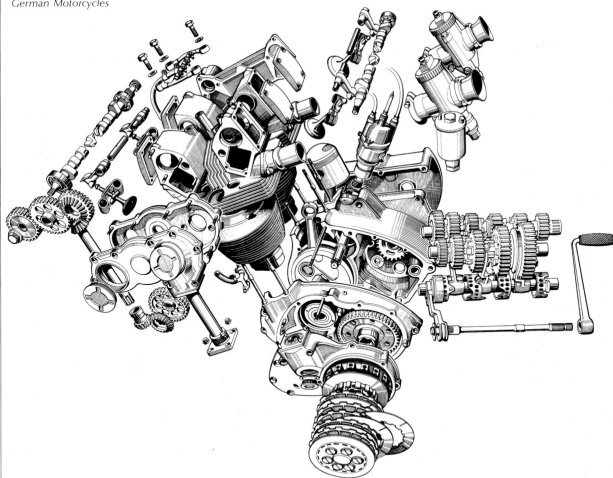

32.7, against 30 bhp of the earlier unit. In reality it was 36 bhp at 11,200 rpm. It had given 32 bhp at 11,000 rpm in 1953 and 27 bhp at 9,000 rpm in 1952. The spine frame was little changed from the 1953 model, as were the forks and rear suspension, but the rear sub-frame structure was constructed from pressings instead of tubing. Also the front fork links had been lengthened to improve suspension geometry. Front brake torque reaction, as before, was transmitted to the structure by a tension strut but the brake operation was on the left of the hub. Both brakes now had twin leading shoes.

Previously the streamlining of the Rennmax consisted of a front mudguard with side valances extending to the hub, a faired rear mudguard and a steering head fairing which extended rearward below the riders arms and embodied a small, curved windscreen. Taking into account a relaxation of FIM regulations on mudguarding, a front one was no longer fitted, and shielding for the front wheel was provided by the streamlining. The shape of the NSU aluminium cowling was reminiscent of the previous year's Moto Guzzi type, with its 'bird beak' projection over the front wheel. However, the NSU cowling completely embraced the handlebar and extended downwards to the base of the engine to shield the rider's arms and legs.

A detailed technical drawing of the 1954 version of the 247 cc Rennmax racing engine.

Cooling air for the engine and exposed clutch entered through an opening in the front of the cowling, and improved airflow over the rider's head and shoulders was provided by an increase in the height and width of the curved windscreen. Extensive use was made of wind tunnel facilities at the Stuttgart Technical College to establish the most favourable shape for the fairing.

Some likened the resultant profile to a dolphin's snout. NSU mechanics accordingly dubbed it the 'dolphin', and later in 1958 when the FIM had banned full fairings, *dolphin* was the term used to describe the new type of permissable fairing.

Rennmaxes were ridden at Floreffe by Baltisburger, Müller and Hollous. The former two had the latest 1954 specification engines, whilst Hollous used a 1953 type. In addition, Baltisburger and Hollous' machines had alloy 'bird beak' fairings and Müller a totally unstreamlined bike.

The race developed into a duel between Ken Kavanagh (Guzzi) and Hollous, who despite using an older motor knocked two seconds off the class lap record and, when rain began to fall towards the end of the race, drew away from Kavanagh to win by 100 yards. A faulty distributor was blamed for Müller being forced in for two pit stops, and it was noticeable that the new engine, on Baltisburger's machine, appeared to be running unevenly.

The 'circus' training session then went to Hockenheim, where a week later, on 9 May, the problems with the new 250s seemed to have been resolved with World Champion Haas winning from Müller. Haas also put in the fastest lap at 107.37 mph. This race followed the 125 event where the team took the first four places on their speedy Rennfox singles. Haas again took the chequered flag.

Though the basic dohc 125 cc engine design remained unchanged engine power had been boosted to 18 bhp at 11,500 rpm. As before a six-speed gearbox was employed because of the need to keep the engine operating within its effective power band. But now as a result of new streamlining and increased power, top speed was some 5 mph quicker. Twin leading shoe brakes were fitted on both wheels, but even so the weight was reduced from 184 lb to 177 lb. This advantage, however, was off-set by the burden of the full streamlining.

The 1954 Rennfox's frame was revised and carried similar streamlining to the latest Rennmax. Firstly, there was a 'bird beak' dolphin design with a large hand-beaten alloy fuel tank and tail fairing. Mid-season, this was replaced by an ugly full dustbin with 'droop snout', followed by more shapely 'blue whale' streamlining. Finally NSU settled upon blue whale streamlining on the definitive design used for the Sportmax models in 1955.

In the last 'warm up', a week before the first of the classics – the French GP – the NSU team appeared on 23 May, at the 17th international Eifelrennen at the Nurburgring. That man Haas set the all-time (until then) outright lap record during his winning ride in the 250 race on his Rennmax. He sped round the tortuous track in just 10 min, 52.4 sec – a speed of 78.12 mph. To understand what an achievement this was, the fastest lap put up in the 500 race by winner Ray Amm on a Norton was a mere 77.44 mph. This is still a record for the class.

Ruppert Hollous won the 125 event and these two NSU results were to prove an accurate guide to the final outcome of the forthcoming World Championships. Battle was joined at the French GP on Sunday 30 May. The Grand Prix was staged for the first time at the exceptionally fast 5.18 mile Rheims circuit. There was no 125 class in France and because of the event's nearness to the TT, only NSU and Gilera were there in any force. The factory riders set such a pace in their respective classes, that most of the privateers were completely outstripped.

Haas and Müller in the 250 race both notched speeds well in excess of Pierre Monneret's winning speed in the 350 class. The Frenchman rode a triple knocker works AJS. Yet the two NSU riders, together with Hollous and Baltisburger, all had 1953 power units. The new engines were reserved for the more strenuous and more important bid for Isle of Man honours. The Rennmax machines appeared with a new style of streamlining which totally enclosed the front wheel.

From Douglas, Isle of Man, *Motor Cycling* reported in the issue of 10 June, 'Herr Germer, the NSU boss, has set up shop 50 yards away from the Italians and was kindness itself when we called there this afternoon. Arist Crawley was given a petrol tin to sit on; models – all in the two-fifty class – were shifted around to suit Eric Coultham's camera, exposure meter and the brilliance of the afternoon sun. What beautiful, watch-like pieces of mechanism these semi-streamlined '250s' are. And if this lightweight class is likely to be won by careful staff-work, the quiet efficiency of the Neckarsulm factory camp practically has the Trophy in the bag even at this stage'.

And so it was. Run in brilliant weather on Monday 14 June the 1954 Lightweight TT proved to be as much of a triumph for NSU Werke as had been the 250 class of the French Grand Prix at Rheims. With five machines entered, four of them finished in the first four places and the other came home sixth. Werner Haas not only led the race from start to finish, but created a new lap record on each of his three laps. He finally covered the 37.73 mile circuit at 91.22 mph and brought his race record up to 90.88 mph. Ruppert Hollous just beat Reg Armstrong into second place, with Hermann Muller a close fourth. Hans Baltisburger was sixth.

The 125 TT was rather different. After a closely fought battle which lasted for 107.9 miles over the 10.79 mile Clypse circuit on 16 June, the 22 year old Austrian Ruppert Hollous took a well-deserved victory from Italy's Carlo Ubbiali and Britain's Cecil Sandford on MV

Rennfox 125 cc single with 'bird beak' fairing at the Isle of Man TT, June 1954.

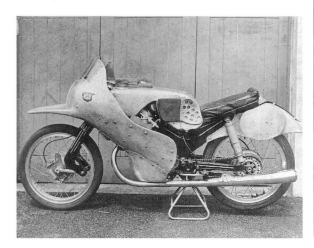

Agustas. Hollous, who put in the fastest lap at 71.53 mph, took 1 hr 33 min 32.5 sec, to cover the 10 laps, averaging 69.57 mph, and finished only 4 seconds ahead of Ubbiali, who had contested every yard of the distance with him. The only other NSU finisher was Baltisburger in fourth place. Haas retired after twice falling off on roads which had been left wet by the overnight rain which had ceased, fortunately, before racing commenced. Müller retired on the second lap after suffering misfiring problems from the start.

Extremely adverse weather, a week after the TT, with rain and gale force winds and the non-appearance of several riders of Italian machines combined to spoil some of the glitter surrounding the third round in the World Championship series, the Ulster GP, the second to be held over the 7 mile 732 yd Dundrod circuit, near Belfast.

The 250 race on Thursday 24 June had five NSU riders on the grid. The TT quartet was joined by Ireland's own Reg Armstrong. Baltisburger led from Haas and Hollous, with Müller a steady fourth. Armstrong fell back early on, and was later to retire with ignition trouble. By the seventh lap, Haas and Hollous had caught the leader, but towards the end of the 11 lap, 96.4 mile race Hollous suffered the same ignition failure which had put Armstrong out. Haas nudged in front of Baltisburger to take victory by a few yards.

In the 125 event, run two days later on Saturday 26 June, Hollous repeated his Isle of Man victory, followed by Müller, Baltisburger and Haas. There were three works MVs and Johnny Grace on a Spanish Montesa. Only MV team leader Ubbiali caused problems, but after setting the fastest lap crashed after running into trouble at Wheeler's Corner. Here a sudden gust of wind caught his fully faired MV and sent him into a bank. His race was over.

At the Dutch TT at Assen, on Saturday 10 July, the 250 race came first and soon became monotonous. Haas and Hollous, about half a mile apart, held their lead and only the possibility of a fight for third place between Baltisburger and Australian Guzzi rider Ken Kavanagh kept the crowd's interest alive. But by the end with his Guzzi failing, Kavanagh had to settle for fourth in front of Müller. With this win Haas made certain of retaining the Championship title for a second year.

The 125 race again saw Hollous take victory from Müller, Ubbiali (MV), Baltisburger and Haas. Trying to keep up with the flying NSUs, MV riders Sandford and Copeta were both forced to retire with wrecked engines.

Solitude, Germany Sunday 25 July – the Grand Prix of the Fatherland – was held beneath a sweltering Sun

World Champion Werner Haas screams his fully-faired Rennmax around the twists of the 1954 Dutch TT. Yet again he was first home at this 10 July meeting.

over a 7.1 mile serpentine circuit among beautifully wooded hills overlooking Stuttgart. Race and lap records were pulverized in all classes before a massive crowd of half-a-million spectators. The first of NSU's new sleekly streamlined 125's appeared on the grid at this meeting. Evolution of the *Blauwal* (Blue Whale) had begun.

The 125 race started the proceedings and it turned out an exact repeat of the Dutch result – Hollous, Haas, Ubbiali and then Müller. Continuing his triumphant progress, Hollous pushed the lap record up to 79.92 mph during the 71.12 mile race. His victory assured him and NSU of the 125 World Championship.

Next came the 250 race. Moto Guzzi withdrew the four factory entries, even though the riders wanted to race. It was an admission that Moto Guzzi could not hold the NSU steamroller. Ironically, NSU strength was reduced by the absence of Baltisburger. He was in hospital following a practice crash.

Hallmeier, on a two-stroke Adler twin, surprised everyone by making a lightning start to lead the pack into the first corner. However, his glory was to be short lived and it was no surprise when Haas headed team mate Hollous over the line at the end of lap one. Müller was chased for third spot by the Adler rider, but the NSU was noticeably quicker although Müller was later forced to pit with a loose streamlining shell. This allowed Hallmeier and the Adler to finish third behind winner Haas, and Hollous. Müller eventually rejoined the race and pulled back up to eleventh. The fastest lap was set by Hollous at 85.95 mph – a new record.

With the 250 cc classes in the German and French Grand Prix won at higher speeds than the 350 cc events, the obvious thought by some pundits was that NSU should bore out a two-fifty and enter it in 350 cc class racing. The thought obviously did not escape the

Neckarsulm engineers. At the German national championship event at the Noris-Ring, Nürnberg on 1 August a 288 cc Rennmax was piloted by Hermann Müller. All that had been done to the engine was to increase the stroke (rather than the bore) giving dimensions of 55.9 × 60 mm and a power output of 40.4 bhp at 11,200 rpm. Not only did the machine win against opposition from the factory three cylinder DKW's and Ray Amm's works Norton, but it averaged a speed of 76.94 mph – only 0.13 mph slower than Amm's winning speed in the 500 event. Moreover, it made the fastest lap of the day at 79.36 mph. The factory policy as stated by team manager Germer at Nürnberg was that NSU would use these larger motors only in German races in 1954, with a view to a full scale assault on the 350 World Championship in 1955.

The following weekend, 8 August, Müller was again on the 288 cc Rennmax. This was the penultimate round of the German championship series and held at the narrow Schotten cobblestone circuit in front of 170,000 spectators. A larger model was also ridden by 250 World Champion Werner Haas who fell during the race. The two Neckarsulm machines led from the start. The result was another win for Müller, who was followed home by Amm (Norton), Hobl (DKW) and Haas, who had remounted to finish fourth.

Sunday 22 August was very wet for the Swiss GP. *Motor Cycling* summed it up like this; 'It has been raining all night; it was raining throughout yesterday and the day before; and still it rains'. With no 125 event, NSU interest was focused exclusively on the 250 race. This was won easily by Hollous, after champion Haas failed to make it even to the end of the first lap. He slid off within about a mile of the start. At this meeting the new streamlining first used by the 125's at Solitude on 25 July was fitted.

The 288 cc Rennmax models were out again on Sunday 5 September, in the final German championship meeting of the year. The Eilenreide was run over a fast three mile circuit in a park at Hanover. On one of them, Müller again finished first in the 350 class at a speed of 83.8 mph. He was followed home by Haas on another '288' and Ray Amm rode a Norton into third place.

Monza was the eighth of the nine World Championship meetings in 1954. The Italian GP opened on a tragic note. In the final practice session the previous day, the brilliant 24-year-old Austrian Ruppert Hollous, who had just turned in a record breaking 125 lap at 93.09 mph on a Rennfox with full tail and frontal fairing, came off on the Lesmo curve and sustained head and back injuries from which he died a few hours later. As a mark of respect to Hollous the NSU team withdrew from the meeting. Hollous was already the 1954 125 World Champion, and second in the 250 series.

This tragedy was to have far wider implications than

At the end of the 1954 season NSU announced its withdrawal from Grand Prix racing. This photograph shows many of the factory sponsored motorcycles, including the GP racers and Baumm's sleek record breakers.

was at first apparent. Not only did NSU not race in Italy, they missed the final round in Spain as well. Then in a radio interview at Stuttgart on 7 October the managing director of NSU, Dr Gerd Stieler von Heydekampf, stated that it was quite possible that the NSU factory would take no active part in racing during 1955.

He said that this was under serious consideration and was influenced by two things. First, NSU as a firm had been subject to considerable criticism by a section of the German press. It was held responsible for the complete elimination of competition and hence of interest in racing during 1954. He said that it was remarkable that the same section of the press, only a few years previously, had been demanding the production of German machines which could compete in international Grand Prix racing and an appeal was made to NSU to do something about it. Now that they had done something that brought success to Germany, the company was being criticised for it. The second 'official' reason was that 'NSU would be devoting much more of its attention to meeting the world demand for more comfortable, more reliable, and cleaner touring machines'.

Another consideration put forward, at least by the motorcycling journals of the day, was a possible shortage of good riders with which the Neckarsulm factory would be faced the following year. This position was made more acute as it was company policy to employ only the smallest and lightest jockeys. Not only was Hollous dead and Baltisburger seriously injured from his practice crash at the German GP, but Müller – then turned 45 – was reported to be retiring. The same was said of Haas. He was just in the process of entering business as a filling station proprietor. Haas was the proud owner of a new services on the autobahn near his home town of Augsburg.

Speculation by von Heydekampf became reality on 22 October 1954 when it was officially announced that NSU would not be contesting the 1955 series of road racing World Championship meetings with a works team. In part compensation for the void left by the decision not to race the Rennfox or Rennmax, NSU announced that distribution of the 247 cc single cylinder Sportmax production racing machine was to begin in early 1955. This generously gave privateers ample time before the racing season got under way.

The prototype of what was to emerge as the Sportmax was first seen at the end of the 1953 season during the Spanish GP at Montjuich Park, Barcelona. Thereafter, development continued both on the track and in the test shop. The first machines made their appearance on 9 May 1954 at Hockenheim. Here one finished in sixth place against international opposition. But it was 22 August that year that the NSU single really showed its character when Georg Braun finished second behind Hollous at the Swiss GP and in front of Müller. Both Hollous and Müller were on Rennmax twins. In addition other Sportmaxes came home eighth and eleventh.

At the Italian GP, 12 September, Sportmax machines were privately entered by Kurt Knopf and Georg Braun. They duelled with Englishman Arthur Wheeler on his home streamlined and prepared 'privateer' Guzzi single. Wheeler eventually won, Knopf was third and Braun retired.

All these early development machines were essentially similar to the 'production' models, but used a smaller diameter front brake and had other minor differences. Karl Kleinbach was responsible for the development of the Sportmax, but there has always been some confusion as to just how many genuine Sportmax models were actually produced by the factory. NSU publicity officer Arthur Westrup stated seventeen whilst other well informed sources go as high as thirty-four. In addition, a number of other machines were built later from spare parts when the race shop was sold to the Herz family in the late 1950's.

Then again many people converted the various Max, Special Max and Super Max roadsters into so called Sportmax replicas. Some were very crude. The roadster frames and forks, not to say anything of the brakes give these spurious copies away.

The genuine Sportmax or Type 251 RS (250 one cylinder Rennsport) had a capacity of 247 cc (69 × 66 mm) and a compression ratio of 9.8:1 giving 28 bhp at 9000 rpm (maximum safe revs 9500 rpm). The piston was a forged 3-ring Mahle and an Amal GP $1\frac{3}{16}$ carb was used. The distinctive 22-litre tank was in hand-beaten alloy and the dry weight was 246 lb. Front tyre was 2.75 × 18 and the rear 3.00 × 18. Top speed was 124 mph and a wide variety of sprockets was available for alternative gearing. Compared with the prototype which had 180 mm diameter front brakes, the production machines sported massive 210 mm units.

Meanwhile, in the rough and tumble world of the International Six Day Trial, NSU eagerly awaited the 1954 event staged around Llandrindod Wells, Wales between the 20–25 September. The team and factory believed they could equal the successes of 1953.

By now, NSU could no longer be ignored by the German team selectors, and Neckarsulm machinery was selected for national duty in both the Trophy and Vase contests. The disaster of 1952 had been finally erased. The Trophy team consisted of Pohl and Deike (175 Maicos), Best (248 Hecker) and a pair of Geländemax machines ridden by Westphal and Stelmar. Meanwhile the whole Vase A team was Geländemax mounted – Haas, Frey and Sauter.

After six punishing days the German Trophy team came sixth and the Vase A team tenth out of a field of 19. Seven Geländemax riders won gold medals: Colin, Frey, Mann, Westphal, Haas, Stucker and Staab – while Falton won a bronze. NSU retirements were limited to Sauter (Friday) and Staab on the same day, the latter piloted a Geländemax and chair. All-in-all, an excellent showing for the marque.

In December 1954 the world 75 cc flying start kilometre and mile records, which Gustav Baumm had established with his 49 cc streamliner the previous April, were broken by Ghiro riding the Italian Ceccato. To combat this, NSU modified the engine of the Baumm machine from 3.2 to 4.1 bhp by altering the port timing, and eliminated a troublesome power loss by substituting spur gears for sprockets and chain in the primary transmission. Another reason for this change had been that during the record runs in April, the 11 tooth engine sprocket had worn rapidly and caused deterioration of the primary chain. Baumm calculated what the theoretical effects of the additional 0.9 bhp and was quietly confident that he could regain the records lost to the Italians.

At the same time another move which seemed likely in the NSU record-breaking programme was the installation in Baumm's second streamliner of one of the new 123 cc Superfox units. It was moderately tuned

Right **Gustav Baumm with one of his astounding feet-forward world record breakers. He proved the validity of his highly original approach with consummate ease.**

to give around 12 bhp and was used in an attempt upon the Romolo Ferri Lambretta speed record described earlier in this chapter. But the ultimate aim was to capture the flying start kilometre and mile records in all solo classes.

The earlier lukewarm reception by NSU to the novel 'Flying Hammock' layout, was now transformed into enthusiasm for it being used exclusively for future record attempts by Baumm. The small frontal area and incredibly low air drag of the design permitted the achievement of exceptionally high speeds with very low power outputs. NSU felt that the use of moderately-tuned production engines for record-breaking would have an important psychological effect upon rival world record teams.

As a matter of policy, the Neckarsulm factory did not intend to improve on records they already held, but openly stated that they would attempt to recapture any titles which might pass to another marque. However, it was acknowledged that an exception to this rule would be considered in the case of the world's maximum speed record in category A – the solo class – then currently held at 180.17 mph by Wilhelm Herz with the streamlined supercharged 498 cc NSU parallel twin.

The German team had also set themselves a goal of 'maximum speed with minimum engine capacity'. Since it was realised that long distances were required if a rider was to accelerate to high speeds when using low power output, NSU were prepared to travel to the Utah Salt lakes in the western USA for their major record

attempts in future. As early as December 1954 2.00 × 16 tyres had been laboratory tested up to 240 mph.

NSU then told the press that its world record programme would start 27 April and continue until 5 May 1955. As before the venue was a closed section of the Munich-Ingoldstadt Autobahn and it was expected that the 50, 75, 125 and 250 flying mile and flying kilometre records would be attempted.

On Tuesday 10 May, later than previously announced due to unsuitable weather, NSU established a total of 22 world records in the 50, 75, 125, 175, 250 and 350 categories with 50 and 125 cc machines. The records were set by Gustav Baumm on a pair of streamliners of the same type used on his previous record spree. One machine was fitted with the tuned Quickly-based engine described previously. The other was equipped with one of the 1954 123 cc Rennfox works racing engines.

Six of the previous records were already held by Baumm, and all the others, save two, were in Italian hands (Ceccato, Lambretta and Moto Guzzi). One of the exceptions was the 75 cc five-mile record which had been established by Englishman Hall in 1929 on a Rocket-JAP. No 50 cc figure had previously been created for five miles.

Each of the Baumm NSUs attacked the flying start kilometre, mile, five kilometre and five mile distances. The 50 cc machine recorded mean speeds of 93.2, 93.8, 90.4 and 91.3 mph for the respective distances, setting up records in both 50 and 75 cc classes. The margin

over the earlier speeds varied from 56.5 mph in the case of Hall's record to 9.3 mph for the 75 cc kilometre record.

Equally remarkable was the performance of the 125 streamliner in covering the distances at respective mean speeds of 134.8, 135.4, 129.8 and 131.0 mph. These speeds brought NSU the appropriate records in the 125, 175 and 250 cc categories, also the 350 cc five kilometre and five mile records. The smallest gain was approximately 2.5 mph on the previous 250 cc kilometre speed. In contrast, Baumm's old five mile 125 speed was bettered by nearly 24 mph.

Later, at a dinner party for delegates to the FIM Congress in Dusseldorf, given by the NSU management held on Thursday 12 May, Baumm was guest of honour. One of his record machines was also on show, together with the two engines used in the successful attempts.

There were distinct differences between the two streamliners used. The smaller engined machine was higher and shorter than its bigger brother. The larger record breaker had a less rounded top to its shell.

Interestingly, although Baumm was officially described as an artist, he was in fact a highly skilled designer who had worked on aircraft development during the war. It was little publicised at the time but Baumm was incorporating the aerodynamic lessons of his record breakers into a projected passenger car. But this was a private venture without the support of NSU.

So carefully had Baumm worked out the contours of his feet-first machines, that even with a gusty 12 mph side wind blowing, the steering he claimed after the record attempts 'was unaffected'. Baumm also revealed that the flatter shell of the '125' might be thought to have been aimed at keeping the front wheel on the road. However, experience had shown that as speed rose, so more weight was transferred to the front wheel. The effect was so great that very powerful springs had to be incorporated on the front suspension of the larger model.

The wind on the day of the successful attempts had been blowing so hard that Baumm claimed to have lost around 500 rpm from the maximum figures for both engines on preliminary testing. In the case of the 49 cc two-stroke unit, which ran on alcohol fuel, this meant that instead of turning over at 9,000 rpm, at which engine speed it had an output of 4.7 bhp, it was only running at 8,500 rpm.

The unsupercharged dohc Rennfox engine employed fuel injection. Originally there had been plans to run it on alcohol but the performance characteristics of these units when using premium grade petrol were so exactly determined and documented that NSU technicians decided to rely upon the known, rather than to introduce an element of experimentation.

When asked about what would be the safe limit at which his streamliner could be navigated, Baumm estimated 'about 150 mph', but revealed that a similar design built for higher speeds might be able to approach 300 mph if propelled by a 500 cc engine.

Sadly, a mere eleven days after the Dusseldorf dinner, on Monday 23 May, Baumm was killed at the Nurburgring testing a prototype of the Baumm streamliner with which it was planned for NSU to make a comeback in the 1956 125 and 250 Grand Prix. Unfortunately, Baumm lost control and ran off the circuit into some trees. He suffered a fractured skull and died from his injuries. It could not have helped to have been testing on a track shared with Porsche sports cars.

And so ended not only the dreams of the bearded 36 year old Bavarian, but many of NSU's future plans. Baumm was not only developing the machine which was to be the basis for NSU's racing comeback, but also a series of production versions in the hope of achieving precise handling, improved speed and dramatically better fuel consumption for any given capacity. The company received a rough handling from the press about the Baumm accident. Management, therefore, shelved the project and returned to planning for car production.

All that remains today of the Baumm era is one of his machines, owned by the Herz family, in the new Hockenheimring Museum. This bullet shaped car is the one used by Müller in his endurance/fuel consumption trials at the 'Ring' in May 1956. It is a sole survivor of the shelved racers. Dimensionally it is shorter than the record machine, but longer than the proposed roadster. It is rumoured that a shell from one of the record breakers still exists but is in private hands.

On a happier note, without a doubt the Sportmax proved even more successful than NSU could have ever dreamed. During the 1955 classic racing calendar, Hermann Peter (Happy) Müller astounded the very people who said at the end of 1954 that he was about to retire. On a semi-works Sportmax he scooped the 250 World title.

In achieving this feat the 46-year old veteran was third in the opening round in the Isle of Man, won at Nurburgring on home ground, fourth at the Dutch TT, sixth in Ulster and fourth in the final round at Monza. However, more than anything his Championship will be remembered by the controversy it created. Müller had the same points at season's end as Englishman Bill Lomas, but Müller was awarded the title following the latter's down grading at Assen. Here, Lomas who had been first across the finishing line, had been demoted to second place by the international jury for having filled up with petrol without stopping his engine.

Bitter controversy raged following this decision, but Müller won the title and promptly retired from a racing career which spanned more than two decades. He competed not only on two wheels, but also raced cars with great distinction. Immediately before the war he raced the fearsome rear-engined Auto-Union Grand Prix cars.

In 1955 NSU offered the Sportsmax ohc single production racer to anyone with the money. Müller became World Champion in the same year with a very similar machine.

Several other prominent stars campaigned the Sportmax in 1955, these included Hans Baltisburger, Georg Braun, John Surtees, and Pierre Monneret. Baltisburger, recovered from his 1954 German GP practice crash and concentrated on the German championship. Although he won the national title he had to be content with second spot in the final GP of the season, but he was ahead of Ulsterman Sammy Miller on another Sportmax, World Champion Muller and Bill Lomas. He lost only to Carlo Ubbiali on his factory MV.

Sammy Miller had earlier been second on his Sportmax back home in the Ulster GP. It was a race dominated by Surtees on yet another of the fleet Neckarsulm singles. Surtees was invincible that year on the Sportmax in British short circuit events. In fact this was to be just the start of a run of successes for the Sportmax. Its record of placings in the top six was unequalled by any other production 250 racer during the decade. Even into the 1960s, a well-ridden and well-prepared Sportmax could offer a serious challenge. Ultimately, of course, it was outclassed by the two-strokes like the watercooled Bultacos and early Yamahas in the middle of the decade.

There were more triumphs in other fields. In July 1955, German rider Manfred Frey, who had taken a gold medal in the 1954 ISDT on a Geländemax, rode his Special Max to become the only competitor to complete the tough 1500 mile Liege-Milan-Liege Sporting Rally, run by the Royal Motor Union, without loss of marks. In this Belgian event he beat competitors from all over Europe, including Britain.

For the 1955 ISDT, 13–18 September, at Gottwaldov, Czechoslovakia, in the Trophy team the Germans chose only two-strokes from DKW and Maico. The Vase A team had BMWs, but the Vase B was given NSUs. These Geländemax models were ridden by Haas, Frey and Westphal. It was a good year for Germany in the ISDT. It won the Trophy and was third in the Vase (NSU Vase B team), while in the manufacturers team contest, NSU entered two teams and both finished. Only four did so from thirty-six factory entries. Gold medals went to Haas, Frey, Westphal on solos, while Sauter, Marnet, Dollmann gained them on Geländemax sidecars. Compared with previous years there were far fewer medals awarded in this event, so NSU's performance was extremely good, even taking into consideration the retirements. A silver went to Colin while Lettko gained a bronze (both on Geländemax). Eight NSU machines retired, one ridden by former world road racing champion Werner Haas.

More records fell in 1956. May saw a 125 NSU streamliner used by Müller to achieve 62.5 miles in an hour on around two pints of petrol. Müller's machine was an adaptation of the intended 1956 racing Baumm streamliner. It was powered by a modified 125 Superfox unit, which was rear-mounted behind the driving seat with carburettor forward, and exhaust straight up at the rear. The machine was a mere 86 cm high to top of cockpit and its top speed was 97 mph. It also achieved 236 mpg.

For 1956, the first round of the classic road racing season was the Isle of Man TT races in June. There were four Sportmax machines entered – Hans Baltisburger, Sammy Miller, Horst Kassner and Australian Eric Hinton, who was a non-starter, but the other three more than made up for this.

With the race run over the Clypse circuit, the Lightweight TT was held on Wednesday 6 June. The opening laps suffered from atrocious conditions. Heavy rain was coupled with a strong biting wind. Retirements were numerous. At first Mondial mounted Cecil Sandford led, followed by the NSU trio, but Miller soon took the lead when the Mondial's battery leads came adrift. At the end of lap 3 Miller still led, followed by the MV pair of Ubbiali and Colombo, with Kassner in fourth, but on lap 4 Miller's Sportmax cried enough and the Irishman was out with a seized engine. On the 7th and final lap, Kassner and Baltisburger reached Signpost Corner side-by-side, and it was Baltisburger who crossed the line in third place, 50 yards to the good and having put up the fastest lap of the race at 69.35 mph.

In the rest of the season's 250 Grand Prix, Sportmaxes achieved several good positions. In the Dutch TT at Assen Kassner was fifth, while in the Belgian GP at Spa, the leaderboard read third Kassner, fourth Koster (Holland), fifth Simons (Holland), sixth Bagle (France). The German GP at Solitude saw fourth go to Baltisburger, fifth Brown (Australia), sixth Heck (Germany). Sammy Miller came second in the Ulster GP at Dundrod with Coleman fourth and sixth going to Bula (Switzerland). Finally Miller was sixth in the Italian GP at Monza.

Meanwhile, NSU returned to record-breaking attempts on the Munich-Ingolstadt autobahn. Herman Müller was there with the 'Baumm II' revised version of Gustav Baumm's original Rennfox powered streamliner. Wilhelm Herz was given the 'Delphin III', the latest version of the 1951 record breaker. This had a completely redesigned form of streamlining, with enclosed cabin, nose window, heightened tail fin and various other changes which like the smaller machine had been developed in the Stuttgart Technical College wind tunnel. The result was a cut in the drag co-efficient from 0.29 in its original form to 0.19. NSU claimed that with its 110 bhp supercharged engine, the reconfigured twin could better 125 mph in first gear.

Another version of a Baumm inspired machine had a Rennmax 250 racing twin GP engine. This fulfilled a dream of the late Gustav Baumm, who together with Dr Froede had planned this record breaker.

The purpose of this testing was part of a massive effort to hold the maximum number of world records. To this effect no expense was spared. As rumoured before, NSU was really determined to race on the Bonneville Salt Flats in the USA. Accompanying the tri-coloured machines to Utah (to improve the ease of spotting them against the salt the models were red on top, white in the middle and blue/grey below) was a party of 30, including timing experts from the Longines factory. The riders were Herz and Müller. Werner Haas went as a reserve rider but was not used. All save Herz left on 23 July aboard a chartered KLM airliner, flying by

way of Glasgow and Newfoundland to New York and Chicago, then by road to Wendover in Utah. Here it was planned to stay a fortnight. Herz left by ship from Genoa.

On the 29 July, a day before the full record-breaking attempt had been due to start, Herz and Müller made some experimental runs which were not claimed as records. Herz with the 350 supercharged twin bettered 180 mph for both the kilometre and mile. In addition, he clocked over 182 mph on the 5 km and 5 mile runs, while Müller with a 125 was close to 140 mph in both the 1 km and 1 mile dashes.

Herz also took a turn on the unblown 250 Baumm Special. Reported to have been moving in excess of 200 mph he was struck by a blast of wind from the side which overturned the machine, but amazingly he escaped with no more than bruises. However, the damage to the shell was enough to retire it from any further use.

The Rennmax engine was then transferred to a more conventional streamliner for further record attempts. Rain having made the surface of the lake tricky, the programme was delayed until Wednesday 1 August. Knowing the capabilities of the 350 had not been reached, Herz again ran this machine while Müller made a repeat test in the 125. On the return run for the first round trip of the day Herz was again plagued with problems. This time he hit a patch of wet salt which veered him off course enough to wipe out a timing light stand.

Fortunately, he was still able to return to the pits under the machine's own power. But damage to the nose needed surgery. In any case, the still damp surface postponed any further attempts by Müller for the balance of the day.

The next day, 2 August, the following records were broken by Herz with the 350: flying start 1 km 188.5 mph; 1 mile 189.5 mph; 5 km 183 mph. On the same date Müller took out the 125 Baumm-type machine to claim the following flying start records (all of which were then held by the late Gustav Baumm): 1 km 150 mph; 1 mile 150.78 mph; 5 km 148.5 mph; 5 mile 149 mph.

Then two days later on Saturday, 4 August, a new 'World's Fastest' motorcycle speed was achieved. Herz, the 46 year old from Ludwigshaven, piloted his enclosed 500 supercharged parallel twin over the Bonneville Salt Flats at an average speed of 210.64 mph for the two-way run. This represented a 25 mph increase over the existing record set by New Zealander Russell Wright on 2 July 1955, with an unblown 998 cc Vincent V-twin. It was also 18 mph faster than the

Left **Seen on the left is a standard production Sportmax near one of the record breaking machines built for thundering over the Bonneville Salt Flats in Utah, USA. Intensive work throughout the summer of 1956 at the factory was absolutely vital to outcome.**

Helpers manhandling the supercharged 500 cc parallel twin record breaker in October 1956 at Bonneville. The streamlining shell is still waiting to be fitted.

unofficial record at 192 mph established by American Johnny Allen with a 649 cc Triumph engined cigar streamliner on 25 September 1953.

Also on 4 August four 100 cc flying start records were set by Müller following Herz's successful run. He drove a Baumm II machine powered by a stroked and sleeved-down racing Rennfox unit (99.7 cc 56 × 40.5 mm 15.5 bhp at 11,000 rpm) to set the records at: 1 km 137.86; 1 mile 137.86 mph, 5 km 136.62 mph; 5 mile 137.24 mph.

Strong winds then caused more record attempts to be cancelled for a couple of days. When they resumed, Müller then broke the standing 10 mile two way average with a speed of 151 mph on the 125 streamliner. On the blown 49 cc two-stroke unit he averaged 119 mph over the flying mile. Herz with the 250 Rennmax engine in the Delphin averaged 152 mph over the same distance.

When all the dust settled NSU claimed a total of 54 new records. Besides the obvious outright speed record, the most noteworthy was the bettering of the 10 km and 10 mile 350 cc class records by a Baumm II streamliner powered by a 125 Rennfox engine. Since the previous figures were achieved only the previous October by Dickie Dale on a 350 Guzzi works racer the NSU performance deserved high praise.

With its marathon American record session over, the team returned to Germany. The last chapter of NSU's glorious post-war speed story was over. The factory was then left to gain the maximum amount of publicity, at a time when good press for the firm could not have been more timely in the face of falling sales.

Sadly, 26 August 1956, Hans Baltisburger, at the age of 33, was killed while competing on his Sportmax during the Czechoslovakian GP at Brno. It was not even a Championship event.

At dawn, against the dramatic light of a rising Sun, NSU team members ready themselves for another record breaking run over the Bonneville Salt Flats.

The 1956 ISDT was centred on Garmisch-Partenkirchen in Bavaria from 17–22 September. Not unexpectedly, the Germans scored well on home ground. The weather throughout the week was consistently fine, but the course, about 1,200 miles, was severe, with every variety of surface included from running water to virgin rock. The German Vase A team was exclusively NSU mounted with Frey and Haas on 250 Geländemaxes and Westphal and Stecher on 300 models.

In the Trophy, the Germans came fifth overall, while in the Vase contest, Germany A lost no marks, and entered the final day's speed tests level with Holland B. The speed circuit was set up over a triangular 4.349 mile course at Ettal. When the time came for the Vase speed event, tension was high between the four teams in contention – British B, Dutch B, German A and Polish A. All the machines were of 250 cc or less except the German 300s and the British 500s.

As a speed spectacle, it quickly developed into a battle between a couple of Ariel and Matchless big singles and the 300 NSU-mounted Westphal. The other three NSU riders also very much to the forefront. As

Motor Cycling put it; 'Before long it was clear that if these 90 mph NSU's could not only keep up with, but pass, our 500s Britain hadn't a hope and our men were signalled that they should forget the Vase 'race' and make sure of their golds.'

But the Germans had to press on, for the Dutch, with more favourable, smaller capacity motorcycles were putting up a formidable challenge. Their determination was rewarded. It was a close-run thing, but Germany was second in the Vase with the NSU team conceding victory to the Dutch B team on a small difference of merit points.

All four Vase A team members took golds, as did Leinsfer (247 Geländemax), Wagenschieber (125) and Rittinger (125). The two 125s were special Geländesport models based on the Superfox roadster. Silvers went to two Belgian 247 cc NSU Geländemax riders – Kempeneers and Colin – while the third Belgian rider de Junckheer retired. Three 250 sidecar outfits were entered. Marnet and Sauter both gained golds, but Ullmar retired. So out of 13 NSU machines on the trial there were nine golds, two silver and two retirements.

This was the last year of official NSU participation in the event, even though both NSU manufacturer's teams finished intact. However, it was not to be the end of NSU machinery in the ISDT, even at team level. As late as 1963 Erwin Schmider took a gold medal as a member of the Trophy team on a 300 Geländemax. Schmider competed successfully on the larger Geländemax from the 1959 ISDT, in which he won silver as part of German Vase B team, until the 1963 event. He returned in 1965 for the last time.

The end of 1956 saw another tragedy for the racing world with the death on 13 November of Werner Haas – perhaps Germany's finest ever road racer – when the private aircraft he was piloting crashed shortly after take-off at Neuburg/Danube airport. Haas was then 29 years old.

Compared to previous seasons, NSU machinery (in other words the Sportmax) did not gain too many top six placings in the classics during 1957.

At the German GP at Hockenheim the former Adler rider Hallmeier, now Sportmax mounted, came home sixth behind MV Mondial and Guzzi machinery, and finished third in 350 race on a 305 Sportmax.

Next, at the IoM TT, where the Swiss sidecar ace Florian Camathias, who also rode 125/250 solos at the time, brought his Sportmax home ninth. The only other NSU finisher was Irishman David Andrews in eleventh

Herz at speed with Delphin III. The photograph gives a vivid impression of the comprehensive streamlining.

place. Australian Bob Brown had been during the race but had fallen before the finish.

NSU then only figured in the first six at one more GP. This was in Ulster, where star of the future Tommy Robb first showed his mettle by finishing third behind the Mondial of winner Cecil Sandford. Dave Chadwick on a factory MV Agusta was second. Sandford was World Champion that year.

Tommy Robb, David Andrews and Sammy Miller were able to race with the Sportmax because of the sponsorship of Terry Hill, the Northern Ireland agent for NSU. Hill owned five Sportmax models at the time, and had also constructed a 50 cc racer from a standard Quickly N model.

Elsewhere, without factory opposition, the Sportmax reigned supreme. John Surtees was outstanding with his NSU when his factory MV contract would allow. Other successful Sportmax riders in 1957 included Horst Kassner, German 250 championship winner, and Helmut Hallmeier who took the 350 title on a 305 Sportmax.

During the winter of 1957/8, Stanley Michael Bailey Hailwood – Mike Hailwood – the 18 year-old Englishman from Nettleton, Oxfordshire, put together a string of successes on a racing tour of South Africa in his

DELPHIN III

first season. Hailwood campaigned with the ex-John Surtees NSU Sportsmax. There were two other Sportmaxes in the Hailwood camp.

Former World Champion Geoff Duke made an accurate forecast in *Motor Cycling* 1 May 1958 when he stated; 'If the results in South Africa are anything to go by, the name Mike Hailwood should appear on many leaderboards'. Upon his return to Britain in late April 1958, Hailwood soon got off to a flying start for the British short circuit season. He had a pair of wins at Crystal Palace in the 200 race (on an MV) and the 250 with one of his NSU's.

Hailwood was not only a naturally gifted rider, but unlike many others, his father, Stan Hailwood, was in a position to provide almost unlimited sponsorship for the Ecurie Sportive team. Throughout Britain during the summer of 1958 Mike Hailwood and his NSU's were described in headlines as 'Untouchable' and 'Giant Killer'. His victories and lap records included Brands Hatch, Crystal Palace, Mallory Park, Aintree, Snetterton, Scarborough and Aberdare. At the end of the season, the youngster had claimed no fewer than three of the four ACU solo Road Race Stars (the British Championships), the 125, 250 and 350 cc classes.

He shone no less brightly on the international scene too, starting with a memorable finish in second place behind race winner Sammy Miller in the 250 class of the North West 200 in Northern Ireland on Saturday 17 May.

Then came Hailwood's first IoM TT. In his first race on

Right **A seated Mike Hailwood on Sportmax with reknowned tuner Bill Lacey, May 1958.**

the Clypse Circuit, in the Lightweight TT on 4 June, he had a long duel with the experienced Australian rider Bob Brown on another Sportmax. It ended with the 19 year old Mike Hailwood passing his rival to take third place. In this event there were 10 NSUs including those of Hailwood and Brown. The others were Eric Hinton (7th), Tommy Robb (8th), Fron Purslow (9th), David Andrews (10th) and Glen Henderson (12th). Alan Povey retired on lap 2 and Alan Harth and Peden retired on lap 1. New Zealander Neil McCutcheon was a non-starter.

First in the international calender was the non-championship Austrian GP on 1 May, where Italy's Carlo Ubbiali took his MV to victory. Sammy Miller was second on a works CZ four-stroke. Sportmax machines took the next four places with the following order Hallmeier, Autengruber, Scheider, and Thalhammer respectively. This meeting was followed by the international Rhein Pukal Rennen, at Hockenheim on Sunday 11 May. It was won by hard-riding Horst Kassner on a Sportmax, ahead of a pair of Adler two-stroke twins.

The Terry Hill NSU racing equipe from Ireland. Left to right *Motor Cycling* **journalist John Griffiths, Tommy Robb in the helmet, helper, Terry Hill on Sportmax and on a converted Quickly is the team mechanic in the late 1950's.**

First of the Continental European classics was the Dutch TT at Assen on Saturday 29 June. Hailwood, on his first visit to the circuit, was first Sportmax rider home with a fourth behind the works MVs and an Adler twin. Kassner was sixth, and Thalhammer eighth, who were followed by several other NSU competitors.

A week later in Belgium there was no 250 class, so it was at the Nurburgring for the German GP that battle resumed on Sunday 20 July. A brief dice between MV riders Ubbiali and Provini enlivened the first few laps of the 250 event, but ended when Ubbiali fell without injury on the third circuit after rain has made the track surface unpredictable. NSU hopes suffered a setback when first Hailwood went out in the first lap with a binding front brake. Then, Dickie Dale on another Sportmax, retired with a seized engine on the last-but-one lap after a battle for third spot with Dieter Falk (Adler) and Horst Kassner. At the end it was Falk who finished third, behind race winner Tarquinio Provini (MV) and Horst Fugner from East Germany on an MZ twin. NSU riders were fourth placed Kassner, fifth Heiss, sixth Reichert, seventh Schneider, eighth Klager, and Holthaus was tenth.

Hailwood made amends at the Swedish GP at the 4.51 mile Hedemora circuit. Here, 50,000 spectators witnessed some memorable racing on Saturday and

Sunday 26/27 July. Sunday's 18-lap 250 race seemed an MV certainty. In reality, things panned out somewhat differently. Ubbiali was forced out on lap 12 with gearbox trouble. He was followed shortly after by Provini, who nearly a minute ahead of the pack pulled in to retire after a few frantic moments of pit work. It was diagnosed that he had a cracked gearbox casing. This left MZ-mounted Fugner to win from Hailwood, with British rider Geoff Monty third on his home constructed GMS special.

The Ulster GP at Dundrod on Saturday 9 August provided a sensation. With MV and MZ works teams present it was local lad Tommy Robb aboard Terry Hill's Sportmax which had the crowds all around the 7 mile 732 yard circuit cheering when they realised that Robb was not just with the leaders, but was actually overtaking them. Robb fought off a determined challenge from the MZ riders Ernst Degner and Fugner – and MV-mounted Chadwick – to take second behind race winner Provini.

Both Hill's Sportmax machines had just been modified by fitting Manx Norton front brake hubs, as well as the front suspension was altered to accept modified Girling units. Hill said that the changes had resulted 'in greatly improving braking'.

At the final Grand Prix, the Italian at Monza in

September, Autengruber was fifth and was the only NSU rider in the top six. Even so, having missed both the Belgian and Italian events and retired in the German, Mike Hailwood still managed to finish the season 4th in the 250 World Championships.

Not content to 'put his feet up' during the winter he then went on another South African Safari during the 'closed season'. During the 1958 season Hailwood won a total of 16 races with his Sportmax and was awarded a vast number of trophies, of which perhaps the most prominent was the Pinhard Trophy for the most notable contribution to motorcycling by anyone under 21. Later, in 1959, he transferred to an ex-works Mondial, then Desmo Ducati twins which had been specially constructed for him, before becoming a full works rider with MV Agusta and Honda amongst others. However, Hailwood owed much of his apprenticeship to the NSU single.

Another notable racing personality campaigned one of the Neckarsulm machines in 1959. This was ex-World Champion Geoff Duke, who through Reg Armstrong (now retired) had the use of the only ex-works Rennmax twin to 'escape' from Germany. Originally, so the story goes, both Armstrong and Duke had expected a 1954 six-speed example. In this hope they were to be sorely disappointed. The machine that arrived was one of the

John Dixon on his Manx Norton front-braked Sportmax sweeps through the home straight at Scarborough in 1960.

earlier four-speed 1953 models with the 'Y' drive to the dohc on the right of power unit. Before being raced it was converted early in 1959 to something of a special using a Reynolds frame and front fork assembly, Manx Norton front wheel and Lyta alloy fuel tank.

In what was to be his last season, the association between Duke and the Reynolds/Rennmax was never happy. Even at the Austrian GP at Salzburg 1 May, the machine was fractuous, and where it insisted it would fire only on one cylinder. Then came the IoM TT, where in practice on the Clypse circuit using, so Duke claimed, 'a mere 9,000 rpm instead of the NSU's permitted 10,400', the engine suddenly slowed. A rapid withdrawal of the clutch was imperative.

When stripped, it was found that the gudgeon pin on the right hand cylinder had broken. Fragments of metal had then found their way into the oil pump, and starved of lubrication the gears sheared. With spares of this nature unavailable, Duke had no alternative but to advise his sponsor Armstrong that he would be a non-starter in the Lightweight TT.

After the TT Duke accepted the offer of a works ride on a Benelli single and so the NSU went back to Reg Armstrong. It was then sold to Glen Anderson from Ayr in Scotland. After this in 1963 it passed on again, this time to North Shields rider Eddie Johnson. Finally, in early 1969 it was sold to its present owner John Kidson – well known for his exploits in the IoM during the 1960s on Moto Guzzi singles.

TWN Triumph

Although it was known as TWN in Germany's export markets to avoid confusion with the British Triumph, in many ways the German marque had as much claim to the name as its English counterpart. In fact, it was two Germans, Siegfried Bettmann and Maurice Schultz who founded the British company in Coventry during 1897.

For the first few years their output concentrated on bicycles, but in 1902, the first motorcycle bearing the Triumph name appeared. It was powered by a 220 cc Belgian Minerva engine.

The following year, in 1903, when Triumph officially entered the motorcycle business, it also opened a German factory in Nürnberg. In the early days, most of the German-built Triumphs had engines and other components supplied by the Coventry works. This arrangement continued until 1929 when the two companies went their separate ways. From then on, both companies used the Triumph brand name in their home markets.

The German firm also adopted the name TWN (Triumph Werke Nürnberg). Orial was also used as a brand by Nürnberg. The British Triumph was known, especially in Germany, as TEC (Triumph Engineering Co. Ltd).

Following the break, the German factory used its own 198 and 294 cc two-stroke engines, together with a range of Swiss MAG engines from 347 to 742 cc. The MAG units were all four-strokes with either ohv or inlet over exhaust valve operation. Very soon TWN secured a license from MAG to build these engines in Germany.

In 1931 the Nürnberg company employed Otto Reitz as chief designer. He was the father of the majority of the various two-strokes which TWN built during the next quarter of a century. One of his most interesting designs was a 198 cc 'stroker with shaft drive, unit construction engine and pressed steel frame. These features on such a small machine at that time was considered trend-setting design. Racing also came into the picture, with 348 and 493 cc ohc singles ridden by riders such as Fleischmann and Ley.

The largest capacity machine built at the works was a 846 cc side-valve V-twin, but it was the two-stroke range in late thirties that dominated the company's interests and production lines. These models included the B350 which first appeared in 1938 – a 346 cc (72 × 85 mm) unit which turned out 12 bhp. Almost the whole output went to the German military.

A far more significant innovation of the late 1930's was TWN's first two-stroke split single. The BD250 was supplied first in civilian guise, then in military trim. It featured two pistons carried on a single, forked con rod, and had a capacity of 248 cc (2 × 45 × 78 mm).

Unlike the 350, the BD250 was supplied in large numbers. Over 12,000 were purchased by the *Wehrmacht* alone. In army service, the machines were known as the BD250W. During wartime, Triumph developed prototypes of a three-speed 125 scooter which could be dropped by parachute, and a TWN-engined NSU tracked personnel carrier. Neither went into production before the war ended.

TWN was among the earliest motorcycle manufacturers to resume production after the Second World War. The bulk of its output in the late 1940s was concentrated on two models, the BDG125 and BDG250. Both machines were directly descended from the pre-war B125 and BD250 models, with the larger model powered by the same 248 cc split single four-speed engine, with dual exhaust system and fully-enclosed rear chain. Except for the substitution of telescopic front forks in 1949, the bikes were of a pre-war specification.

The BDG125H was launched in 1950 and was a split single. It had a 123 cc (2 × 35 × 62 mm) engine with a compression ratio of 6.4:1 and a power output of 6.5 bhp at 4800 rpm compared to the earlier model's 4 bhp. The BDG125H also featured the Nürnberg factory's first application of plunger rear suspension.

However, as a result of the technical advances, the dry weight rose from 176 lb to 204 lb, and the machine was substantially more expensive. So why had TWN added cost and complication to its machines? There were two very good reasons.

The first was that the two piston layout endowed the engine with a much smoother power delivery. No 'four-stroking' was evident and top gear performance for such a small power unit was superb. It had the ability to run down to 10 mph. Secondly, there was also a 20 per cent improvement in fuel consumption figures.

When one of the new BDG125H models was tested in Germany during April 1950 by the editor of *Motor Cycle*, Arthur Bourne, summed up the TWN as 'A handleable, likeable, lively mount with an excellent riding position and the most interesting 125 cc two-stroke of the present day'.

TWN also pioneered new engineering practices with the use of light alloy cylinder barrels in which the bores were plated with dull chromium honeycombed with minute identations. This ensured not only much closer tolerances, but also enhanced lubrication. Today, this process is almost universally used on two-strokes, but when it was introduced by TWN, no other company had tried it.

The BDG250H, which was launched in 1951, not only followed the 125 by adopting plunger rear suspension, but also incorporated a redesigned engine with a shorter stroke (2 × 45 × 78 mm) giving a capacity of 246 cc. Power was up to 11 bhp at 3800 rpm, and with the dry weight unchanged at 303 lb, performance was much crisper, offering a true 62.5 mph top-end speed.

It was none of these features, however, which came in for the most praise when leading British designer Bert Hopwood conducted a technical review of German motorcycle design in *Motor Cycle*, 13 December 1951. He stated that one of the outstanding aspects of the BDG 250H was, in his view, the protection of the rear chain. TWN used a system which is still found on contemporary East German MZ roadsters. Hopwood went on, 'The TWN scheme, with its slideable, flexibly mounted connector ducts housing the top and bottom runs of the chain is, to my mind, a very commendable layout'. What was not stated at the time was that this

Classic formula for a split single. This drawing shows the principles of the scavenging system. For German Triumph models both before and after the Second World War this was the normal arrangement. Shown here is 1953 BDG 250 L.

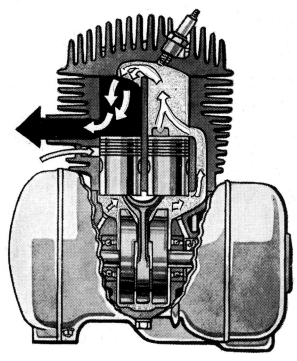

had been used on the 250 and 350 TWN models from as early as 1938.

During 1952 the two model range continued unchanged. However, following an excellent result in the 1951 ISDT, which was held around Varese in northern Italy, there was a suggestion that one of the official German Vase teams should use a trio of 250 TWN sidecar outfits. This did not happen, but the factory gained a pair of gold medals in the 1952 ISDT, Guth on a 125 and Durschinger mounted on a 250 were the successful riders at Bad Aussee in Austria.

Much of 1952 was taken up with the development and testing of a larger capacity machine now that Allied controls on such models had been relaxed. TWN's machine emerged with the designation of the 350 Boss. Its debut was at the 23rd Geneva Show in March 1953. Like the others in the range, the new model had total enclosure of the rear drive train and used plunger suspension.

The Boss engine was a new split single design with a capacity of 344 cc (2 × 53 × 78 mm) and used the same type of chrome-plated light alloy bores already in service on the smaller models. Two Bing 1/24/66 carbs with separate air filters were fitted, and there were also twin exhausts. However, the normal principle of split single operation remained unchanged. The object of the two carburettors was to ensure (so TWN claimed) that both pistons were properly cooled by the incoming fresh gas. With larger cylinders, the factory considered this aspect vitally important.

Twin exhaust pipes were fitted, although the exhaust outlet ran from the left-hand bore only. Part of the exhaust gas travelled through the exhaust pipe on the left, while the remainder passed through an internal passage across the front of the cylinder barrel and then into the exhaust port on the right.

The exhausts were specially manufactured for TWN by Eberspacher and were the other major innovation by the factory for 1953. Best described as bulbous, they were also used on the smaller models, which, however, only had single pipes. The idea of the design was to improve both performance and noise level. Naturally, the marketing department leaped on the last point and rushed out publicity material that proclaimed; 'TWN Producers of the Whispering Motorcycle'.

From a technical viewpoint, the increased diameter of the bulbous design provided high volume expansion chambers for the wider section of the pipe, which then reduced to a more normal size for a low-level horizontal length before terminating in a large and effective silencer fitted with fishtail ends.

With a maximum power output of 16.5 bhp at 3800 rpm and nearly 11 bhp at a mere 2500 rpm, the newcomer appeared to offer engine characteristics which were eminently suitable for work with a third wheel. As if to prove the point, at Geneva, one Boss was displayed hitched to a single seat sports Steib sidecar.

Pride of the 1953 German Triumph range was the 344 cc two-piston split-single Boss. It first made its debut before the general public in May 1953 at the Geneva Show. The model had hydraulic rear brake.

This was mounted on a revolving dais, and was an imposing and impressive exhibit.

Another Boss feature was a hydraulically operated rear wheel and sidecar wheel brake that was activated by a single foot brake pedal. The master cylinder was built integrally with the engine crankcase and incorporated the stoplight switch. Alfred Teves manufactured the hydraulics for TWN. Both wheels carried alloy rims and 160 mm full-width drums. They were interchangeable, and when used with the Steib sidecar, a spare was carried.

Also making its debut at Geneva was the Knirps cyclemotor. The term Knirps is not directly translatable but has the sense of a lively child who would like to do brave things, amongst other meanings. Anyway, it was available with either belt or chain drive. And another change for 1953 was the introduction of two new 250s, the S and the L. The latter replaced the H, but not only was it less powerful (10.5 bhp at 3600 rpm using a Bing 2/24/15 carb) – at 321 lb, it weighed more. With the deeply valanced heavyweight mudguards introduced on the 350 Boss it was strictly for touring. The S

delivered 12 bhp at 4000 rpm and had a respectively more sporting performance. Although it was hardly any faster than the original H, acceleration was improved by narrow mudguards and other weight saving measures.

Both 'new' 250s sported a single version of the 350's expansion chamber pipe and silencer on the right. Like the 350, they used Noris 6 volt electrics with a 60 watt generator and a 7 amp/hour battery.

July 1953 was the company's Golden Jubilee, and to commemorate 50 years of motorcycle production, TWN duly celebrated by announcing what was hailed as one of the smartest lightweights of the era.

Named the Cornet, it had a 197 cc (2 × 45 × 62 mm) split single engine with a 6:1 compression ratio, giving 10.1 bhp at 5000 rpm. A Bing 2/26/26 carburettor fed the combustion chamber with a 20:1 petroil mix. The exhaust system was based on the Boss' architecture. Primary drive to the four plate clutch was by chain, and there was a fully enclosed pressed steel guard for the rear drive chain. Performance was well up to the class standard with a top speed of 63 mph and a dry weight of 266 lb.

The model's most outstanding feature was its full swinging arm rear suspension (the first to appear on a TWN machine). Oil-damped telescopic forks together with a sturdy frame made it supremely comfortable for its class and time.

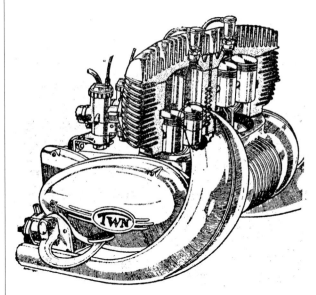

Above **A cutaway view of the intriguing 250 Duplex. Unfortunately, this engine never went into full production.**

The specification included a 12-litre fuel tank, 19 inch tyres, 125 mm full width alloy brake hubs, and 6 volt electrics with a Noris 60 watt generator and a 7 amp hour battery for the coil ignition. Neat detailing included the housing of horn and battery under the left-hand toolbox. A tyre pump was carried underneath the rear sub-frame tube. Unlike the majority of other German lightweights of the time, the Cornet was supplied with a foam rubber single rider's seat as standard, while a 'companion's' seat was available as an extra. This bolted to four points on the rear mudguard which was an integral part of the frame. The companion's seat was styled to match the rider's seat, and came with a large grab handle at the front. A rear carrier was also listed in the accessories catalogue.

With all the newcomers to its range over the preceding few months, TWN were hardly expected to come up with anything new for the Second International Motorcycle Exhibition at Frankfurt in October 1953. But in Hall 10 TWN surprised the industry with an all new 500 cc machine. In effect this was an enlarged Boss 350 split single, but as events were to prove this was largely an exercise to boost show interest rather than a serious production model. The 500 was hardly ever seen again after the Frankfurt exhibition.

Another TWN which went no further than the prototype stage was the interesting Duplex. A 250 model powered by a twin, double-piston two-stroke. The engine had a three bearing crankshaft and twin carburettors. It was claimed to produce 14 bhp, giving the machine to which it was fitted a maximum road speed of over 71 mph. Another noteworthy feature was a hydraulically-operated rear brake. The Duplex was originally scheduled to enter series production.

Right **A sales brochure of the early 1950's which typified Triumph's determination to project a family touring image.**

Management, however, is thought to have shelved the project because the machine lacked significantly improved performance to warrant any further major investment. Nevertheless, development continued until 1954.

In January 1954 TWN stated that further research and development work was needed on the four-piston Duplex 250. The main unresolved area was the choice of materials for cylinders, piston and rings. This can be interpreted as hinting at possible seizures. Another reason why the Duplex never entered mass production was that owners of German two-strokes had by then become used to expecting some 30,000 miles normal use before needing a major engine overhaul. It was unlikely a complex, four piston engine could be reliable for such a lengthy service interval.

The 1954 model range consisted of the Knirps bicycle with auxiliary engine, BDG125 (now called the L), Cornet 200, and three versions of the BDG250 (the L, S, and SL). The latter had the 12 bhp engine of the S with the touring equipment and valanced mudguards of the L.

The 29th ISDT at Llandrindod Wells, Wales from

Below **Comic scene depicting the quietness of the then new Cornet model. It was introduced to coicide with the company's Golden Jubilee in motorcycle production. The fifty year milestone was reached in July 1953.**

TRIUMPH WERKE NURNBERG A.G. NUREMBERG

Monday 16 to Saturday 25 September 1954 was a success for a trio of 350 Boss models. Strohe took a gold medal, while Hartner gained a silver and Kussin finished with a bronze. Against this, Meunier's 173 (a sleeved-down Cornet) and Hermand's Boss had to retire on the Wednesday of the event.

At around this time, the German Triumph finally came to Britain. Manchester based D. Salem Limited were appointed in October as importers. Initially only three models were available – the Cornet (£199 7s 9d), 250L (£219 12s), and Boss (£248 8s).

Also during 1954, TWN determined that it would take advantage of the small-wheel boom which was then in full swing. The result was the Contessa scooter. Its split single engine came from the Cornet motorcycle, but suitably modified for its new use by having fan cooling, an electric start and 12 volt Noris electrics. Suspension was by leading arm front fork and swinging arm rear.

The first apperance of the Contessa was at the 38th Brussels Salon in January 1955. But in Britain the Contessa was not available until February 1956, when a batch was imported by Industria (London) Ltd of Maidenhead, Berkshire. Industria fixed the retail price at £229 8s, 0d.

Meanwhile, TWN had entered a manufacturers' team for the 1955 ISDT at Gottwaldov in Czechoslovakia. In the 175 class, Stump took a gold medal, while Strohe and Hartner both on 350s took golds. Bonvoisin

of Belgium took a silver on his 175, while his compatriot Mernier (175) and the Swiss Del Torchino (350) were forced to retire.

Early in 1956 the 200 Cornet was updated, gaining 12 volt electrics and an electric start. To achieve this two 6 volt batteries were connected in series and were housed in a new location beneath the rider's seat. Another change was the addition of an easy-to-operate neutral selector which worked directly from any gear. The lever was located behind the conventional gear lever and operated by the rider's heel, like the similar Royal Enfield system. Otherwise, the machine was largely unchanged.

At the same time, a new moped and scooter were added to the range. The moped was the 47 cc Fips which used a proprietary Sachs power unit. Its specifications included trailing link front forks, swinging arm rear suspension, full-width front brake, built-in luggage carrier, speedometer and horn. The scooter was the 125 cc Tessy, which proved a dismal failure and only remained in production for a short time. However, both models were imported into Britain by Industria in August 1956 and sold for £184 15s 3d and £84 18s 10d respectively.

The 1956 ISDT was held at Garmisch-Partenkirchen in Bavaria from 17–22 September. TWN entered an official manufacturers' team. Zellhofer rode a 175 Cornet for the German Vase B team. Zellhofer won a gold medal, but other team members failed to live up to his fine performance. They netted only a bronze and a retirement for their week's effort.

A tripartite pact between TWN, Adler and Hercules acknowledged the mid-fifties over-production crisis in the German motorcycle industry. All three manufacturers' stands at the Frankfurt Show displayed Sports Fips. This was essentially a superficially enhanced standard model. Badge engineering was rampant on the three stands. Apart from the Sports Fips, TWN had nothing new to add to the line-up of BDG125L, BDG250SL, Cornet, Boss and Contessa – plus the standard Fips moped line.

An interesting aftermarket novelty was available for TWNs. This was a new silencer from Rokal called the 'Frankfurter Topf', consisting of a cast light alloy expansion chamber containing a maze of cunningly contrived baffles and connected to a long tail pipe. A demonstration of the efficiency of the new system was given for the press. The ladies and gentlemen of the Fourth Estate learned how to transform the healthy note of a high-efficiency two-stroke into a car-like whisper in which the loudest noise came from the pistons without seeming to affect power output. But another, perhaps far more significant event at the same show was the launch of Karl Altenberger's design for the world's first tubeless tyre for use in a spoked wheel.

Proof of the seriousness of TWN's lack of sales and over-production first was confirmed in early June 1957.

Cutaway drawing of 197 cc Cornet two-stroke, double-piston engine (2 × 45 mm bore, 62 mm stroke). Alloy cylinder had hard chrome running surface. The patented process was pioneered by Triumph in Nürnberg.

A batch of 300 1956 model Cornets with electric start, were imported into Britain as a 'job lot' by the London dealer Claude Rye Ltd. They sold at the bargain price of £159 9s 3d.

But by then, TWN's life as a motorcycle producer was almost over. The company ceased two-wheel production in mid-1957 to concentrate on making office equipment and typewriters. In July 1958 both TWN and Adler were taken over by the massive Gründig electrical combine. Gründig, had by that time already gained a controlling interest in both companies.

Two famous and well-respected marques thus effectively ceased to exist, but an interesting footnote to the TWN story was that a couple of models lived to fight again under other colours.

These were the Sports Fips moped and Contessa

In early 1956 the Cornet was updated. It was now equipped with 12-volt electrics, electric start, plus a selector which allowed engagement of neutral from any gear.

scooter. Both were acquired by former rivals Hercules. The moped was then marketed as the 219, while the scooter became the Viscount, with a 200 Sachs engine replacing the split single Triumph unit.

In Britain, these models were imported by Industria and sold as Priors (the name which replaced Hercules as the brand name in Britain). Industria was at the same time selling the Czechoslovakian Jawa/CZ range. A brochure of the period shows the German and Iron Curtain machines together. But the Nürnberg machines were at least allowed to retain the dignity of a seperate identity.

Victoria

Founded in Nürnberg by Max Frankenburger and Max Offenstein, the Victoria bicycle factory began trading in 1886. After thirteen successful years, the company switched from muscle power to the internal combustion engine.

Victoria began by fitting single cylinder Zedel and Fafnir power units into frames of their own manufacture. These machines were sold until 1918 but after the Great War, production concentrated on 493 cc motorcycles with horizontally-opposed twin cylinder power units.

As the engine layout might suggest, Victoria used proprietary power units built by BMW. These were early M2B15 blocks with fore-and-aft cylinders, not the more familiar transverse flat-twin engine. In 1923 when Munich-based BMW decided to build complete motorcycles, Victoria quickly engaged BMW's former designer Martin Stolle. He developed a family of new ohv engines with a very similar layout. These were built for Victoria at the Sedlbauer factory in Munich. But in the late 1920's Victoria bought the engine factory and continued producing 498 cc flat twins. A 598 cc version was produced at a later stage.

Stolle remained with the company for only two years, and was succeeded by Gustav Steinlein. In 1925 Steinlein designed the first supercharged German racing machines. He chose a 498 cc flat-twin engine for the honour. Once again, the cylinders were in-line with the machine, and in 1926 one of these broke the German speed record at almost 104 mph.

New single cylinder models were introduced in 1928 using Sturmey-Archer engines of 198 to 498 cc, and Victoria also fitted a 348 cc ohv version of the Sturmey-Archer engine built by Horex (Columbus) under licence. In the 1930s, Victoria raced an official works team in which a string of well-known German riders took part. Usually the 348 cc engine was used, but the 499 cc single and the 598 cc flat twin were also built into racers.

Victoria used designs from Albert Roder and Richard Küchen as well as Stolle. Among normal production roadsters built in the inter-war period were several two-strokes ranging from 98 to 198 cc, a 497 cc inlet-over-exhaust unit and some ohv twins designed by Stolle. These had triangular pressed steel frames and completely exposed unit-construction engines.

After 1945, production initially concentrated on small capacity two-strokes, ranging from a 38 cc engine for attachment to a conventional pedal cycle to a 247 cc motorcycle, the KR25 Aero. This was available from 1948. The KR25 Aero had a twin-port engine giving 6 bhp at 3200 rpm, four-speed gearbox, rigid frame, blade forks and 19 inch wheels. It weighed 292 lb.

Like other manufacturers of the period, Victoria soon found that demand outstripped supply, and by the end of the 1940s, they were firmly re-established and in full production.

In March 1950 Victoria rather missed the boat and failed to ready its new models in time for the Frankfurt Show. These were not available until the following year, when an improved 250 appeared. This was the KR25HM, with 9 bhp at 4000 rpm and generally uprated performance. But the biggest news was a completely new 125, the KR125 Bi-fix. This had a capacity of 123 cc (51 × 60 mm) and gave 4.5 bhp at 3000 rpm. With a three-speed gearbox, the 182 lb machine was good for 50 mph.

The next major event was Victoria's first post-war four-stroke – the V35 Bergmeister (Mountain Master), which first went on show in 1951. The shaft-driven

Victoria's 38 cc record breaker which appeared in the immediate post-war period was little more than a pedal cycle with limited streamlining

Bergmeister had an unusual 347 cc (64 × 54 mm) V-twin engine designed by Richard Küchen, which produced 21 bhp at 6300 rpm on a compression ratio of 7.5:1. The engine was transversely mounted, with its cylinders across the frame. Its exceptionally clean lines of the castings completely concealed the Bing 2/24/26 carb and its large air filter. Hidden under another cowling was a Noris dynamo, 7 amp/hour battery and a 6 volt coil ignition system. There were several interesting features, including a gear-driven camshaft located between the cylinders, and pushrod tunnels cast in the cylinder barrels and heads.

The frame was, for the times, extremely modern, with telescopic forks and plunger rear suspension. The 19 inch wheels had 180 mm full-width alloy brakes that were well able to haul the 389 lb machine to a standstill. It was a machine with an impressive specification – the only snag being that it was over two years before customers were actually able to buy one. Ultimately, the Bergmeister almost ruined the company because it needed four expensive years of development work before serious engine vibration could be cured.

Bergmeister 347 cc V-twin with Steib chair was exhibited at 1953 Frankfurt Show.

The English journalist John Thorpe was lucky enough to be the first of the British press to test the latest version at the Geneva Show in early 1954. At low speeds, Thorpe found the steering heavy, but as the machine was accelerated its navigation became 'delightfully positive'. The front forks 'coped admirably' with the various bumps, while in Thorpe's opinion, the rear plungers proved that for purely touring purposes a good set of plungers could be made as comfortable and efficient as the more popular swinging arm.

Of the engine's performance he had this to say; 'It would be difficult to speak too highly, the power coming in smoothly from walking pace right up to a maximum which had not quite been reached when the speedometer needle was climbing past the 120 kph (75 mph) mark. Even allowing for possible error in the instrument, that places the Bergmeister in the 70 mph class'. Victoria claimed 130 kph – 81 mph.

Gear selection was described as light and positive, although it was essential to make a slight pause when ringing the changes at high revs. The penalty for undue haste was a marked refusal of the dogs to engage, as Thorpe soon discovered.

There was one 'fly in the ointment', as John Thorpe described it. This was the throttle action, which was of

KR 26 Aero Sport was an attractive twin-port 246 cc single, circa 1953.

the slow-action type popular in mainland Europe at the time. However, British riders commonly found these took more than a little practice to become proficient at judging the lag between the movement of the grip and the response of the engine. *Motor Cycling's* man commented; 'I for one would have felt happier had a direct action throttle been fitted'.

That said, the Bergmeister proved almost ideal. On the twisting climb up one of Switzerland's minor Alps it acquitted iself well. It could be 'heeled right over until the centre stand fouled the ground noisily', as Thorpe vividly described it. Whatever the surface, the machine remained steady and changes of direction could be made rapidly.

Of the dreaded torque reaction which was then a feature of most transverse engines, there was no sign. Even with the machine at a standstill, blipping the throttle failed to produce a noticeable reaction. Thorpe noted; 'the firing was unusually even for a Vee engine; the "works" mechanically quiet and the silencing excellent – the last named a happy state of affairs engendered by Germany's strict new laws on the subject'.

The first Victoria V-twin went on sale in 1953, the same year that the KR26 Aero became available commercially. This was a much-improved version of the earlier KR25NM, and came in two variants; the KR26N and the KR26 Sport. Both were extremely well made, and robust. In the 25 June 1953 issue of *Motor Cycling* even went so far as to describe the newcomers as 'massive'. The difference between the two amounted to cosmetic changes only, with the standard model having a 14.5-litre tank and single seat, while the Sport had a larger 16-litre tank with chrome sides and a plush dual saddle. Both 247 cc engines produced 16 bhp at

5250 rpm, Bing 2/24/24 carbs and a compression ratio of 7.35:1.

The frame was a huge single front downtube design, with tele-forks and a plunger rear end. Wheels were 18 inch, and 180 mm full-width drums were fitted. Drive was via a fully-enclosed rear chain.

In 1953 at the second Frankfurt International Motorcycle Show, Victoria introduced a scooter called the Peggy. This was not only luxurious, but practical, with excellent weather protection and a lusty 198 cc horizontal single-cylinder two-stroke engine. Wheels were 16 inch in diameter, suspended via leading link forks and a swinging arm at the rear.

A new lightweight, the Vicky III, was introduced in 1954. However, despite its technical qualification as a moped, it was almost universally regarded as a scooter. This was underlined when a Vicky finished in first place in a scooter rally at Merano in Italy in April that year. The course, laid out in the Tyrolean Alps, attracted entries from Britain, Switzerland, Denmark, Austria, Belgium and Germany, who witnessed Wilhelm Steiner, the Vicky rider, cover 376 miles on 1.9 gallons of fuel.

The Vicky had a 48 cc (38 × 42 m) piston-ported single cylinder two-stroke engine, with a hand starter and two-speed gearbox. This was carried in a simple frame with leading-link forks using rubber suspension elements. The rear suspension was by progressive coil springs. Both wheels were 20 inches in diameter with 2½ inch section tyres.

The lines were very clean indeed, and set off by a combined instrument panel and headlamp unit

Right **In 1956 the Swing was hailed as revolutionary. This 197 cc model had pushbutton gear changing and a unique form of rear wheel and engine suspension.**

mounted on top of the steering column. This panel covered the centre section of the handlebars, and very unusually for such a humble machine, included a fuel level gauge.

At the Brussels Show in January 1955, there was an interesting exhibit from Sparta – then Holland's largest motorcycle manufacturer. Its new 250 was shown with a Victoria KR26 Aero engine in place of the usual Ilo unit. Interestingly, the KR26 itself was enjoying a modest boom. Amongst other successes, in 1954/55 it achieved higher sales than any other model on the Danish market.

Early January 1955 brought the first acknowledgements of a new Victoria motorcycle. The newcomer was the KR21, shown in trials trim, and the 24 February issue of *Motor Cycling*, referred to it in the following terms: 'an unconventional model is this prototype Victoria KR21, a high performance German "200". Its engine, which uses Elektron castings, develops 9.5 bhp. Combined with a weight of 240 lb this gives a very good power/weight ratio'.

The shows during March in Copenhagen and Amsterdam both had examples of this model in production form. It entered the market as the 200 Swing.

The unit-construction engine was an extremely advanced design, borrowing heavily from scooter practice and mounted almost horizontally in the duplex cradle frame. The 197 cc (65 × 60 mm) power pack was fixed rigidly to an internally ribbed cast-iron strut which carried the rear wheel. The wheel was linked to the spindle of the four-speed gearbox by an enclosed final drive chain tensioned by an eccentric jockey sprocket. In order to provide rear suspension, the engine unit pivoted from the frame below the crankcase. The upper rear portion of the frame and the rear mudguard were integral welded-up pressings, reinforced to take the upper mountings of the twin, adjustable rear shock absorbers. This system precluded the use of a conventional foot-controlled gearchange, so this was effected from the handlebar by twistgrip.

The rear of the engine was concealed under detachable panels fitted to the frame. Front suspension was provided by leading links connected by covered links to a bridge piece which bore on a coil spring with co-axial damper fitted in front of the steering head. A small fairing was built into the top of the forks, and this

Right **A sample of the publicity material published by newly formed Zweirad Union in early 1960's.**

carried the headlamp and speedo. Both wheels had 16 inch rims with 3.25 inch section tyres. Other details included a large dual seat (in two sections), and an equally massive (and effective) silencer running down the left of the machine.

Power figures of the production model were a definite improvement to those quoted for the prototype, with 11.3 bhp at 5300 rpm. And for the 1956 season, the specifications of the 60 mph 288 lb lightweight were increased even further. This included the fitting of an electrically-operated fuel gauge and brake warning lights. But the major publicity and comment was reserved for a new method of gearchange. From a small control panel on the left hand handlebar, the rider could change gear at the press of a button. The system was remarkably simple, consisting solely of a powerful electromagnet which operated the gear selector pushrod. There was an emergency circuit for use when the battery went flat.

Below **By the end of the 1950's Victoria was reduced to manufacturing small lightweights and mopeds. Typical of the breed was this 1959 Avanti sports moped. In the same year, Victoria joined the Zweirad Union.**

DKW VICTORIA EXPRESS

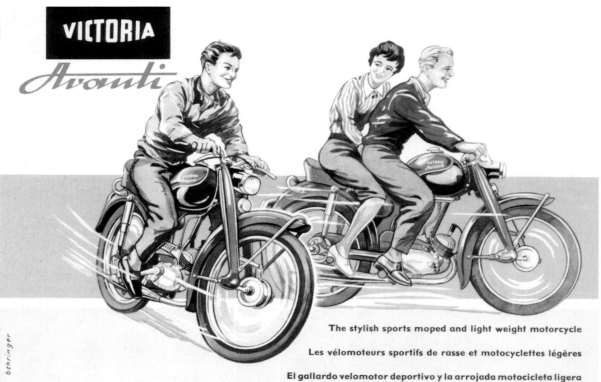

VICTORIA Avanti

The stylish sports moped and light weight motorcycle

Les vélomoteurs sportifs de rasse et motocyclettes légères

El gallardo velomotor deportivo y la arrojada motocicleta ligera

Mid-1960's Victoria 159 TS Super. It was a fully equipped 49.6 cc motorcycle and capable of a genuine 50 mph. It was the last Victoria built in large numbers.

At the Geneva Show in March 1956 a brand-new two-seater sports three-wheeler called the Belcar appeared. This was powered by a Swing engine unit.

Meanwhile, Victoria was quickly becoming financially unstable. An attempt was made to improve flagging sales by entering into an agreement with the Italian Parilla company. Under the terms of this deal, Victoria arranged to use several of the Italian engines, though not the renowned high camshaft 175 unit. These machines were marketed as Victoria-Parilla models and were displayed for the first time at the giant Frankfurt show in October 1956.

After a period of indecision the company decided to relaunch the Peggy scooter which had been discontinued a few months previously. Interestingly, its unconventional 197 cc engine with 'live' rear axle and push-button gearchange was the same power unit which had been used for the KR21 Swing motorcycle. With its appearance on the Peggy scooter, the wheel had turned full circle.

Several new mopeds also made their bow at Frankfurt, including the Avanti and Tony, together with the Spatz four-wheel light car. But all these new ideas were insufficient to divert Victoria from its fate. Two years later, Victoria was one of three companies which amalgamated to form the Zweirad Union. This was

made possible by Herr Flick, controlling shareholder of Daimler-Benz, parents of Mercedes-Benz. The other parties were DKW and Express, whose factories continued in operation, but the Victoria company's plant in Nürnberg was nominated as the headquarters of the organisation.

Throughout this turbulent period British imports of Victoria machines continued. In 1956, Stacey and Harding of London SW3 were appointed Victoria's importers. The company's asking price for a Peggy scooter was £223 14s 6d. Stacey and Harding also landed the Vicky moped. In October 1957 the concessionaires changed to Europa Imports of Reading, Berks. But Europa was deprived of the Peggy and the Vicky and allowed only to sell the Swing. This motorcycle retailed at £199 12s 0d.

A year later, business appeared to be improving because the range had risen to eight models, including various versions of the Vicky, Avanti and Preciosa – a three-speed scooterette. But a year later, the range was cut down to four – the Avanti K Sports at £98 8s, the Preciosa, Vicky Luxus and Super Luxus. By the mid-1960s, only one Victoria was listed by Europea Imports – the Vicky 117 Mk II at £100 16s.

This reflected mounting troubles in the Zweirad Union. The board of management decided to cease Victoria production in 1966. Shortly afterwards, Express, as a marque, was consigned to oblivion. The Zweirad Union's efforts and resources were then committed to promoting the DKW brand and image. . . .

Zündapp

On 17 September 1917, Zünderund Apparatebau GmbH, better known in the shorter form as Zündapp, was founded in Nürnberg. The new company, which employed 1800 workers was a joint venture between three established firms at the height of the Great War. The commercial stimulus was war production. Zünderund manufactured fuses for artillery guns. At the war's end the new company struggled to find a suitable product to replace the no-longer needed war materials.

Zündapp was acquired in full by Dipl Ing Fritz Neumeyer in 1919. Born in 1875, Neumeyer had first displayed his entrepreneurial skills as early as 1901 by starting a highly profitable metal working company in Nurnberg. This later branched out into various other industrial fields and was active in both home and export markets. For example, one of Neumeyer's best customers before 1914 was Serck Radiators of Birmingham, England.

After the Armistice, Dr Neumeyer not only built Zündapp but established a conglomerate which encompassed such diverse engineering enterprises as cable and radio; farm tractors, and rolling stock repair yards for the German railways. Neumeyer created a financial empire which eventually wielded world-wide economic influence. While its scope and story are outside the bounds of this book, having Neumeyer at the helm undoubtedly provided Zündapp with a strength that few others within the motorcycle industry could match.

Neumeyer's task of discovering a profitable role for Zündapp after the war was difficult. However, in the autumn of 1921, the company found its new identity, and built its first five motorcycles. These were the forerunners of the more than three million machines that the company manufactured over the next 63 years.

The first model built by what was to emerge as one of Germany's premier marques was the 211 cc Z22. It was powered by a British-made Levis engine. This was a deflector-piston type three port two-stroke which produced 2.25 bhp, transmitted to the rear wheel by belt. By 21 October 1922, 1,000 of these machines had been manufactured by a workforce which now totalled 600.

Zündapp's management realised how important motorcycle sport was for a company's prestige. The very first Zündapp built was ridden in the critical North Bavarian reliability trials, 18 September 1921, by the German champion Metsch, who was later to become a legend within the Zündapp organisation for his exploits on the company's products during the 1920s.

By November 1924 other models powered by Zündapp's own engine designs had been added to the range, including one which used a 249 cc version of the original Levis. At the beginning of 1924 Zündapp commissioned its first modern assembly line. By year's end more than 10,000 machines had been assembled on its conveyors.

The German public first bought motorcycles in high volume in 1924. This boom was greatly helped by a national 17 day touring race which aroused the interest of millions. Zündapp scored some impressive successes in this event. Although Zündapp only briefly took a serious interest in road racing, and at that only at the very end of the company's life, it found a special niche in endurance trials which followed the early touring events.

From 1926 onwards Zündapp established branches in all the major commercial centres of Germany. The first was in Berlin, followed by Munich, Cologne and Hamburg. This was the beginning of the establishment of a nationwide dealer and service network.

In that year a total of 4226 machines were purchased. By 1928 this figure was up to 16,877 — and rising rapidly. Several hazardous journeys were undertaken by Zündapp machines in 1928, for example, two students rode the 7,350 kilometres from Berlin to the Black Sea and back on their small Zündapp two-stroke without a single breakdown, despite often dreadful roads.

This was followed by more adventures, including a record-breaking demonstration in 1930 when a Zündapp S300 (again a single cylinder two-stroke) covered the Berlin-Paris route in 17 hours 40 minutes — faster than either an express train or the Mercedes car against which it was competing.

By 1928, the four separate Zündapp plants in Nürnberg were cluttered and congested, so a new plant at Nürnberg-Schweinau was constructed. This opened the following year and was hailed as the most modern in the world. In seven short years Zündapp had risen from nothing to take a place amongst the market leaders. In April 1929, a new monthly output record was set of nearly 4200 units.

In July Hans-Friedrich Neumeyer the son of the founder joined the company. Things may have appeared buoyant, but within a few short months he was to witness a real crisis for the company when by December that year the sales figures had fallen drastically. A miserable 300 machines came off the production lines in the last month of the year.

Zündapp survived, even though for the next three years less than 30,000 machines were produced. Neumeyer's role in the company's survival cannot be underestimated. The Great Depression struck, and over 5,500,000 Germans were unemployed. However, it says much for the commercial drive of the founder of Zündapp, that just when the company was passing through its most difficult period, Fritz Neumeyer prepared to realise a dream he had long cherished, that of a *Volkswagen* – or people's car.

As long ago as 1924 he had considered making a small car under licence from Britain's Rover, but nothing came of his offer. Neumeyer never abandoned the idea. It came to life in September 1931 when a contract was concluded with Ferdinand Porsche. Porsche designed the Type 32 for Zündapp. But although three prototypes were built, the worsening situation in 1932 brought an abrupt halt to this interesting project. Both Zündapp and Porsche had to wait until 1934 to resume work on the *Volkswagen*

project. Porsche's Type 32 was the father of the legendary 'Beetle'.

By 1933 Zündapp and the German economy was making a massive recovery. Not only did the company produce the first of its four-stroke flat twins, with capacities of 398 and 498 cc, but also brought out a flat four of 598 cc. These models were designed by Richard Küchen, and introduced an unconventional, but very successful, chain and sprocket gearbox. The year also saw an upturn in sales, helped by the postal services and police forces ordering large numbers of Zündapp motorcycles.

A new small capacity two-stroke was launched in 1934. This was the Derby, with a 174 cc unit producing 5.5 bhp, which introduced a new three-way scavenging system. This later incorporated into other two-stroke Zündapp models.

By 1935 sales had climbed to 18,822 units, and Zündapp accounted for 15.9 per cent of all new registrations in Germany. Unhappily, this re-invigouration of the marque was overshadowed by the death of its founder Dipl Ing Fritz Neumeyer. He died on 10 September – his 60th birthday.

In 1936, 24,519 machines sold, but in stark contrast to a few short years before demand now exceeded supply. Dealers grumbled about being strictly limited to a set

K600, a revised version of the pre-war flat twin was reintroduced by Zündapp in 1950.

allocation. Zündapp simply could not make more machines.

The Nurnberg-Schweinau plant was enlarged in 1937 with a second complex, but the era of private enterprise and free competition in Germany were fast coming to an end. Rationing, raw material quotas and limitations on model ranges were the first unmistakable signs of state control encroaching seriously on the national economy.

On the initiative of the founder's son Hans-Friedrich Neumeyer, the company began to develop small-capacity aero engines in 1938. First 40 hp units, then 50 and later still 60 hp for light plane civilian use.

More and more, the need for military production governed industrial life – and Zündapp Werke GmbH, the new name which the company took in May 1938, was swept by the Government into its vast network. From this point onwards, arms manufacture pre-dominated, though prior to the actual outbreak of hostilities in September 1939, Zündapp introduced several new models including the KS600 flat twin with a 597 cc engine giving 28 bhp at 4700 rpm using a 25 mm Amal carburettor. The model had the all-chain gearbox featured on the earlier flat twins, and a pressed steel frame with pressed steel girder forks. Another new model, the DS350, was the first of the marque to feature foot pedal gear changing.

A number of records were established in 1939 using the air-cooled four-cylinder ohv aero engines (and after the end of the Second World War, a French pilot broke another two world records with a captured Zündapp engine.) There were also developments for the KS600 motorcycle engine, including a stationary power plant. The production range also included aircraft trans-mission systems. From March 1940, all supplies to civilian customers were discontinued, but unlike many of its rivals, Zündapp retained a majority of its wartime production facilities for the manufacture of motor-cycles. Two decades after its first motorcycle, Zündapp's 250,000th machine, a KS750, left the assembly line on 13 March 1942.

The KS750 was a special 750 cc model developed by Zündapp for military purposes. It had an integral sidecar with its wheel driven via lockable differential. The power unit was an air-cooled flat-twin four-stroke and the KS750 had two sets of four forward and reverse gears. Together with the similar BMW outfit, the Zündapp KS750 was *the* definitive Second World War Germany motorcycle. Though, in reality both had been replaced on the wartime production lines by the simpler and far less expensive 350 DKW two-stroke from 1944.

In 1945, at the end of the war, one third of all Zündapp's production machinery and installations had been destroyed, together with 40 per cent of other buildings. The main office block, repair shops and service premises were occupied by American units. In the heavily damaged facilities, 170 employees (in 1944 there had been 4000) made a valiant attempt to restore order but it was clear that motorcycle production was beyond reach.

So, for the first few months of peacetime, Zündapp made potato mashers, iron axles and various small fittings. Then, using remaining stocks, it built generating sets powered by the flat-twin engine. These were quickly snapped up by the building trade. But the real commercial breakthrough came in the autumn of 1945 when a substantial section of the Zündapp works was committed to the production of urgently-needed equipment for grain mills, principally rollers, extractors and grain cleaning machines. A year later, in November 1946, the two owners of the Zündapp company, Hans-Friedrich Neumeyer and Elizabeth Mann appointed Eitel-Friedrich Mann, Elizabeth's husband, as managing director. But there was no favouritism in his selection. Born in 1910, Dr Ing Mann was a diploma engineer and doctor of political science who had studied in Munich and Braunschweig, then worked from 1935 to 1939 in various sections of the Siemens-Schuckert in Nürnberg. Here he was assistant managing director. As was to be proved by his performance, the appointment was made for commercial reasons alone.

Under Mann's guidance Zündapp soon regained strength. First with improved mill equipment, then domestic sewing machines and finally in August 1947 with the re-introduction of motorcycle production under the auspices of chief engineer Ernst Schmidt. The first motorcycle to enter post-war production was the DB200 Derby. For Zündapp it was a straightforward re-introduction of the pre-war model which had originally entered service in 1935. It was a 198 cc (60 × 70 mm) single cylinder two-stroke engine which produced 7 bhp at 4000 rpm using a 20 mm Bing carb, with a 3-speed foot operated gearbox, tubular rigid frame with pressed steel blade forks and 3.00 × 19 inch tyres.

The interesting KS250, a single cylinder four-stroke with ohv and vertical cylinder, shaft drive, telescopic fork and plunger rear suspension was developed during the winter and spring 1948/49. This advanced machine never went beyond the prototype stage, mainly because it would have been too expensive. However, for 1950 a de luxe version of the two-stroke single was added to the range and the horizontally opposed twins were re-introduced.

First newcomer was the DB201. This had a slight increase in power to 7.5 bhp and a higher output 6 volt 60 watt flywheel generator, but the main differences were its more modern appearance, telescopic front forks and wider section 3.25 inch tyres. Speed was 53 mph.

Memories of pre-war Zündapp flat twins were stimulated by the appearance of the KS600. With its pressed steel frame, inter-connected hand and foot change and dated appearance, this model was to have

Factory rider Georg Weiss raced a close to standard KS601 machine.

no more than a short life before it was phased out in favour of the new.

The chief excitement was reserved for the appearance of the machine which entered service at the beginning of 1951, and would replace the KS600 within two years. The KS601 was a new sports version of the Zündapp flat twin which had a 597 cc (75 × 67.6 mm) ohv engine with a separate 25 mm Bing carburettor for each cylinder, cast iron barrels and light alloy heads. Power output was 28 bhp at 4700 rpm, with electrical power being provided by a 6 volt 90 watt system.

The four-speed chain and sprocket gearbox were in-unit with the engine and there was shaft final drive, with plunger rear suspension matched to a new telescopic fork. A maximum road speed of 87.5 mph was available in virtually all conditions, thanks to the engine's vast amount of torque. The KS601 was the fastest German roadster when introduced.

Besides their solo performance, both flat twins made ideal sidecar machines and were greatly in demand. They were also soon to prove themselves as sporting machines in long-distance trials. A KS601 outfit could top 75 mph. Development had been proceeding behind the scenes since 1947, but even though Zündapp might have wished to re-introduce its big

twins earlier they could not, if for no other reason than that until late 1949 German marques were restricted to motorcycles with a capacity of 250 cc or less.

Zündapp's output rose to 15,000 machines in 1949 – four times the 1948 figure. Not surprisingly, Zündapp then concentrated increasingly on motorcycles once again. The mill equipment division was sold off to a Swiss company, not only because that particular market was becoming saturated, but also to free production capacity for the growing bike business.

Under Mann's leadership there were now plants both in the original Nürnberg location and for the first time in Munich, then steadily becoming one of the most active industrial centres of the new Federal Republic. Here, a brand-new complex was constructed, which was opened in September 1950 and later substantially expanded. When the move to Munich was first mooted, no one at Zündapp could have visualised that this would soon become the mainstay of the company.

By 1951 output was up to 3,000 units a month. And from the beginning of 1952 the plant at Nürnberg came under the direct management of Hans-Friedrich Neumeyer, while the further enlarged Munich complex was under the control of Dr Eitel-Friedrich Mann.

Several prototypes appeared in 1951 which were not developed – a 100/125 class scooter and a two-stroke version of the abortive KS250 shaft-drive motorcycle of the late 1940s. There was also a 175 version, and these machines were coded K250 and K175.

The 1952 production model range comprised the Derby DB202, an improved version of the DB201 with four-speed foot change, the DB203 Comfort with more power, 8.7 bhp at 4250 rpm, the DB204 Norma, KS601 and KS601 Sport. The latter had a more highly-tuned engine offering 34 bhp at 6000 rpm and was faster than before with a maximum of 97 mph.

The new two-stroke singles displayed a considerable degree of original thought. Both the 200 Norma and Comfort models used a new Bing dual carburettor. This was to ensure a more efficient cylinder change and hence improve the smoothness at low speeds, giving, the factory claimed, better flexibility throughout the speed range and an increase in power output at wider throttle openings.

The idea was that this would give these engines a similar amount of power to a twin cylinder power unit, such as Adler's recently introduced MB200. But it would have been more expensive to produce a twin. For example, in late 1952 the 200 Adler with a conventional carburettor developed 9.3 bhp at 5600 rpm and cost DM 1,675 (£144), while the Zündapp Comfort with the dual carburettor developed 9.8 bhp at 4250 rpm and was priced at DM 1,495 (£122).

The principle behind the Bing dual carburettor was that the conventional piston-ported two-stroke engine had difficulty in breathing at low revs; hence a weak mixture was required for it to perform well at that stage.

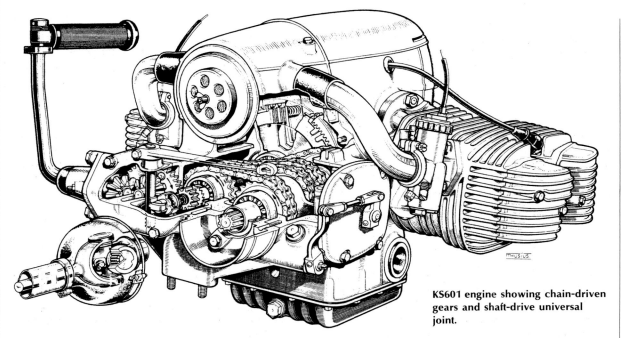

KS601 engine showing chain-driven gears and shaft-drive universal joint.

On the other hand, a more ample supply of fuel was required well before the engine attained the speed at which maximum torque was recorded. To obtain a well proportioned power curve, exact metering of the mixture was of great importance. Half the carburettor was designed to ensure the correct mixture for slow running or running on a light load; the second stage ensured a really efficient flow at an earlier stage than would have been possible with conventional single needle carburettor.

In the Bing dual carburettor, air was supplied through a filter and common air intake to two mixing chambers arranged side by side. Each mixing chamber had its own venturi, throttle slide and attached taper needle which acted within a needle jet. The throttle cable was attached to one slide only, but a bar projected sideways from this slide through a slot in the wall between the two mixing chambers and located in another slot provided in the second slide. Initial movement of the throttle control from the closed position raised only the first slide; this continued until the bar had reached the top of the slot in the second slide, when further cable movement raised both slides.

The other notable design feature of these Zündapp 'strokers was their constant-mesh gearbox. This was a four-speed unit of compact construction and had a minimum number of sliding components.

Inevitably, however, these middleweight machines were displaced in the public's imagination by the flagship model. John Thorpe of *Motor Cycling* magazine was able to ride one of the standard KS601 models, which belonged to Christian Pyx, a Swedish engineering student from Stockholm, who made a visit to London in July 1952.

These were his riding impressions; 'Having been shown the controls, I straddled the Zündapp and a quick jab brought the big machine into purring life. It simply leapt away and, to accustom myself to it, I first made a couple of tours of the block. I found that the engine was delightfully smooth and quiet and that it would respond to the throttle like a racehorse to the turf. Both front and rear braking was one of the most powerful I have yet encountered. Braking for the corners could be left quite late and then a gentle pressure on the lever would result in a very marked deceleration, accompanied by a squeal from the front tyre.

In common with most machines fitted with big, engine-speed clutches, the gear changing was a little tricky until one had the feel of the engine and could judge the right pause in between the 'cogs' – although the Zündapp, of course, has a chain and sprocket gearbox. Once the proper drill has been ascertained, changes in either direction were delightfully easy.

Returning to the little group outside *Motor Cycling's* office, I switched off and examined the finer points of the model. Especially neat was the rubber mounted torque tube enclosing the final drive shaft, light alloy was extensively used – for fork bridges and covers, amongst the things. One interesting detail was the built-in oil cooler in the top of the crankcase casting, while the die-cast light alloy cylinder heads were works of art!'

Not revealed in these comments were the other main features of the KS601's engine construction. Much use was made of light alloys as Thorpe noted. The ignition coil, the DC dynamo and large-capacity air filter, which was connected by ducts to the two 25 mm

Bing carburettors, were all enclosed within the crankcase. Conventional ball bearings were used for the one-piece crankshaft and the camshaft, and needle roller bearings for the rockers. An unusual, though not novel, feature was divided big ends with needle rollers. Each bearing had 30 rollers carried in a divided cage, which could prove to be a source of trouble in high-mileage engines. As Thorpe mentioned the engine was provided with an oil cooler. In addition, another refinement was an extremely effective crankcase ventilation system.

Zündapp made several modifications to the chain and sprocket four-speed gearbox which Thorpe referred to. Although this type of gearbox had been used on the flat-twin Zündapp for almost 20 years, the duplex-type chains for bottom, third and top gears were now all of equal length, while that for second gear was two links shorter. The rear drive transmission shaft had its helical driving pinion carried on two bearings. Whereas the similar BMW arrangement employed a double roller bearing and a needle bearing, Zündapp used a double roller bearing and a porous, oil retaining bronze bush. This arrangement was not only more

compact but also permitted the inclusion of a helical gear speedometer drive.

Another interesting aspect of the KS601 was its telescopic front forks, which employed three hydraulic dampers. One in each leg and the remaining one as a separate unit mounted externally between the upper legs.

More influential than John Thorpe's report was a legendary road-test published by the German magazine *Das Motorrad* in December of 1952. Basing his impressions on the lusty power of the machine and its green paintwork, the magazine's editor bestowed the title of the 'Green Elephant'. It was a name which was to stick to the KS601 throughout its life.

Much of 1952 was spent developing a new range of machinery including not only motorcycles, but moped and scooter projects as well. The Amsterdam show at the beginning of March 1953 saw the debut of the 48 cc (39 × 41.8 mm) Combimot two-stroke engine rated at

Works riders Keitel and Seemann are shown negotiting a tricky hairpin with their KS601 sidecar outfit during 1951 ISDT at Varese, Italy.

1.5 bhp and weighing 13.5 lb. The Combimot had been developed for use with a conventional pedal cycle, either to be bolted into the middle of the frame, or above the front wheel. An interesting technical feature was that the light alloy cylinder had a chromium plated bore.

Initially Zündapp only sold the engine itself as a separate unit for customers to fit into their own cycle, or to rival manufacturers Triumph and Hercules for moped manufacture. It was much later that Zündapp used the Combimot engine for a moped of its own design and manufacture. Later still, an outboard motor was developed from the basic Combimot unit. Whatever their destination, Zündapp benefitted from a monthly output of 15,000 of these tiny engines at the Munich factory.

The original Nürnberg works was not to be outdone by such efforts, and in May 1953 it announced its latest model – a 150 cc scooter. Designated the Bella Motor Roller (Motor Scooter) this was to be a major success story for Zündapp, with the basic design running until 1964. A total of 130,680 units were produced in several variants during its eleven year life.

The first model was the Bella 150, officially coded R150, with a capacity of 147 cc (57 × 58 mm), 7.3 bhp at 4700 rpm, 20 mm Bing carb and 50 mph maximum speed. Its single port unit construction engine had a flat-top three ring piston, cast iron cylinder barrel and alloy head.

There was a geared primary drive to a four-speed gearbox controlled by a rocking foot pedal, and the rear drive chain was fully enclosed in a case arranged to

Making its debut in 1952, the DB203 Comfort was a development of Zündapp's first post-war design, the DB200 Derby of 1947.

pivot with the swinging fork rear suspension assembly. Open coil suspension springs were used, controlled by a single hydraulic damper fitted on the left of the fork. The front wheel was mounted in leading axle telescopic front forks, and the larger 12 inch alloy wheels with 150 mm brakes were shod with 3.50 section tyres.

The frame took an unusual form, principally consisting of a large diameter downtube and two backbone members arching over the engine and rear wheel. Over this frame was fitted pressed steel bodywork offering a large expanse of protection both front and rear. Included in the body was a fuel tank with a capacity of 8.5-litres.

A cooling duct allowed air in at the front and directed it over the cylinder through to a vent behind the rider's seat. An optional pillion seat could be fitted on top. Cast alloy open grilles on each side of the rear wheel were hinged so that they would fold down to become pannier luggage supports, while a spare wheel and carrier could be purchased as extras.

Also new for the 1953 season was the Elastic 200, code named DB205. The word Elastic was used in recognition of its luxurious suspension system. This combined oil-damped telescopic forks at the front with a spine frame and pivoted fork rear suspension with twin hydraulic shock absorbers.

Both the latest version of the Norma, now called the DB234 Norma Luxus, and the Elastic 200 used the Bing

New for the 1953 season the Elastic also had the code DB205. The marketing department chose Elastic as the model name as a reference to its hydraulically damped suspension.

dual carburettor described earlier, but now both the intake ports were circular. This modification offered a much more even gas flow, resulting in a smoother and more flexible performance throughout the speed range. The cylinder barrel of the Elastic 200 was inclined forward at 30 degrees, and a unique feature of the model was the neat underseat tray providing lockable storage space for the tool kit. There was another version of the DB205 which only reached the prototype stage. This used a horizontal engine and was given the serial DB251.

Throughout the early 1950s, Zündapp had a remarkable line of triumphs in long distance endurance trials with specially prepared versions of the 597 cc KS601 model hitched to sidecars. This run of success had started in the 1951 ISDT based at Varese in northern Italy, where four such outfits put up a wonderful show of reliability by gaining four gold medals.

This was repeated the following year when another four Zündapp outfits gained golds in the ISDT staged at Bad Aussee, Austria. A further gold was gained by a competitor riding a 200 Zündapp solo. But for the 1953 ISDT no Zündapp entries were made. Although it had been rumoured that one of the German teams would be equipped with 600 cc Zündapp sidecar outfits.

At the massive international Frankfurt Show 1953,

Zündapp exhibits stole much of the thunder with a brand-new horizontally opposed ohv 247 cc (54 × 54 mm) twin, the B250, a larger version of the recently released Elastic, the DB255, with a 246 cc (67 × 70 mm) single cylinder two-stroke engine – and what was described as the most talked-about scooter of the show, the Bella which was already in mass production.

The B250 had an exceptionally clean engine design with alloy heads and barrels with reborable cast-iron liners. The dimensions were square and the three-ring pistons gave a 6.8:1 compression ratio. Power output with twin Bing 24 mm carbs was 18.5 bhp at 7000 rpm. Perhaps the model's most notable feature for its capacity was the use of shaft drive. The engine had needle roller big-end bearings of a similar type to the larger 597 cc KS601 engine. To the forward end of the three bearing crankshaft was attached the armature shaft of a DC dynamo. A four-speed gearbox was flange-fitted to the rear of the crankcase, and the drive was through a large diameter, single plate car-type clutch. The 'gearbox', like that of the larger flat twin, actually contained a range of sprockets linked by duplex roller chains.

A novel approach to frame design on the newcomer was that the transverse flat twin engine was carried below two widely spaced, large-diameter tubes which ran downward and rearward from the steering head. The tubes terminated above and slightly in front of the rear wheel spindle to form upper supports for the rear suspension shock absorber units. As the engine mounts were close to the horizontal plane through the crankshaft axis, the arrangement was claimed largely to

B250 flat twin, although it aroused considerable interest when it was exhibited at the Frankfurt Show in 1953 the machine was never to go into production.

counteract the effects of torque reaction.

A pivoted front fork was employed, and in this case the pivot was visible and was carried at the bottom of a sturdy, channel section pressing which, in turn, was mounted on the bottom of the steering column. The shock absorbers had totally enclosed springs. Both wheels had 180 mm full width alloy brake hubs, with 16 inch rims and 3.50 section tyres. Other cycle parts included a 15-litre fuel tank, a deeply valanced front mudguard and an almost totally enclosed rear section aft of the engine unit.

Although stand personnel were saying the B250 would enter production the following spring, this never happened. The design was to be one of the few Zündapp failures of the immediate post-war era. Unlike other Zündapp models which only appeared as prototypes, the fact it chose to launch this one in such a blaze at Germany's premier show suggested the factory really intended to go into production and the model's eventual demise must have been due to an undisclosed problem. In fact, the model was influenced by the similar Hoffman 250 flat twin of 1951, and was built by Zündapp specifically to create a show sensation as it was too costly to build in series. The only object of the exercise was to gain the maximum publicity for the company.

The larger version of the Elastic used an identical set of running gear to the original, the only mechanical difference being the 250's larger cylinder bore and 26 mm Bing carb. Power had been increased to 13 bhp at 5200 rpm and maximum speed was up to 63 mph.

Late in 1953 a British importer was appointed. This was UK Concessionaires Ltd of Ascot, Berkshire, who was also the manufacturer of Ambassador motorcycles that used Villiers engines.

Initially, only the Bella 150 scooter was imported. *Motor Cycling* tested one of the first Bellas in Britain in December 1953. The magazine commented in particular on its imposing appearance, wide use of alloy for many parts including the wheels, high level of comfort, and above average handling and roadholding abilities. The latter was referred to in the following terms; 'It would be difficult to speak too highly of the Zündapp's navigational properties. Though a slight roll would manifest itself at low speeds, once the model was on the open road and motoring at anything over 30 mph the steering became rock steady. Corners could be taken as fast as the rider wished, with never a waver from the desired line, while even deliberate attempts to provoke front wheel deviation met with no success. Undoubtedly, part of the credit for this must go to the use of wheels which, with 3.50 by 12 inch tyres, are rather larger than those generally employed on vehicles of this type'.

Another area which won praise was the flexibility of the 147 cc single cylinder engine. As *Motor Cycling* put it; 'With a small capacity engine pulling a comparatively high top gear, it would have been reasonable to suppose that full use would have to be made of the gearbox. This, however, was not the case. Minimum non-snatch speed in top gear proved to be 14 mph, and from a standstill the highest gear could be engaged by the time 18 mph was registered on the speedometer, from which point the Bella would accelerate smoothly up to its maximum speed!'

The only two real niggles came from a twistgrip operation which was unduly stiff and that for serious touring the 8.5-litres (just under 2 gallons) fuel tank was too small, even though the test machine averaged 95 mpg throughout the test period. As tested by *Motor Cycling* the British price was £180.

Zündapp was also one of the first of the German marques to be represented in the USA after the war. The importer, who began operations in 1953, was the International Motorcycle Co. of New York. An interesting adaptation of the Bella for the North American market was the Suburbanette. It was a standard Bella stripped of much of its rear bodywork and fitted with a dual seat. In addition a motorcycle type front mudguard was used, allowing the telescopic forks to be seen. All this gave the machine a totally new line.

By May 1954 no fewer than 10,000 Bella scooters had been produced since production begin the previous August. To meet demand from its customers for improved acceleration at a higher maximum speed, Zündapp had been working on a larger capacity version. This was released that month, and was a 200 cc machine incorporating numerous changes and dubbed the R200.

To achieve the larger 198 cc capacity, both the bore and stroke measurements had been increased to 64 and 62 mm respectively. This gave slightly oversquare dimensions. The compression ratio was now 6.3:1 and, as before, a light-alloy cylinder head and cast iron barrel were fitted. A larger air filter with oil-damped filtration material was fitted to protect the engine from airborne dust.

The crankshaft assembly had been beefed up to withstand the greater output of 10 bhp at 5200 rpm. A heavier duty primary chain drove through a strengthened clutch, and as with the smaller engined model, alternative solo and sidecar gear ratios were available.

An important modification, which was now also featured on the 150 Bella, was the adoption of a 90 watt flywheel generator in place of the earlier 60 watt type. This ensured more reliable current for ignition and the 35/35 watt bulb in the 150 mm headlamp. Previously a 6 volt 7 amp/hour battery was installed under the bodywork behind the engine. But now a larger capacity 8 amp/hour battery was fitted at the extreme rear of the machine. An unusual location, but one which combined accessibility with good protection.

Mounted on the horizontal frame tube loop which embraced the rear wheel was a die-cast, light alloy box which contained both the rubber mounted battery and the tool kit. The box had a hinged lid secured by a single knurled nut, and also embodied the rear light and number plate holder. The whole assembly was extremely neat and practical. Chromium-plated quarter bumpers were fitted on each side of the battery/tool box, and direction indicators could be specified in the original equipment at an extra cost.

Frame, wheels and brakes remained as before, but the front fork action had been found slightly on the hard side and so both models of the Bella now had lengthened fork travel. A hydraulic steering damper was also added.

Several alterations were made to body styling. The headlamp was mounted higher on the front fairing and the horn was built in below the lamp. Improved weather protection was provided by a deeper front mudguard which was taken further forward at the front and nearer to the ground at the rear.

Zündapp make the decision in 1954 to manufacture its own moped. It was marketed the Combinette Type 408, and used a version of the well proven and popular Zündapp Combimot 48 cc unit increased to 49 cc. It was a very simple and basic moped, essentially a conventional bicycle with 26 inch wheels and a power unit. However, it sold well and as the first of Zündapp's own mopeds was very much a pointer to the future. November 1954 brought the news that the Combinette 408 units were to be assembled under licence and sold in Britain by Ambassador Motor Cycles for £59 each.

On the sporting front, in September Zündapp rider Hessler gained a gold medal at the ISDT in Wales, on a single cylinder 246 cc Elastic model. This was a fully prepared enduro machine based on the production roadster. A motocross version without lighting equipment was also built.

For 1955, a de luxe version of the Combinette moped appeared with two-speed gearbox, smaller 23 inch wheels and the appearance of a real moped rather than

By May 1954 more than 10,000 Bella scooters had been produced since the model's introduction in August of the year before. R200 is illustrated.

a motorised pedal cycle. This move had been brought about in response to a new German law introduced on 1 December 1954, when a driving licence became compulsory for machines over 50 cc capacity. Many people believe this was the beginning of the end for those companies which did not respond in the same positive manner adopted as Zündapp.

But even without its change of attitude, for Zündapp as for many other motorcycle producers 1955 was a record year, with an unparalleled amount of business to keep its 4,000 strong workforce at full stretch in both the Nürnberg and Munich complexes. Not only did they make record numbers of the best-selling Bella scooter, but also built large numbers of the new moped and a full range of motorcycles.

Owing to the breathtaking success of its Bella scooter series, Zündapp built and developed a new 125 class scooter in 1955 using a horizontal engine. Although a good deal of their R&D budget went on the project it was ultimately discontinued. So the only brand new model to enter production in 1955 was the 200S. This eventually replaced the Elastic models and spawned a whole range of motorcycles which were to

Zündapp began selling the 48 cc Type 408 Combinette moped in 1954. The Combimot engine, however, was the same as the unit sold to other moped manufacturers.

stretch into the next decade.

The new model had an engine which owed much to the earlier machine and shared the 30 degree inclined cylinder angle. But was, in fact, almost a total redesign. For a start, unlike its forerunner the 200S was a short-stroke, with bore and stroke measurements of 64 × 62 mm. This gave a capacity of 197 cc, 12 bhp at 5400 rpm, and a maximum speed of a claimed 62.5 mph from its four-speed gearbox.

The most obvious change, and one which was to be a trend-setting innovation, was the deep radial finning on the alloy cylinder head. Carburation was by a conventional 24 mm Bing instrument, while the sparks came from a 6 volt system, with a 90 watt Noris flywheel mounted generator. The fuel tank was a much more shapely design, and the 16 inch alloy wheel rims with 3.25 section tyres and full-width 160 mm alloy brake hubs were the same as used on the Elastic models. Except for the abortive B250 flat twin, all previous Zündapp post-war motorcycles had used 19 inch wheels.

In March 1955 three Zündapp models were listed in Britain – the two versions of the Bella scooter at £170 8s and £186 and the 48 cc Combinette motorised cycle at £67 16s. But at the end of May it was announced that the range was to be increased to include the 246 cc Elastic. Both *Motor Cycling* and *Motor Cycle* were able

to run the rule over an example provided by the importers in Ascot. The latter magazine summed it up as 'A luxuriously comfortable, medium weight two-stroke of high yet flexible performance, with first class steering, and braking.'

Even allowing for an amount of the over-praise prevalent in the period these were glowing comments. *Motor Cycle* also noticed the 'Meticulous attention to detail which characterised the whole design'. On the road they found it offered 'quite an outstanding performance for its class'. And, 'Though engine power is above average for a two fifty two-stroke, high torque is produced over an unusually wide engine speed'. Like the Bella there was criticism concerning the twistgrip, the journalist continued; 'Of typical continental pattern, with the cable enclosed within the handlebar, the control was slow in action, requiring 180 degrees of rotation for full throttle movement.'

Although both magazines were in agreement on most matters concerning the Elastic, descriptive details differed widely on the matter of clutch action. *Motor Cycle's* conclusion was that it was 'A trifle heavy in operation, the clutch freed perfectly and took up the drive smoothly', while *Motor Cycling's* view was that the 'Clutch take-up tended to be rather on the fierce side, and the tester was rarely able to get under way without an initial jerk, which caused the front of the machine to rear up on its soft suspension.'

Held in gruelling conditions, the 1955 ISDT in Czechoslovakia from 13–18 September saw Zündapp

Rudolf Hessler won a gold medal in October 1954 at the ISDT. His mount was a Zündapp 246 cc Elastic. That year the international competition was held in Wales.

enter two manufacturers teams, although they were again not part of the official German entry. Despite this, Zündapp showed up well in the results, with three gold medals, a silver and a bronze, and only two retirements. The golds were gained by Gehring and Lohr on 250s and Kritter had a 600 flat-twin with sidecar.

Late in September 1955 both Bella scooters were considerably revised. Restyled bodywork and new frames, dual seats, and 12 volt electric starting were added. The all-welded steel frame had been extensively altered to marry up with the new bodywork, which was not only of a cleaner style, but also more practical. The front legshields now swept in a more flowing line and the edges were strengthened. The body proper now had internal ducting to improve the cooling draught to the engine, plus a re-arranged exhaust outlet. At the lower extremity of the front mudguard was a small mudflap, and on the rear guard the number plate was mounted so it could be hinged down out of the way. The toolkit, previously housed there, was moved into a watertight compartment on the right hand cast-aluminium foot board. Its lid was secured by two screws with slots for a coin. To suit the new frame the fully enclosed rear chaincase had to be redesigned.

A new car-type Bing carburettor on which the float chamber was cast in one with the mixing chamber superseded the previous motorcycle type. At the same time a redesigned filter was employed. The choke slide lever was dispensed with, and its place was taken by a trigger on the handlebars so that after turning the engine over on the electric starter, a flick of the finger would fully open the choke.

But the major innovations concerned the electrics. The new starter motor was mounted on the left hand end of the crankshaft, while the high tension coil and condenser were now carried on a small platform attached to the frame. The 12 volt supply was from twin 6 volt batteries wired in series. Switchgear and instruments were all mounted in a console to the top rear of the steering head and shrouded by a steel pressing. Both models now used the larger headlight previously only fitted to the 200 version.

Other notable detail improvements were a cast iron spanner for rear brake adjustment, a strap across the dual seat, intended to assist in lifting the machine onto the centre stand; and purpose-built luggage equipment as a factory-made optional extra.

Finally, the new frame had two attachment points for fitting a Steib single seat sidecar. This used a Bella cast alloy wheel, interchangeable with those on the scooter, and swinging arm, rubber in torsion suspension. Weighing 102 lb it could be supplied in the correct matching colour scheme.

By then, at least some of those in power at Zündapp were aware of the problems facing the German two-wheel industry caused by improved living standards. Dr Neumeyer wrote at the end of 1955; 'The situation might make one pessimistic if one looks only at the motorcycle market'. But he continued; 'Those firms may consider themselves lucky who recognised the coming development in good time and turned for compensation to the scooter or moped business, or better still both. It seems reasonable to expect that firms which kept the market under careful observation, converted their production in time and can offer a product tailored to public demand at a suitable price, will stay in business and do well. . . .'

Zündapp management had already set the wheels in motion by developing its own range of scooters, mopeds and small cars. Now it also planned to open a new light alloy die-casting shop, both for the company's own use and as a service it could sell to outside customers. The principle of relying on one's own production facilities instead of depending on outside suppliers was ultimately to prove a life-saver for the company. Rival manufacturers were often crippled by the failure of vital component sub-contractors. Even the difficult to manufacture internal major engine parts, including crankshafts, clutches and gearboxes, were not bought in. The same principle applied to metal fabrication; not only the front forks and swinging arms, but also tanks and chaincases were made in-house.

Zündapp was able to survive, not through vast advertising, or fielding world beating Grand Prix racing teams, or even dynamic state of the art models but simply by making the correct commercial decisions as each problem was faced. This included seeing the value and importance of developing export markets for their products before most of its rivals.

January 1956 was the launch date of another change for the popular 146 and 198 cc Bella scooters. Pivoted suspension for the front wheel was introduced. Initially this was for home market machines only and export models continued with the previous telescopic type. The basis of the new suspension was a single, curved stanchion member concealed within the mudguard. Welded to the lower end of the stanchion was a pivot tube, in which the pivot spindle ran in plain bearings. The left hand arm of the fork was welded to the spindle, while the right hand arm was secured to it with a cotter pin. Springing was by means of a large diameter shock absorber with hydraulic damping, mounted on rubber bushes between the left arm of the fork and a lug on the stanchion at the base of the steering column. This provided wheel travel of over 140 mm. The brake backplate was anchored directly to the left arm of the fork.

The first export market to get the new version of the Bella was the USA, where the importers, International Motor Cycle Co, listed the 150 Bella at $389 and the 200 at $499. Other models on sale in North America in 1956 were the latest version of the venerable KS601 flat twin, now with swinging arm rear suspension at $995, and called the KS601 Elastic. Less than 300 of these were sold to the US and in reality it was the end of the road for the model both at home and abroad. Also on offer were the $200, sold as the Challenger in the States at $449, and the 250 Motocross scrambler at $549. All the roadsters including the two Bella scooters had cowhorn 'Western' handlebars as standard equipment. At that time Zündapp was well publicised in Canada and the USA by full page advertisements in such popular magazines as *Cycle*.

The 1956 ISDT was staged at Garmisch-Partenkirchen in the shadow of the Bavarian Alps. A total of 317 riders from 19 nations competed over 1,180 miles. Though the route was no shorter than usual, it was one of the most compact ISDTs ever held because each day's route consisted of two laps of the circuit. Conveniently, the lunch stops as well as the start and finish were at Garmisch for the first five days of the six day event.

For once the German team selectors had not totally ignored Zündapp in their selection process as the Vase B team included the 250 Zündapp rider Hessler. There was a total of 23 riders on Zündapps ranging from a trio

Right **The 200S came in 1955. Ultimately it replaced the Elastic model range while spawning its own family of machines. The last 250 Trophy S was made in the 1960's.**

of 175 solos to four 600 sidecar outfits. Between them they amassed ten gold medals, five silver and two bronze and only six retirements. The International Vase was won by the Holland B team, which included Frits Selling on a 250 Zündapp. None of his four team members lost any marks. After this solid performance Zündapp could be said to have firmly re-established its pre-war reputation as serious long distance trials performers.

Following the ISDT in October came two large international motorcycle shows – Paris and Frankfurt. As the French event came first Zündapp could have reasonably been expected to hold all its new releases until the home exhibition. However, obviously realising the importance of the export market the company launched a brand new model, the 250S and marketed it as the Sabre in the USA. As its code name suggested, this was a larger version of the 200S, but one which merited additional interest by having Earles-type front suspension and a massive silencer.

Its 245 cc (67 × 70 mm) engine was based on the smaller unit, but both the bore and stroke measurements differed, although it shared many components and used the 200S-type radial head finning. The head and barrel were inclined at the same 30 degrees. Using a 26 mm Bing carb it gave 14.5 bhp at 5500 rpm, and a maximum speed of 69 mph.

Also on view in Paris was the 175S – the 200S with a sleeved-down cylinder so that its 174 cc engine had dimensions of 60 × 62 mm and pumped out 10.5 bhp at 5400 rpm with a 24 mm Bing carb. Its speed was 59 mph, and the running gear was exactly as the 200S, telescopic forks and all.

At Frankfurt, Zündapp exhibits were in two separate halls. The main stand featured the Earles-forked 250S which had made its debut in Paris, together with the 175 and 200S models. The various Bella scooters and the big flat twin four-stroke KS601 shared space with the company's new four wheel 'bubble' car, the Janus. This used a single cylinder 245 cc (67 × 70 mm) two-stroke unit which produced 14 bhp at 5200 rpm driving through four forward and one reverse gears.

Zündapp reasoned that it could capture the motorist whose rising income made his thoughts turn towards a car. It was also believed that customers who had purchased Zündapp motorcycles would display a brand-loyalty and buy Zündapp four-wheelers. This was a revival of the old dream of pre-war years, and so management decided once again to offer a 'peoples car'.

The curious name Janus came from the two-faced Roman god. It was used because of the car's rearward facing rear seat. The Janus design originated with the earlier, and very similar, Dornier Delta which had a 197 cc Ilo single cylinder engine. This was built as a prototype only early in 1955, but the design had caught the attention of the Zündapp management. After meetings between Dr Mann and Dornier, Zündapp took over the Delta design. It was then refined and re-engined before appearing as the Janus.

From the front, the four wheeler appeared almost identical to the rival BMW Isetta. But a major difference

was the rear section of the car which had a single outward folding door like that at the front to allow access to the rear seat. The Isetta had only a front door. Even though the Janus was well received by the press on its debut, it nonetheless did not prove much of a sales success. Only 6900 were produced before production ceased in 1958. These sales figures never matched those of the more popular miniature cars.

At the same time, on the initiative of Dr Mann, the Munich plant was at work on the development of a low-cost sports car. Pininfarina, the famous Italian designer, produced a streamlined body shell with advanced styling, however, this project progressed no further than the prototype stage.

Back at the 1956 Frankfurt show the other hall taken by Zündapp was filled with far less glamorous machinery, but was nonetheless to point the way forward for the company. Combinette mopeds and a new luxury moped, the Falconette, which was almost a motorcycle were the heart of the display. The very latest Combinette, the 423S, shared with the Falconette a frame in which the centre section was formed by a lightly alloy die casting. The Falconette was equipped with a three-speed foot change, tuned version of the 49 cc (39 × 41.8 mm) engine which could trace its beginnings right back to the 'clip-on' Combimot unit of 1953. Although, along the way it had been almost totally re-designed and gained a kickstarter and multi-speed gearbox in unit with the crankcase.

The Falconette, the 425, produced 2.3 bhp at 5400 rpm, and was fitted with a 13 mm Bing carb, 6 volt 17 watt flywheel magneto and 90 mm full width hubs laced into 23 inch rims with 2.50 section tyres. Maximum speed was 35 mph. And its full size motorcycle type appearance, with 7.3-litre fuel tank, front and rear suspension, with a unique four-shock – two units each side – system, and acceptable performance soon made it a popular machine. Throughout its production life it was steadily updated and improved, until replaced by the first KS50 in the early 1960s.

Together with the Combinette mopeds, the Falconette sold in huge numbers, and fully justified the company's move in the direction of smaller capacity machines. Amongst all German motorcycle manufacturers, Zündapp was best able to weather the storm through a combination of having just the right product line and the fact that they had followed a strict production policy of making only enough machines to meet orders. This meant none of the stockpiling which led to some of the competitors building up a year's supply which eventually no one wanted to buy. And unlike the opposition, Zündapp's experience of 1957 was relatively free from trauma.

It was this understated success compared to the turmoil all around which led the German selectors to pick Zündapp, together with another relatively

KS 75 Falconette lightweight motorcycles were seen on Zündapp's production line 1959–62. It was a popular model and sold in large numbers.

unaffected company, Maico, to form the country's Trophy team for the 1957 ISDT at Spinleruv Mlyn in North Bohemia from 15–20 September. The team consisted of Zündapp riders Specht (175), Hessler (250) and Leistner (262) plus three Maico riders. It was inspired choice of men and machines because at the end of the week it had won six of only 25 gold medals awarded that year. The performance was good enough to win the coveted Trophy for West Germany for only the second time since the Second World War.

But even these figures conceal just what a great victory it really was. The 32nd ISDT was the first to be held in the Krkonose Mountains (the Giant Mountains) in Czechoslovakia. The little resort of Spindleruv Mlyn welcomed the 246 starters with the foulest possible weather. Apart from fogs, the only interruptions to the rain were sleet and snowfalls. Inevitably, there was a toll in riders, 81 of whom gave up on the very first day. This event was one of the most arduous ISDTs of all time. The Germans lasted the whole six days without losing a single penalty point, a performance which absolutely eclipsed the previous year's winners Czechoslovakia, who were second with 700 points adrift, while Italy came third with 1613 marks lost.

At the end of 1957 it was announced that the KS601 was finally to be taken out of production. The end of the road for Zündapp's four-stroke flat twin family and a lineage which many consider today as the classic of the marque. The Sport turned out 34 bhp at 6000 rpm and was good for 97 mph. Over its final two years, when it was produced as the KS601 Elastic Sport and KS601 EL, it had finally been available with a full swinging arm frame. But with demand for large capacity motorcycles in Germany at an all-time low, only 700 of the swinging arm models were produced. All of them were made at the Nürnberg plant, and most of the production went for export.

At the beginning of 1958 Hans-Friedrich Neumeyer fell ill and was hospitalised. But under his direction on 1 July that year the Nürnberg plant was sold to Bosch, the electrical machine conglomerate. This permitted an expansion programme to begin at the remaining Munich complex.

At the same time, the latest version of the Bella scooter, the 204, arrived in Britain, priced at £205 16s 9d. The 198 cc engine, although still having the same 64 × 62 mm bore and stroke, had its cylinder inclined at 30 degrees like the S range of motorcycles and the power was increased to 12 bhp at 5400 rpm.

For the 1958 ISDT, held in the hills, at Garmisch-Partenkirchen, the selectors again relied on Zündapp and Maico. The German team came third, with a total of 38 points lost.

For the 1959 season a larger capacity Falconette, the KS75, was introduced. This had its barrel bored out to 48 mm to give the larger capacity. Now with four speeds, more power, 5.6 bhp at 6200 rpm a 17 mm Bing carb, more powerful 6 volt 45 watt flywheel magneto and smaller 21 inch wheel rims, it was also equipped with wider 2.75 section tyres. The appearance was more modern too, with a larger 11.5-litre fuel tank and more

Dieter Kramer, 1964 German enduro champion, in action on his KS 100 in mountainous terrain.

substantial bodywork. Although heavier at 162 lb (formerly 147 lb) performance was much better with the KS75 able to achieve 53 mph.

Five Zündapp models were available in Britain: the Combinette moped, 50 and 75 Falconettes and the 154 and 204 Bella scooters. Potential British purchasers of the latest Bella 204 were able to read for themselves the various improvements of the latest model over the earlier 203, when the 1 January 1959 issue of *Motor Cycling* concluded it was 'excellent' and 'amongst the best scooters on the market'.

Mid-1959 was chosen for the appearance of the 49 cc Falconette updated as the 435 and it replaced the original 423. Power was improved from 2.3 to 3.6 bhp, a larger 16 mm Bing carb was fitted, there were larger 120 mm brake hubs (from the 75 cc model) and maximum speed was up to 41 mph.

Throughout the year the Munich plant continued to expand and launched a new range of automatic sewing machines which were still an important part of the company's revenue. But 1960 was the year of the great comeback for Zündapp with two wheeler production showing a large increase over the past few years. In the same period many of the previous competitors had disappeared.

But the driving force behind the company's survival and revival, Dr Eitel-Friedrich Mann, unhappily did not live to see the fruits of his work. He died suddenly on 11 August 1960 shortly before his 50th birthday while in the thick of the reorganisation and construction work that the transfer to Munich, and development of a radically revised model range had entailed. Still, Zündapp itself was to benefit from Dr Mann's foresight and emerged into the new decade much improved by his 'slimming down for better health' campaign.

Zündapp produced 75,000 machines – mopeds, motorcycles and scooters – in 1961 and was at the head of the German two-wheel industry. The only new model was the Bella R175S. This featured a 174 cc (60 × 62 mm) engine with 204 chassis and a power output of 11 bhp at 5400 rpm. With only 2,000 produced from 1961–64 this was the least popular Bella model.

The company also made a return to endurance trials in 1961. It not only won four classes of the German national championships, but again provided part of the German Trophy squad and one machine for the Vase A team for the 1961 ISDT in Wales. The 1,200 mile ISDT was staged at the beginning of October. Zündapp was the backbone of the winning team. Germany took the Trophy for the third time post-war, with no marks lost. Zündapp's total medal haul was five golds, including those of the two Trophy men Specht (175) and Hessler (250), plus a bronze. Six out of six entries won medals. An impressive debut was made by a pair of 75 cc models and a lone 50 cc midget trials iron. Together with similar machines from Kreidler these flyweights amazed observers by their speed and lasting power.

The successful Zündapp record breaking team at Monza in April 1965.

A proper motorcycle returned to the Zündapp line-up in Britain from January 1961. This time the model concerned was the 250 Trophy S which sold in Britain as the 250S Super Sabre. This differed from the earlier 250S by having telescopic forks, in place of the original Earles type and gave the machine a better appearance. When *Motor Cycling* tested one for the 13 July 1961 issue the price was £202 13s, and the concessionaires were still Ambassador Motor Cycles of Ascot, Berkshire.

The test was headlined 'Pleasant, 70 mph "250" with excellent roadholding'. The best one way speed (prone) was 70.7 mph, and although the performance was around the 'norm' for a touring quarter-litre the tester reported; 'But a balanced touring performance, rather than a spectacular top end figure, has obviously been the aim of the Zündapp designers. In fact, all-out speed is about the least important of this model's attributes. Far more useful was the excellent acceleration obtainable'. And the test concluded; 'For the daily rider, in 1961's hurly-burly traffic, a characteristic of this sort is worth its weight in gold'.

Features which failed to gain the tester's approval included the idling which was 'erratic', and 'lumpy' and slow running. The fuel consumption figures for the whole test averaged 64 mpg over 1600 miles. When run-in, it was found that main road cruising at 60 mph was well within the machine's capabilities. But the biggest praise was reserved for the outstandingly good steering with comfort, both solo and with a passenger. The standard of silencing, from what was suggested to be 'the biggest silencer in the world' and 'first class' lighting also were well received.

November 1962 saw the machine, now renamed the

Trophy (in line with its name in Germany) drop in price to £169 11s 9d. This was exceptional value for the British market. The Super Sabre name was then adopted in America.

In January 1962, Ernst Leverkus, professional motorcycle journalist, arch-enthusiast for the marque, Green Elephant-and-Steib owner, organised a rally for fellow Zündapp KS601 owners. It was the depths of winter and hardly a time to drive an outfit to a site chosen near the Solitude race track, but the rally caught the imagination of enthusiasts to the extent that it has become an institution. Taking its name from the machine that inspired Leverkus, it is known universally as the Elephant Rally and continues as an annual event.

The British Zündapp concession changed hands in September 1962. The new importer was Motor Imports of London SW9. This company handled several marques including Moto Guzzi. Motor Imports was an offshoot of Pride and Clarke, at the time one of Britain's largest motorcycle dealers. Initially it only imported two models, the latest version of the long running 200 Bella scooter and the KS75 lightweight motorcycle. These were priced at £179 19s 6d and £124 19s 6d respectively.

The KS75 gave the new importers a good start by taking 'gold' in the 1962 ISDT at Garmisch-Parkenkirchen, Bavaria. Here the West German Vase B team won the International Silver Vase. Zündapp machines were used by Kramer and Sengfelder and by two of the Trophy team, Specht (175) and Hessler (250).

When *Motor Cycling* tested one of the KS75 roadsters in the 28 November 1962 issue it was found to

Horizontally engined 49 cc record breaker with its enveloping streamlined shell comes on fall chat around a deserted Monza Autodrome.

European Trial Champion 1965, Gustav Franke is astride 246 cc Zündapp.

offer an excellent combination of value between a proper-motorcycle and a utilitarian moped. The only two black marks were a tendency to jump out of bottom gear (which was acknowledged as being true only of the test machine) and a rock hard dual seat. Otherwise it received much praise and was summed up as follows; 'All-in-all, this was an excellent ultra lightweight. It was nippy and well mannered, silent yet lively and safe and speedy (50 mph). Sturdily built to a luxury specification by a famous German factory, it is a first class example of a mount that fills a void in the two wheeler market in the United Kingdom'.

The end of the line was in 1963 for the remaining 'S' motorcycles, the 175 Trophy S and 250 Trophy S, with Zündapp's decision to concentrate on the smaller classes below 100 cc.

But in the sporting world Zündapp made a significant move into one day trials with a range of machinery up to 250 cc. At the season's end Zündapp had captured three German national trials championships, while in the enduro class, it gained three titles, the Alpine Cup, and one victory each in the 50 and 100 cc classes of the German six day event.

In the ISDT, held from 2–7 September in Czechoslovakia, 17 Zündapps were entered in the 50, 75, 100, 125, 175 and 250 classes. But only Sengfelder (50), Roth (75) and Kramer (100) gained gold medals.

The following year Zündapp's 'strokers maintained their off-road competitiveness by taking eight German championship titles, the Alpine Cup and victory for the first time in the important Valli Bergamasche event in northern Italy. But most interesting of all was a prototype 250 machine for one day trials. This bike was

more successful than anyone at the factory could have imagined.

On the production front, the factory arranged the debut in April 1964 of the all-new Roller 50, and RS50 Super. This pair of modern scooters had the same basic 49 cc (39 × 41.8 mm) engine which was based on the Falconette power unit. Sharing the same running gear, the Roller 50 was the standard machine with 2.9 bhp at 4900 rpm and three gears, while the de luxe RS50 Super offered a 41 mph performance thanks to its higher output of 4.6 bhp at 7000 rpm and four-speed gearbox.

Both machines were styled very much in the Italian Lambretta/Vespa mould, with the headlamp up on the enclosed handlebars, large, quickly-detachable side panels over the engine, 10 inch pressed wheels with 2.50 section tyres, 120 mm diameter brakes, twistgrip operated gearchange and two-tone dual seat.

The appearance of the two ultra-lightweight scooters signalled the end of the remaining two Bella models. The R175S and R204 were finally taken out of production towards the end of the year. This brought to a close the career of the marque's most successful machine of the 1950s. In its 12 year life the Bella range, together with the NSU Prima and Heinkel Tourist, were Germany's mainstream machines of the scooter era.

By 1965, sales of mopeds, lightweight motorcycles and scooters were at near record levels for the Munich-based company. And in reaction to this Zündapp made a big effort in motorcycle sport. This included not only one day trials and endurance trials, but also two new

Pinnacle of Zündapp's sporting achievement came in 1968 when a team of six Zündapp riders with machines ranging from 50 to 125 cc ended East Germany's five year domination of the ISDT Trophy. Andreas Brandl on a 50 cc motorcycle is seen against backdrop of Italian Alps.

ventures with the appearance of a streamlined record breaker and a road racer.

The record-breaking machines were largely the initiative of Dieter Neumeyer, grandson of the company's founder. And their appearance followed the successes of a year before, when a specially prepared standard KS50 Super clocked up 12,247.5 kilometres in 144 hours, representing an average speed of 85.05 kph (just over 53.125 mph). Zündapp was determined to be even more successful.

The first outing was in April 1965 at Monza in Italy, where the team made an attack on world records then held by rivals Kreidler. But the attempt was abandoned when the bike proved to be down on power. However, after additional work and tuning the team returned to Italy the following month. Between 13–15 May the air around the Monza Autodrome was filled with the high pitched note of the 49 cc two-stroke whose horizontal single cylinder engine, like the rest of the machine was wholly enveloped in an aerodynamic glassfibre shell.

In those three days the revised streamliner broke six world records on the high speed Monza bowl. Volker Kramer took the 10 km at 95.355 mph, and the 100 km at 100.668 mph, plus the hour record at 101.045 mph. Zündapp's team riders took the 1000 km at 91.121 mph, 6 Hours at 91.841 mph and 12 Hours at 85.156 mph. All the records were ratified for both the 50 and 75 cc classes, and the last record also counted in the 100 and 125 cc categories.

For decades the name Zündapp had stood for reliability rather than speed, but the Monza record spree changed all this. With the company concentrating on small capacity machines, it was felt important to display that the marque meant both reliability and speed. However, this was not quite the change of policy which it first appeared. As far back as 1937/38, the Nürnberg plant was secretly working on a machine which would challenge existing world records. But this was something totally different to the diminutive Monza record breaker. It was a supercharged four cylinder 1000 cc monster with a Rootes blower, designed for speeds in excess of 187.50 mph. And this brave attempt was snuffed out not by lack of technical expertise, but the political situation and the pressure which the Nazis put on Zündapp.

Developed in line with the Monza record breaker was a 50 cc class road racer. This was constructed by the Kramer brothers, Volker and Dieter, both of whom were employed at Zündapp. This semi-factory sponsored effort had a 49 cc horizontal air-cooled single cylinder unit of a similar type to the record breaker with a single rotary valve, coil ignition and ten speeds. Claimed power output was 10 bhp at 11500 rpm and a twin gearbox link-up provided ten gear ratios. A five-speed foot-change box was linked to a second gearbox with two ratios, which could be swapped by hand lever, doubling up the ratios in the main 'box'.

Although it was not raced in the World Championships, the 50 cc Zündapp racer showed up well against the leading privately-entered Kreidlers in German national events that year. The main reason the racer was not developed further was due to the level of success Zündapp achieved in off-road sport, where in the world of One Day Trials, the combination of Gustav Franke and Zündapp was to prove hard to beat in 1965.

Zündapp's first water-cooled roadster was the super-sporting KS 50 of 1972.

Above **Factory GS 125's at 1972 IDST which was based that year in Czechoslovakia.**

Even Sammy Miller on his Bultaco and Don Smith on the highly-competitive Greeves were hard pressed to match the German pair. Franke and Zündapp were 1965 European Trials Champions.

The contest was staged over three rounds. The first was at Bielefeld in West Germany on 2 October. Here Gustav Franke won, with compatriots Hans Kramer and Fritz Kopetzky second and third, and Belgium's Victor Gigot fourth. *Motor Cycle* reported 'Fantastic Franke, with a ride that left little doubt that he is the best trials rider on the continent, West German, ace Gustav Franke (247 Zündapp) took top honours'.

The next round was the St Cucufa Trial on the outskirts of Paris in early November. Here the winner was Sammy Miller, with Don Smith in second. Franke finished a lowly 13th.

The final round was held in Belgium over an extremely tough course in the Ardennes on a cold wintry day on 30 January 1966. The hazards were mainly of stream crossings, muddy banks and rocks. They were

Right **KS 50 engine and radiator assembly on display at the 1972 Paris Show.**

made more difficult by a film of ice, and on the second lap most riders lost marks on time as they plunged through steadily thickening fog. Although Franke was fifth at the end of the first circuit, on the second he made a fantastic recovery to get round with a penalty of only 11 marks – easily the best performance of the day. This put Franke in second spot behind winner Don Smith. For the European Championship award, Franke amassed 55 points from the three trials, while Smith and Miller, both of whom missed the opening round, came second and third with 48 and 45 points respectively.

In endurance trials 1965 was another successful year for the marque, with eight German championships, the Alpine Cup for the third successive year and best performance for a 50 cc machine in the Isle of Man ISDT. As a measure of just how popular the ISDT was in West Germany at the time, national team manager Otto Sensburg stated that the whole 300 entries for the 1965 event could have been filled by West German riders who would have liked to compete.

Zündapps were entered in both the Trophy and Vase teams with 50, 75, 100 and 125 cc class machines. Gold medals were won by Lehner (50), Kamper (75), Gienger (100) and Specht (125). The Trophy team came home fifth, whilst the German Vase A team came second, and when one considers that of the 299 starters, only 82 finished, Zündapp showed up well.

But perhaps the potentially most hair-raising event of the whole competition came when Zündapp factory star Dieter Kramer took a wrong turning on a moorland section in misty conditions and nearly met his end. Having scanned the ground ahead for a firm path (or so he thought), he opened the throttle wide and promptly shot into a deep bog. Within seconds his machine had almost disappeared and he was in up to his chest. Prompt work by officials and spectators extracted him, white-faced and shaken by his experience. Even though his machine was a small one – 100 cc – it took the combined efforts of several men to retrieve it. Amazingly, Kramer continued and finished the week to win a silver medal.

All the under-125 cc classes for trials and enduro in Germany were dominated by Zündapp in 1966.

The third Neumeyer generation was at the helm when Zündapp celebrated its first 50 years in 1967. Dieter Neumeyer, born in 1931, had graduated in economics and like the late Dr Mann had gained much practical experience of both the technical and commercial side of business at Siemens-Schukert. On 8 May 1963, the Zündapp management appointed him joint General Manager with director Schulz, and by 1966 he was running the company himself. As a former endurance trials rider of the early 1950s, Dieter Neumeyer's enthusiasm for motorcycle sport was unabated in the years following his appointment.

The Jubilee year saw 1800 workers employed at the Munich complex who assembled 55,000 machines of

Right **KS 350 water-cooled twin-cylinder two-stroke at the Cologne Show, September 1976.**

which half were exported to 138 countries. And despite the large workforce, a large amount of capital was spent on cost-saving automation.

In stark contrast to Zündapp's own ultra-lightweight 1967 model line, one German Zündapp enthusiast decided to join the pursuit of the *Buffel* (Buffalo), which was the pet name for the biggest and most impressive bike. At that time the publicity given to Friedl Münch and his monster NSU-engined Mammoth had spurred several other of his countrymen to build car engines into motorcycle frames to create the ultimate *Buffel*. But one who did manage to create something really special was a 30-year old Bonn hairdresser, Horst Kreutzer. He married together a fabled KS601 Green Elephant and a 898 cc Borgward Isabella four cylinder transverse engine.

Kreutzer chose the Isabella car engine because, although it was slightly heavier than the old Zündapp twin, it had a power output of 45 bhp at 5300 rpm compared with Zündapp's best figure of 34 bhp at 6000 rpm for the sports version of the Nurnberg flat twin. Borgward even officially helped by supplying him with a factory reconditioned engine for only £70. So, he had a frame (one of the original plunger-types) and a gleaming engine. And that was where the problem really started.

Although the Borgward engine was shorter than the KS, because the Zündapp had a front mounted dynamo, a flange was necessary to make a satisfactory union between car engine, bike gearbox and clutch. And a large Bosch dynamo was mounted atop the engine, necessitating a slight alteration to the frame. The dynamo and water pump both came from a larger capacity Borgward car, the 1100 cc Hansa, as the pump could cope with a larger volume of water. This was because the twin radiators, from an Opel 1500, were of a smaller capacity to the four-wheeler's. The rest of the machine was KS Zündapp, with the exception of the custom-built seat, 5-gallon capacity tank and super large, 200 mm Mercedes headlamp. All-in-all, Horst Kreutzer could be justly proud of his Super Elephant.

In 1969 Zündapp also 'dabbled' at road racing again. This had been spurred by some members of the sport's international governing body, the FIM, wanting to limit 50 cc racers to a maximum of six gear ratios in order to eliminate factory freaks.

With this in mind, in the summer of 1967 Zündapp was testing an air cooled 50 cc six-speeder with development rider Dieter Kramer. The machine had basically a tuned ISDT-type motor mounted in a one-off racing chassis.

Lower right **The 49 cc Roller 50 scooter which made its introduction to the market in 1964 and was still available in the early 1980's.**

That year Zündapp won the Europe Cup. This was the FIM organised European Enduro championships. In both the two 100 and 125 cc categories Zündapp led all season. Again Zündapp won the three German trials titles. And for the first time a 100 cc machine won overall victory at the important Greenhorn Enduro event in the USA.

But the biggest sporting achievement of the 1960s for Zündapp was to come the following year, when East Germany's five year supremacy in the ISDT came to an end among the Alps of northern Italy in early October 1968. It was shattered by six Germans from west of the Iron Curtain mounted on six lightweight Zündapp two-strokes ranging from only 50 cc to a maximum of 125 cc.

In a near miraculous performance, the West Germans were the sole competitors out of 29 national Trophy and Vase teams to complete the rugged 788 mile route, often against ultra-tight team schedules, without losing a single mark for lateness at a control.

From this tremendous result was ultimately to come a new range of ultra-lightweight roadsters and off-roaders to carry the marque into the 1970s. The most glamorous of these were the GS/MC 125s – a pair of fire-breathing dirt irons for enduro (GS) and motocross racing (MC). Both shared the same 123 cc (54 × 54 mm) five-speed engine developed from the highly successful

This later KS 50 was projected by the Zündapp marketing department as a close cousin of the KS 175. The KS 175 was the most popular 'real' motorcycle for Zündapp in the late 1970's.

Dr Dieter Neumeyer (left), the head of Zündapp, with Wilhelm Lyding of the ADAC – the West German governing body for motor sport and similar to Britain's RAC. The machine is a GS 100 enduro.

ISDT bikes. The GS gave 18 bhp, the MC 19 bhp – both at 7900 rpm. The bikes both carried 27 mm Bing carburettors and were equipped with near bullet-proof multiplate clutches with helical geared primary drive.

The brace also shared 150 mm full-width brake hubs, 21 inch and 18 inch front and rear high tensile wheel rims and 3.00/3.50 section tyres, 10.2-litre alloy fuel tank, double cradle chrome moly frames, 32 mm telescopic forks and near-vertical rear shocks. On both models the black expansion pipe exhaust system exited centrally between the two front downtubes, passed underneath the engine and came out on the right of the machine. The enduro version differed by having an additional tailpipe silencer, and for the US market a built-in spark arrester.

The majority of GS and MC models went to North America, where they were highly regarded. For example, in a giant 15 bike enduro test in the American magazine *Motorcycle Buyers Guide* in 1972 the GS125 came out top in every rating. For 1973 production of both was increased. The GS sold in the USA for $950 and the MC $900.

Just as successful on the roadster front for Zündapp was the KS125 which used a detuned version of the GS/MC five-speed engine. However, this exceptional lightweight was good for over 70 mph and offered its owner a well-built, fast but reliable sportster.

The factory also exported large numbers of Zündapp engines to power a variety of other manufacturers' machines around the world. This policy had begun as far back as the late 1950s when a new company, Metalurgica Casal was established in Portugal. Casal had enlisted the aid of Zündapp to supply engines and technicians. The last Zündapp engineer was not to leave the Casal work until as late as 1971. Even well into the '70s the majority of Casal designs showed a definite Zündapp design influence, especially the engines which ranged from 50 to 125 cc.

Other manufacturers to benefit from Zündapp technology were the Spanish Sanglas company who used Zündapp power for the 72 mph 100 Sport in the mid-1960s. Rickman in Britain sold large numbers of 125 Zündapp-engined motocross and enduro bikes mainly to the USA, and in the early to mid-1970s also supplied a number of Zündapp-powered models to the British police. Laverda in Italy also used the later water-cooled 125/175 engines for its smaller roadsters. Another Italian company, TM chose watercooled Zündapp KS50 engines. Finally, Mototrans in Spain produced a pair of sporting 50 cc featherweights with air-cooled Zündapp power during the early 1980s.

In 1972 Zündapp introduced its first water-cooled roadster, the super-sporting KS50. This replaced the air-cooled KS50 Super Sport which had been launched together with the standard KS50 Sport in 1967. Besides the KS50 water-cooled model, another newcomer in 1972 was the KS50 Cross trail bike. Both models pumped out 6.25 bhp at 8400 rpm and had five-speed gearboxes (as did the original KS50 Sport). Output of the KS125 Sport had been increased from 15 to 17 bhp, with maximum speed now 78 mph.

The RS50 and Roller 50 scooter continued unchanged as did the large range of mopeds, which in Germany were sold either as Mokick or Mofa depending upon their speed and whether they were started by pedals or kickstarters.

In Britain there had been no importer for the Zündapp range since Motor Imports ceased handling them in the mid-1960s. But in September 1975 a new company called Zündapp UK was set up at Beeston near Sandy in Bedfordshire to sell the new range of motorcycles. The men behind the company were two South African brothers, Doug and Bob Aldridge. Both were known for their sponsorship of leading South African road racers who had included Martin Watson and Kork Ballington on the European circuits.

The first machine offered, with a price tag of £599, was the GS125 ISDT replica. Also available was the KS50 Special, tailored to fit Britain's sixteener laws. This four-speed 'sports' moped produced 6.4 bhp and was priced at £329. The final machine to be offered, at £600, was the latest version of the MC 125 motocrosser. This was claimed to be a true replica of the bike that won the European 125 motocross series in 1973 and 1974 and finished second to Suzuki in 1975.

Zündapp UK had plenty to shout about, at least from a results point of view, when the West German Trophy team, which was exclusively Zündapp mounted, took the 1975 ISDT Trophy. This event was staged in the Isle of Man for the third time in ten years. The opening day of this, the 50th International Six Days Trial, was marred by the death of Bren Moran, a Canadian Can-Am rider. This fatality was only the second in the event's history, the first being the Italian Serafini who had crashed in 1955. Although the German team won, it was not a repeat performance of the earlier 1968 Zündapp zero mark epic.

Even as early as the first day, despite holding the lead, the team had dropped 32 points. On day three German team member Hau collided with one of the other competitors and damaged his machine. He was penalised for a delay of two minutes, saddling his team with 120 points. His fellow team member Grisse also had two crashes that day, but he succeeded in repairing his Zündapp within the time allowed.

Another member of the West German Trophy team Weber did not stop at a time check, and this failure was brought before the International Jury. By the narrow margin of eight votes to seven Weber was allowed to continue. But eventually, even though Zündapp had had problems all the other teams suffered worse, leaving West Germany and Zündapp to score yet another ISDT Trophy victory.

At the very end of the year, in the 31 December 1975 issue of *Motor Cycle News*, tester Brian Crichton put one of the newly launched KS50 'Sixteener Specials' through its paces. The headline 'Cracking the clock – our fastest moped' said it all. *MCN* electronically timed the flying fifty at 55.15 mph – 2 mph faster than the previous best, gained by the popular Suzuki AP50. The Zündapp also recorded the fastest acceleration over the timed quarter mile. It took 22 seconds compared to its nearest rival, the Puch Grand Prix, at 23.25 seconds. Considering the excellent performance *MCN* found fuel economy 'surprisingly good'. Riding the KS50 to its maximum produced 92.5 mpg.

The only criticism concerned the high price. This latter point and the limited resources of Zündapp UK to compete effectively against Suzuki, Honda, Yamaha and Puch, sadly ensured that very few Zündapps were sold in Britain during the short-lived Zündapp UK reign. Also affecting the new company's performance was the changing moped laws. These came into effect in 1976 and imposed a blanket restriction of 30 mph as a top speed.

After an interval of sixteen years, the 51st ISDT was held again in Austria. In comparison with the 1960 event at Bad Aussee the Austrians made a much better job of the 1976 event. Its centre was at Zeltweg within the new Osterreichring autodrome. Here once again, the combination of West German riders and West German Zündapps proved unbeatable.

At the biennial Cologne show in September Zündapp caused a stir by displaying a completely new water-cooled twin cylinder model, the KS350. However, this advanced and superbly styled machine was never to reach production. Its features included a 27 bhp, 326 cc parallel twin with single 36 mm Bing carb and five-speed gearbox. There was a full cradle duplex frame, cast alloy wheels, fully enclosed rear drive chain with rubber bellows, hydraulically operated disc front brake, stainless steel mudguards, 12 volt electrics, 16-litre fuel tank and a metallic gold/black finish with up-to-the-minute styling.

Also displayed were new versions of the KS50 and KS125 water-cooled models. Both with cast alloy wheels, single disc front brake and a de luxe specification which included lots of chrome work, fork gaiters and a large instrument console that housed matching speedometer, rev counter and warning lights.

A selection of Zündapp mopeds available in 1983. Left to right ZL, 25, ZS 25 and ZE 40.

Zündapp won the European 80 cc road racing championship in 1983 with this machine.

The abortive KS350 did bear some fruit in the shape of a brand-new Zündapp which appeared at the beginning of 1977. The KS175 was a watercooled single cylinder two-stroke based on half the KS350 engine unit. With its short stroke 62 and 54 mm bore measurements this gave the KS175 a capacity of 163 cc. With a compression ratio of 7.8:1 and 28 mm Mikuni carburettor the engine turned out 17 bhp at 7400 rpm. There was a five-speed gearbox with ratios of 3.4, 2.16, 1.53, 1.26 and 105:1. Maximum speed was 58.125 mph.

For the day, the new Zündapp's reliance on a petroil mixture (50:1) could be considered a little crude, but its only really bad point were the 6 volt electrics, even if these had a reliable Bosch transistorised unit. Fuel tank capacity was 14.25-litres. Standard equipment included cast alloy wheels and a 280 mm front disc with Grimeca caliper, 160 mm rear-drum brake, fork gaiters and grab handle, plus twin mirrors.

The KS175 was refined in 1979 with a restyling exercise which included a neat seat/tail fairing, chrome carrier, improved bikini fairing, Brembo caliper mounted at the rear of the new Marzocchi fork legs, and new graphics. Beside the inevitable mofas, mokicks

and mopeds the Zündapp line now consisted of the RS50 Super scooter, KS50 Super Sport (air cooled) and the KS50 TT. The latter was a new model in the same style as the KS175 and was given a claimed maximum of 53 mph. This performance was actually less than some of the earlier Zündapp 'fifties', while it had a whopping DM3550 price tag.

From a high point of 115,000 units in 1977, Zündapp declined badly in the 1980s with 1980 production down to 70,000. In 1981 it fell to below 60,000 and by the 1982 Cologne Show Zündapp were struggling badly, having lost some 41 per cent of the previous year's figure.

This was not for the want of new ideas. The KS80 was unveiled in 1981. This had a 78.1 cc (46 × 47 mm) five-speed watercooled engine unit which with an 11.2:1 compression ratio and Bing carb gave 8.4 bhp at 6000 rpm. Brakes were a 220 mm disc at the front, and a 150 mm drum rear. There were cast alloy wheels with 2.75 × 17 and 3.00 × 17 inch tyres. All this added up to a dry weight of 231 lb and a speed of 50 mph. The model was actually offered in two guises; a touring version with a stepped seat, high bars and exposed forks while the Sport came with a Bikini fairing, fork gaiters and flat bars. Both had a large carrier and twin mirrors as standard equipment.

In 1983 a completely revised, air-cooled version, the

Above **Zündapp's 1984 RSM 80 GP racer could reach an outstanding 137.5 mph with its 79 cc engine which developed 30 bhp at 14,800 rpm. Transmission was six-speed.**

K80, was wheeled out to the press. It had many changes not only to the power unit, but also to wheels, tank, seat, exhaust, fairing and side panels.

Then came the startling news that Zündapp would be fielding a new machine in the 80 cc road racing championships, which for 1983 were to be a Eurooean championship.

Power output of the racer was claimed to be 28 bhp at 14,000 rpm but at the time Zündapp refused to give away any further details. The team was to be headed by 24 year old Hubert Abold and sponsored by Krauser, Metzeler and Shell.

The 1983 European rounds were held 13 March at Jarama, Spain; 27 March Santa Monica, Italy; 29 May Donington Park, Britain; 28 August Brno, Czechoslovakia; 11 September, Assen Holland and the final round was 25 September at Hockenheim, West Germany.

Even though Zündapp was struggling with its production models the RSM80 racer was unbeatable and ended the season as Champion of Europe. For 1984 the 80 cc racer was refined further and at long last its technical detail was revealed. The heart was a 79 cc (46 × 47 mm) single with disc valve induction, 16:1 compression ratio, 32 mm Bing carb and Bosch transistorised ignition, giving 30 bhp at 14800 rpm

through a six-speed box. The power unit was finished in white and housed in a sheet aluminium monocoque frame, with adjustable air-sprung oil-damped Marzocchi forks, taper roller head bearings, box-section chrome moly swinging arm using plain bearings and cantilever rear suspension. There was a 10-litre fuel tank and five-spoke Campagnolo cast magnesium 18 inch wheels fitted front and rear with Michelin 80/70 and 80/80 tyres. Brakes were Zanzani aluminium discs (220 mm front and 180 mm rear) with Mozzi Motor aluminium calipers. The 1983 machines had smaller triple discs and calipers of a different design, made by Brembo. Altogether, this added up to 123 lb dry weight. Maximum speed was claimed as 137.5 mph.

Riders were Abold and 35 year old Stefan Dörflinger. As *Motor Cycle News* reported in the 29 August 1984 issue Dörflinger needed only a seventh place at the final

Right **Swiss rider Stefan Dörflinger piloting his Zündapp to victory in 1984 80 cc Austrian GP at the Salzburgring. He became the first World 80 cc Champion that year.**

round, the San Marino GP the following weekend, to take his third World title. The previous two had been on 50 cc Krauser-backed Kreidlers.

Dörflinger's team-mate Hubert Abold had been instructed that he could only beat his fellow Zündapp rider if engine trouble struck and Dörflinger was not going to make the points he needed to win the crown. But in fact the result was never really in doubt with Dörflinger scorching home to give Zündapp its first-ever World road racing title.

The same machine took the Championship again in 1985 ridden by Dörflinger with Krauser's backing and under his name. However, this was of little use in stemming Zündapp's financial haemorrhage. The result was that a few short days after the triumph Zündapp went into liquidation.

This was just as the Cologne show was starting. At such short notice that the show's official catalogue inside front cover displayed one of the company's full colour advertisements as there was no time to re-print.

In the following months the liquidator searched for a buyer. Unexpectedly, one was found in the People's Republic of China.

Enfield Explorer, still available today and made under licence in Madra, India, with K 80 79 cc engine.

The factory's name, tooling and stock were shipped east to start a new life on a new continent under new ownership.

When the sale of Zündapp had been completed special trains travelled overland from China to the Zündapp works in Munich. Each covered rail wagon carried large packing cases to house the remains of the plant for their journey to their new home. Around 1500 Chinese made the trip, and to save on cost the personnel slept inside the packing cases while loading operation took place. This took several weeks during the summer of 1984.

Another twist to the Zündapp saga came in 1986 when it was announced from India that the Enfield India company was producing the K80 model complete with 'Zündapp' name on both the engine castings and petrol tank! Did Enfield India conclude a licensing deal with Zündapp before 1984 or with the Chinese after the sale? At any event, the name, if not the original company, survives.

Zündapp was in many ways the greatest of all the German marques. Certainly it was at the forefront of the industry for a longer period than its competitors. And it deserves to rank with the true pioneers of the industry, along with Triumph, Norton, BSA, Harley-Davidson and Gilera.

Other Marques

This chapter sets out to catalogue the vast number of smaller post-war German marques. Some were quite significant pre-war producers whose fortunes waned after the end of the Second World War. Others were new companies which sprang up in the aftermath of war and although they produced reasonable quantities of motorcycles, scooters, mopeds or three-wheel cars never made a lasting name. There are still others who either appeared only briefly on the scene, or made prototypes only. And, of course, there were several small producers who built solely racing motorcylcles.

Whatever their claim to fame, however small, they are here, to prove the truly staggering post-war economic miracle that was the German motorcycle industry.

Achilles
1953-57

In the days before the First World War Achilles built motorcycles in the Austro-Hungarian empire. When it returned to motorcycle manufacture after two world wars, Achilles produced a wide range of scooter-like small bikes, with 98 and 123 cc Sachs power units. After closure in 1957, the tooling was purchased by the British Norman motorcyle works.

AMO
1950-55

Based in Berlin, AMO-Motorengesellschaft GmbH marketed a range of mopeds, including one fully enclosed model on the lines of a large wheel scooter. All the machines were powered by a 48 cc two-stroke unit of AMO's own design and made by Westendarp and Pieper, a company which built motorcycles under the TX banner in the 1920's.

Amorette
1954-58

Sachs-powered de luxe moped, with front and rear suspension, similar in appearance to the NSU Quickly. Imported into Britain during 1957 by A Goldsmith & Co of Willesden, London NW6.

Anker
1949-58

Once a famous German bicycle factory, which post-war turned to building Ilo and Sachs-powered mopeds and motorcycles. All had two-stroke engines from 48 to 244 cc. From 1958 it was known as Pamag. Afterwards the company concentrated on business machines, including cash registers, but closed down in 1976. Motorcycle production was transferred in 1952 to a branch factory at Paderborn. The main works was in Bielefeld.

Ardie
1919-58

Started in Nürnberg in 1919 Ardie took its name from its founder Arno Dietrich who had been a chief designer for Premier. The company's first efforts were 305 and 348 cc two-stroke singles with deflector-type pistons. But after Dietrich was killed in a racing accident in 1922 the firm passed into the hands of the Bendit factory and from 1925 used British JAP engines. These were from 246 to 996 cc, but the best selling models used the 490 cc overhead valve engine. Very refined machines, these featured duralumin frames and many luxury fittings. In the mid-30s JAP engines were supplanted by those from Bark, Küchen, Sachs and Sturmey Archer. The firm reverted to tubular steel frames, presumably to cut costs. In 1938, Richard Küchen designed an interesting 348 cc ohv V-twin with transverse engine but this never went into volume production.

Following the Second World War, the company was owned by the Bartel-controlled Dürkopp company of Bielefeld, but remained under independent management. Unlike most firms of the time, Ardie built its own power units because its engineering director Dr Noack created a range of new crossflow-two-stroke engines from a 122 cc single to a 344 cc twin. These were used to power a range mainly consisting of modest but well-engineered commuter-type machines. From 1953 Ardie also produced mopeds. After record sales in 1955, Ardie suffered the same drastic decline as many other producers in Germany. It finally went into liquidation in 1958.

Ardie B251 two-stroke single with twin exhaust ports and Jurisch plunger rear suspension at Amsterdam Show, 1951.

ARO

see also Chapter 6 dealing with Fath

AWD

See Wurring

Bastert
1950-56

Based in Bielefeld, Bastert produced a wide range of motorcycles powered by Ilo and Sachs engines of 98, 123, 147, 174 and 197 cc. Also it made the *Einspurauto* (Single track car) luxury scooter, which was available with either a 174 or 197 cc Ilo engine. The *Einspurauto* was very similar to the Maicomobil.

Bauer
1936-58

Another well known bicycle factory. Pre-war, Bauer produced lightweight moped-type machines with 74 or 98 cc Sachs engines. After 1945 (production restarted in 1949) came a range of motorcycles with 97, 123, 147, or 174 cc Ilo or Sachs two-stroke engines. Initially these sold well, but in 1952 the company suffered from the introduction of a brand new machine with a Bauer built 247 cc engine. The ohv single was an unusual design which had the carburettor at the front and the exhaust port at the rear of the engine. The layout led to overheating, and the technical problem caused it to be a commercial failure. Bauer gave up making motorcycles in 1954, although bicycle production continued.

Beckmann ASB
1953

Displayed at the 1953 Frankfurt Show, this interesting moped-type machine had its 48 cc Zündapp Combimot engine mounted over the front wheel. It transmitted its power via a chain to a sprocket on the front wheel. The motorcycle-type exhaust system ran down the left of the wheel almost to the ground, and a built-in leg shield, foot board and partial rear enclosure gave the machine a scooter-like appearance. Only a very limited number were produced, selling at DM690.

Bauer B250 featured ohv engine of company's own design. The developments cost crippled the firm.

Binz
1954-55

Very basic scooter with 20 inch wheels and a choice of 47 cc Sachs or 49 cc Ilo engine.

Bismarck
1904-57

Old established German marque which originally produced massive V-twins with Anzani, Fafnir and Minerva engines up to 1300 cc. Motorcycle production stopped in 1908, but began again in 1931 with 75 and 98 cc motorised bicycles.

Post-war motorcycle production resumed in 1950 with a range of machines designed by Emil Fischer. The LM125K came first, powered by a 123 cc Ilo two-stroke single. This featured twin exhausts, telescopic forks and an unsprung frame. Other models were the LM98TG, LM100K, LM98K, M150K and finally in 1953, the M175K. All used either Sachs or Ilo single-cylinder engines. Bismarck Werke finally ceased production 9 November 1957.

Brütsh
1952-58

Mainly a producer of small four-wheelers with either

Lloyd of Sachs engines, Brütsh also built a small number of the Mopetta. A tiny three-wheeler best described as a bullet shaped shell with room for just the driver and its 49 cc Sachs engine. Only 14 were sold.

Bücker
1922-55

Founded in 1922, Bücker was a relatively large company and pre-war assembled a vast number of machines with proprietary engines and capacities ranging from 98 to 996 cc. Engine suppliers included Cockerell, Columbus (Horex), JAP, Blackburne, Bark and MAG.

Post-war production resumed in 1948, with a range of machines from 123 to 247 cc and all powered by Ilo two-stroke engines.

In the late 1940's, Friedl Schön rode a pre-war 248 cc Bücker with an ohv British JAP engine to victory in the 250 cc German road racing championship. The final model was the Ilona II, powered by a twin-cylinder Ilo unit with four speeds and a range of singles with the TZ prefix. Although production ceased in 1955, it was still possible to buy a Bücker machine as late as 1958.

Cityfix

See Delius

CL
1951

Offered a mini scooter with a 48 cc two-stroke engine, but only a very few machines were produced.

Condor
1953-54

Unrelated to the major Swiss Condor company, the German Condor built a small number of scooter-like lightweights with a 48 cc two-stroke engine.

Delius
1950-53

Sold under the Cityfix label. Two models were produced; the Cityfix 49, with a Lutz 49 cc engine, and the MR 100 with a 98 cc Sachs unit. Both were primitive scooter-type machines, with girder forks, leg shields, 16 inch wheels and a rigid, unsprung, step-thru frame.

Diebler
1951-55

The Berlin firm of Arthur Diebler manufactured and sold, mainly for export (to Thailand, India and South America), a motor tricycle with a 200 Sachs engine. The power unit was mounted with the fuel tank above the front wheel and power was transmitted via a chain to a sprocket on the front wheel hub. The driver (rider) steered the machine, which had seating capacity for two passengers and twin rear wheels, with conventional motorcycle handlebars and controls.

Dornier

See Chapter 16 dealing with Zündapp

Dürkopp
1901-1960

Best remembered for its contribution to the post-war scooter boom, the Dürkopp marque was one of the true pioneers of German motorcycling. Founded in Bielefeld in 1867 by Nikolaus Dürkopp, the company

Right **Dürkopp tried to capture young buyers with publicity material of this kind for its 1952 MD 200. The company was best known post-war for the Diana scooter.**

198 c. c. · 10,2 H. P. · 60 mph 96 km/h · 2,4 liters per 62,5 miles/100 km

DÜRKOPPWERKE AKTIENGESELLSCHAFT BIELEFELD / GERMANY

FOUNDED IN 1867

PHONE: *63161 · CABLES: DÜRKOPPWERKE BIELEFELD · TELETYPE: 0932802

made bicycles from 1898 and motorcycles as early as 1901. By 1905 it made not only singles and V-twins, but also an aircooled in-line four.

Motorcycle production ceased just before the Great War, but began again in the 1930's in the form of bicycles using 'clip-on' power units of 60, 75 and 98 cc capacities. 'Real' motorcycles were not made again until 1949 when models powered by 98 cc Sachs and 123 cc Ardie and Ilo engines appeared. In 1951 it introduced a 150 cc machine fitted with a Dürkopp engine, followed by similar 175 and 200 cc models. From then on no further proprietary engines were used.

In 1954 Dürkopp introduced the 194 cc Diana scooter. This high-quality, stylish model was the cornerstone of its motorcycle business during the mid-1950's boom and helped it to weather the depression that followed when most of its other two-wheelers were taken out of production. In any case, Dürkopp was a flourishing general engineering company and was not wholly reliant on motorcycle business. Production of the various Diana models ceased in 1960, by which time 24,963 had been made.

Express
1903-1958

Express-Werke AG was founded in Neumarkt, Nürnberg in 1882 to make pedal cycles and in 1903 added Fafnir engines to become a pioneer of German motorcycling. Its V-twin racing model of 1904 had a

mighty 8 hp engine but soon the company reverted to pedal power.

In 1933, it tried again with a range of two-stroke lightweights but with the coming of war returned to bicycles and were the major suppliers to the German armed forces.

Post-war, by 1950 Express was making large numbers of pedal cycles and lightweight motorcycles using Fichtel and Sachs engines. Through the early 1950's there followed a host of sophisticated new models of up to 250 cc, plus mopeds. Express motorcycles managed to continue selling through 1956 and 1957 when many other famous names were hard pressed. At the beginning of 1958 there was little to suggest an upset for the firm which had just celebrated its 75th year, but by November it merged with DKW and Victoria to form Zweirad Union. The plant did not feature in the corporate plans and was soon closed. With it went all the marque's identity, and even the name was dropped after only a few months.

FA
1952

Small *cabin-scooter* powered by a 175 cc Sachs engine.

Express 147 cc Radex 154 illustrates the firm's unique forward link front forks. Virtually every model it produced during the hectic mid-1950's had some variation of this theme to attract riders.

EXPRESS
RADEX 154

Faka
1952-57

Produced a range of scooters' Tourist, Commodore 175 and Commodore 200 with Ilo engines. The firm also made three-wheeler, again Ilo powered, called the Dreirad-Lastenroller.

Falter
1952

Exclusively a producer of mopeds and mafas, usually with 49 cc engines. The Bielefeld company is still in existence today and also sells models under the Stoewer Greif name.

Fend

See Messerschmitt

Ferbedo
1953-54

A neatly designed, but unsuccessful scooter, called the R48 and powered by a 48 cc Zündapp engine, that was manufactured in Nürnberg.

Fiame
1951-53

Used the same 123 cc two stroke single cylinder engine for both a motorcycle and scooter.

Forelle
1955-58

Mopeds powered by 49 cc Ilo and Sachs engines were among the products of the Forelle bicycle factory.

Fuldamobil
1951-65

A range of three-wheeler passenger light cars, the prototype of which first appeared in 1950 and was powered by a Zündapp engine. The first production model, the N1, appeared in 1951 and was fitted with a 247 cc Baker and Polling single producing 8.5 bhp. All the later models, N2, 52, 54 and 57 used Sachs motors, and a total of 1,738 Fuldamobils were sold. Marketed in Britain as the Nobel, and first imported in early August 1955.

Geier
1934-54

Pre-war, Geier built lightweights with 73 and 98 cc two stroke engines. Resumed production in 1950 with a large range of motorcycles from 98 to 174 cc. The ten model line-up used either Ilo or Sachs power and included the Motri. It was a three-wheel truck with the front half of a motorcycle, and the rear half of a pick-up van.

Glas-Goggo
1951-66

Major producer of scooters and small four-wheel cars. The scooters used 123, 148 and 197 cc single cylinder two-stroke engines of Ilo design and were offered between 1951 and 1956. A total of 46,181 units were produced. There were also various versions of the *Lastenroller* (goods scooter) with a pick-up truck rear section.

But it was the twin cylinder 247, 296 and 395 cc Goggomobil light cars which really made the company's name. Over a twelve year period from 1955-67 a total of 357,200 were built. Hans Glas sold, at the height of his success, to BMW in 1966 and following this all the Dingolfing, Bayern, plant's machine tools and production facilities were shipped to South Africa to establish a BMW facility there.

Gnom
1950-51

Three-wheel car powered by 123 cc Ilo engine and built at a plant in Berlin.

Goebel
1951-79

Goebel exclusively produced mopeds, latterly with 49 cc Sachs engine units.

Gold-Rad
1952-81

For many years a manufacturer of mopeds with either Sachs or Ilo engines, more recently concentrated on importing Italian engines and some complete machines, including the Moto Graziela range.

Göricke
1903-79

One of the pioneers of the German motorcycle industry. Originally a bicycle manufacturer, Göricke's motorcycles were always something of a sideline. Its most famous designer was Alfred Ostertag and the earliest machines used both single and V-twin engines. In the 1920s Göricke used 172 and 247 cc British Villiers two-stroke power, as well as 346 and 496 cc inlet over exhaust (touring) and ohv (touring) Swiss MAG units, plus some Blackburne engines.

Post-war production resumed in 1949, with first 98, 123, 147 and 174 cc motorcycles and then in 1951 a new scooter with a 98 cc Ilo engine. Later the Gorette moped, with a choice of either 47 cc Sachs or 49 cc Ilo engines, was offered in addition to the Go 200 S motorcycle.

By the late 1950s only mopeds and ultralight motorcycles were available including the 100S, which, introduced in 1960, offered a full motorcycle specification. In this form the company survived until the late 1970s.

Gritzner-Kayser
1903-62

A well known manufacturer of sewing machines which early on turned to making Gritzner motorcycles powered by Fafnir singles and V-twins. It also made three-wheelers under the Kayser name in 1901. After The Second World War motorcycle production restarted in 1953 with Sachs engined machines of 98, 147 and 174 cc – the latter in two versions, the 175F and 175S. The final Gritzner was an attractive 49 cc ultra lightweight known as the Monza and originally designed by the Mars factory. It had sporty looks with low handlebars, two-tone dual seat, flyscreen and carrier as standard equipment. At the same time the firm also built under licence a KTM-designed de luxe scooter.

Hecker
1922-57

Founded by Hans Hecker in August 1922, the firm became a major factory pre-war. production included 245 cc two-strokes, then 346 cc ohv models, both with engines of Hecker design. Then came a range of machines powered by British JAP motors and a 746 cc V-twin with ioe valve operation manufactured by MAG. During the 1930s, Hecker built a pair of lightweight models with square tube frames and either 73 or 98 cc Sachs two-stroke engines.

Post-war production recommenced in 1948. Initially it was purely a one model range – the K125 powered by a 123 cc Ilo two-stroke single. In 1950 the V200 appeared, which used a British Villiers 197 cc unit. Also available were the K175 (1951-54), K175V (1954-56), K200 (1953-56) and K250 (1953-56). All these latter machines used single cylinder Ilo power.

Hecker machines also did well in the ISDT, gaining several gold medals in the early 1950s. The highlight came in 1954, when Best, a member of the German Trophy Team struck gold riding a 248 cc Hecker in Wales.

The factory finally ceased on 2 May 1957, although no complete motorcycles were manufactured after the end of 1956.

This Gritzner late 1950's de luxe special was really an Austrian KTM built under licence.

Heidemann
1949-52

Heidemann was well known for its bicycles and also produced a lightweight motorcycle, the KR125 powered by a Sachs two-stroke unit.

Heinkel
1951-1965

Together with Claudius Dornier and Hugo Junkers, Ernst Heinkel became virtually synonymous with the resurgence of German aircraft between the wars. He began his company in 1922 and with the importance placed in aviation in the 1930s after the rise to power of the Nazi party, the firm developed many innovative designs. Inevitably, it was not long before they were stretching the production facilities to the utmost for the war effort.

The cessation of hostilities brought a ban on aircraft manufacture which meant that Heinkel had to find another outlet. It chose to produce mopeds, scooters and three-wheel cars. After a slow start, development began in 1951. The 149 cc four-stroke Tourist scooter was launched in January 1953, followed in 1954 by the 49 cc Perla moped. The Tourist later became available with a 174 cc engine. In 1956, Heinkel launched the Kabinen 'cabin scooter' with car-type steering and independent suspension powered either by the 174 cc Tourist engine or a 198 cc version of the unit. Like the later BMW Isetta access was by a single front opening door.

In 1957 Heinkel launched the Roller 112, an unsuccessful 125 cc scooter. The following year Ernst Heinkel died and three-wheeler production began in Southern Ireland. They were later imported to Britain under the Trojan name in the early 1960s. In 1960 the Tourist was updated to the Mark II and in 1962 a new

Above **Technically, the Heinkel Perle was very advanced. Among many noteworthy features was a cast alloy frame. Remarkably, the company was able to design and enter production with this model in just six weeks in 1953.**

Below **Heinkel added to its reputation for quality engineering with its Tourist ohv scooters. Apart from commuter duties, the machines also enjoyed a vogue for competition as these three examples prove.**

scooter was introduced and named the Heinkel 150. Both scooters were discontinued in 1965 as aircraft production returned to a healthy level, by which time over 100,000 Tourists had been made.

Hesco
1984-86

Manufactured sporting roadsters powered by the 500 or 600 cc Austrian Rotax four-stroke single cylinder engines.

Hoffmann
1949-54

Founded by Jakob Oswald Hoffmann with the production of two Ilo-powered 125 cc motorcycles at a plant in Bezirk, Düsseldorf and given a boost by acquiring the rights to build Vespa scooters under licence in mid-1949. Production moved to a new factory at Lintorf in 1950 and the next year took over half of the German market for 125 cc scooters. 1951 also saw the introduction of a 175 cc motorcycle with Ilo engine and a 250 cc horizontally-opposed twin called

Imme 100 had a horizontal 99 cc two-stroke engine. It was available in the early 1950's.

the Governeur. This used Hoffmann's own power unit designed by Richard Küchen and its only real failing was the high production cost. For the next two years the company built up its export markets and then in 1953 launched a host of new machines powered by Ilo two-strokes of 200 and 250 cc capacity. There was also a new 250 and a 300 using a development of the 250 cc flat twin. These were intended to take over from the Vespa models, for the licence agreement would end in 1954 and Hoffmann lacked the cash to renegotiate. Unfortunately, sales never met the hoped-for level and Hoffmann became the first casualty of the post-war industrial recession.

Hummel
1951-55

Hummel-Sitta-Werke of Sittensen, Bremen sold a large number of scooters under the Sitta label – the 118 cc 120G, 123 cc 125G and 149 cc 150G. All were powered by Ilo single cylinder two-stroke units. Hummel also made a small range of motorcycles, again with Ilo engines from 49 to 248 cc.

Ilo (engine manufacturer)

The Ilo factory in Pinneberg built complete lightweight motorcycles in the 1920s until the popularity of its proprietary engines led the company to concentrate on manufacturing power units alone.

Imme
1948-51

The first Imme was designed by Norbert Riedl, and was a highly unorthodox and interesting horizontal 98 cc two-stroke housed in a pressed steel frame. The engine assembly and rear wheel were suspended together pivoting below the seat, and the connecting frame also formed the exhaust system. At least one of these unique lightweights was imported into Britain. Imme also built a 148 cc twin cylinder model on the same lines, but this was only produced in very small numbers before the Imme factory closed.

Isetta

See BMW

Karrenburg
1968-69

Jurgen Karrenburg was an enthusiast who built some highly interesting two-stroke racing machinery at the end of the 1960s.

His most famous design was a three cylinder 350 using a similar layout to the mid-1950s DKW with the middle cylinder jutting forward horizontally between two near vertical outer cylinders, although unlike the DKW, the Karrenburg three was watercooled with a separate circulating pump. An unusual feature was that both exhaust and inlet ports were on the same side of cylinder. The port layout meant that the SSI Dell'Orto racing carbs for all three cylinders had to be tilted to allow the expansion chambers to clear them. The finned transfer port covers were removable, as on certain MV Agusta 'strokers of the early 1950s, so that different patterns could be tried out during development work.

Jurgen Karrenburg's three-cylinder 350 cc special hit the headlines in 1968.

The gearbox was a six-speeder and another technical feature was positive lubrication for the main bearings from a mechanical pump. A full duplex cradle frame was used together with Italian Ceriani forks and Oldani brakes.

A 125 cc version, with one horizontal cylinder, was also built.

Kleinschnittger
1950-57

Mainly a producer of mini-cars, in 1954 Kleinschnittger also constructed around 50 examples of a scooter like machine powered by a 48 cc Ilo engine. Called the Roller, this had large 20 inch wheels, full enclosure and the headlamp mounted on the front mudguard.

Kramer
1977-85

Originally a dealer, Franz Kramer made his name tuning Maico off road machinery. In early 1977 he ended his association with the Maico factory, and from then on produced his own bikes. All these featured cantilever rear suspension – usually with twin Dutch Koni units. Rider Rolf Dieffenback left Maico with Kramer and thereafter rode as the official Kramer rider in motocross events. By 1980 a full range of not only motocross but

also enduro mounts were available – the latter under the prefix ER in 124, 174, 244 and 280 cc sizes. All used Rotax based power units. Kramer machines also competed with distinction in the ISDT, later known as the ISDE (International Six Day Enduro). The motocross machines were imported into Britain during the early 1980s by H & S Accessories of Bordon, Hampshire.

Krauser
1976-

Another dealer who ultimately has become a manufacturer is the Munich BMW specialist Michael Krauser. He is perhaps most famous for his range of luggage equipment sold under the Krauser brand. But his first foray into the motorcycle manufacturing field came in 1976 when he spent a lot of money building an eight valve (four per cylinder) BMW Rennsport engine with centre crankshaft bearing and fuel injection for Grand Prix sidecar driver Otto Haller. Drive to the dohc was by toothed rubber belt, with peak revs of 12,000.

Krauser had himself raced BMWs in the 1950s and at the same time as preparing the sidecar outfit described above ran the official BMW factory endurance solo racing team. This later led to the design of a new triangular trellis chassis for the flat twin engine. First for racing, then with BMW's approval, a batch of 200 MKM1000 sports roadsters were constructed. These

Above **Krauser rider Stefan Dörflinger was 80 cc World Champion in 1984 and 1985.**

Left **Krauser MKM 1000 superbike had full BMW warranty.**

used a standard BMW R100 engine and as such the Krauser MKM1000 carried a full BMW warranty.

But at least one MKM1000 was built purely as a racer. This was campaigned by Englishman Paul Iddon in the 1984 Battle of the Twins series. He finished second overall. Besides the usual race preparations this machine also used four valve heads (an aftermarket Krauser accessory), oil cooler, larger discs and stronger three spoke cast alloy wheels. In pure speed it was a match for its rivals but handling was not up to that of the Ducati V-twins. Krauser also bought both the Kreidler and Zündapp Grand Prix racing teams, and as Krausers these machines made a great impression on first the 50 and later the 80 cc road racing World Championships during the early/mid 1980's.

Lambretta

see NSU

Leopard

Name used in certain export markets, including Britain, for German Panther marque.

Levante
1954

Five hundred of these 34 cc Rex engined scooter type mopeds were built in Hamburg. The engine was mounted above the front wheel and was belt driven.

Lohrlein
1981

Designed by Peter Lohrlein, a prototype enduro-type machine was completed in March 1981 using a Sachs 250 engine and unique trailing link front forks of own design. No production was undertaken.

Lutz
1949-54

Lutz produced its first machine, the R3, in 1949. This was a scooter with a Lutz designed 58 cc two-stroke engine. A distinctive feature was the 'wire mesh' in place of the conventional side panels which other scooters had at the rear of the machine.

In 1951 a larger model, the R175 appeared. This featured a highly streamlined enclosed bodywork and an extensive equally streamlined front section which extended from the front wheel spindle right up to the handlebars. This too had a Lutz designed engine of 174.3 cc, which produced 6 bhp.

Mammut

See Meister

Mars
1903-58

Prior to the First World War, Swiss Zedel and German Fafnir engines were used in the Nürnberg factory's machines. Then in 1920 chief engineer Franzenberg designed one of the company's most well known models, *Der Weisse Mars* (The White Mars), with a box square section frame constructed from welded and riveted pressed sheet steel. The engine for this machine was made exclusively for Mars by Maybach, who were famous as both aircraft and car engine manufacturers. This was a 956 cc side valve flat twin, with the cylinders

Mars S50 ultra-lightweight was introduced in 1951 and was seen the same year at the Amsterdam Show.

pointing fore and aft. Initially this machine sold well, but the company ran into financial difficulties in 1924 at the time of hyper inflation in Germany and production was not able to restart until 1926. Then Karl and Johann Müller, two leading engineers at the Mars plant, reopened it with new financial backing. However, they were for a considerable period unable to use the Mars title, instead they marketed the machines under the MA name.

During the late 1920's and throughout the 1930's various imported engines were used, including Sturmey-Archer, JAP, Villiers, plus Sachs 75 and 98 cc units were used. There were also a few other models including one with a 60 cc power unit.

Post-war production, now under the original Mars

name, resumed in 1950, when Rudi Albert, normally chief designer with Allright und Phänomen, joined Mars. His first effort, launched in 1950, was the S50, a neat 98 cc Sachs-powered ultra-lightweight with two speed hand gearchange, and undamped telescopic front forks But Albert's most notable design for Mars was without doubt the Stella, which featured exceptionally low lines for a motorcycle. This was helped by its 16 inch wheels, with 3.50 section tyres. The first Stella, the 190, appeared in 1951, powered by a Sachs 147 cc (57 × 58 mm) unit construction two-stroke single, which produced 6.5 bhp at 4500 rpm, offering a maximum speed of 50 mph. Later, larger engined Stellas featured full swinging arm rear suspension. The final model, the 175DS, used a 174 cc (62 × 58 mm) Sachs engine and had leading link front forks, a fully enclosed chain and a luxurious dual seat.

The 175DS lasted until 1957, by which time Mars was struggling. It did however, partially fight back by bringing out the Monza. A sporting ultra-lightweight which was taken over by Gritzner-Kayser when Mars closed in June 1958.

Meister
1949-56

Meister Fahradwerke began trading in August 1921 as a cycle manufacturer, and it was not until 1949 that the company began producing powered two-wheelers. These were designed by Alfred Ostertag and included 49 cc Zündapp engined mopeds, and a wide range of 98, 123, 147, 174, and 197 cc models with engines from either Ilo or Sachs, plus the M41S scooterette. Also sold under the Mammut and Phänomen brand names.

Mars Stella 175 S was produced only in 1954. It had a Sachs 174 cc four-speed, two-stroke engine. Mars as a manufacturer continued until 1958.

Messerschmitt
1952-64

Like Heinkel, Messerschmitt was an aircraft manufacturer which found itself with production facilities but nothing to make after the war. Its solution was a joint venture with Fritz Fend to manufacture Fend's *Kabinenroller* (cabin scooter) three-wheeler. The design looked something like a fighter aircraft cockpit with two seats in tandem. Production began at the Regensburg aircraft works in 1953. The new machine, the KR 175 powered by a 175 cc Sachs engine was an instant success, and in 1955 a 200 cc version, the KR200 was launched. Germany was permitted to re-arm in 1955 and Messerschmitt began making aircraft again. Fend, with funding from the State Bank, then took over production and the Messerschmitt name. In the same year a new model was launched, the 200 Super, which set three speed/endurance records at Hockenheim.

Despite falling demand, the company was aided by acquiring the Vespa manufacturing rights from the defunct Hoffmann marque and over the next three years built two versions of the scooter which helped

them to survive. Three-wheeler production continued at lower levels and in 1956 an open tourer, the KR201, was introduced, while in 1958, a further model, the KR200 Sports Cabriolet appeared. The model range remained the same until 1964 by which time 41,190 three-wheelers had been built. Fend had left by then to work as an independent consultant, but his original design had already outlasted all of his competitors.

Meyra
1949-56

Originally established by Wilhelm Meyer, Meyra Werke concentrated on three-wheelers and never produced any two-wheelers. There were two main models, the 55 and 200-2.

Miele
1899-1962

Formed in 1899 by Carl Miele and Reinhard Zinkann, Miele was a large bicycle manufacturer. In the 1930s Miele produced 73 and 98 cc Sachs engined motorised bicycles. But it was not until 1950 that the company introduced a range of motorcycles all powered by Sachs engines – The K21, K30, 100 and 190. Although never sold in vast quantities Miele motorcycles built up a good reputation for high quality.

Messerschmitt, 29/30 August 1955, established innumerable world records in the under-250 cc three-wheel category with a specially prepared and highly tuned version of the KR200 Kabinenroller on closed roads.

Miranda
1949-54

The Miranda name was first used when the Pirol factory based in Dortmund took over manufacture of the Schweppe scooter, a design with motorcycle-style swinging arm and offered with a choice of either a 173 cc Sachs or 198 cc Richard Küchen-designed two-stroke engines.

Mota
1955

Prototype scooter with a 98 cc engine, unusual in several ways including bulbous leg shields, large disc type wheels and strange extended leading link front suspension. No production was undertaken.

Mota-Wiesel
1948-52

A combination of scooter and moped using small wheels and 74 or 98 cc engines. It was originally called the Motra-Wiesel.

Nera
1948-50

The Nera was one of the first German-made scooters to appear after the Second World War – although few were made and the company soon folded. Designed by Wolfgang Neuscheler, the engines were either 120 cc Ilo or 149 cc Sachs.

Opti

Operated solely as an engine manufacturer.

Pamag
1958-59

For a short time, Pamag took over Anker production, making a range of machines with, 123, 174 and 197 cc Ilo or Sachs engines. Success limited because market was in decline.

Panther
1896-1975

Not to be confused with the British Panther factory of Cleckheaton, West Yorkshire. The only thing the two companies shared was a trademark featuring a panther's head. Panther AG was formed in 1896 as a bicycle manufacturer and did not produce any powered two-wheelers until the mid-1930's. These were motorised bicycles with either Sachs or Ilo engines.

Post-war, like many German makes, production was initially slow to restart after 1945. Panther's first model, the TS98, was delayed until 1950. Thereafter, a whole range of machines appeared, all with Sachs engines from 98 to 173 cc.

When the German Panther range was offered in Britain during the late 1950's, the name was changed to Leopard to avoid confusion with the British Panther. The marque continued until the early 1970's and offered mainly 50 cc machines.

Patria
1925-1952

Always interesting, the first models from the factory founded by Hans May had 248 and 348 cc Roconova single cylinder ohc engines designed by Johannes Rossig. However, after 1927 until the Second World War only mopeds were produced. When production resumed in 1949 a three model range powered by Ilo engines of 123, 147 and 173 cc was launched. Neatly engineered machines with telescopic forks, plunger rear suspension and sleek modern lines. However, in 1950 the owner of the Patria factory died suddenly and the leaderless company soon folded.

Permo
1952-54

Exclusively a producer of mopeds with 38 cc Victoria designed and built engines.

Phänomen

See Meister

Pirol

See Schweppe

Prior

Export name for Hercules in Britain and other export markets.

Progress
1953-60

Based in Stuttgart, Progress was unrelated to an earlier pre-war maker of the same name. It manufactured a range of Sachs-powered large wheeled scooters, with 98, 147, 174 and 191 cc engines, mostly known under the Strolch brand. A unique innovation was the headlamp which although mounted in the legshields swivelled with the handlebars Other features included leading link forks and motorcycle type wheels, with full width alloy brake hubs and a silencer of unusually large capacity.

The 174 and 191 cc engined models were imported into Britain for a short period from the spring of 1956 by Carr Bros. Garages Ltd of High Street, Purley, Surrey.

Several models were fitted with a single seat Steib sidecar. This combination made its debut at the 1955 Geneva Show. Final variants introduced for 1958 sported new styling, which included doing away with the pivoting headlamp.

Rabeneick
1933-63

August Rabeneick founded the company in Bielefeld during the summer of 1933. Pre-war it produced exclusively lightweights, mainly with Sachs engines.

Post-war, Rabeneick branched out into larger machines, including a four-stroke, large capacity flat twin in 1951. They also built a large range of two-strokes with Ilo or Sachs units from 98 to 247 cc, including a 244 cc Ilo powered twin, the F250/2, which was manufactured from 1951 to 1957.

But perhaps the most interesting Rabeneick was the Swiss Universal-engined 250 four-stroke ohv single with shaft drive. It was first seen at the 1953 Frankfurt Show, and was sold in limited quantities thereafter. The Rabeneick Universal's 247 cc (70 × 64 mm) engine had a high compression ratio and produced a claimed 15.2 bhp. It featured telescopic forks, swinging arm rear

Rabeneick drew informed observers to its stand at the 1953 Frankfurt Show with its innovative engineering. Power came from a Swiss Universal 250 cc ohv engine.

suspension and a dual seat. However, although boasting a superb specification it proved too expensive to produce.

After 1958, the company concentrated on smaller machinery and by 1962 its largest model was the LM100/4 lightweight motorcycle, powered by a 98 cc Sachs four-speed engine. The balance of the range were all 50s – the Saxonette moped, Binetta Super 4 (four speed) and Super 5 (five-speed) motorcycles (both with Earles-type forks), and the R50 scooter. In 1963 Rabeneick was swallowed up by Hercules, which itself became part of Zweirad-Union three years later. The Rabeneick plant's fate was finally, in the 1970s to be used by Fichtel and Sachs to recondition automobile clutch assemblies.

REH
1948-53

Designed by Richard Engelbrecht, the REH motorcycles were never anything more than limited-run, almost hand-built luxury lightweights, that were available with a choice of Ilo engines – either 173, 198, 244 (twin) or 248 cc.

Rex
1948-64

Not to be confused with the well known Rex Acme, a famous name in British Veteran and vintage circles, or for that matter the Swedish Rex. The German Rex company built 'clip-on' engine units for bicycles, with capacities of 31, 34, and 40 cc. Later, the firm made mopeds and ultra-lightweight motorcycles with its own 48 cc two-stroke power units, as well as a lightweight motorcycle employing a British Villiers 123 cc engine.

Riedl

See Imme

Rixe
1921-85

Originally a bicycle manufacturer, Rixe first produced a powered two-wheeler in 1934. Until 1939 a range of motorised cycles was marketed with a choice of either 73 or 98 cc Sachs engines. Post-war it offered a large range of motorcycles from the 98 cc austerity model K98 first made in late 1949, through to final closure of the factory in 1985 with a range of lightweights headed by a sophisticated water-cooled 79 cc sportster. In between came an array of other models. The 1950s launched the KT125 (1950-52) the K98 (available until 1959), KT150 (1950-52), KT175 (1950-53), R150 (1953-55), R175 (1953-56), R200 (1953-54), R250/2 (1953-54), RS250/2 (1954-58) and finally the RS175 (1955-59). The 1960s witnessed a change to smaller machines, including various Sachs-engined mopeds, even including one specially adapted for tradesman, with large front and rear carriers. There were also two 100 class motorcycles, again with Sachs power. The RS100 Tourer had Earles forks, low-level exhaust system, comprehensive mudguarding, 16 inch wheels, full chain enclosure, high bars and rear carrier. The sporting version was the RS100 Sport. This not only had a tuned engine, but also a larger 13.5-litre tank, high-level exhaust, flat bars and sprint type mudguards.

Into the 1970s production concentrated purely on 50 cc mopeds and mokicks (lightweight motorcycles), still with Sachs engines.

The 1980's Rixe attempted a fight back. This came during 1982 with a new range headed by the RS80W. This was powered by the new Sachs watercooled 80SW motor. Its 79 cc (46 × 48 mm) unit provided 8.5 bhp at 6000 rpm, giving a top speed of 50 mph. It also boasted five gears, a duplex twin front down tube frame, cast alloy wheels, Bikini fairing, rear carrier, twin disc front brake, matching speedo and tacho, and silver finish. However, together with such well known names as Kreidler and Zundapp, the Bielefeld factory found the going too tough to survive.

RMW
1925-55

During its thirty year existence the RMW company not only had to face a long World War, but also intense competition. As proprietary engines were mostly used, it was in effect an assembler, rather than a real manufacturer, but its first machines were an exception. A pair of 132 and 148 cc two-stroke single cylinder engines of the company's own design were made in-house.

Later, larger versions were built before a change to bought-in power units from companies including Sturmey-Archer, MAG, JAP and Küchen. RMW took over the Phoenix marque and thereafter the output from the Neheim-Ruhr company included designs from Phoenix which embraced the 198 and 246 cc two-strokes.

Post-war, both Phoenix and RMW attempted to re-establish themselves in the motorcycle market without any real success and very few machines were made by either company.

Röhr
1952-57

Röhr was a farm machinery factory whose sole two-wheel product was an Ilo 197 cc powered scooter. It had very similar lines to the successful Zündapp Bella series.

Ruwisch
1948-50

A small scooter was powered by a 38 cc Victoria engine. Only limited production undertaken.

Sachs (engine manufacturer)

Schnell-Horex
1952-54

Produced by the Horex factory and designed by engineer/racer Roland Schnell, these machines used 248, 348, and 498 cc single cylinder engines with gear driven dohc. Riders included Erwin Aldinger, Georg Braun, Hermann Gablenz, Hermann Müller, Fritz Klager and Robert Zeller. Schnell also rode his own machinery.

The 350 proved the most successful, gaining placings at even the highest level. See Horex chapter for full story.

Schürhoff
1949-53

Besides producing the MR123Z and MR175Z motorcycles, both powered by single cylinder Ilo units, the

Gevelsburg marque also offered a wide range of bicycles and mopeds.

Schweppe
1949-54

Also known as Pirol, a range of attractive scooters was produced, starting with the Pirol 145 in 1949. This had an Ilo 143 cc engine. Then came the Küchen 198 cc Pirol 200 in 1951 and finally in 1953 the last of the line, the Miranda. This used a 174 cc Sachs motor. See also Miranda.

Seith
1949-50

Built mini-scooters for children, powered by 38 cc Victoria two-strokes.

Servos
1953

A small scooter built in Augsburg with a 38 cc Victoria engine mounted over the front wheel.

Sitta
1950-55

Built Ilo engined motorcycles from 123 to 247 cc from 1953-55 including the twin cylinder 244 cc model. Sitta also made scooters, again Ilo powered, with capacities of 119 or 123 cc, and finally 49 cc mopeds.

Solo
1949-

Has always concentrated on machines with an engine capacity not exceeding 50 cc, and has been a survivor

Solo City bike of 1974 had automatic two-speed engine and die cast magnesium wheel rims. Virtually unknown outside Germany, the company continues to make two-wheelers.

without too much publicity. However, in 1974 not only introduced the new City Bike model with automatic two speed transmission, cast alloy wheels and a large seat but also what was claimed to be the world's first watercooled moped engine. Then in 1980 the 350 road racing World Champion Jon Ekerold was sponsored by the company.

Steinbach
1981-85

Produced replica classics using large capacity four-stroke Austrian Rotax single cylinder engines.

Strolch

See Progress.

Stüdemann
1953

Another small manufacturer who used the 38 cc Victoria two-stroke engine.

Sudbrack
1949-51

Bicycle factory, who for a short period manufactured a small range of mopeds and a pair of motorcycles powered by Ilo 98 and 123 cc engines.

Tornax
1925-55 and 1982-84

Tornax built up an enviable reputation in the years before the Second World War as makers of quality motorcycles using JAP and Columbus (Horex) engines. The Wuppertal-Langerfeld company also built a small sports car from 1934-36 that used a three-cylinder DKW two-stroke engine.

After the war, production did not restart until 1948, when the company reorganised by new owner Ernst Wewer. In that year the first of a new breed of Tornax machines appeared, powered by 125 and 175 cc Ilo engines. Unlike most of their contemporaries, these machines had an air of glamour rather than austerity. Both models sold well in Germany, Belgium and Holland. But by 1952, the management was aware that the seller's market was almost over and that they were under increasing threat. An intensive, expensive development programme produced new 200 and 250 cc Ilo-powered machines and a new 250 cc four-stroke parallel twin. These appeared in 1953 but although they were successful, in truth, it was too little to justify their development cost. With restricted cash and too few sales, the marque joined Hoffmann in 1955 as early casualties of recession.

Below **Reborn for a short time in the early 1980's, Tornax offered a range of 50 and 80 cc models with Italian Minerelli engines. The photography shows a 80RX. In its first incarnation, Tornax had used JAP engines amongst others.**

Above **Tornax K125 S Luxus initially made its mark in 1950. It seemed to offer the allure of speed and endurance from its Ilo two-stroke engine. Among its selling points were twin carbs and dual high-level exhausts.**

But almost three decades later the name was briefly revived on a range of 50 and 80 cc machines using Italian components that included Minarelli engines. Launched in 1982, it was a mere two years before this, too, was just a memory.

Torpedo
1928-53

A famous bicycle factory who before the war built 198 cc Blackburne engined motorcycles. Post-war, like many others, the Torpedo used either Sachs or Ilo power. The 63 had a 98 cc Sachs and was offered only in 1951. The mainstays of the range were the 125 (Ilo 123 cc), 150 (Sachs 147 cc) and 175 (Ilo 174 cc). In 1953 the production of motorcycles ceased to allow Torpedo to concentrate on mopeds and bicycles.

Tramnitz
1951

Tramnitz marketed a 98 cc Ilo engined scooter with a de luxe specification.

Troll
1948-51

Ugly three-wheeler, built with a range of engines – 60 cc VMO and 98 or 118 cc Ilo. Had the appearance of a lawnmower with a carrying compartment at the rear.

UNO
1980-

Offers a range of sports roadsters with various engines including Honda XL500, Yamaha SRX600 and even rebuilt Ducati 450 units. All fitted into a monoshock frame with *café racer* styling.

UT
1922-59

One of the most important of the lesser known post-war German marques. The 1920s gave UT the opportunity to launch motorcycles with a variety of engines including Bekamo, Blackburne and JAP units. The latter two were large capacity ohv singles. At the same time the factory gained a considerable amount of publicity by taking part in road racing events. Notable riders included Blind, Frenzen and Kohfink.

In the 1930's, following the Great Depression, Bark and Küchen engines were also used in the production machines. Post-war, the first machines, which used Ilo two-stroke singles, were the KTNs, with 123 and 174 cc capacities. These first appeared in 1951.

A major sales push in 1953 was accompanied by the new KTV 175. It had both front and rear suspension. A larger version, the KTV200 was also announced. In addition, three new machines appeared with swinging arm suspension, (the KTV's had plunger). These were the TS200, TS250 and TS252 (a twin-cylinder model).

In 1955 came the TS175F and TS175J. Finally in 1956 emerged the VS100, using a Sachs engine, as did the TS175J, and the VS252 twin. 1958 and 1959 were spent selling off remaining stocks.

URS

See Fath

Van Veen

See Kreidler

Varel
1952-53

Small factory which produced mopeds and mini-scooters with its own 43 cc engines. Also a larger 99 cc Mota two-stroke engine was used to power a bigger scooter.

Venus
1953-55

Only manufactured scooters. First model, the MS150 appeared in the summer of 1953. Shortly afterwards joined by similar MS175. The following year the DS100 was added to the range. All had Sachs engines but none were ever produced in quantity.

Ducati 450 cc engined UNO cafe racer in 1981.

Vespa

See Hoffmann and Messerschmitt.

Volkswagen
1986

Rumours about the car giant VW's interest in motorcycle production have been around for several

Van Veen's German subsidiary was responsible for building and marketing the OCR 1000 1-litre superbike in the late 1970's. It was powered by a Wankel twin-rotor unit.

years, but have always come to nothing. However, in 1986 VW displayed an interesting prototype three-wheeler called the Scootar. The rear section followed BMW swinging arm practice. The front end running gear was lifted from the popular four-wheel VW Polo car. In fact, in development the 1050 and 1400 cc Polo engines were installed. In the process, some very

A 1955 brochure shot showing a top-of-the-range UT VS 252. Its kilometre-eating urge came from a twin-cylinder Ilo two-stroke. The company vanished in 1959.

impressive performance figures were recorded. It will be interesting to see if the gull winged Scootar will go beyond the prototype stage and reach production.

Walba
1949-52

Walter Baibaschewski designed the Walba range of scooters powered by Ilo engines from 98 to 173 cc.

Westfalia
1952-53

Extremely basic three-wheeler with motorcycle-type steering and a choice of either 174 or 191 Sachs engine. There was also a Westfalia motorcycle company in Germany's pioneer days.

Wimmer (engine manufacturer)

Before the Second World War, Wimmer built a number of motorcycles including 137 and 172 cc watercooled ohv singles, and aircooled models in a range of capacities up to 497 cc. The watercooled 172 had a good record in competitive road racing, and the company also manufactured a trials model with an engine by Bark. After the war, no more motorcycles were made and the company concentrated on manufacturing its proprietary engines.

Wittenkind
1952-54

Komet engines of 40 cc were fitted to the Wittenkind company's mopeds.

Wittler
1924-53

During the 1920s, Wittler offered a machine fitted with its own 249 cc two-stroke single, but after 1949 it concentrated on manufacturing mopeds with either Sachs or Zündapp engines. A lightweight motorcycle with Sachs power unit was also in the range.

Wurring
1921-59

Founded by August Wurring and also sold under the AWD brand, Wurring for many years designed a number of excellent motorcycles powered by a wide variety of engines including DKW, Blackburne, JAP, Küchen, Sachs and Villiers. It also constructed a number of successful racing machines for several leading pre-war riders.

Post-war, a large range of motorcycles was produced, including the SZ100, 125, 150, SZ175/1 and 175/2, SZ200, SZ250 and SZ252 – the latter was a twin-cylinder design using an Ilo 244 cc (52 × 58 mm) unit.

Zweirad-Union
1958-74

First formed by the merger of DKW, Express and Victoria in 1958. The conglomerate then added Hercules in 1966. For full details refer to respective chapters in main text. Was eventually absorbed into the giant Fichtel and Sachs group

Automotive giant Volkswagen went through this three-wheel design exercise. Given the congestion and pressure on inner-city space the concept is appealing.

Index